CLEAN BREXIT

LIAM HALLIGAN AND GERARD LYONS

CLEAN BREXIT

WHY LEAVING THE EU STILL MAKES SENSE

— BUILDING A POST-BREXIT ECONOMY FOR ALL —

Biteback Publishing

First published in Great Britain in 2017 by
Biteback Publishing Ltd
Westminster Tower
3 Albert Embankment
London SE1 7SP
Copyright © Liam Halligan and Gerard Lyons 2017

ISBN 978-1-78590-258-1

10 9 8 7 6 5 4 3 2 1

A CIP catalogue record for this book is available from the British Library.

Set in Adobe Garamond Pro

Printed and bound in Great Britain by
CPI Group (UK) Ltd, Croydon CR0 4YY

MIX
Paper from
responsible sources
FSC® C020471

The views expressed in this book are solely of the authors – and not necessarily those of any organisation with which they are affiliated.

CONTENTS

FOREWORD

While the majority of people have rejected the bad union that the EU has become, they have not rejected the good union of the nations of the United Kingdom. The strength of that union is based on a much deeper sense of shared destiny and it will continue as long as the political structures of the UK represent and express the views of the people effectively and fairly.

The 2016 referendum was a vote on a political establishment that had become disconnected from the majority of the people. Now, with Brexit, there is an opportunity to address our domestic challenges. The coming months must be guided by three basic principles.

First, the broad outline of the referendum decision is clear. The British people want their own Parliament to have the final say over UK laws, immigration policy, trade negotiations and taxation. We should not stay in the single market or try to adopt Norway's approach when redefining our relationship with the EU, as this would not respect the referendum outcome. As this book makes clear, we must seek a new path outside the EU.

Second, we enter the talks with the EU as equals. The UK is one of the world's largest economies and a permanent member of the United Nations Security Council. We are the EU's second-largest net budget contributor. Just as trade with the EU is important to the UK, so UK trade is important to the EU. Free and frictionless trade is in everyone's interests.

The UK will have to accept that the cohesion of the Eurozone will be the driving imperative for the EU 27. But the European Commission will have to decide what it can and cannot do in the future, as there seems little appetite among member states to increase their contributions to make up for the loss of the UK. There will be a bit of sniggering and condescension as these Article 50 negotiations get serious, but our negotiators are there to implement the will of the UK.

The third basic principle is that these negotiations will be as simple or as complicated as we choose to make them. Liam Halligan and Gerard Lyons have put forward a clear, credible approach for the UK to take – Clean Brexit – and have outlined how it can be achieved. This is a welcome rebuttal to those who speak only of stopping a chaotic Brexit because they still have not come to terms with the outcome of the referendum. Britain and the EU do not want a messy divorce, but instead an approach based on extensive future cooperation and shared values.

Brexit is about allowing the British electorate, and in turn Parliament and the government of the day, greater future scope to pursue the domestic economic policies that the country needs. One of the important points that Halligan and Lyons make is that Brexit allows Britain to take a leadership role in global affairs. Arguably, the last time we articulated a coherent and outward-looking approach to our role in the world was during the first term of the 1997 Labour government.

Leaving the EU provides an opportunity to rewrite some of the rules, take back responsibilities and adopt a strategic approach, rather than a collection of tactical responses to events which lack strategic underpinning. From striking fairer trade deals with developing countries to lowering rates of VAT at home to help those on lower incomes, our ability to make these decisions again will enable us to more closely reflect our values and priorities.

In *Clean Brexit*, the two authors, whose work in this area I greatly admire, have provided an excellent framework within which we can continue the debate, with a positive outlook towards Brexit and what lies ahead.

Rt Hon. Gisela Stuart
August 2017

PREFACE

'We are with Europe, but not of it. We are linked but not compromised.
We are interested and associated, but not absorbed.'
WINSTON CHURCHILL, 1930[1]

How will Britain fare outside the European Union? During the Article 50 negotiations, what should the government's priorities be? Theresa May's hand has clearly been weakened by the June 2017 general election – which resulted in a hung parliament, with the government commanding no overall majority. Is Brexit still going to happen? Could there be a second referendum on EU membership? Would that be a good idea?

Can Britain and the EU maintain good relations, despite testy Brexit talks? Will EU imports and exports continue even if we leave with 'no deal' on trade? Is the danger of the cliff edge real and is 'falling back on World Trade Organization (WTO) rules' really the disastrous outcome that many suggest?

What does Brexit mean for UK-based car manufacturers, for the City and our farmers, for British universities and our fishing industry? Will our new immigration system mean fewer EU nationals living and working here? Can the UK itself hold together once we have left the EU, given ongoing calls for Scottish independence and concern about fresh tensions between Northern Ireland and the Irish Republic?

How will Brexit affect the EU and the single currency? What does the rise of nationalism across the EU mean for the European project? Could the euro and even the EU itself collapse? If that happened, would Britain get the blame?

Clean Brexit tackles all these questions and more. Amidst the confusion, spin and rhetorical barbs, this book addresses, honestly and openly, the vital Brexit-related issues the politicians try to avoid. While a single volume cannot consider all the technical aspects of unravelling the decades-long formal UK–EU relationship, *Clean Brexit* doesn't shy away from detailed analysis of the economic, commercial, diplomatic and geopolitical issues that the UK faces as it undergoes its most significant negotiation since the Second World War.

The British economy, having performed quite well since the EU referendum in June 2016, still faces genuine difficulties. Brexit will not be entirely straightforward – we are realistic about the near-term challenges and outline how they should be addressed. But this book is, nonetheless, unashamedly optimistic. Leaving the EU will obviously cause some upheaval, with both winners and losers. But we genuinely view Brexit as an opportunity – to reassert the UK's sovereignty, reinvent our economy as both more productive and inclusive, while reclaiming Britain's rightful place as a premier global trading nation.

Under a Clean Brexit, the UK will be outside of the single market, but will still have access to and trade extensively with the EU – as do the US and many other leading economies. They trade with the EU without diluting their democracies or making multi-billion-pound annual contributions. Also, outside of the EU's protectionist customs union, we will be able to cut trade deals with the world's major and fast-growing economies, which Brussels has largely failed to do. The UK can then conduct more business with non-EU countries, which accounts for about 80 per cent of the world economy – a share set to go even higher.

By avoiding a potentially explosive Messy Brexit that tries to trade off freedom of movement and single market membership and could ultimately end in stalemate, Clean Brexit provides the best chance of a constructive Article 50 negotiation. That bodes well for the continuation of healthy UK–EU trade volumes and ongoing cooperation across a range of important areas – from education and research to environmental protection, from military and security matters to cultural exchange. We are leaving the EU, not Europe, after all.

This book draws on the authors' long experience in economics, business, journalism and finance, as well as extensive discussions with leading politicians and diplomats from the UK and beyond. It argues that the Article 50 process, if cool heads prevail, can be simpler and less disruptive to citizens and businesses than is often suggested.

Part I – Before Brexit – outlines how the EU has changed since it was formed, as the European Economic Community (EEC) in 1957. The world economy, also, has changed unrecognisably over the last sixty years, with Europe accounting for an ever-falling share of global commerce.

In Part II – Choices for the UK & EU – we discuss the Brexit model we believe works best for both Britain and the EU, while highlighting the significant choices the EU must urgently make. Is 'Project Europe' still about 'ever closer union' – as outlined in the 1957 Treaty of Rome? Is that possible? Or what the people of Europe want?

Part III – Taking back control – focuses on the Article 50 negotiation, the relative bargaining strengths of the two sides and the approach Britain should take before we formally leave in March 2019. We discuss the early skirmishes of the Article 50 negotiation – relating to the 'divorce bill' and the rights of EU citizens in the UK, and their British counterparts living on the Continent.

Explaining why trading under WTO rules is not to be feared, we outline a temporary transition plan – a bridge to Brexit rather than a cliff edge. We then highlight opportunities for the UK, as we seek to build on our growing non-EU trade by striking deeper commercial relationships with the broader world – not least the large, populous emerging markets, where Britain already has long-standing ties.

Part IV – The UK after Brexit – maps out a new economic and industrial landscape for Britain's domestic economy outside the EU, outlining the future of regional and industrial policy. We discuss the automotive sector and financial services, along with agriculture and fishing. Rather than blindly deregulating and pursuing a race to the bottom, Brexit is a chance to create an enabling environment that encourages not only wealth creation, helping the UK to grow in a fast-changing global economy, but also better consumer protection – another area where Brussels has fallen short.

A system of managed immigration is proposed – to be determined and implemented during the Article 50 window, ready for when we leave. We need immigration controls that provide the skilled and unskilled labour that businesses need while restoring the confidence of our broader population. Measures to promote a significant increase in the rate of house-building are proposed – injecting demand into the post-Brexit economy while encouraging ongoing collaboration between UK and EU universities. We discuss arrangements for Scotland, Wales and Northern Ireland once we have left the UK, including the prospect of further devolution. We then consider the important relationship between Britain and the Republic of Ireland.

Part V – Moving on – argues against a second referendum. Another public vote, involving a potential default back to EU membership, would betray the UK's June 2016 referendum result. The prospect of a repeat referendum, in addition, seriously harms the UK's Article 50 negotiating position, carries economic and financial risks and would further polarise the British electorate. After Brexit has happened, the return of sovereignty to Westminster, with laws once again decided by directly elected MPs, allows the broadest possible democratic engagement in shaping not just our domestic agenda but Britain's relations with the EU and the wider world.

Clean Brexit is written in a constructive spirit. The authors are independent economists, not front-line politicians with axes to grind. While we both advocated a Leave vote ahead of the referendum, we came to that conclusion based on careful consideration of the evidence, rather than any ideological or party affiliation. We also both decided to argue for Brexit only after then Prime Minister David Cameron's failure to secure a different deal with the EU – an outcome we felt reflected badly on the European Commission and other leading member states, as well as on ill-judged UK negotiation tactics.

Following the 2016 Brexit referendum, the British government has a clear mandate to take the UK out of the EU, which means leaving both the single market and the customs union. To be a member of either is incompatible with being sovereign outside the EU. While the outcome of the June 2017 general election makes the process of Brexit more complicated, given the tighter parliamentary arithmetic, that does not change the referendum result, or the fact that over 80 per cent of voters backed parties standing on a platform to implement Brexit.

The UK is now in a high-stakes negotiation, with significant challenges. Mistakes will be made on both sides. The general public, exposed to the daily political sniping, could become disillusioned with Brexit. Business leaders could also lose patience. We identify and address these challenges, while fully recognising that the government must be scrutinised by Parliament and held to account at all times.

The twenty-seven EU nations, though, each have their own interests to consider, too. The European Commission is a powerful, self-serving bureaucracy. And within the UK itself there are politicians in both Houses of Parliament who want to undermine Britain's negotiating hand and provoke a loss of public confidence. Then, of course, there are various financial and big business lobbies that are also determined to keep us in the EU, because it suits their current interests. To them, it is of little consequence that the British people have twice expressed their clear wish to leave the EU – both in the referendum of June 2016 and the general election twelve months later.

There are still those, at home and abroad, who are trying to frustrate and even prevent Brexit. All the more reason for the government and the broader electorate to maintain a clear vision of how these Brexit talks should be conducted and, beyond the rhetorical exchanges, the larger issues at stake. That is the purpose of *Clean Brexit* – a book dealing with technical subjects, but written in clear language for a broad audience. After all, the vast majority of British people, regardless of how they voted in either the referendum or general election, now want the government to get on with delivering a successful Brexit that works for them.

Britain should not fear the Article 50 process. Since June 2016, the UK economy, while still fragile against an uncertain global backdrop, has held up well. Although these negotiations will be testing, at a time when Britain has many other policy issues to address, we sincerely believe Brexit will unleash a wave of energy, investment and reform as the UK rediscovers its global vocation. We believe that being outside the EU, with a renewed entrepreneurial spirit, will also reinforce Britain's position as Europe's premier destination for inward investment.

The UK cannot hide from the deep-rooted structural issues we face. There is a long-overdue need to rebalance our economy, so growth is driven more by investment and exports rather than consumption. If Britain is to prosper in the twenty-first century, we need the positive engagement of both the private sector and the state. We must enhance our infrastructure, while focusing relentlessly on vocational training and skills, as we reconnect fully with the international markets upon which this nation's wealth was built. Britain has a chance to forge a new strategy and identity, unlocking our vast intellectual property while building a modern, regionally balanced economy less dependent on London and the broader south-east.

The EU, instead of being the seemingly dynamic and outward-looking organisation we joined in 1973, now looks isolationist and dated. Despite noble early intentions, the European project has become remote and anti-democratic, pitting nation against nation. Its authority and broader consent are under serious threat. Elections in Holland and France during the first half of 2017 saw 'centrist' candidates prevail, but their populist opponents polled significantly stronger than in previous elections – reflecting growing public discontent. From over-bureaucratic regulation and an insistence on freedom of movement, to the disastrous and dangerous single currency, the EU needs fundamentally to change to counter the rise of extremist politics.

With our unwritten constitution, code of common law and global perspective, the UK and the EU have never fully accepted one another. The authors believe, along with the vast majority of British voters, that any European supranational body ultimately needs to be looser, less statist and more democratic. This vision, rather than 'ever closer union', will more likely result in pan-European prosperity and peace.

Despite that, the Article 50 negotiations need not be acrimonious. The vision at the heart of *Clean Brexit* is one of good relations and ongoing UK–EU cooperation. The nations of Western Europe should engage in free trade while collaborating across a broad range of areas. It is our sincere hope that we continue to do so after March 2019, and, indeed, for generations to come.

Liam Halligan and Gerard Lyons
London, August 2017

GLOSSARY

4IR	Fourth Industrial Revolution
ACER	Agency for the Cooperation of Energy Regulators
ASEAN	Association of Southeast Asian Nations
CAP	Common Agricultural Policy
CBI	Confederation of British Industry
CDU	Germany's Christian Democrats
CET	Common External Tariff
CETA	Canada–EU Trade Agreement
CFP	Common Fisheries Policy
CPI	Consumer Price Index
DUP	Democratic Unionist Party
EASA	European Aviation Safety Agency
EC	European Commission
ECA	European Court of Auditors
ECAA	European Common Aviation Area
ECB	European Central Bank
ECJ	European Court of Justice
EEAA	European Economic Area Agreement
EEA	European Economic Area
EEC	European Economic Community
EFCA	European Fisheries Control Agency
EFTA	European Free Trade Association
EIB	European Investment Bank
ENISA	European Network and Information Security Agency
ETS	Emission Trading Scheme
ESA	European Space Agency
ESMA	European Securities and Markets Authority
ESRB	European Systemic Risk Board
EU	European Union
FCA	Financial Conduct Authority
FDI	Foreign Direct Investment
FSB	Financial Stability Board

FTA	Free Trade Agreement
GATS	General Agreement on Trade in Services
GDP	Gross Domestic Product
GPTs	General Purpose Technologies
GTA	Global Trade Alert
GVA	Gross Value Added
HDC	Housing Development Corporation
ICAO	International Civil Aviation Organization
ICJ	International Court of Justice
IMF	International Monetary Fund
IoD	Institute of Directors
IoT	Internet of Things
MAC	Migration Advisory Committee
MNC	Multinational company
MFF	Multiannual Financial Framework
MRA	Mutual Recognition Agreement
NAFTA	North America Free Trade Agreement
NDC	National Development Corporation
NPLs	Non-performing loans
NTB	Non-Tariff Barrier
OMT	Outright Monetary Transactions
OECD	Organisation for Economic Co-operation and Development
OPEC	Organization of Petroleum Exporting Countries
PBS	Points-based system of immigration
PD	Italy's Partito Democratico
PISA	Programme for International Student Assessment
QE	Quantitative easing
SMEs	Small and medium-sized enterprises
SPD	Germany's Social Democrats
TiSA	Treaty in Services Agreement
TRIPS	Agreement on Trade-Related Aspects of Intellectual Property Rights
TRIMS	Agreement on Trade-Related Investment Measures
TRQs	Tariff Rate Quotas
TUC	Trades Union Congress
T-Tab	Temporary Transition Agreement for Britain
UKTI	UK Trade and Investment
UKMBA	UK Municipal Bonds Agency
UN	United Nations
UFT	Unilateral free trade
WHO	World Health Organization
WPS	Work-permit system of immigration
WTO	World Trade Organization

CLEAN BREXIT IN BRIEF

Below, we outline our Clean Brexit negotiating strategy: twenty-five principles we believe the government should adopt during the Article 50 negotiations ahead of March 2019. These bullet points relate largely to the first half of the book.

We then present our 'Blueprint for a post-Brexit Britain' – in twenty-five additional bullet points. These suggest domestic economic policy priorities – the main subject of the second half of this book.

TWENTY-FIVE ARTICLE 50 NEGOTIATING PRINCIPLES

Clean Brexit

1) *Rule out single market membership*

   The benefits of single market 'membership' are grossly overstated. Inside the single market, Britain remains liable for multi-billion-pound annual payments to the EU, while accepting European Court of Justice (ECJ) jurisdiction and freedom of movement rules. This is not Brexit. The single market requires all UK firms – not just exporters – to comply with unnecessary and expensive EU rules. The single market in services barely exists – which penalises the UK, the world's second-largest services exporter.

2) *Rule out customs union membership too*

   Inside the customs union, Britain cannot cut free trade agreements (FTAs) with the four fifths of the world economy that exists beyond the EU. The EU's Common External Tariff (CET) makes UK imports more expensive – including food – and results in us sending additional millions of pounds to Brussels every year.

3) *Explain that Clean Brexit is the best option for both the UK and EU*
Under a Clean Brexit, the UK leaves the single market and the customs union. As such, Britain quickly regains control of sensitive issues relating to our money, borders, laws and trade. Clean Brexit avoids cherry-picking, leaving the EU's 'four freedoms' intact. This is better for Britain, the EU 27 and the vital relationship between them – given the benefits of ongoing cooperation across a range of headings.

4) *Do not attempt a potentially explosive Messy Brexit – aka Soft Brexit*
A Messy Brexit seeks to trade off single market membership against freedom of movement rules. This gives Britain no control over the central aspects of leaving the EU. Taking this route maximises 'cliff-edge' dangers and business uncertainty – and could result in a disastrous stalemate. So-called Soft Brexit, while rhetorically appealing to some, does not exist. Attempting to break EU treaties would actually result in Messy Brexit, risking a systemic crisis that could tear the EU apart.

Opening three issues

5) *No 'divorce bill' to be agreed until the end of the Article 50 period*
The UK is under no legal obligation to pay the EU to leave. But we want to exit on good terms. If we are to pay anything, the sum should be finalised at the end of the Article 50 period, so we extract maximum concessions from each incremental increase in agreed payment. The final total should be transferred over several years – perhaps as part of a transition agreement. The total payment should reflect the extent of goodwill and cooperation shown by the EU ahead of March 2019.

6) *Take the initiative to resolve EU citizens' rights*
While standing firm on cash, the UK should guarantee the residency rights of the 3.1 million EU citizens living in Britain, subject to criminal checks and proof of 'means of financial support'. That makes sense for them and UK businesses employing them. This issue has become embroiled in the dispute over ECJ jurisdiction, allowing the EU to portray Britain as intolerant. A unilateral guarantee, under British law, would force the EU to reciprocate

– or be accused of 'using people as bargaining chips'. The rights of the 1.2 million EU-based UK citizens are covered by the Vienna Convention.

7) *Work closely with the Republic of Ireland to maintain open borders*
The EU will try to exploit sensitivities over a 'hard' Irish border, not least because the government's House of Commons majority relies on support from the Democratic Unionist Party (DUP). Ensure controls on goods across the Irish land border are electronic and 'frictionless'. Confirm information-sharing agreements with Dublin to facilitate ongoing freedom of movement between the UK and Republic of Ireland – an arrangement much valued by both countries that long predates the EU.

Trade with the EU

8) *Offer to keep trading under existing EU tariff-free arrangements, but state that, if this isn't possible, Britain is happy to trade under WTO rules*
Trading under WTO rules is often presented as damaging or irresponsible. This is alarmist nonsense. WTO tariffs are relatively low and falling. The US, China and many other leading economies conduct extensive trade with the EU under WTO rules – Britain can do the same. Much of the UK's trade with the non-EU, over half our total trade, is largely under WTO rules.

9) *While WTO rules are fine, the UK would prefer a free trade agreement (FTA) with the EU. But this can be agreed after Article 50 expires.*
With WTO rules as a solid platform, it is by no means essential to strike a UK–EU FTA by March 2019. Failing to grasp this reality amounts to a major strategic error. Negotiating a complex, multi-sector FTA with twenty-seven governments, themselves with conflicting interests, plus ratification by national Parliaments and the European Parliament, may anyway be impossible in the Article 50 timeframe. The UK should remain open to negotiation, though – including on less ambitious sector-based deals (relating to automobiles, for instance, or financial services).

10) *Under Clean Brexit, we prepare for WTO trade rules with the EU*
Having declared Clean Brexit, the UK re-introduces systems to manage

cross-Channel immigration and customs checks. Unless we are logistically prepared for WTO rules, the threat to reject a disadvantageous FTA is not credible. The UK leaves the single market fully compliant with EU regulations, by definition. Before leaving the customs union, we reoccupy our WTO seat and adopt our own tariff schedules. This ordered approach contrasts with the last-minute brinkmanship of a Messy Brexit – which could result in political, diplomatic and even economic chaos.

No deal?

11) *'No deal is better than a bad deal.' State this clearly and often*
'No deal' simply means we don't strike a UK–EU FTA before March 2019. Again, this is by no means a disaster – and has its benefits. Negotiating up against a hard deadline, the terms of any FTA with the EU, which we must live with for years, would be far worse than a deal settled under less time pressure. Under 'no deal', UK and EU exporters pay relatively low WTO tariffs. Britain's EU trade deficit would generate substantial net tariff revenues, which could be used to compensate UK exporters.

12) *'No deal' is very different from 'just walking away'*
'No deal' is a coherent position, in terms of both negotiation and outcome – with UK–EU trade operating under WTO rules, as we look to cut an FTA after March 2019. 'Just walking away', in contrast, means failing to settle administrative issues such as mutual recognition agreements on goods and aircraft landing rights. No one is advocating such an approach. It is unthinkable that existing and uncontroversial EU protocols granted to countless other non-EU members would not apply to the UK, not least as we leave the EU fully compliant. For Brussels to deny Britain such rights would breach both WTO and EU law, while incensing EU businesses and voters by threatening billions of euros of profit and countless EU jobs.

13) *Announce a 'no deal' administrative deadline*
The UK government should set a deadline – perhaps the autumn of 2018 – after which we announce that FTA negotiations will take a back seat, with Britain focusing instead on preparing to trade under WTO rules. If an FTA

is impossible to agree and ratify during the Article 50 period, that should be acknowledged early – so WTO rules can be introduced as smoothly as possible. While continuing with UK–EU trade negotiations after this deadline – including sector-based deals – the change of emphasis will make sure the EU knows Britain is serious about trading with no FTA.

Negotiation tactics

14) *If the EU imposes WTO tariffs, make clear the UK will reciprocate*

Some economists want the UK to grant the EU tariff-free access, even if they impose WTO tariffs on us. While sympathetic to this view, on balance we disagree. 'Unilateral free trade' is attractive in theory, and lowers prices, but would be politically naïve. We would advocate a gradual reduction of import tariffs. Once outside the EU, trading under WTO rules, the UK will anyway be well-placed to negotiate a future tariff-reducing FTA with the EU. Having WTO tariffs in place that we can offer to remove strengthens our hand.

15) *Compile a sector-by-sector menu to help guide our FTA negotiations*

Ahead of detailed Article 50 talks, the government must plan how to treat key sectors. Ministers should identify what sector-specific transition measures and additional temporary subsidies are needed after Brexit – and if so for how long. Sectors to consider include autos and related supply chains, agriculture, fishing, pharmaceuticals and financial services. Industry leaders should be closely consulted, but negotiating priorities should not be publicly disclosed until closer to March 2019.

16) *Ensure 'strategic issues' feature in the Brexit negotiations*

There are many 'strategic' areas where the EU would benefit from future close ties with the UK – whether in defence, security, environmental protection, scientific research or educational and cultural exchange. Britain has a leadership role, of value to EU members, across numerous non-economic headings. The Article 50 negotiations should reflect this reality.

17) *Recognise the strength of the City*

The City – with its formidable combination of skills, knowledge and infrastructure – is largely Brexit-proof. London will remain the financial capital of Europe and, free of EU constraints, could even enhance its status as a global financial hub. While some firms may lose EU 'passporting' rights, the overall impact should be manageable and financial services will anyway benefit from 'regulatory equivalence'. While Brussels may threaten punitive regulatory action, EU-based firms and governments rely on the City to raise capital and for other specialized financial services.

Global Britain

18) *Negotiate FTAs with the rest of the world*
Some EU officials claim the UK cannot discuss or agree trade agreements with non-EU countries before March 2019. This is wrong. Any FTA negotiated before March 2019, that does not come into force until we have left breaches no EU treaty obligations. Our FTAs should focus on access for the services sector and investment flows, safeguarding of intellectual property rights and a commitment to remove tariff and non-tariff barriers (NTBs).

19) *Be clear that non-EU FTAs need not be in place before March 2019*
It would be helpful, during the Article 50 talks, if the EU sees Britain making progress on non-EU FTAs. Such deals, though, are not vital – and rushing into them could, again, result in unattractive terms. The UK already sells 56 per cent of its exports outside the EU, the majority to countries where the EU has no FTA. The notion that we must have a string of non-EU trade deals in place before the Article 50 window closes, or our trade will collapse, is nonsense.

20) *'Port over' existing EU FTAs and other trade facilitation agreements*
The EU has FTAs with a handful of large economies – including South Korea and Mexico – and lesser trade facilitation agreements with others. The UK should propose an 'exchange of notes' with these nations so, where possible, existing EU deals apply to the UK after Brexit. This is far less complex than cutting FTAs and other deals from scratch.

21) *Act as a cheerleader for free trade, but remain pragmatic*
Outside the EU, the UK should, as a point of principle, promote free trade

around the world, encouraging the eradication of both tariffs and NTBs. Lowering import tariffs, ultimately to zero, benefits UK consumers and importers of intermediate goods – even though we prefer a gradual approach. This pragmatism should extend to recognising the dislocation that changing tariff regimes could cause some sectors – reinforcing the importance of the UK's industrial and regional strategy.

Ready for Brexit

22) *Agree on a T-Tab to make Brexit as smooth as possible*

If the 'no deal' deadline passes, with an FTA deemed unlikely ahead of March 2019, the UK and EU should minimise business disruption by agreeing a 'Temporary Transition Agreement for Britain' (T-Tab). Subject to negotiation, this could comprise a 'zero-for-zero' tariff deal and mutual recognition agreements – to remain temporarily until they are updated or, better still, subsumed under a comprehensive UK–EU FTA. A T-Tab would also include specific government support for certain domestic sectors. The length of transition should be, at most, two years – and the UK should take care to remain free of ongoing ECJ jurisdiction.

23) *Keep the 'Repeal Bill' as simple as possible*

The European Union (Withdrawal) Bill – known as the 'Repeal Bill' – brings EU law relating to the UK onto the British statute book. On 'Brexit Day', then, nothing changes across a range of sectors – lessening cliff-edge dangers. The Act should be entirely uncontroversial, amounting to 'cut and paste' – so as to minimize the danger of parliamentary wrecking tactics. Repatriating a vast body of law will allow MPs of all parties to consider which aspects they want to scrap or amend – emphasising that Brexit is, above all, about empowering British democracy.

24) *Scale-up Whitehall, but use some imagination*

There have been reports that say the UK does not have enough skilled staff in key areas of Whitehall and the broader civil service – including trade negotiators and customs officials. Such warnings should be taken seriously. Senior trade negotiators need to be trained and recruited, including from

overseas. The civil service should be restructured in order to prepare for the
return of competencies from Brussels.

25) *Decide how best to use 'our EU money'*

In 2016, the UK paid a net figure of £165 million a week to the EU. After
March 2019, even if we are making staged 'divorce payments' as part of a negotiated T-Tab, or paying to be part of future projects, lower net payments
and tariff revenues should produce a 'Brexit bonus'. This money could be
earmarked to help certain sectors or regions adjust or, indeed, for spending
on the NHS. It should emphatically not be used to 'buy' some form of
ongoing single market 'membership' – paying to tie the UK into EU regulations and the continued weakening of our democracy.

BLUEPRINT FOR A POST-BREXIT BRITAIN

Brexit provides a unique opportunity to reinvigorate the British economy. Below, we present a summary of our recommendations for UK economic policy, particularly after March 2019. We have included opportunities arising from Brexit, as well as some long-standing issues the UK should have addressed while in the EU.

People

1) *Protect workers' rights – avoiding a genuinely Hard Brexit*

   Leaving the single market and the customs union isn't Hard Brexit. It is Brexit. A genuinely Hard Brexit would involve a 'race to the bottom' on working conditions once the UK is no longer obliged to comply with EU rules. This must be avoided at all costs – and is, anyway, highly unlikely. After March 2019, laws and regulations will be determined by Parliament – answerable to UK voters. Many existing UK-derived rules on pay and labour conditions are already more progressive than those applying elsewhere in the EU – such as our minimum wage and equal pay legislation.

2) *Put skills and vocational training at the heart of government policy*

   British-based firms have under-invested in UK staff over many years, in part due to the EU's freedom of movement rules. The UK must become a high-wage, high-productivity economy – which means, above all, more investment in skills. Align the UK's tax, training and education policies to meet publicly stated skills goals, overseen by a Cabinet Minister for Training and Skills. Overhaul student loans, providing a heavily discounted education for those taking economically vital subjects – particularly science,

technology, engineering and mathematics. University numbers are too high
and vocational training numbers too low. Both trends should be reversed.

3) *Build new homes on a large scale*
    Take immediate steps to ensure that 300,000 new homes are built each
    year over the next decade – double the current rate of construction. While
    this will require additional planning permissions, the immediate priority
    is to ensure large builders implement permissions already granted. Revive
    the 'garden cities' movement, with local authorities setting up 'new town
    companies'. This will limit building on greenbelt land and other sensitive
    sites – but some greenbelt will need to be shifted. The UK's housing short-
    age is now so serious, and causing such economic and social damage, it is
    not feasible to hope the situation will change without radical reform.

4) *Use a 'National Development Corporation' to break the building logjam*
    Central government should establish a National Development Corporation
    (NDC) that purchases green- and brownfield land suitable for housing, while
    managing existing state-owned land. The NDC grants itself planning per-
    mission on selected holdings, before selling it in lots to private developers.
    The captured 'planning gain' – the huge rise in land values once planning
    permission is granted – then funds schools, hospitals and other infrastructure
    at no net cost to the Exchequer, lessening local objections to additional hous-
    ing. Every UK economic recovery over the last century has been associated
    with a sharp rise in house-building – except that since 2008: the slowest,
    most subdued recovery in modern history. That is not a coincidence.

Business
5) *Create an enabling environment for business based on low and simple tax*
    As we leave the EU, Britain needs to forge a domestic economic policy
    based on high growth and investment. This is less about 'picking winners'
    than creating an enabling environment for business. The key principles are
    low and simple taxation, world-class transport and broadband connectivity,
    reasonably priced energy, a steady supply of skilled and unskilled labour and
    maximum access to international export markets.

6) *Ease the regulatory burden while retaining global industry standards*

The Treasury, working with the Department for Business, should examine where regulatory gains can be achieved as we prepare to leave the EU. While fully recognising global industry standards, not least to facilitate trade deals and protect consumers, a particular effort should be made to ease the regulatory burden on our all-important small- and medium-sized enterprises (SMEs) – the engine room of UK employment, innovation and growth.

7) *Close the 'Macmillan Gap' – finally*

The UK banking sector has failed for several generations adequately to finance domestic companies, particularly SMEs. This is the 'Macmillan Gap' – first identified in 1931. Explore regulatory changes that will help SMEs to access capital, not least for investment, helping them bridge the long-standing gap between fickle bank loans and far more complex equity finance.

8) *Prepare the UK to play a leading role in 4IR*

As the Fourth Industrial Revolution (4IR) has gathered pace, based on digital and nanotechnology, Britain has developed some world-class 'tech clusters'. But there is a disconnect between the presence of tech giants in the UK, and a relative lack of domestic investment and related employment. Our broader training policy must include a focus on digital and technical skills. Bolster efforts to make the information superhighway a reality across Britain, with super-fast broadband viewed as a utility, like access to water or electricity.

Control

9) *Pass legislation on UK immigration*

Prior to March 2019, the UK must prepare to return to the system of managed immigration that Britain operated for decades prior the EU's freedom of movement rules. Creating a system that is business-friendly and humane – with provision for all types of skilled and unskilled labour – will reassure many who voted Remain. Demonstrating that the UK government is now in charge, and immigration will be managed, will reassure many others who voted Leave.

10) *Implement a 'return of competencies' plan*

A comprehensive Cabinet Office assessment is needed of the 'competencies' and legislative powers returning from Brussels, outlining the extra policy tools and levers available. Once the UK is outside the EU, there will be much that can, over time, be abandoned or improved upon – examples include competition law, state aid, regional policy, the precautionary principle that hinders research and the terms granted to UK firms in domestic procurement. Much work is happening behind the scenes in Whitehall – and we are conscious of this in making this recommendation.

11) *Immediately fund necessary practical steps to make Brexit work*

The Treasury has not shown enough urgency in funding areas necessary for Brexit to succeed. Resources are needed, for instance, to train new customs officials, for a technology upgrade at UK ports and for new patrol boats and other unmanned devices to monitor our 200-mile exclusive economic zone. Such expenditures, across a range of sectors, must continue once we have left the EU. Brexit is a process, not a one-off event.

Economy

12) *Emphasise regional policy, with a focus on infrastructure*

Freed from EU state aid rules, and with a return of competency for 'cohesion funds', there is much scope to boost UK regional policy. Efforts to address the UK's regional divide should focus on infrastructure spending. Transport can play a transformative role – regional airports should be expanded significantly and HS3 prioritised, to help create an alternative UK growth centre in the north-west. We need new bridges, tolls roads and enhanced rail links beyond the south-east. Leaving the EU allows low-tax free ports to bring enterprise and prosperity to coastal areas.

13) *Create an investment fund to boost infrastructure spending*

The Labour manifesto was right to propose a National Transformation Fund to invest £250 billion over ten years in the UK's transport, communications and energy infrastructure. This should be seeded by central government – taking advantage of low long-term interest rates. We would put greater emphasis, though, on infrastructure bonds, with the private sector channelling institutional pension and life assurance savings into infrastructure investments that generate a regular income stream, matching long-term revenues with long-term liabilities.

14) *Ensure universities play a major role in economic strategy, beyond education*
Build on the role leading universities play in regional growth, encouraging stronger links between higher education, academic research and industry. Look for lessons from the US university sector, the only global challenger to the UK, yet more successful in transferring business ideas from campuses to commerce. Showcase UK universities when building the case for ongoing inward investment. Re-examine the funding of universities, exploring how more money can be attracted to research.

15) *Exclude students from migration numbers*
International students should not be included in migration figures – they are not permanent residents and attracting overseas students delivers significant gains for the economy. Students should only count if, having completed their UK education, they then stay. While not guaranteed residency, recently graduated foreign students should be favoured if they hold industry-specific qualifications. Justifiable concerns must be addressed about the abuse of student visas in 'fake colleges'.

Reform

16) *Commit to fiscal devolution*
Fiscal devolution is necessary and desirable once the UK has left the EU. The recommendation of the London Finance Commission should be adopted nationally, with stamp duty from property transactions retained at the local level. While the UK will remain a 'unitary' state, municipal bonds could play an important role in funding specific local infrastructure projects. Work to maintain a UK-wide consensus for Brexit by sharing regional powers returned from the EU with respective administrations in Edinburgh, Belfast and Cardiff.

17) *Make a radical reassessment of government spending*
The UK needs to decide on the appropriate size of the state as a share of

GDP. We favour a radical approach, bearing down on public spending, consistent with a sustainable tax take. If voters want higher government spending, we must be honest about the implications, taking steps to raise the necessary taxation. It is not acceptable to keep borrowing every year, loading debts onto future generations.

18) *Appoint a Royal Commission to consider a Bismarckian approach to welfare*
The UK should consider whether our welfare system needs to become more 'contributory', moving from a Beveridge system of universal provision to a Bismarckian system where personal contributions play a greater role in determining levels of entitlement. Such an inquiry is necessary – given our growing and fast-ageing population – and should be conducted with an open mind, with any recommendation not detracting from minimum subsistence benefits or 'free-at-the-point-of-use' health care.

19) *Take a fresh look at our institutional infrastructure*
The role, structure and stated priorities of the UK's main macroeconomic institutions need to be examined – including the Treasury and the Bank of England. The Treasury has become too powerful, while the Bank of England probably needs to show more independence. We believe that more 'outsiders' from industry and elsewhere should be seconded to such bodies, in order to tackle 'group think'.

20) *Implement our own Emissions Trading Scheme (ETS)*
Ensure our post-Brexit approach to the environment is positive for UK people and firms. We should only remain in the European Emissions Trading System if our obligations are outside the jurisdiction of the ECJ, where they currently fall. Better still would be a UK-specific ETS, along with a UK-wide carbon tax. Britain's desire to simplify its carbon pricing policy, with just one carbon price after 2021, will be more achievable outside the EU's ETS.

Global

21) *Outline a positive post-Brexit vision based on reform and enhanced trade*
Our thinking has been anchored in the EU for over forty years. Yet inside

the EU, our record on investment and productivity has been poor. Amidst inevitable near-term uncertainties, it will take time for the entire country to feel 'comfortable' outside the EU. But the potential Brexit upsides are huge – not least the forging of deeper trade links with fast-growing economies beyond the EU. Outlining an upbeat vision, combined with bold and constructive domestic policies, will ultimately positively impact how Britain sees itself, while bolstering the UK's reputation across the world.

22) *Spearhead a 'Go Global' and 'Britain is open for business' campaign*
Brexit provides a unique opportunity to reinvigorate the British economy. A 'Go Global' campaign should dispel misplaced fears that the UK will be more isolationist outside the EU. Since June 2016, the UK has attracted sizeable inward investment. The need for world-class export promotion must be taken extremely seriously, drawing on the experience of Austrade, Enterprise Ireland and other examples of international best practice.

23) *Make the Department forInternational Trade permanent*
While building up expertise in trade negotiation during the Article 50 process, the UK needs to maintain a permanent trade secretariat that will manage our existing FTAs and constantly seek to widen the scope of our trade relations around the world.

24) *Work with other countries to address migration 'push factors'*
The scale of immigration from the Middle East and North Africa into Europe is too large to be ignored. Work with other nations to address 'push factors' encouraging people to leave such regions. Redirect some of our overseas aid budget towards preventing emerging economies from losing talented people – aligning some aid flows to the export of UK university courses, to help such nations gain the human capital and international contacts that will drive future growth. Work on 'agriculture for services' trade deals under which low-income nations sell more farm produce to wealthy Western countries.

25) *Develop the UK's leadership role on global issues*
Having left the EU, Britain needs to adopt a leadership role at the WTO,

building support to cut tariffs and NTBs, particularly on services. We
should push to eradicate all trade barriers and global subsidies discriminat-
ing against underdeveloped countries, particularly in agriculture. The UK
should remain a signatory to the Paris Agreement on climate change. As the
largest military power in Western Europe, post-Brexit Britain must consoli-
date its leadership role within NATO.

INTRODUCTION

'A vote to leave the EU would result in an immediate
and profound shock to our economy.'
GEORGE OSBORNE, MAY 2016[1]

As is so often the case, the 'smart money' was wrong. Ahead of the UK's referendum on EU membership, the overwhelming consensus among political analysts, backed up by successive opinion polls and investors, was that Britain would vote Remain.

Less than a week before the vote, online prediction markets became emphatic. As campaigning reached a crescendo, the weight of money bet on either side suggested an '80 per cent probability' of continued EU membership.[2] Among 'decided' voters, the pollsters put Remain ahead, with most analysts then assuming the 8–10 per cent of 'undecided' voters would be 'most likely to stay with what they know'. There was a self-reinforcing prediction, echoed across the print and broadcast media and reflected in financial markets, that an 'inherently cautious' UK electorate would take the stern advice of Prime Minister David Cameron, Chancellor George Osborne, HM Treasury, the Bank of England and pretty much the entire British and international establishment. Surely UK voters wouldn't take a 'leap in the dark'.[3]

On the morning of Thursday 23 June 2016, foreign exchange markets were skewed heavily towards Remain winning – a victory that almost all mainstream economists expected to be hugely positive for the UK economy. For the entire week leading up to the referendum, the pound had climbed steadily, as uncertainty regarding the outcome dissipated, crystallising into a conventional wisdom 'baked into' financial markets that Britain would vote to stay in the EU.

That's why the announcement of a single result in a single constituency in the early hours of 24 June produced such a violent market reaction. When news came through that Sunderland, a largely working-class city in the industrial north-east, had voted decisively to leave, sterling plunged 3 per cent against the dollar. This was an extremely dramatic fall, given that Sunderland was just one of 382 voting districts across Britain, and only the third district to declare.

Although Sunderland had been expected to vote Leave, the recorded victory margin was a massive twenty-two percentage points, almost four times more than expected. This was a result so decisive it suggested the entire Leave vote may have been underestimated, right across the country. At a stroke, although vote counts in 99 per cent of the referendum districts were ongoing, Sunderland caused billions of dollars of 'smart money' to unwind on foreign exchanges across the globe. The world suddenly realised that Brexit was on the cards.

An area known for car manufacturing, and a beneficiary of significant foreign direct investment, Sunderland had shown real defiance. From that result onward, it was clear that the UK's EU referendum could produce a major political upset. The overwhelming majority of political pundits and investors who believed them were soon exposed as having misjudged the national mood.

Six hours after Sunderland, when the nationwide vote count was over, sterling had dropped to its lowest dollar level in more than thirty years. When the London Stock Exchange opened on Friday morning, the FTSE 100 nosedived a nerve-jangling 8.7 per cent. Investors then watched aghast as the British Prime Minister resigned outside Downing Street. By lunchtime, gold prices had spiked 10 per cent.

But despite the early stomach-churning headlines – '£150bn wiped off the value of stocks in a single morning' – financial markets proved remarkably resilient. After the initial drop, the FTSE 100 recovered. By close of play on Friday, the day after the referendum, London's main stock index was down just 1.9 per cent compared to the day before the referendum – and slightly up on the weekend before. Having plunged following the Brexit vote, sterling similarly staged a partial recovery. And, after a few weeks, what with the UK sporting a large current account deficit, many concluded a lower pound would benefit the UK economy, giving it a much needed export boost.[4]

CLEAN, NOT SOFT

Since the summer of 2016, the UK economy has held up rather well. Prior to the Brexit referendum, a HM Treasury study that was widely cited by then Chancellor George Osborne warned that the very act of voting to leave the EU would produce 'an immediate and profound economic shock'.[5] Treasury mandarins warned that if voters backed Brexit in the June referendum, the UK economy would contract by 1 per cent between July and September, compared to the same quarter in 2015, before shrinking another 0.4 per cent from October to December. Merely the decision to leave the EU, then, as opposed to actually leaving, would push the UK into recession.[6] This alarming forecast was, during the referendum campaign, repeatedly described as 'fact' by the Remain camp, not least the Chancellor himself.

The reality has been rather different. From July to September 2016, despite the referendum outcome, UK GDP grew by 0.5 per cent – only slightly less than the 0.6 per cent during the three months before the vote and the complete opposite of the Treasury forecast. Growth stayed buoyant from October through to December 2016, with GDP expanding by 0.7 per cent – once again, defying all official predictions. At the time of writing, official data points to 0.3 per cent growth during the second quarter of 2017, above the increase seen in the first three months, but having lost momentum ahead of the unexpected general election. The service sector, accounting for three quarters of the UK economy, remains strong, having expanded 2.3 per cent over the year since the referendum.

The performance of the British economy since the Brexit vote has been somewhat of a tale of two halves – with a strong showing during the second half of 2016 followed by more moderate growth between January and June 2017. Consumer spending surged before Christmas last year but as inflation has gone up, with prices of goods and services rising faster than wages, consumption has been squeezed.

This rise in inflation – from 0.6 per cent in June 2016 to 2.6 per cent in June 2017 – was partly due to weaker sterling pushing up import prices. It is often overlooked, though, that the inflation from mid-2016 was seen globally, with price pressures rising across the US, Germany and the Eurozone too.[7] Since the spring of 2017, inflation has eased elsewhere, but remained more elevated in the UK. The Bank of England, writing in its August 2017 Inflation Report, expects

UK inflation to peak towards the end of the year, before falling. This is the pattern it followed in the wake of sterling's depreciation after the 2008 global financial crisis. If this happens, it will ease pressure on real incomes, helping spending to recover. In July 2017, the International Monetary Fund (IMF), which was also very critical of Brexit ahead of the referendum, predicted the UK economy will expand by a relatively buoyant 1.7 per cent in 2017 and 1.5 per cent in 2018.

While the Brexit vote has caused some business uncertainty, and will continue to do so, the Treasury's 'immediate and profound economic shock' prediction now looks absurd. Since the referendum, UK unemployment has fallen to a 42-year low. The Treasury's pre-referendum forecast pointed to 500,000 job losses during the first twelve months after any Leave vote. Britain's factories have benefited instead from steady growth and strengthening exports, helped by a more competitive pound and a broader rebound in the global economy. At the time of writing, a new survey from the Confederation of British Industry (CBI) shows manufacturing output growing at its fastest rate since 1995.[8]

A continuation of the UK's relatively solid economic performance should bolster the country's position during Brexit negotiations with the European Commission and the EU 27. The Eurozone, despite deep-rooted structural problems, is meanwhile set for some cyclical rebound in coming years, after a decade of weakness, finally responding to strong simulative policies from the European Central Bank (ECB).

There is much speculation regarding what 'deal' the Article 50 negotiations might produce between the UK and EU – in terms of trade access, any 'divorce payment' and the residency and working rights of citizens – ahead of our planned leaving date in March 2019.[9] It is a central argument of this book that the UK's Brexit negotiations could and should be kept as simple as possible.

Under a Clean Brexit,[10] the UK will be outside both the EU's single market and customs union. The economic benefits of the single market and the customs union are grossly exaggerated, as this book will explain, and in net terms are probably negative. Clean Brexit also means ruling out the permanent adoption of 'off-the-shelf' solutions – such as retaining European Economic Area (EEA) membership, known as the 'Norway model', or selecting the 'Swiss option' and permanently joining the European Free Trade Association (EFTA). Both are problematic and, anyway, do not amount to Brexit.

The UK could try to break apart the EU's four freedoms and seek single market membership along with a special dispensation from freedom of movement rules and other related conditions.[11] Efforts to achieve such a bespoke deal, however, would all but guarantee an extremely acrimonious negotiation. The UK's determination to assert its newly reclaimed sovereignty would be put in direct conflict with EU core principles, which, if seriously breached, could tear the bloc apart. While this cherry-picking option is often called Soft Brexit, we refer to it as Messy Brexit because it risks causing chronic business uncertainty, last-minute decision-making and diplomatic chaos.

Since the general election in June 2017, many, mostly Labour Party, politicians have been calling for Soft Brexit – combining single market membership with UK controls on migration from the EU. While sounding attractive, this outcome almost certainly is not available and, if the UK did manage somehow to achieve it after an extremely heated negotiation, it could spark seismic political instability across the EU, as populations in other member states demanded the same deal. Soft Brexit would anyway still mean UK law remains under the jurisdiction of the ECJ along with continued multi-billion-pound payments to Brussels – in sum, a betrayal of the referendum result.

Attempting such a Messy Brexit would generate serious political conflict, risks setting back UK–EU relations for a generation and would imperil the EU per se. Those pursuing this route are either disingenuous, politically naïve, or both. It makes far more sense to pursue Clean Brexit, accepting that Britain will be outside the single market and the customs union – a position that benefits an open, services-oriented economy. Other large economies conduct extensive EU trade from outside the single market and the UK can do the same. Outside the customs union we can also cut trade deals with nations beyond the EU, many of which have far better growth prospects than Europe.

Leaving the single market and the customs union isn't Hard Brexit. It is Brexit. The Hard Brexit label, designed to make leaving the EU sound extreme and unreasonable, is used by those determined to reverse the referendum result. Clean Brexit accurately describes an approach that aims to keep the negotiations as simple and productive as possible. It minimises uncertainty, while making every effort, at a time when the EU is extremely fragile, not to further antagonise UK–EU relations or disrupt the EU – with the precarious single currency at its heart – in a manner that could send shockwaves across global financial markets.

Acknowledging that the UK will be outside the single market and the customs union by March 2019 also means the government can use the Article 50 period to make the necessary preparations for when we leave – putting in place updated immigration and customs clearance facilities, for instance. That helps avoid the cliff-edge scenario highlighted by business leaders. Leaving a legal construct after more than four decades obviously involves upheaval, raising difficulties and concerns. The groundwork needs to be laid across a range of areas, from port technology to confirming various mutual recognition agreements that facilitate trade. And while these arrangements can be managed, a sense of urgency is required.

Under Clean Brexit, Britain can actively negotiate free trade agreements (FTAs) with non-EU nations during the Article 50 window – precisely because we know that we will soon be outside the single market and the customs union. Clean Brexit is also the most democratic outcome. It quickly and decisively re-empowers Westminster, allowing a whole raft of EU-derived legislation, which will once again be under UK jurisdiction, to be confirmed, amended or repealed by directly elected MPs.

NO MORE FINGER-WAGGING

The EU, while still a major economic region, is not the force it once was. In 1973, when the UK joined the EEC, the resulting nine member states accounted for 26 per cent of the world economy. Now, with no fewer than twenty-eight members, the EU's share of global GDP is just over 20 per cent.[12] Credible forecasts suggest the EU 27 'will account for less than a tenth of the world economy by 2050 ... which will be less than India'.[13] While the EU has been shrinking as a proportion of global GDP, the share of UK exports that are sold in the EU has also been falling – from 61 per cent in 1999 to 56 per cent in 2006 and 44 per cent in 2015.[14] The direction of travel is clear.

Slow-growing and tied up in red tape, the Continent looked like the future when the UK voted to stay in the EEC in 1975. Now, attempts to bind nations together in a regional supranational body, surrounded by protectionist barriers, seem to be backward-looking, in denial of globalisation and rapid technological change. Since the UK joined the EEC, treaties including Maastricht and Lisbon have radically altered our relationship with what is now the EU, considerably diluting British sovereignty. The European Commission, with its unaccountable bureaucrats, and the European Parliament, a rubber-stamping factory for Commission diktats, are now powerful entities in our national life. The UK is subject to numerous EU directives and treaty obligations, regardless of what our own MPs and government think, even though the 1975 referendum asked us only to stay in 'the common market'.

Of course, the UK must keep trading with the EU 27 after Brexit. It makes complete sense for Britain to attempt to negotiate an FTA during these Article 50 talks. Our £71 billion trade deficit in goods and services with the bloc means that powerful German auto producers, French wineries and Italian furniture makers, those for whom this deficit represents revenue and profit, will want a deal to happen.[15] But even if an FTA isn't struck immediately, UK–EU trade will continue. Trade deals, while useful, aren't necessary to trade. The US and the EU have no formal FTA, yet they trade to the tune of hundreds of billions of dollars a year. Brazil and China have no FTA either, yet they trade too, with China having several years ago displaced America as Brazil's biggest trading partner.[16]

Trade happens, in the end, because entrepreneurs and companies see commercial opportunities and act upon them, selling their goods and services overseas, building relationships with foreign agents, counter-parties and end buyers. Trade happens because businesses make it happen, not because politicians and diplomats hold summits and sign pieces of paper. Trade deals are useful in helping to keep bureaucracy and red tape in check, but most trade happens between countries that haven't signed formal FTAs.

If the UK and EU fail to sign an FTA during this two-year Article 50 window, or even the several years following, Britain can exercise its right to trade with the EU under rules laid out by the WTO – the same rules under which the UK currently trades with the US, our biggest single-country trading partner. Under WTO rules, most cross-Channel trade flows will continue regardless, even if across some categories of goods and services relatively small tariffs are payable and regulatory boxes need to be ticked. And, during any period when we do trade without an FTA with the EU, our trade deficit with the EU 27 means the UK Exchequer will benefit from billions of pounds of import tariffs.

It would, in our view, be a major strategic error for the UK government to think that an FTA with the EU simply must be agreed before March 2019, and that somehow disaster looms if no such deal is struck. Nothing could be further from the truth. What matters above all is the quality of any UK–EU FTA, and striking a good deal means understanding that the British economy won't collapse if such a deal is delayed or, ultimately, doesn't happen.

The UK's trade with the EU will continue regardless, then, and will form an important, if declining, share of Britain's overseas commerce, as our trade with the rest of the world grows. The UK specialises in 'weightless' services. In an increasingly interconnected world, geography is becoming less significant. Any trade lost with the EU simply isn't economically important enough for Britain to have to succumb to an undemocratic supranational political body, the membership of which costs billions of pounds a year and deeply compromises British sovereignty. None of this is to ignore the economic uncertainties linked to Brexit. Leaving the EU is obviously disruptive to some UK residents and companies. Overall, though, we believe the upheaval is manageable and will be offset by new opportunities.

Ahead of the referendum, HM Treasury claimed British households would be £4,300 a year worse off by 2030.[17] The Organisation for Economic Co-operation and Development (OECD) warned of a Brexit shockwave. Such 'studies' were, in our view, all part of 'Project Fear' – a misjudged exercise in establishment finger-wagging, a coordinated attempt to scare voters away from exercising their democratic rights. Involving not only deeply partisan economic analysis, Project Fear was also politically ill-judged. It was a disastrous campaigning tactic that only served to galvanise the Leave side, as millions of undecided voters grew sick of clumsy attempts to frighten them.

Trade between the UK and EU could certainly experience some temporary disruption after March 2019. There is every chance, though, that the UK, free from onerous EU directives and the common tariff on non-EU imports, could move onto a faster growth path. After Brexit, Britain can focus more on trade with dynamic, populous emerging markets in Asia and elsewhere – nations set to dominate the global economy. The EU status quo, such as it is, suits big UK corporates, banks and professional firms, given that Brussels-based lobbying and tortuous regulation keeps smaller challengers at bay. That's why so many small- and medium-sized firms, accounting for much of Britain's creativity, innovation and employment, voted for Leave.[18]

OVERCOMING DIVISIONS

'Europe' isn't working – a trend illustrated most starkly by monetary union. The single currency, which 'most economists' said the UK must join back in the late 1990s, is doing untold damage, spreading economic stagnation across much of southern Europe. Locked in a high-currency straitjacket, Greece and Spain are suffering from 40–50 per cent youth unemployment. Italy, having barely grown since the euro's launch in 1999, could face a major banking crisis which, given the size of the Italian economy, has the potential to spark a global systemic meltdown. Unable to depreciate their currencies, less productive Eurozone members are being sacrificed on the altar of 'more Europe' – the mantra of further centralisation. And if the euro ever did implode, which looks entirely possible at some stage, the big EU economies would pick up the tab. For now, global reflation, which is boosting the world economy, has provided a temporary reprieve.

We also believe the EU's freedom of movement rules, while theoretically appealing, are dangerous and naïve. Massive wage differentials between EU members have driven record UK net immigration – up from 50,000 in 1997 to over 330,000 in 2016, double that number if gauged by new national insurance numbers issued. Immigration has long been a net-positive for the UK economy. The country has benefited enormously, over the centuries, from Huguenot, Jewish, Irish, Afro-Caribbean and Asian immigration, along with countless migrants from elsewhere. Successive waves of immigration have brought millions of talented and hard-working people to British shores.

A near sevenfold rise in annual immigration over twenty years, though, raises questions that cannot be ignored. Convenient for employers and the wealthy, such a rapid influx has suppressed the wages of many low-income workers, worsening their financial insecurity, while further stretching the public services on which poorer citizens disproportionately rely. For the overwhelming majority who backed Brexit, immigration concerns relate to economics and public services, not race. Such problems must be addressed, in part by the reintroduction of flexible and humane border controls, with immigration continuing at a pace that benefits the British economy but also restores public confidence.

During any referendum, the whole country is like one big general election constituency. Every vote counts with equal weight and there is only one winning side. Ahead of the UK's EU referendum, the public were repeatedly told they faced a 'once-in-a-generation' decision. The reputations of many driven and ambitious people were on the line, along with the future of the world's fifth biggest economy and the broader European project. It was inevitable the political environment would become febrile, even fraught. And the divisions exposed by the referendum ran deep.

'Brexit is often characterised as either a catastrophe or a much-needed liberation,' says Jonathan Hill, a former EU Commissioner. 'Beyond the rhetorical war, though, the overwhelming likelihood is that it will be neither.' Hill, a Remain voter and consummate Brussels insider, resigned the day after the EU referendum. He has since worked to bring together UK politicians and campaigners from both sides of the Brexit divide. He is particularly critical, rightly, of the still-polarised nature of the UK debate – with 'Remoaners' being accused of wanting Brexit to go wrong, while 'Brextremists' are told their optimism shows they are out of touch. 'There will clearly be winners and losers from Brexit and to say so isn't Remoaner defeatism,' Hill insists. 'But neither is it swivel-eyed utopianism to see new and exciting opportunities for the UK outside the EU.'[19]

The UK's EU referendum was always likely to generate passionate and combative political debate. Rather than marking an end to rhetorical acrimony, since June 2016 the discourse has possibly become even more bad-tempered – particularly since the June 2017 general election. Britain boasts a generally positive and vibrant political culture that, one must hope, will reassert itself soon. In this regard, UK politicians can learn much from the business community. Most firms, in the authors' experience, are now pragmatic about the reality of the UK leaving the EU. The vast majority of business leaders, whichever way they voted, generally want the details of Brexit decided and implemented with a minimum of diplomatic theatrics and political fuss. We believe our Clean Brexit model provides such a solution.

Beyond the UK's political and media classes, the majority of voters, including those who voted Remain, now want the government to get on with Brexit. A poll conducted in June 2017, after the general election, suggested that 70 per cent of the public feel that Brexit now needs to happen.[20] It is the sincere intention of this book to promote an approach to Brexit that we believe will result not only in the best deal for Britain but also the greatest chance of continued strong and harmonious relations between the UK and EU.

'The only project I'm interested in is Project Fact,' declared then Prime Minister David Cameron during the referendum campaign, rejecting allegations of fearmongering. 'Project Fact is about saying: "Stay in and you know what you'll get."' As a campaigning device, that statement fell flat. Voters could see that, far from standing still, the EU is constantly changing and has, in recent years, become alarmingly unstable.

The EU has been transformed since the six founding members signed the Treaty of Rome in 1957. Such change has accelerated since 1975, when the UK voted to stay in 'the common market'. It has been the thrust of such changes, away from a free trade zone of sovereign states, towards a proto super-state issuing directives overruling domestic laws, which many in the UK have found alarming, contributing to the Brexit vote which dumbfounded the establishment. The ongoing march towards 'ever closer union' is concerning electorates across much of the rest of Europe, too. There is, contrary to David Cameron's statement, no EU status quo.

Part I of this book outlines how 'Project Europe' has developed since it formally began sixty years ago. It also highlights how Europe's place in the broader global economy has changed. Britain, from the outset – by dint of geography, history and culture – was an awkward member of the European club. And Europe, while still an important region, now accounts for a smaller share of the global economy, and a much smaller share of UK exports, than when Britain joined the EEC in 1973.

PART I

BEFORE BREXIT

CHAPTER 1

THE EUROPEAN UNION AT SIXTY

'Europe will be forged in crises, and will be the sum
of the solutions adopted for those crises.'
JEAN MONNET, 1978[1]

On 25 March 1957, the heads of government of Belgium, France, West Germany, Italy, Luxembourg and the Netherlands met in the Palazzo dei Conservatori. Set on Rome's Capitoline Hill, the fifteenth-century palace has, over the centuries, been adorned with balustrades, statues and huge Corinthian pilaster strips, part of a façade redesigned by Michelangelo.

It was in such suitably historic and sumptuous surroundings that, sixty years ago, the Treaty of Rome was signed, establishing the European Economic Community (EEC), the main precursor to today's EU. Explicit in its aims, the Treaty of Rome sought to 'lay the foundations of an ever closer union among the peoples of Europe'. The goal was 'common action to eliminate the barriers which divide Europe' so as to improve living and working conditions. Attempting to bring peace and prosperity to a continent ravaged by war twice over the previous half-century, the Treaty's signatories were driven by noble intentions.[2]

The European Coal and Steel Community had already been formed in 1952, to help Europe's reconstruction efforts and lessen the threat of future conflict by establishing mutual economic reliance. The creation of the EEC five years later – with the aim of promoting food and energy security, social cohesion and intra-European trade – was seen as the logical next step.

Throughout the 1960s and into the 1970s, the six member states gradually dismantled tariffs on international trade in goods, mindful that such barriers had scarred international relations during the 1930s, so gradually creating 'the common market'. At the same time, the EEC was transformed into a protectionist 'customs union' that imposed a 'common external tariff' on all products entering the bloc from third countries.

The UK, from the very beginning, had an uneasy relationship with the EEC. Britain initially refused to participate, in part due to commercial, political and psychological ties to the former Empire. Many previously colonised countries had been brought together under the banner of the Commonwealth in 1949, less than a decade before the Treaty of Rome was signed. While the UK backed pan-European free trade, there was a reluctance to join a customs union, with British officials wanting to keep control over tariffs on imports from non-EEC countries.

In addition, the political establishment and the broader UK population were somewhat concerned about a project whose long-term aim was to pool the sovereignty of nation states to form supranational 'European institutions'. While the UK considered signing the Treaty of Rome, Conservative governments during the mid- to late 1950s, led by Winston Churchill, Anthony Eden and Harold Macmillan, felt the loss of sovereignty was too great and the EEC's plans too ambitious.[3]

However, during the years that followed the ceremony in Rome's Palazzo dei Conservatori, the six EEC members flourished. Their economies were buoyant, driven by post-war reconstruction efforts and inward investment, outpacing growth in the US while the UK endured a stark relative decline. It was from an economic imperative, then, that Britain reconsidered. By 1961, Macmillan had applied for the UK to join after all, only to be rebuffed by Charles de Gaulle. The French President argued that the UK's strong links to the Commonwealth and especially to the US would dilute Britain's commitment to the European project.

In 1967, when Britain applied again under Labour Prime Minister Harold Wilson, de Gaulle vetoed once more, accusing the UK of 'a deep-seated hostility' towards the EEC.[4] After the more conciliatory Georges Pompidou replaced de Gaulle at the Élysée Palace, Prime Minister Edward Heath took the UK into the EEC on its third request to join in 1973, along with Denmark and the Republic of Ireland.

EARLY WARNING SIGNS

When Parliament passed the European Communities Act in 1972, in preparation for EEC entry, the rather heated debate and resulting slim majorities in the

House of Commons were warning signs of what was to come. A fundamental tenet of the UK's unwritten constitution is the sovereignty of Parliament, making British legislature the supreme power of the state, passing statutes that are the principal form of British law. The unequivocal effect of the 1972 Act, though, was to enshrine in UK law the fundamental supremacy of the EEC, with European law prevailing. As such, the ECJ became the de facto 'Supreme Court of Europe', with judgments binding on all member states.

Such concerns, while highlighted by some MPs and other campaigners, were pushed to the fringes of the UK's political consciousness. The pressing issue was that Britain's ailing economy, with its sluggish growth and embittered industrial relations, was destroying the self-confidence of a country which, just a generation before, had been a leading global power. The 1973 oil price shock, which saw the price of crude oil quadruple in a year, as the OPEC exporters' cartel embargoed several Western countries that supported Israel in its war with Egypt and Syria, added to the feeling of economic vulnerability.

Ahead of entering the EEC, the UK was widely referred to as 'the sick man of Europe'.[5] As such, most of the country's political and commercial leaders put any constitutional squeamishness out of their minds. It was far more important to reverse Britain's decline and not miss out on the EEC's 'economic miracle'. For many, with memories of the Second World War still fresh, the notion that West Germany's *Wirtschaftswunder* economy was booming, while the UK struggled, was particularly galling.

The outcome of the UK's 1975 referendum, which was held to confirm EEC membership that had begun two years earlier, came as no surprise. Wilson's government made strenuous efforts during the campaign to keep the debate focused on the economic advantages of 'staying in', and away from seemingly arcane constitutional issues. Some leading political figures, such as then Secretary of State for Industry Tony Benn, who helped convince Wilson to hold the ex post EEC referendum in the first place, emphasised sovereignty. 'Continuing membership of the Community would mean the end of Britain as a completely self-governing nation and the end of our democratically elected parliament as the UK's supreme law-making body,' Benn wrote, in his famous pre-referendum letter to his Bristol constituents. His warnings were largely ignored.[6]

Even the question posed on the 1975 ballot paper: 'Do you think the United

Kingdom should stay in the European Economic Community (The Common Market)?', seemed designed to focus attention on the economic aspects of EEC membership. Faced with an apparent choice between British decline and European prosperity, and with practically every national newspaper supporting 'Yes', 67 per cent of voters backed remaining in the EEC.[7]

Over the four decades since the 1975 referendum, being 'in Europe' has clearly come to mean a lot more than the 'common market' the British electorate voted to join. Most obviously, the nine nation states of the mid-1970s EEC have become the twenty-eight members of the EU – a bloc that is home to more than 500 million people with a GDP of some $16,400 billion, second only to the US and accounting for just over one fifth of the world economy.[8] A succession of treaties since 1975 has also radically altered our relationship with the EU, further diluting the sovereignty of member states. Institutions including the European Commission and the ECJ have become extremely influential, exerting powers that manifestly trump those of the UK and our democratically elected MPs and leaders.

Building on the tariff-free intra-EU trade in goods established by the original customs union, the 1987 Single European Act emphasised not just the free movement of services and capital, but also people. The 1995 Schengen Convention then went further, removing border controls completely and creating a common visa policy.[9]

Prior to that, the Maastricht Treaty of 1992 had created the EU's 'pillar system', extending cooperation deeper into criminal justice, the military, foreign policy and the judiciary. By far the most ambitious and integrationist treaty since the Treaty of Rome, Maastricht also paved the way for the single currency, which was eventually launched in 1999.

To some observers, Maastricht was a Franco-German fait accompli, with Paris accepting the reunification of East and West Germany in exchange for Berlin agreeing to give up the Deutsche Mark – a powerful symbol of the country's post-war rejuvenation. With the constitutional significance of further European integration now screamingly obvious, Maastricht met with fierce resistance at Westminster. Under enormous pressure, not least from many of his own Tory backbenchers, Prime Minister John Major secured an 'opt-out' from the European Commission, allowing Britain to remain outside the single currency.

It is a widely held view, in the UK and beyond, that the advent of monetary union marked the moment when, to paraphrase Robert Browning, the EU's 'reach exceeded its grasp'.[10] There is certainly a very strong argument that many of the significant difficulties facing the 'European project' today, difficulties that seriously threaten its future, have their origins in the launch of the euro.

RISING DISCONTENT

Back in 2007, the leaders of EU member states, including a recently elected Chancellor Angela Merkel of Germany, assembled in Berlin to celebrate the fiftieth anniversary of the Treaty of Rome. They could look forward with confidence to another half-century of European nation-building. The EU's economic model, the Berlin Declaration stated, combined 'economic success and social responsibility' and was built on 'a euro that makes us strong'.[11]

Just three years earlier, under the 'big bang' enlargement of 2004, ten new nations had joined the EU, including Eastern European and Baltic states previously under Soviet control. The 'unnatural division' of Europe was 'consigned to the past', the Berlin Declaration triumphantly concluded, describing Europe as a continent where people had learned to 'live together as was never possible before'.

The reality is that for some years prior to 2007 there had been growing evidence of public antipathy towards the EU's pursuit of 'ever closer union'. In 1993, a majority of Danish voters rejected their country's ratification of Maastricht, protesting the loss of sovereignty. After certain concessions were granted, not least the same single currency opt-out as Britain, Danish voters eventually accepted Maastricht in a second referendum.

Irish voters rejected the Treaty of Nice in 2001, believing proposed changes to EU voting weights marginalised smaller countries, while undermining Ireland's military neutrality. Minor concessions were made and, following an intense campaigning effort by a strongly pro-EU Irish government and national media, the Treaty passed in a second referendum sixteen months later.

The Danish and Swedish electorates, in referendums in 2000 and 2003 respectively, chose not to join the single currency, even though it had launched relatively successfully and was up and running. Most spectacularly perhaps, in mid-2005, voters in both France and the Netherlands, two founding Treaty of Rome signatories, rejected the 'EU Constitution' that proposed more 'qualified majority voting', expanding the EU's power by dropping the need for unanimous agreement from all member states across a broader range of policy areas.

After these French and Dutch votes, previously announced referenda on the EU Constitution in Portugal, Poland, Denmark and the UK were quietly shelved. The centralising measures in the draft constitution were nevertheless recycled and presented in the form of the 2007 Treaty of Lisbon. Responding to protests that Lisbon was a rehash of policies previously rejected in two national referenda, official denials were somewhat discredited by Valéry Giscard d'Estaing. 'All the earlier proposals will be in the new text,' said the former French President, who had overseen the creation of the original EU Constitution, before the Treaty of Lisbon was finalised. 'But they will be hidden and disguised in some way.'[12]

After a huge lobbying effort by Brussels, only the Irish government held a referendum on the Lisbon Treaty, as required by its own constitution.[13] Again, Irish voters said no, as they had in 2001. And again, after more cosmetic concessions – contained in letters from the European Commission to the Irish government, separate to the Treaty and containing no legal force – an exasperated Irish public finally approved Lisbon in a second referendum just over a year later.

While such political difficulties could be shrugged off at the fiftieth anniversary of the Treaty of Rome, the atmosphere that surrounded the sixtieth anniversary was somewhat different. By March 2017, the 'European project' was marred not by contained national disputes over various treaties, but widespread economic frustration and blatant EU-wide political rancour. A project based on wholly laudable aims, that had hoped to heal divisions resulting from bloody conflict, had become increasingly beset by new and threatening divides.

Proclaiming that 'Europe is our common future', the 2017 Rome Declaration, signed in the same Palazzo dei Conservatori as the original Treaty sixty years before, asserted the EU's aspirations of a 'unique union with common institutions and strong values, a community of peace, freedom, democracy, human rights and the rule of law'.[14] Behind the pomp and ceremony, though, clear concerns showed through. On the eve of the Rome Declaration, EU leaders met with Pope Francis at the Vatican. While offering a blessing for the EU, the Pope issued a warning: 'When a body loses its sense of direction and is no longer able to look ahead, it experiences a regression and, in the long run, risks dying,' he said, in comments released by the Vatican press office.[15]

Even the Rome Declaration itself, amid defiant assertions that the EU remains 'undivided and indivisible', was forced to nod towards reality. 'The EU is facing unprecedented challenges, both global and domestic,' the text stated, including 'regional conflicts, terrorism, growing migratory pressures, protectionism and social and economic inequalities'.

There was also, of course, a glaring absentee from the sixtieth anniversary celebrations. There was no delegate for the UK – just as there hadn't been at the original signing ceremony, in the same Palazzo hall sixty years before. A few days after the anniversary on 29 March, Prime Minister Theresa May was due to trigger Article 50 of the Lisbon Treaty, starting the clock on a two-year timetable to leave the EU.

MONETARY DIS-UNION

Current discontent towards the EU is in part the result of a poorly performing economy. This wasn't always the case. For a quarter of a century, following the Treaty of Rome until the early 1980s, the EEC's national income per person grew at an almost identical pace to that of the US. Europe slowed during the late 1980s and early 1990s, around the time of German reunification and various exchange rate crises, but growth then picked up again. During the ten years from 1997 onwards, EU GDP expanded at an average of 2.3 per cent a year, only slightly behind the 2.6 per cent average US growth.

The global financial crisis of 2007–08, though, hit Europe particularly hard. The EU then endured a sovereign debt crisis in 2012–13, centred on the Eurozone, which sent the region into a double-dip recession that the US managed to avoid. In the decade since 2007, America's per capita GDP grew by a historically lacklustre 0.6 per cent a year. But the EU figure was just half that at 0.3 per cent.

The EU has not only grown very slowly since the financial crisis, but what growth we have seen has been very uneven. By the end of 2016, the German economy had, in real terms, grown by around 12 per cent since 2007. The equivalent Spanish and Italian numbers were 1 per cent and -7 per cent. Almost a decade on from the crisis then, Spain has barely recovered, while Italy remains a long way from recovery. In 2017, the Greek economy is still 20 per cent smaller than it was in 2007, having endured a decline steeper and longer than that suffered by America during the Great Depression, a plight that rocked US capitalism to its core. Flirting once again with sovereign default, Greece remains an economic basket case, with more than one in five workers unemployed.

The underlying cause of the EU's disappointing and disjointed economic performance since the global financial crisis, which has seen Germany and other rich member states fare quite well while others have suffered, is the single currency. The centrepiece of the European project, the euro has, for many millions, been an unmitigated disaster. By binding members across the south of the EU into a high-currency straitjacket, it has condemned countless workers to live in economic stagnation. Youth unemployment in Italy, Greece and Spain is over 40 per cent – a human tragedy.[16] Italy, one of the world's largest economies, has not only failed to recover since the 2007 financial collapse but the country has barely grown since the euro was launched in 1999.

Rich countries such as Germany and the Netherlands, for whom the euro is undervalued compared to their productivity, have benefited hugely from single currency membership. Yet there is no appetite among voters in wealthier Eurozone nations to bail out poorer neighbours such as Italy, Greece, Portugal and Spain – economies throttled by a currency that, given their somewhat lower productivity levels, is far too high. The resulting rows over soaring sovereign bond yields, subsequent rescue plans, 'austerity measures' and failed repayments, have seen violent protests on the streets of Madrid, Lisbon, Rome and, in particular, Athens – protests marred by blatant anti-German sentiment, involving Nazi iconography. Far from promoting 'unity' or 'cohesion', Europe's monetary experiment is stoking the kind of cross-border division and nationalism the EU was supposed to have consigned to history.

By early 2010, the uneven impact of the euro across its constituent member states could be denied no longer. As weaker, more indebted nations struggled to cope with the fallout of the biggest financial collapse in almost a century, without the buffer of a depreciating currency, the resulting 'spreads' – or difference between the respective sovereign bond yields of wealthier and poorer Eurozone members – threatened to tear the single currency apart. As bailout packages were prepared and paid, voters in richer northern Eurozone countries, their views long hidden under the cloak of 'European solidarity', were loath to see their governments rescue southern members whom they saw as profligate.

Those nations being 'rescued', some that had been dictatorships only a few decades previously, deeply resented the 'austerity' conditions imposed on them by much wealthier neighbours. The euro has 'sown division across Europe', in the words of Yanis Varoufakis, the academic economist turned politician who served as Greek Finance Minister during 2015. 'The euro has turned Europeans against Europeans.'[17]

The first Greek bailout was in May 2010 and amounted to €110 billion. Coordinated by a self-styled 'Troika' of the ECB, the European Commission and the IMF, it was the biggest financial rescue in history. Since then, despite such efforts, the Eurozone has lurched from crisis to crisis. Three bailouts later, Greece is still struggling to survive in the cruel economic trap that is the single currency. During the summer of 2017, now on its third bailout, Greece has again been on the brink of a potentially catastrophic default. There is widespread agreement that this Greek stagnation will only end, making way for a recovery, if the vast debts Athens now owes other Eurozone members are partially written off. But such debt relief would be extremely controversial among richer northern members.

Portugal, Spain, Cyprus and Ireland are four other Eurozone member states that have also been assisted in the face of sovereign default since 2010 – and, to varying degrees, have managed to recover. In all four countries, though, the harsh conditions imposed have seriously knocked the popularity of EU membership. And still, in the cases of Portugal, Spain and Cyprus, the gap between sovereign bond yields and those of Germany remains alarmingly wide.

Financial markets are most nervous about Italy – given the country's size, which could make any bailout impossibly expensive. The Eurozone's third-largest economy, Italian GDP is around ten times that of Greece. Economic stagnation and high unemployment within the single currency have seen Italy's national debt spiral to 133 per cent of GDP. This loan-pile represents 'a major source of vulnerability' for the single currency, observed the European Commission in February 2017.[18] In response, Rome says the Commission and other EU member states should cut Italy 'more slack', not least because the country's geographic location means it is disproportionately affected by another important issue that has seriously impacted the EU.

PERFECT STORM

Along with ongoing concerns about the single currency, the EU has also, since 2015, had to deal with an extremely serious refugee crisis. Mass migration, mostly from the Middle East and Africa, and its related tensions are seriously threatening the EU's internal rules, broader unity and political stability.

Over the last decade and a half, Western Europe has absorbed millions of migrants from former Communist countries.[19] Some 20 million people have emigrated from central and south-eastern Europe since the 2004 'big bang' enlargement, around 80 per cent of them heading to richer nations within the EU, many in search of higher wages.[20] Ten years later in 2014, while such migration from 'new' EU nations hadn't caused political outcry, there were signs of contained resentment.[21]

Over the past three years, though, public attitudes have been transformed. Civil war in Libya and Syria, as well as broader regional instability, has sparked an accelerating immigration from outside the EU. Countries across southern Europe – Spain, Greece and Italy – have seen the biggest waves of illegal immigration, as instability in north Africa and the Middle East have resulted in widespread people smuggling.

Asylum applications from outside the EU increased from 250,000 in 2010 to 1.3 million 2015 – a fivefold rise. This acceleration abated after the EU struck a deal with Turkey to stop migrants from entering Greece. But, still, an additional 1.2 million new asylum seekers entered the EU in 2016, only slightly down on the year before.[22] Rather than registering migrants in the country in which they enter the EU, countries in southern Europe have allowed migrants to travel illegally across EU territories unregistered to wealthier northern European nations, particularly Germany, where they perceive better economic opportunities. During 2016, even though the overall number of asylum seekers entering Europe fell slightly from the previous year, those registering in Germany rose from 442,000 to 722,000.

The flow of migrants and asylum-seekers into Europe, and their distribution within the EU, has been causing political turmoil not only between but also within nations, spreading instability and uncertainty across what were previously among the world's most stable democracies. Yet that flow will surely continue.

Considerable bitterness in Germany, among politicians and the broader population, is now directed towards other EU members. They have shown little 'solidarity' in registering and accepting asylum seekers, the argument goes, despite the understanding Germany has shown during bailout talks. There is also anger across the richer EU nations towards Eastern European members – particularly Poland. Warsaw has refused to accept practically all refugees, openly flouting EU rules it must do so, despite being recipients of many billions of euros in EU structural funds.

Sixty years on from the Treaty of Rome, then, as the EU grapples with north–south tensions resulting from the inherent flaws of the single currency, it is also dealing with east–west divisions stemming from a serious migrant crisis. As a result, five EU nations have 'temporarily' suspended the Schengen Agreement, as we will discuss in Chapter 3. Amidst public outrage at large inflows of people, the idea of borderless, passport-free travel – one of the EU's most cherished principles – is now being challenged. The euro crisis and the migrant crisis have combined to generate a perfect storm, which is seriously testing the EU's durability.

The impact of this twin crisis on the respective domestic politics of various EU members has, of course, been considerable. Millions of EU citizens are anyway fundamentally frustrated by a decade of economic stagnation and related unemployment and austerity measures, often blamed on membership of the euro. Among the economically vulnerable, such concerns are now coupled with a migration crisis that they feel is also the fault of the EU. Mass migration, from within the EU but more importantly from outside, has sparked a rise in nationalism. Terror attacks in various EU capitals, often with an Islamic connection, have unfortunately generated a fear of foreigners that is increasingly expressed as xenophobia. And even among wealthier, generally more liberal EU voters, tough new policies limiting refugee flows from war-torn countries in Africa and the Middle East have caused dismay, given the EU's claims to moral leadership on human rights.

ROME REDUX?

During the early 1990s, in leading member states such as Germany, France, Italy and Spain, EU membership generally received opinion poll approval ratings of 70–80 per cent. Such polls now produce scores not much above 30 per cent.[23] Since 2015, voters in Greece, Denmark and Holland have rejected EU proposals put to them in referendums – and that was before the UK's dramatic Brexit vote in June 2016.[24]

Support for parties wanting to hold a referendum on membership of the EU and/or the euro has risen dramatically in recent years. Populist anti-EU politicians are now well-established, building an infrastructure and challenging for power. They are tapping into deep-seated concerns among many voters that the EU would be better off as a group of freely trading nations, rather than continuing to pursue 'ever closer union'.

In December 2016, Italy's pro-EU Prime Minister Matteo Renzi was comprehensively defeated in a constitutional referendum. Now that Renzi has resigned, elections must take place in early 2018. Italy's three main opposition parties, including the Five Star Movement, have all supported leaving the single currency, amidst widespread perception that euro membership is hindering Italian growth. Headed by comedian turned political leader Beppe Grillo, Five Star has benefited from a split in the ruling Partito Democratico (PD). From 2015 to 2017, opinion polls have suggested support for Five Star rising from 20 to around 30 per cent – with some polls showing the populist party in first place, ahead of PD. Local election successes in June 2017 for the centre-right coalition led by former Prime Minister Silvio Berlusconi and the far-right anti-immigration Northern League have muddied the waters of Italian politics. But, at the time of writing, following a reaffirmation of its pledge to hold a referendum on euro membership, Five Star is once again polling neck-and-neck with PD.[25] Were Italy to vote to quit the euro, then successfully leave and benefit from a competitive devaluation, other struggling nations would surely seek to follow.

In March 2017, there were sighs of relief in Brussels when the party of Dutch Prime Minister Mark Rutte beat that of Geert Wilders, who strongly opposes the EU. Although Wilders lost, his party won over 30 per cent more seats than in 2012, while Rutte's party won almost 30 per cent fewer. Recent support for Wilders has certainly forced mainstream politicians – Rutte included – to adopt a more Eurosceptic tone during campaigning. And with Wilders now the leader of the biggest opposition party in the Netherlands, he is well placed to keep growing his support base, further challenging Dutch acceptance of the broadly progressive politics of the EU establishment.

There was positive jubilation among mainstream politicians across the Western world, when in early May 2017 Emmanuel Macron beat Marine Le Pen by a margin of 66 per cent to 34 per cent in the second and final round of the French presidential election. While Le Pen lost in what was widely hailed as a defeat of populism, it is worth noting that she attracted a vote share that was almost double what her Front National party had received in the 2012 presidential contest and over three times bigger than that of her overtly racist father, Jean Marine Le Pen, when he contested the presidency in 2007. The 2017 French election was also marred by record abstentions. For every five voters backing Macron, another four refused to vote or spoiled their ballot.

From 2012 to 2016, under President François Hollande, the French economy grew by just 0.7 per cent a year, compared to 1.3 per cent in Germany and 2.1 per cent in the UK and US. At thirty-nine years old, and having never held elected office, Macron must now tackle France's deep-seated economic and social problems – including unemployment of 10 per cent, with youth unemployment at a shocking 25 per cent. Polling evidence taken immediately after the 2017 presidential contest suggests almost 60 per cent of Macron's voters chose him primarily to block Le Pen – with only a fifth saying the former investment banker spoke to their concerns.[26] Le Pen's supporters, in contrast, are committed and determined. Already, she has vowed to contest the next presidential election in 2022.

Committed to taking France out of both the EU and the single currency, a Le Pen presidency could lead to 'Frexit', which, in turn, would surely mark the end of the broader European project. During the spring of 2017, as her support built, the gap between French and German ten-year sovereign bonds quadrupled to almost ninety basis points – a level not seen since the height of the euro crisis of late 2011 and early 2012. This spread fell sharply once Macron prevailed, but remained at around forty basis points, having averaged around ten basis points in 2016 and half that the year before.

Federal elections are also due to be held in Germany in September 2017. The anti-euro Alternative für Deutschland (AfD), founded only in 2013, already holds seats in thirteen of Germany's sixteen regional Parliaments. AfD now looks extremely likely to enter the Bundestag, roughly equivalent to the UK's House of Commons, by winning more than 5 per cent of the national vote. While other parties have ruled out forming a coalition with AfD, and it has been riven with infighting, it will still be the first party to enter Germany's Parliament on a platform to the right of the Christian Democrats in over sixty years.

At the time of writing, the Christian Democrats look well placed to prevail in September, with Angela Merkel winning a fourth term as Chancellor. Populist parties seem unlikely to upend German politics this autumn, with the main challenge coming from the Social Democrats under Former European Parliament President Martin Schulz.[27] In a recent official survey, though, 45 per cent of Germans said 'immigration' was the most important issue facing their country, a higher share than any other major EU nation.[28] This reflects, perhaps, the disproportionate burden Germany has shouldered in terms of registering and accommodating asylum-seekers entering the EU in recent years. Such concerns about migration, as well as the bailouts associated with euro membership, are likely to shape German politics for years to come.

Despite the defiant words of the 2017 Rome Declaration, the EU is under intense pressure. For the first time since 1957, the bloc can no longer take its future survival for granted. Amidst a host of global challenges that have brought national identity back into focus, widespread discontent towards the EU has seriously discredited the idea that membership of a supranational body can deliver economic stability and prosperity. 'I know about the state of the EU,' said Sigmar Gabriel in January 2017, who has since become Germany's Finance minister. 'It is no longer unthinkable that it breaks apart.'[29] The EU seems to be just one bad election, one geopolitical event, one Eurozone bond crisis away from a great unravelling.

Sixty years on from the Treaty of Rome, a lot has been achieved. For a considerable part of its lifetime, the EU has been a force for economic prosperity, cross-border cooperation and social progress. But for much of the past twenty years, and particularly since the 2008 financial crisis, the EU economy has underperformed, as the single currency has condemned some countries to low growth and high unemployment while others have thrived. The related bailouts and attached conditions have generated much discontent, with intra-EU relations deteriorating as the Continent has struggled to respond to the migrant crisis. This is the backdrop against which the UK voted for Brexit and will now conduct the Article 50 negotiations.

'Europe will be forged in crises, and will be the sum of the solutions adopted for those crises,' wrote Jean Monnet, the spiritual father of the European project. The EU now, though, is in a deeper crisis than it has ever been before. Since 1957, much has happened within Europe that has made the vision of the EU's founding fathers more difficult to implement. Yet the pace of change across the European continent has been nothing compared to the pace of change across the rest of the world.

CHAPTER 2

HOW THE WORLD HAS CHANGED

'People think I live in a cave all year and come out in December,
shouting: "It's Chriiisstmasss!"'
NODDY HOLDER, 2015[1]

One thing that should be fully appreciated is context. To understand the future economic changes that the UK is about to experience as we leave the EU, it is crucial to look at the past, starting in 1973. The EEC that Britain joined was very different to the EU we voted to leave in 2016. The world economy, too, has changed considerably over the last half-century, and looks set to change even more in the years to come.

The UK in 1973 was 'the sick man of Europe', as explained in Chapter 1. The 'three-day week' – which lasted from December 1973 to March 1974 – seemed fully to vindicate the 'sick man' label. Factories' operating times were significantly limited as the UK, contending with an energy crisis, was marred by power cuts, industrial unrest, a miners' strike and political uncertainties that were to trigger two general elections in 1974.

It was this sense of despair that led Slade, one of the leading pop groups of the time, to release their iconic song 'Merry Christmas'. While that classic track now celebrates seasonal festivities every year, for those of us around in 1973, it serves also as a reminder of the grim atmosphere in the UK at that time. 'Merry Christmas' is one of those wonderful feel-good songs, and one of the main reasons for its release, according to the band's lead singer and co-writer Neville 'Noddy' Holder, was to give hope for the future. It did.

Some might say joining the EEC was also about providing hope for times ahead. There was a common perception in Britain that the EEC had somehow discovered the key to economic success. That was a central feature of the 1975 referendum on remaining in the 'common market'. For many British politicians and voters, 'being in Europe' provided a route out of the UK's seemingly endless post-war demise.

OIL PRICE SHOCK

Whether or not 1973 was a turning point for the UK, it marked a moment of significant change for the broader, global economy. From 1946 until the 1973 oil price crisis, world economic growth soared. Global GDP expanded on average by 5 per cent a year during those early post-war decades, an unprecedented stretch of sustained growth, never seen before or since across the Western world over such an extended period.

There were many reasons for this – not least reconstruction efforts, and the potential for 'catch up' after the Second World War. Japan and other Asian economies also enjoyed big advances, helped too by the aftermath of the Korean War, with Japan surging from 3 per cent to 10 per cent of the global economy. Europe grew strongly too, particularly Germany and the other war-torn nations of Western Europe that went on to form the EEC. There was considerable financial assistance from the US through the Marshall Plan, as Washington sought to contain the rise of Communism. By 1973, Western Europe appeared to have discovered the secrets of economic success.

Encouragingly for a country that has a huge overhang of public borrowing today, Britain began the post-war period with even bigger outstanding state loans – a debt to annual GDP ratio of 240 per cent, the stock of state borrowing some two and a half times the size of the entire economy.[2] Along with untold human suffering, the Second World War also left Britain on the edge of financial ruin. By the end of the 1950s, though, strong growth had allowed debt levels to fall sharply, and Prime Minister Harold Macmillan was proclaiming the British people had 'never had it so good'.[3]

Debt levels can be reduced in a number of ways – inflating debt away is always an option, but never recommended. Austerity, sharply reducing expenditure, is another method, but it rarely works. The lesson of the 1950s is that the best way to reduce a debt burden is for the economy to grow, so the liabilities become a smaller share of overall GDP. But as we moved through the 1960s and into the early 1970s, the UK seemed to lose its way and growth faltered. In an ironic twist, Britain joined a fast-growing EEC in 1973, just as growth in Western Europe was about to slow.

The 1970s proved to be a difficult period for the UK and, in fact, for the economies of the entire Western world. The new economic buzzword was 'stag-flation', describing the combination of low growth and high inflation that was to inflict itself upon the advanced industrialised economies for much of the rest of the decade.[4]

While there were various explanations for stagflation, its origins lay partly in the Middle East. The October 1973 Yom Kippur War, which saw Syria and Egypt unexpectedly attack Israel, marked a shift in the balance of global bar-gaining power. OPEC gained the upper hand, with the Arab world imposing an embargo on crude oil exports to the US, punishing Washington's support for Israel. The fourfold rise in oil prices saw Western consumers suffer. It was also a sign that change was coming in terms of a shift in economic power between 'the West and the rest'.

Currency markets also became more turbulent, just as the UK joined the EEC. During much of the post-war period, currencies has been tied to gold and fixed against one another. During the early 1970s, though, the reverberations of the US decision to abandon the dollar's link to gold in 1971, effectively ending the 'Bretton Woods' system of fixed exchange rates, began to be felt. As the world's major currencies started to float once more, foreign exchange specula-tors were reborn and the UK was one of the first major economies to feel the effects. In mid-1972, there was 'a massive speculative attack against the pound sterling' in the words of the IMF. 'On June 23rd, the UK authorities decided not to maintain margins for that currency in the exchange markets and withdrew from the narrow-margins arrangement of the EEC,' reported the IMF in its 1973 annual report, describing the UK authorities' response to the fall.[5] On the same day, forty-four years later, there was another sudden drop in sterling, as the UK voted to leave the EU.

NEW KIDS ON THE BLOCK

One of the most dramatic changes in the global economy since both the Treaty of Rome, and particularly since the UK's EEC entry in 1973, has been the rapid growth of China, India and other emerging economies. The Chinese economy has expanded, on average, by more than 9 per cent a year since the mid-1980s. The Four Asian Tigers – South Korea, Singapore, Hong Kong and Taiwan – have meanwhile grown by 6 per cent per annum. Back in 1980, the advanced economies accounted for 70 per cent of global GDP. In 2013, that share fell below 50 per cent, as the emerging markets surpassed the G7 and the rest of the Western world in terms of overall economic size.

By 2016, the advanced economies accounted for 46 per cent of the world economy. They remain extremely important and will continue to grow – albeit rather slowly compared to the emerging markets. As the cake of world GDP gets bigger, even though the size of the slice representing the West is also growing, it accounts for a diminishing share of a much bigger cake. This West-to-East shift of the balance of global commerce is one of the economic mega-trends of our time. Another, as we discuss later in this chapter, is the technological revolution.

As relatively faster growth across emerging markets continues, the West's share of the global economic cake will keep shrinking. Back in 2010, Standard Chartered's 'Super-cycle Report' forecast that during the two decades to 2030, two thirds of economic growth across the world would come from emerging economies, led by China.[6] The European Commission, in a more recent study, predicted that over the next twenty years around 90 per cent of global growth will come from outside the EU.[7] There is a similar view among most private-sector forecasters.

As the emerging markets develop and their economies become more sophisticated, they are now accounting for a growing share of the world's most important companies. A report by the McKinsey Global Institute predicts that by 2025, the emerging markets will be home to 229 of the leading 500 companies of the world, as represented by the Fortune 500, up from just twenty-three in 1980.[8] Back then, Western Europe accounted for 168 of the Fortune 500, falling to 143 in 2000 and 128 in 2013. McKinsey expects the EU will be home to only eighty-six such companies by 2025, less than two fifths of the number based in emerging markets.

The key economic relationship to the future of global commerce is that between China and the US – the world's two biggest economies. The most important region overall, though, in commercial terms, will be the Indo-Pacific, which includes the USA, Japan and South Korea, China and the ASEAN economies of Southeast Asia through to India. A vast combined economy, with huge domestic markets, the Indo-Pacific region is home to 4.9 billion people, around two thirds of the world population, and will soon account for around three fifths of global GDP.

After Brexit, it is vital for the UK to retain a good relationship with the EU, but also to establish much stronger commercial links with the rest of the world, not least the large emerging markets – given that they are, increasingly, 'where the growth is'. In many respects, the UK needs multiple networks of ties across the globe. These should include the EU, our allies in the US, the huge growing markets across Asia and Africa and like-minded countries elsewhere, including Canada, New Zealand, Australia and others.

There is ample scope to open up vast opportunities in India, the demography of which is conducive to enormous future growth. We must also seek more financial and business opportunities with China as it expands its 'One Belt, One Road' initiative into third countries, across central Asia, Eastern Europe, southern Asia and Africa.[9] This initiative – representing an enormous boost to the stock of global infrastructure – is already well under way. As a sign of what is possible, the first direct-route freight train carrying goods directly from China to the UK left from Zhejiang province in eastern China in January 2017, arriving in east London's Barking Station, 7,400 miles away, just eighteen days later. Completing the same freight journey by sea would take around six weeks – and the 'One Belt' journey time is likely to come down significantly in years to come. The train route, moreover, naturally goes through Kazakhstan, Russia, Belarus, Poland, Germany, Belgium and France before reaching Britain, providing enormous scope for additional trade. In 1957, such a route would have been impossible but also seen as unnecessary. Today, these growing East–West links are of huge potential commercial significance.

When the EEC was created in 1957, the population of the whole of Europe – west, central and east – was 588 million, about 21 per cent of the global total. By the time the UK held its EEC referendum in 1975, Europe was home to 677 million people, with its share of a fast-rising global population falling to 16.6 per cent. By 2015, Europe's population was 738 million, just under 10 per cent of the global total. And, according to UN projections, by 2050, the fast-ageing population of Europe will have shrunk, in absolute terms, to 707 million, or 7.3 per cent of the global total.[10]

Regions, and the individual countries within them, can remain important, of course, even if their population share declines. But these numbers highlight the need to think not of Europe as '*the most*' important part of the world but '*an*' important part – one with which Britain obviously wants to retain a close relationship. But in a multipolar world economy, the UK needs to think in global terms.

This historic shift in the weight of the world population presents an opportunity. The large emerging markets of Africa, India and China represent fast-growing domestic markets for the UK to sell into. There are challenges too, though. One of which is migration flow – an issue the EU has struggled adequately to address. Africa has the fastest-growing population in the world, but 'has failed in the past to create enough good jobs despite higher economic growth' according to the African Development Bank.[11] In 2014, no fewer than 435 million Africans were below the age of sixteen, pointing to a huge future expansion of the workforce. By 2030, Africa's working population will rise to match the combined workforce of India and China.

Although we are optimistic about Africa's economic prospects, if only 10 per cent of those 435 million young Africans migrated to Western Europe in search of a better life, that would mean 8,000 people arriving every day for the next fifteen years. The UK, like other Western European countries, cannot and should not cut itself off from international labour flows. But the EU's lack of effective efforts to manage migration from beyond the EU, combined with freedom of movement within, is a major reason for rising nationalism and discontent with 'Europe' – as we discuss in later chapters. Engaging with the world means addressing the challenges as well as the opportunities – and Brussels' inability to tackle migration flows has been a major failing.

One determinant of trade flows is geographic proximity. The EU will remain more important for the UK than its actual size in the world economy would otherwise warrant. But even allowing for such 'gravity effects', as economists call them, the UK should be focusing its trading efforts way beyond Europe. The weight of economic commerce is shifting east, at a relentless pace. Yet the EU, despite years of trying, has not cut any FTAs with China, India or any of the other large emerging markets. Striking such deals when negotiating as a group of almost thirty countries, many with conflicting commercial agendas, is extremely tough. It may well be easier to strike FTAs with other large economies when negotiating as a single country. That has certainly been the experience of a variety of other nations, as will be discussed in subsequent chapters.

Having grown rapidly over recent decades, if not always steadily, the large emerging markets are no longer indebted to the West. The notion that the rest of the world is dependent on Western largesse, and craving Western approval, is a badly out-dated cliché. The sovereign bond markets of major Western nations, on the contrary, are now increasingly reliant on the continued backing of China and other non-Western creditors. The four largest emerging markets of China, India, Russia and Brazil control between them an estimated $4,150 billion of foreign exchange reserves, much of it held in the form of the IOUs of Western governments. The G7 nations have $2,100 billion of reserves, falling below $900 billion if Japan is excluded. The EU nations have less than $800 billion. In an increasingly interconnected world, large foreign exchange reserves represent not just wealth, but independence and an ability to weather inevitable economic and financial storms. As the weight of global population, growth and raw economic power continues to shift eastwards, it is vital that the UK raises its sights from Europe, putting far more emphasis on commercial, economic and political relations with the rest of the world.

TECH BOOM

Such is the pace and scale of change in the world economy that people and businesses everywhere need to have an open mind about what lies ahead. Just think how the internet has changed the way we find out information, interact with one another and communicate. The Internet of Things takes this much further.[12] A new industrial revolution is already under way. This is good news, given the need for additional growth across the Western world in the face of increasingly severe fiscal and demographic pressures.

While there is disagreement as to whether there have been three or four industrial revolutions throughout history, we are definitely now in the early stages of another. The first industrial revolution happened when the age of mechanisation and steam power came to the UK over 200 years ago. The second was at the end of the nineteenth century, with the age of electricity, and the economic rise of America, Russia and Germany. The third industrial revolution took place in the mid-twentieth century, with the increasing use of plastics and petrochemicals. This one is often overlooked, but was a game-changer in many ways. Then, over the last quarter of a century, we have witnessed the age of digital technology. Why, you might ask, does this influence the debate on Brexit, the UK and the EU?

The EU was founded in a different era to the one we live in now. Since the Treaty of Rome, the pace of technological change has made the inability of the EU to adapt and reform sufficiently even more stark. The world economy of the early part of the twenty-first century is already very different from that of the late twentieth century, let alone the mid-1950s, in the aftermath of the Second World War, when the European project was launched.

Consider some of the profound aspects of those changes that are already under way. There is the rise of artificial intelligence and of robotics. The focus on the 'green economy' is leading to dramatic changes in behaviour, whatever your views on 'global warming'.[13] Then there are many different types of technology: green, bio, nano and financial technology – or 'fintech'. The advent of small-scale and remote manufacturing through 3D printing is also creating all sorts of new opportunities.[14]

We are seeing great advances in stem cell research, medicine, life sciences – and the widely discussed advance of 'big data', the manner in which information and analytics can be used to provide products and services to customers.[15] There are undoubtedly more. Each one of these developments alone would be eye-catching. The fact they are occurring all together points to profound future change.

This new industrial revolution goes to the heart of much of the current debate about the long-run rate of growth in Western economies. The economist Paul Ormerod has written extensively about what he calls 'general purpose technologies (GPTs)', which become pervasive across a wide range of industries. 'The essence of a GPT is that it is widely adopted, improves over time and the price of the technology falls as it becomes more widespread,' observes Ormerod. GPTs spark innovation in both products and processes across a wide range of industries, he explains, with some 'representing marginal improvements to existing products' while others 'incorporate GPT in entirely new products, both those aimed at consumers and those which are innovative capital goods'.[16]

The adoption of GPTs across the economy 'can lead to turbulence as existing products and processes are challenged and established production techniques for both goods and services become obsolete,' Ormerod continues. This is an issue to which we will return in Chapter 8, when discussing the UK economy after Brexit. The point for now is that GPTs are here, and there is a need for the UK to position itself so its workforce and broader economy can benefit from this new industrial revolution – and to do so while outside the EU.

SHARING SUCCESS?

Looking at the history of the EU since 1957, three major developments stand out. First there is the creation of the single market and the enshrining of the four freedoms of free movement of people, capital, goods and services after 1992. Then there is the launch of the euro in 1999 and, finally, the eastward 'enlargement' from 2004 onwards.

The last of the three was a direct consequence of an external event – the 1989 collapse of the Berlin Wall, and the demise of Soviet-era communism. Joining the EU significantly changed the politics of the accession countries, moving them towards Western liberal democracy. It also triggered significant migration. When countries had similar levels of income and benefits across the EU, the incentive to move was less. But once workers in a host of poorer, low-income nations were part of the EU, and permitted to move to Western Europe due to freedom of movement, the incentive to do so was considerable.

The fall of the Iron Curtain also led to the dissolution of East Germany and, while that came at a considerable initial financial cost for West Germany, the combination of unification and the creation of the euro cemented German dominance of the EU. France, once on a par with its neighbour and ancient rival, may still regard itself as politically at the centre, but in economic terms it has moved closer to the periphery. Indeed, the relative convergence in the political thinking of the EU's members since 1973 is in stark contrast with their sharp divergence from an economic point of view. And that reality, in turn, has fuelled recent moves towards political extremes.

The UK may have escaped the excessive problems of euro membership, but it has still been impacted by the challenge of sharing economic success across the domestic economy. For many people in the UK, there has not been much, if any, improvement in their lives, despite economic growth. Many localities are caught in a rut, just as they were decades ago, before EEC membership. If being 'part of Europe' was viewed as a salvation for less-advantaged parts of the UK in the early 1970s, that sense of hope has now gone. 'While joining the European Community in 1972 may have been seen as the only way to cure Britain's "sick man" economy, by 2016 the argument no longer held,' argued a recent report from the Centre for Social Justice.[17] Poorer households voted strongly for Leave in the EU referendum in June 2016, while richer households overwhelmingly backed Remain. Only 38 per cent of voters living in homes with an annual income below £20,000 chose to stay in the EU – not much more than one in three. In contrast, 65 per cent of those from households earning above £65,000 chose Remain, roughly two in three. Many from poorer backgrounds felt that they had not benefited from the broader economic progress of the past four decades, or from being 'in' Europe.

From the ashes of the Second World War, six European nations created the EEC – to trade more, generate mutually dependent prosperity and prevent conflict. During those early years, while the EEC thrived economically, Britain suffered a relative decline. As the UK joined, the 1970s became a troubled decade of oil shocks and stagflation for the entire Western world, the EEC included. Britain then took a different turn, adopting 'supply-side' reforms in a some-times painful but largely successful bid to promote competition, innovation and growth. By the 1990s, it was Germany that had become the 'sick-man of Europe' – before a reunified nation rediscovered the ability to grow, itself adopt-ing UK-inspired labour market reforms and other supply-side measures.

'Correlation' is not 'causation'. If two things happen at the same time, one does not necessarily cause the other. Yet the UK's relatively strong economic per-formance during the second half of the 1980s and onwards until the 2008 global financial crisis was probably not due to its membership of the EU. It surely had more to do with the energy and ingenuity of a nation determined to work hard, innovate, shake off the economic torpor of the 1970s and compete. One illustration of this is the 'big bang' – which established the City, from the mid-1980s onwards, arguably the world's financial capital. The UK's 'Wimbledon Effect' has, at the same time, become more pronounced. Britain may not always own the best companies in the world, but very often hosts them, with numer-ous leading multinationals using the country as a global platform – resulting in considerable UK-based jobs and commercial activity. In recent years, the UK has attracted no less than one third of all foreign direct investment (FDI) into the EU.[18] Britain's recent economic renaissance may have happened while in the EU, but it was not caused by EU membership.

The pace and extent of change across the world since 1957 helps to explain, in many respects, why Britain being a member of the EU is like walking the wrong way on an escalator. The UK has sought to – and indeed needs to – embrace globalisation, technical change and innovation. Much of the EU, led by Brussels, has been heading the opposite way, emphasising regulation, centralisation and bureaucratic control.

The EU has also been heading in a different direction from the UK politically – given that there is almost no British appetite, among those who voted Leave or Remain, for 'ever closer union'. In a May 2016 survey, just 6 per cent of British voters felt that 'national governments should transfer more powers to the EU'. No less than 65 per cent agreed that 'some powers should be returned to national governments', while another 25 per cent felt 'the division of powers should stay the same'.[19]

The EU has, indeed, changed markedly from the 'common market' that the UK joined back in 1973 – becoming far more than a free trade zone. With almost every incremental act of integration, from the creation of the single currency to freedom of movement, UK voters have become less enthusiastic about being 'in Europe'. Once the world's economic powerhouse, the EU now accounts for a diminishing slice of the world economy. The large emerging markets, set to dominate this coming century, are meanwhile expanding fast.

As the Article 50 negotiations begin, the UK must decide how to approach these highly sensitive talks. 'Brexit means Brexit,' says Prime Minister Theresa May, but what does 'Brexit' mean? In truth, the UK government has, since early 2017, given clear signals regarding the terms on which it wants to leave the EU – as we discuss in Chapter 3.

It is also clear, amidst considerable rhetorical sniping between London, Brussels and other European capitals, that the EU itself faces considerable choices. Aside from how to respond to Brexit, the 27-member bloc, now much more unwieldy than the original group of six, must somehow try to arbitrate between opposing forces of integration and convergence. This is the subject of Chapter 4.

While Slade may have caught the mood of 1973, it is worth noting the name of the no. 1 hit record in the UK pop music charts on 25 March 1957, the day the Treaty of Rome was signed. It was a record by Tab Hunter called 'Young Love', a song of teenage affection and broken promises, its concluding lyrics: 'Don't say goodbye, please.' But after forty-three years of EU membership, Britain did.

PART II

CHOICES FOR THE UK & EU

CHAPTER 3

WHAT KIND OF BREXIT?

'The single market and its four freedoms are indivisible.
Cherry-picking is not an option.'
MICHEL BARNIER, 2016[1]

As the UK's Article 50 negotiations get under way during the summer of 2017, the British government has already made clear the UK will leave the EU's single market and the customs union. It is important the government does not backtrack on this in the wake of the 2017 general election result and subsequent pressure from various interest groups who do not want to upset the status quo. The economic benefits of both the single market and the customs union are wildly overstated and the drawbacks of membership are considerable. It would also be a mistake to attempt to replicate, as a long-term solution, one of the existing country-specific arrangements between the EU and, for instance, Norway, Liechtenstein or Switzerland.

We believe this Clean Brexit approach, explicitly leaving both the single market and customs union, is to the UK's economic advantage. It also offers the best chance of maintaining good UK–EU relations in coming years. More detailed analysis of how Britain's negotiations with the EU are going, and how they may develop, is contained in Chapter 5 and Chapter 6. This chapter explains why Clean Brexit should be our starting point, and why adopting this position provides the best chance of delivering a relatively orderly, constructive outcome, which works for the UK, the Eurozone and the broader EU 27.

Since the 2016 referendum, there has been much talk of Hard Brexit versus Soft Brexit. While such labels have dominated political discussion of the Article 50 talks, they are misleading. Leaving the single market and the customs union isn't Hard Brexit – a name coined to sound extreme and painful. It is simply Brexit. Staying inside the single market and customs union, meanwhile, is not Soft Brexit, a name suggesting a comfortable and harmonious future. It amounts, instead, to a failure to implement Brexit, despite the clear implication of the 2016 referendum result.

OUTSIDE THE SINGLE MARKET

The EU's single market is an economic area where most barriers to trade between member states have, in theory, been removed. Within the single market, there are no tariffs (charges) or quotas (physical limits) on trade in goods. The single market also removes many non-tariff barriers (NTBs) to trade, such as differing technical specifications, safety standards or labelling requirements. This arrangement is supposed to extend to trade in services – such as finance, insurance, law and accounting – where the UK has a significant comparative advantage. In reality, significant restrictions on trade in services remain within the EU, very much to the UK's detriment.

Under a Clean Brexit, Britain ceases to be a member of the single market and doesn't attempt to negotiate such membership. As a member, after all, the UK would remain subject to the EU's *acquis communautaire* covering goods, people, services and capital, bound by the full body of EU law in such areas and under ECJ jurisdiction.[2] Single market membership would also mean continued multi-billion-pound annual payments to the EU, while probably also accepting freedom of movement. Such conditions do not amount to Brexit, and, in the eyes of millions of UK voters, would be a betrayal of the referendum result.[3]

Beyond sovereignty issues, the economic benefits of the single market are grossly exaggerated. While membership allows free trade in goods, the EU has over recent years been the slowest-growing economic bloc in the world and, as such, accounts for a diminishing share of UK trade. In 1999, some 61 per cent of British exports went to the EU, falling to 56 per cent in 2006 and then 44 per cent in 2015, despite single market membership.[4] That share is expected to drop further, to around 35 per cent, by 2025. Even on current figures, the share of UK exports going to the EU could be 40 per cent or below, due to the so-called Rotterdam Effect, as a sizeable share of goods sent to Europe's busiest port are bound for non-EU markets.[5, 6]

As a member of the single market, the UK sells £241 billion of exports (of goods and services) to the rest of the EU while buying £312 billion of imports, resulting in a hefty £71 billion EU deficit (of goods and services). Beyond the EU, Britain delivers £307 billion of exports – 56 per cent of all the goods and services we sell abroad – while buying £273 billion of imports. That amounts to a £34 billion non-EU surplus.[7] So, the UK's trade within the single market already accounts for the minority of our exports, a share that is fast diminishing. Such EU trade, moreover, drives Britain's very sizeable and potentially destabilising overall trade deficit. The UK's non-EU trade, in contrast, provides markets for the majority of British exports. Such trade is quickly growing and generates a sizeable surplus.

These basic facts must cast doubt over whether the single market is so economically beneficial as to warrant all the costs and limitations on national sovereignty that membership entails. The EU is, moreover, a systemically slow-growth region, beset by demographic, fiscal and other structural issues that are likely to curtail future growth. The UK's non-EU trade is with some of the fastest-growing and most populous countries in the world, the economic superpowers of tomorrow – markets where there is huge scope for us to forge deeper commercial links.

Trade with the EU will remain important for the UK, of course. Yet such trade can continue, and even grow, from outside the single market – not least if the UK becomes more competitive and innovative outside the EU. Many opponents of Brexit claimed before the referendum, and continue to claim, that leaving the single market would be 'an economic disaster'.[8] In reality, there is no need to be 'in' the single market to trade extensively with the EU. The world's leading economies all enjoy 'access' to EU markets as long as their exporters comply with the relevant regulations and pay relatively low tariffs. Exports of goods from the US to the EU, for instance, totalled €247 billion in 2016, despite the US being 'outside' the single market. Chinese merchandise exports to the EU were even higher, at €345 billion, while Russia and Japan sold €119 billion and €66 billion of goods respectively within the EU in 2016.[9] UK exporters can also enjoy such 'access' to the single market, with the EU remaining a major export destination for Britain as it is for other large non-EU economies, but without the huge costs and obligations of membership.

Along with sizeable goods exports, many non-EU economies similarly sell plenty of services within the EU – an important observation for a services-oriented economy like the UK. While services exports into the EU don't attract tariffs, they can be subject to NTBs, which many who backed Remain have claimed would be impossible to surmount. Despite that, countries outside the EU sold service-sector exports into the bloc exceeding €600 billion in 2015, the US alone accounting for €202 billion of this total.[10]

It is a myth, then, that the UK can only trade extensively with the EU from 'inside' the single market. The US, China and Japan are not single market 'members'. None of them even has an FTA with the EU. Yet they all trade extensively with the EU under WTO rules – a subject that will be further explored in Chapter 6. While conducting significant EU trade, these nations don't accept the raft of costs and obligations – including annual contributions, ECJ jurisdiction and freedom of movement – that come with single market membership.

Some claim that Brussels will impose 'punitive' measures on UK exports after Brexit happens, so that other nations are not also tempted to leave. Such statements, once again, are scare tactics. Trading under WTO rules 'in practice, prevents discriminatory or punitive tariffs being levied by either the EU on the UK, or vice versa' according to the highly respected House of Commons Library.[11] Under WTO rules, the UK is protected from indiscriminate or spiteful EU trade barriers. Trying to punish the UK would also go against the EU's own treaties.[12]

Every member of the WTO – some 164 countries at the time of writing, including over 130 not in the EU – has guaranteed 'access' to the single market. Many non-EU nations are doing extremely good business with the EU – and, after Brexit, the UK can do the same. That's because the most important feature of the single market is that standardised product requirements apply across all member countries. So exporters, be they from France or America, Germany or Japan, can produce a single range of goods for all EU member states. This helps Chinese exporters as much as it does exporters in Italy. And it will continue to help UK exporters once we have left the EU.

The UK has, since 1973, paid billions of pounds in annual EU membership fees in return for single market membership.[13] Yet the extent to which membership has helped the domestic economy isn't clear. On joining the EEC, the UK's share of the market for goods in the countries of the six founding members was just 4 per cent. Lower trade barriers associated with the common market saw that share climb to almost 8 per cent by the mid-1980s. Since then, though, Britain's market share in those same six countries has fallen back below 4 per cent – with the EU as a whole accounting for an ever-decreasing proportion of our exports.[14]

That's because, since the 1990s, the EU has implemented incrementally lower external tariffs as a result of WTO-level 'multilateral' trade agreements, including the pivotal 'Uruguay Round' signed in 1991 – which has lowered trade barriers everywhere. As a result, competition from the rest of the world has significantly reduced the benefits of single market membership for UK goods exporters.

The gains from single market membership are particularly questionable regarding trade in services. Despite having no FTA with the US, the UK recorded a US services surplus of £32 billion in 2015, but a services surplus with the EU of just £21 billion. In practice, the single market in services is far from 'complete'. Numerous protectionist restrictions remain in place, which mean the trading of services across the EU is far less free than goods trade. This raises more doubts about the benefits of single market membership for a services-oriented economy like the UK.

A European Commission staff report in 2007 found 'little difference between trade (in services) between EU member states and trade between the EU and third countries'.[15] Service exports within the EU and beyond were roughly the same, the authors concluding that 'the internal market does not yet fully play its role in the services sector'. A later Eurostat report in 2015 suggested, once again, that intra-EU trade in services was only marginally higher than the EU's trade in services with the rest of the world.

In attempting to assess the efficiency of the single market in services, the European Commission's preferred measure of market integration is the ratio of service-sector exports sold within the EU compared to those sold beyond. Yet academics and other researchers, over many years, have found it remarkably difficult to access such data from Brussels. One independent study, involving detailed comparisons of available information on intra-EU and extra-EU services exports over a ten-year period, concluded in early 2016 that 'no one can say for sure if the single market for services exists'.[16] Another report found that although EU directives 'oblige' member states to liberalise their service sectors, facilitating services trade between member states, successive proposals have been 'heavily

amended in the legislative process'. That has led to 'a great deal of ambiguity …
and often resulted in poor implementation across the EU'.[17]

In March 2016, after a lengthy investigation sparked by EU companies complaining about ongoing barriers to services trade, the European Court of Auditors (ECA) – an EU-affiliated body – acknowledged that it is 'widely recognised
the services market had not achieved its full potential'. Containing repeated
references to the need for more 'transparency', the ECA's judgement criticised
the Commission for 'a reluctance to launch legal proceedings' against infringe-
ments by EU members unlawfully protecting domestic markets for services. 'The
European Commission is not looking after the interests of Europe's consumers
or service providers as well as it should,' the ECA concluded.[18] The UK is, by a
long way, the largest service-sector provider of any economy in the EU. As such,
it has been disproportionately harmed by this persistent failure to lower trade
barriers to services.[19]

Since the June 2017 general election, those backing Soft Brexit repeatedly
claim that leaving the single market will 'damage our economy' and 'put jobs at
risk'.[20] Since the single market was created in 1993, annual UK exports to the rest
of the EU have increased by just 0.9 per cent a year compared to a German figure
of 2.6 per cent. The UK's export growth is by far the lowest of any long-term
EU member, and in part reflects the extent to which the single market fails to
help a services-driven economy within the EU. Over the same 23-year period,
US exports to the EU have grown by 2.1 per cent, Canadian exports by 3.4 per
cent and Chinese exports by 13.3 per cent – all from outside the single market.[21]

Staying in the single market does not constitute a 'jobs-first Brexit'. Since the
single market was launched in 1993, manufacturing as a share of UK employment has fallen from around 35 per cent to 10 per cent. It is wrong to believe
single market membership has been good for traditional UK industries, or that
ongoing membership is necessary to counter pro-market 'Anglo-Saxon' policy-
making that would obliterate manufacturing. In France, which has implemented
far more interventionist policies than the UK since the early 1990s, the decline in
the employment share of manufacturing has been almost identical.[22]

The economic benefits of the single market to the UK, then, for all the alarmist slogans of those advocating Soft Brexit, are dubious. What is clear is that,
while inside the single market, all UK businesses, not just exporters, must adhere

to the entire range of the EU's often onerous rules and regulations. This piles extra costs onto the 92–95 per cent of UK companies that do not export to the EU.[23]

That's one reason why SMEs disproportionately backed Brexit, as we mentioned in the Introduction. Their large corporate counterparts, the vast majority of which supported Remain, are far better placed to handle EU regulations and may even view the regulatory burden as a convenient hindrance to the growth of smaller rivals. Large employers also back continued single market membership as it will almost certainly require the UK to retain the EU's freedom of movement rules – or something very close. A virtually limitless, low-cost workforce is understandably attractive to well-established commercial interests.

The public were told, though, that Brexit would result in a more accountable immigration system, managed by the UK government. This is what must now happen. Such controls should allow for an inflow of skilled and unskilled labour based on domestic economic needs. A new system of managed immigration, designed by UK ministers and officials, with the legislation debated and passed by Parliament in the normal way, would admit such overseas labour while retaining broad public support for immigration.

The EU is struggling with a Schengen arrangement that is rapidly sapping public confidence, even fuelling intolerance and nationalism. Brexit, in contrast, gives the UK an opportunity to put its immigration policy, and Britain's inherently positive and generous attitude towards migrants, back on a stable footing. It would be a grave mistake if attempts to negotiate continued membership of the single market, or something close to it, prevented that from happening.

OUTSIDE THE CUSTOMS UNION

While leaving the single market, a Clean Brexit also rules out being in the EU's customs union. This is a highly protectionist body that charges a Common External Tariff (CET) on all goods imported from outside the EU, while preventing Britain from cutting UK-specific FTAs. 'Membership of the customs union means EU member states are severely limited in their ability to operate independent trade policies,' says the House of Commons Library.[24]

The CET varies across different types of goods, and is set at rates that are, by definition, higher than regular WTO tariffs – the customs union acting as a protectionist wall around the EU. In 2014, CET tariffs averaged 2.3 per cent for non-agricultural goods, but on some individual products were higher.[25] The CET gives Brussels 'exclusive competence' over Britain's trading arrangements, preventing the UK from setting a trade policy designed to benefit British exporters, importers and consumers.

One regularly cited reason to stay in the customs union is so the UK remains party to trade deals negotiated by Brussels for the EU as a whole. Reference is often made to the 'clout' the EU brings to trade negotiations. The EU finds it hard to cut meaningful trade deals, though, not only because it is cumbersome and bureaucratic but because when negotiating as twenty-eight nations, objectives often conflict.[26] Despite years of effort, the EU has no FTA with either the US or China – the world's two largest economies. Trade negotiations with the US began in 1990 and those with China in 2005 – yet there is no EU FTA with either nation remotely on the horizon. The EU also has no formal trade deal with India, Indonesia or Brazil – all world-ranking and very populous economies set for considerable future growth.

In June 2017, there was much fanfare about a new EU–Japan trade deal, the announcement of which was timed to coincide with the start of the UK–EU Article 50 negotiations.[27] The EU was also keen to portray the US government as protectionist, ahead of the Hamburg G20 summit, given a recent souring of trade talks between Brussels and Washington. Yet it turns out that the free trade deal between the EU and Japan was merely a non-technical, non-binding political agreement that remains a very long way short of even an outline trade pact.[28]

Of the fifty-three FTAs that have been agreed by the EU, only four are with countries ranking amongst the world's twenty largest economies, with none in the top ten.[29] And only thirty-three of those fifty-three FTAs are signed and fully implemented. The vast majority of active deals are with very small countries, with the combined GDP of the nations covered amounting to well below 10 per cent of the global economy.

The EU's trade deals, apart from their relatively narrow coverage, are also far from UK-oriented. Given the overwhelming influence of the Franco-German axis, Brussels' negotiating approach has long been to 'gold plate' agriculture, protecting it at all costs. The French agricultural sector, compared to that of Britain, is huge and deeply inefficient, accounting for a three times' bigger share of GDP and a four times' larger share of total employment. When EU-level trade deals have been struck, the UK's needs – such as the promotion of trade in services – have not figured highly.

Leaving the customs union will see Britain regain its ability to negotiate its own FTAs, to the benefit of British commercial interests and the broader economy. Such agreements, crucially, can also focus on services – something that EU trade deals, dominated by French and German economic interests, have failed to do. By cutting bilateral FTAs, while acting as a champion for free trade and open markets within the WTO, the UK will be better able to position itself with fast-growing, dynamic parts of the world economy – not least the large emerging markets where Britain may already have a language in common, shared legal codes, institutional practices or other historical ties. The overwhelming evidence is that countries negotiating on their own behalf, free of intra-bloc conflicts, fare much better than the EU when it comes to striking beneficial FTAs. These issues are further explored in Chapter 7, when we discuss UK negotiations with the rest of the world during the Article 50 window and beyond.

While preventing the UK from agreeing FTAs, being in the customs union also makes imports of consumer goods and business inputs from outside the EU more expensive as consumers pay tariffs on goods imported from outside the EU. This argument was rarely aired during the referendum campaign, but it is important. Inside the customs union, British consumers end up paying import tariffs on goods where there is often no UK producer to protect, facing higher prices to shield producers in other EU countries. CETs collected in each EU country are paid into a central fund – with some 80 per cent of such revenues going to Brussels.[30] Because the UK has a much higher share of non-EU trade than any other EU member, our CET burden is particularly high. This is one reason Britain is the second largest net contributor to the EU, paying far more than France even though our economies are of similar size. These CET revenues paid from the UK to Brussels represent the premium that British consumers pay above world prices for goods imported from outside the EU. Some estimates suggest the price of food in the UK is 17 per cent more expensive than it would be outside both the single market and the customs union – given the combination of EU-imposed tariffs on imports from beyond the EU and the Common Agricultural Policy (CAP).[31]

As poorer families spend a large share of their incomes on food, leaving the customs union would not only allow the UK to strike FTAs, but could also help relatively low-income households. When negotiating future FTAs, the UK could then lower tariffs on food and numerous other consumer goods even more, below the WTO tariffs that would automatically apply to UK imports from outside the EU.

When selling to the EU from outside the customs union, UK exporters would be subject to the CET – unless Britain struck an FTA with the EU. The scale of these tariffs, though, should be a manageable business cost, not a deterrent to doing business from the UK. The average EU tariff to be paid is 5.1 per cent in simple 'most-favoured nation' terms and 2.7 per cent in trade-weighted terms. While for non-agricultural goods, the simple tariff is 4.2 per cent and 2.3 per cent in trade-weighted terms, for agricultural products the averages are 10.7 per cent and 8.5 per cent respectively.[32]

Rather than remaining in the EU's customs union in a bid to secure some form of Soft Brexit, Britain should rule out that possibility – not least to facilitate the early negotiation of FTAs across the rest of the world. Even during the Article 50 negotiation period, the Department for International Trade is legally entitled to negotiate FTA deals on a 'heads of terms' basis – providing they are enacted only once we have left.[33] Since the UK's Brexit vote, numerous countries have shown interest in a bilateral UK trade deal.

It is impossible to make significant progress in such negotiations, though, when our non-EU counterparts do not know if the UK will be inside or outside either the single market or the customs union once we've left. So the UK should continue to make clear that we will soon be outside both, allowing ministers and officials to negotiate in good faith, implementing non-EU FTAs as soon as possible after Article 50 expires.

Knowing we will be outside both the single market and the customs union also means detailed preparations can be made ahead of March 2019. The UK must reclaim its WTO seat and tariff schedules. This is a necessary, but relatively simple, process, discussed further in Chapter 6. Being outside the customs union also requires the training of more customs staff and specialists to make 'rules of origin' judgments, so that tariffs can be calculated.[34]

Given that the EU accounts for just under half of our trade, the number of customs declarations will rise sharply, probably almost doubling after Brexit. We also need to agree with the EU the proportion of cargoes to be inspected. This all points to a number of costs, and ports (on both sides of the Channel) must be equipped to cope with an increased inspection workload. This will mean hiring more customs staff.

While there will be extra bureaucracy relating to UK–EU trade, being outside the single market will mean the vast majority of UK firms that do not export are no longer bound by EU red tape. The FTA deals we strike outside the customs union with non-EU countries could further reduce regulation. Leaving the customs union could also kick-start the use of new technology for declarations and inspections. An advanced economy like the UK should be able to ensure goods flow relatively quickly through the ports, with minimal delay, ultimately lowering costs. Increasingly, customs and related processes are electronic and scalable, able to handle ever larger volumes. The average 'dwell time' of consignments of non-EU goods entering via French ports, for instance, is less than six minutes. The US and Canada are not in a customs union, yet more goods cross the US–Canada border each year than do the EU's external border – with no delays.

Providing we get the bodies that check standards for the EU market accredited here in the UK before leaving the EU, the vast majority of UK–EU customs clearance post-Brexit can be done electronically, as happens under the North American Free Trade Agreement (NAFTA).[35] In many cases, the costs of adapting to leaving the customs union are one-off costs. As technology is enhanced, this investment will result in falling variable costs. And while remaining in the customs union would avoid such initial outlays, that would compromise FTAs with the rest of the world – which are ultimately of far more economic significance.

The disruption to the business models of some firms and sectors once we leave the customs union, and indeed the single market, should not be dismissed. For many sectors, though, tariff rates are low and much of the service sector remains unaffected. Given potential disruption, there is scope to agree temporary 'transition' deals, allowing various sectors to adjust, as systems and technology relating to UK–EU commercial flows bed down, before moving entirely to the new trading regime. Again, such mutually beneficial, largely technical deals will be more likely to come to fruition if the UK isn't engaged in heated public argument over high-profile EU principles such as freedom of movement and single market membership, as is the case under Clean Brexit.

OFF THE SHELF?

Several countries have 'bespoke' relationships with the EU. But none of these deals would be suitable for the UK if we are to be outside ECJ jurisdiction with control of our own borders and free of large annual payments to Brussels.

The 'Norwegian model' refers to membership of the European Economic Area (EEA), which includes Norway, Liechtenstein and Iceland.[36] Some cite EEA membership as an acceptable Soft Brexit compromise for the UK. As a member of the EU, Britain is already in the EEA and, while legal opinion is divided, it should be possible to leave the EU while retaining EEA membership. EEA members, outside the EU, can sign non-EU trade deals and have near-full access to the single market. Being in the EEA, though, means ongoing annual payments. As an EEA member, Norway makes a per capita contribution around two thirds that which the UK makes inside the EU. On that basis, Britain's annual net payment, if we stay inside the EEA, would be around £6 billion, compared to £8.6 billion in 2016. In future years, that annual payment could rise further.[37]

EEA membership also means remaining under ECJ jurisdiction.[38] Inside the EU, the UK has at least some influence in shaping such legislation. Being only in the EEA would mean far less – and possibly none. Remaining subject to ECJ judgments, but with scant influence in shaping underlying laws, raises serious sovereignty issues and, with the ECJ increasingly expanding its remit, could leave the UK dangerously exposed. Within the EEA, for instance, with the single currency still likely to face serious future challenges at some stage, the UK government could find itself legally obliged to fund further Eurozone bailouts.

An additional consideration is that because EEA nations are effectively 'members' of the single market, negotiating FTAs with non-EU nations including services would, in effect, remain impossible. Such trade deals for services relate to domestic regulations and, as EEA members, such regulations would not be under UK control. This is a significant problem for a service-driven economy such as Britain.[39] Perhaps the biggest drawback to EEA membership, though, is that it almost certainly means accepting freedom of movement. While not delivering for the UK economy, then, EEA membership doesn't reflect the referendum result either – so is a non-starter.

As this book goes to press, there is much political speculation that the UK could use its existing EEA membership as a 'transition' structure between the end of the Article 50 period in March 2019 and 'full Brexit'. That would mean accepting various conditions – including freedom of movement and annual payments – until the transition period is over. There are fears of a fudge among some, not least if the transition deal is open-ended, with no strict time limit. After all, the EEA is as 'an ante-room, not a departure lounge', as the former Cabinet minister Peter Lilley has put it, being an organisation for those countries that might one day join the EU, rather than those about to leave.[40] We discuss the EEA option as a transition device in Chapter 6.

Despite EEA membership, Liechtenstein has negotiated its own tailored EU immigration policy, leading some Soft Brexit advocates to suggest it as a model that Britain could use once it leaves the EU. Yet Liechtenstein is a densely populated microstate, while the UK is the second largest EU economy and a major migrant destination. Given growing public disquiet across the EU relating to Schengen, it is inconceivable the EU 27 would grant Britain single market membership while waiving freedom of movement. A large economy gaining such a concession would encourage growing demands for EU referenda across other member states – something Brussels and incumbent EU leaders are desperate to avoid.

Switzerland, as a member of the European Free Trade Association (EFTA), has had an FTA with the EU since 1972.[41] The Swiss have partial membership of the single market and can strike their own FTAs with non-EU nations – one example being the China–Switzerland trade deal struck in 2013. Under this complex arrangement, freedom of movement remains a hotly contested issue, with the EU constantly pushing for Swiss acceptance and voters fiercely resisting. In 2014, the Swiss electorate opted to introduce legal quotas on the number of EU migrants who could enter the country. Some EU officials, in response, suggested 'a further referendum' to 'change the logic'.[42] Brussels then refused to negotiate, insisting that free movement is a condition of single market membership, while warning of future trade restrictions. The Swiss government is now working on a compromise, allowing free movement but with hiring preference for Swiss citizens over EU migrants, amidst continued protests from disgruntled voters.

Switzerland shows that when it comes to linking freedom of movement to single market membership, the EU is determined not to give ground. That is particularly true now that Schengen, suspended in several large EU countries, is in danger of collapse. Again, if the UK is granted single market membership while reclaiming control of its borders, other EU governments, backed by vociferous voters calling for national referenda, would demand the same. If the UK tries to 'have its cake and eat it', attempting to bend the EU's core principles to its will, it could seriously damage the EU, even sparking a systemic crisis that tears the bloc apart.

CLEAN, NOT MESSY

'Cherry-picking isn't an option,' declared Michel Barnier in December 2016. The European Commission's Chief Negotiator on Brexit has repeated that statement many times since. The UK should accept Barnier's words in good faith. That is exactly what a Clean Brexit does.

Declaring that the UK will leave both the single market and the customs union brings much of the Brexit process under the British government's control, helps minimise business uncertainty and causes the least possible disruption to the EU itself. The opposite of Clean Brexit is Messy Brexit – attempting to remain 'in' the single market while achieving partial control over borders, or attempting some kind of Swiss-style compromise. This is far more complicated, fraught with economic, political and diplomatic dangers and would probably not be achievable. It is also not what the British public voted for in June 2016. Despite this, it is still promoted as an option by many in the House of Commons and beyond, under a misleading Soft Brexit label.

By maintaining that Britain will leave the single market and the customs union, the UK also increases the chances of striking an FTA with the EU – possibly during the two-year Article 50 negotiation period, but if not soon after. That's because influential business lobbies of major exporting nations such as Germany, France and Italy will be mindful of the benefits of maintaining favourable UK trading arrangements in specific sectors. For EU exporters, Britain is a substantial market accounting for billions of euros of profits and supporting hundreds of thousands of jobs, with the UK's £96 billion annual EU trade deficit in goods clearly illustrating the importance of a UK–EU FTA.[43]

It is vital that corporate leaders in the largest and most powerful EU economies, and the workers they employ, understand unequivocally that the UK is leaving the single market. They will then pressure their political leaders to refrain from 'punishing Britain' and knuckle down to the grown-up compromises needed to strike, as quickly as possible, the multi-sectoral FTA which makes sense for both sides. Under Clean Brexit, the inevitability of Britain leaving the single market puts Europe's powerful export-oriented businesses on the UK's side, as we push for an FTA with the EU.

Attempting to negotiate a Messy Brexit during the two-year Article 50 window is highly unlikely to produce such a trade deal. There would simply be no incentive to come to an agreement if single market membership is seen as even a remote possibility. A Messy Brexit would anyway be entirely dominated by 'headline' emotive issues, not least freedom of movement and ongoing annual payments. An 'up-against-the-clock' diplomatic and political battle, pitting the UK's newly established sovereignty against the survival of the entire European project, would be extremely explosive. During such talks, politicians on both sides, under enormous pressure, would inevitably use rhetoric that stokes up dangerous cross-border tensions. And it could easily happen that, after months of heated discussion, the UK and EU 27 would fail to agree, resulting in a disastrous stalemate. Business uncertainty would then become 'semi-permanent', doing serious economic damage across Western Europe and beyond.

A fiercely negotiated bid for a Messy Brexit, then, is not wise – especially when the EU itself is embroiled in various crises, ranging from migration to the fragility of the Eurozone, which threaten its very existence. Such a deal would only emerge, if it emerged at all, during the final moments before the window closes. Such brinkmanship leads to bad policy-making and chronic business uncertainty. Numerous key policy outcomes, including those related to the UK's immigration system, agriculture and fishing, must not be subject to last-minute, closed-door deals.

Clean Brexit avoids such unaccountable, chaotic decision-making. It is designed to make leaving the EU as smooth as possible for both the UK and the EU 27. By deciding at the outset that the UK will be outside both the single market and the customs union, we can make the necessary preparations ahead of March 2019, helping to avoid the cliff-edge scenario highlighted by business leaders. Taking this stance also provides a lot of negotiating flexibility, as Britain, having made preparations to trade on WTO rules, and fully expecting to do so, can refuse to accept an FTA from the EU if the terms of such a deal are poor.

The short-term disruption of leaving the single market and customs union should not divert attention from the longer-term benefits – including the ability to make UK-specific FTAs, oriented towards trade in services, with nations far more populous and fast-growing than the EU. Clean Brexit also restores unequivocal control over crucial areas of public policy – such as domestic regulation and immigration – to our own elected ministers and parliamentarians, returning vital powers to institutions that are directly accountable to the British electorate.

It cannot be stressed enough that services account for four fifths of the UK economy. Britain exported $84.7 billion of financial services in 2015, the second biggest total in the world, while selling $345 billion of services overall abroad – again, the world's second largest in total. Only Clean Brexit allows the UK to strike FTAs that emphasise services outside the customs union. And it is only outside the single market that Britain has control over its domestic commercial regulations, allowing such service-based FTAs to be struck.

By returning control over our laws and borders to the UK, Clean Brexit allows us to leave the EU in a pre-announced and planned manner, rather than exposing the country to dysfunctional, last-ditch negotiations that would undermine public faith in politicians and broader business confidence. The government has backed this approach. 'We do not seek partial membership of the EU, associate membership of the EU, or anything that leaves us half-in, half-out,' said the Prime Minister, at her pivotal Lancaster House speech in January 2017. 'We do not seek to adopt a model already enjoyed by other countries or to hold on to bits of membership as we leave.'[44]

May's insistence that 'no deal is better than a bad deal', which she made clear at Lancaster House, is correct in our view. Trading under WTO rules is a long way from the 'disastrous' outcome that it is often claimed to be. Most trade in the world already takes place under WTO rules, outside of formal FTAs. Trading with the EU under 'no deal' will be further explored in Chapter 6.

Any Brexit outcome that involves ongoing single market membership, with all the associated conditions, would be deeply undemocratic. Membership is, in any case, of dubious economic value to Britain. Aside from the sovereignty gains, the UK could well enjoy a steeper growth path outside of the EU, less confined by red tape and trading more with the rest of the world, facilitated by mutually beneficial trade deals.

Above all, those trying to remain in the single market and even reverse the UK's referendum result should recognise that the EU is palpably a broken model. For the European Commission and the EU 27, Brexit is rather low on a list of extremely knotty problems. More than anything, the EU 27 needs to fend off multiple ongoing crises while attempting to decide, in the context of 'ever closer union', what they are ultimately trying to become. These profound choices that the EU must make are the backdrop against which our Article 50 negotiations will take place – and are the subject of Chapter 4.

CHAPTER 4

WHAT KIND OF EUROPEAN UNION?

'The euro is in danger – if we do not avert this danger, the consequences for Europe
are incalculable and the consequences beyond Europe are incalculable.'
ANGELA MERKEL, MAY 2010[1]

The sixtieth anniversary of the Treaty of Rome saw two distinct groups of demonstrators on the streets of the Italian capital. Leaders from twenty-seven EU members assembled on 25 March 2017 inside the Palazzo dei Conservatori, where the original Treaty was signed. As they gathered, listening to each other's collegiate speeches, the 'March for Europe' could be heard cheering outside. Several thousand EU supporters, many young and excited, held a celebratory rally close to the magnificent fifteenth-century palace.

Across the city, away from the Palazzo, rather different demonstrations were going on that involved many thousands more. Amidst tight security, including one of Italy's biggest ever deployments of anti-riot police, much noisier protesters, who were generally middle-aged and more careworn, railed against the EU. With sections of the city centre blocked off by armoured vehicles, belligerent groups marched under various right- and left-wing banners and trade unions, loudly voicing their disaffection. There was no hint of celebration.

These demonstrators decried Brussels-based technocrats and corporate vested interests. They protested against the single currency. Journalists were told that the euro unfairly benefits rich nations like Germany, holds back Italy and impoverishes poorer members like Greece. The EU was derided as a 'rich man's club', while 'the banks are always getting saved' by the ECB, and there's 'never any money for the people'.[2] Although smoke bombs went off and tensions rose, the demonstrators did not riot. But some 120 protesters were detained anyway for disorderly behaviour.

Back in the Palazzo, the assembled dignitaries tried to ignore the UK's absence from the sixtieth anniversary celebrations. The departure of the EU's second largest economy, its leading liberal voice on competition and trade and its biggest military power was clearly a blow for the Union. European Council President Donald Tusk said: 'Europe, as a political entity will either be united, or will not be at all.'[3] All twenty-seven national leaders, and the heads of Brussels institutions, signed a new Rome Declaration hailing six decades of the EU. 'Europe is our common future,' it defiantly stated. 'We are determined to make the EU stronger and more resilient, through even greater unity.'[4]

The declaration also pledged to 'listen and respond to the concerns expressed by our citizens'. The only citizens anywhere near the Palazzo, though, were those on the March for Europe, essentially signed-up EU cheerleaders. Much further away, unseen and unheard beyond the rings of armed police and multiple security zones, were thousands of other protestors who were deeply sceptical of the EU, angry – and concerned about their livelihoods.[5]

These two opposing sets of demonstrators in Rome – and in several other European capital cities – on 25 March 2017 illustrate the EU's quandary. The EC and member states could push for 'more Europe', accelerating integration towards 'ever closer union'. Or, instead, they could abandon more ambitious aspects of the European project and choose to focus instead on trade and other forms of collaboration, including environmental protection, criminal justice and tackling terrorism. This choice, in evidence for decades, can no longer be ignored.

Since the Treaty of Rome, European integration has happened in fits and starts. Now, given the dysfunctional single currency and public dissent over internal and external migration, the Commission and the main member states must act. While Brexit is a setback, and the Article 50 negotiations may prove challenging for both sides, 'Europe' is spiked on the horns of a much more serious dilemma. The EU must decide whether to forge a more integrationist future despite rising voter discontent or consign 'ever closer union' to history before truly testing the limits of democratic tolerance. 'With Brussels facing the euro mess and mass immigration, Brexit is just an irritant on the EU's priorities list,' says Mervyn King, former Governor of the Bank of England.[6] The instability of the single currency, EU-wide concern about freedom of movement and the unaccountable nature of the European Commission, are indeed long-standing issues, unrelated to Brexit, and amount to far deeper problems.

European Commission President Jean-Claude Juncker is clearly concerned that if Britain's exit from the EU appears to be successful, other nations could follow suit. Yet the EU faces more pressing concerns than negotiating with the UK – issues raising the most fundamental questions about the future of the European project.

FLAWED AT BIRTH

In April 2016, official Eurostat data showed that the combined economy of the nineteen Eurozone nations had grown 0.6 per cent during the first three months of the year.[7] After an eight-year wait, the Eurozone GDP was finally the same size as it had been during the first quarter of 2008, just before the global financial crisis. The entire world economy slumped after the sub-prime mortgage crisis. The US, EU and Japan all went through a period of contraction. Emerging markets like China and India also slowed significantly. By 2011, though, the US economy was back above its pre-crisis level of activity. Two years later, the UK economy had also fully recovered. However, the Eurozone suffered particularly badly, enduring two successive recessions after 2008 and taking until 2016 to reach its previous peak. Even then, unemployment across the nineteen member states averaged over 10 per cent – a rate twice that of Britain and the US.

With consumer price inflation down at 0.2 per cent in April 2016, a sign of ongoing stagnation, the Eurozone was widely compared to Japan, where the early 1990s real estate collapse and banking bust led to years of economic torpor. Slow Eurozone growth also masked sharp differences between members. By 2016, the German economy was, in real terms, 12 per cent bigger than in 2007, as we stated in Chapter 1, while Italy was 7 per cent smaller. The Greek economy, at the time of writing, remains an astonishing 20 per cent smaller than it was in 2007, with more than one in five of the workforce unemployed.

The underlying cause of the Eurozone's disappointing and disjointed performance is the single currency. 'It's almost a lost decade – a remarkable testimony to the euro's economic failure,' says Joseph Stiglitz, the American Nobel laureate economist, an avowed and long-standing supporter of the EU. 'The crisis began in the US, yet the rigidities associated with the single currency meant the Eurozone wound up the big loser.'[8]

The euro has been, for many millions, 'an unmitigated disaster ... it was flawed at birth', says Stiglitz. By denying less competitive countries the ability to devalue, it has condemned countless workers to live amidst economic stagnation and high unemployment. 'The single currency ... has tied together countries with vastly different economic and social backgrounds, denying them the vital ability to manipulate their exchange and interest rates,' Stiglitz says. Far from promoting European prosperity, peace or influence, 'the structure of the euro is to blame for the poor performance of Europe, its successive crises and increased inequality'.[9]

Across southern Europe, membership of the Eurozone has left economies largely moribund for a generation, causing their banking sectors to deteriorate and public indebtedness to spiral. In Italy, which has barely grown since the euro was launched in 1999, some southern regions are now so poor there is talk of the country splitting into two. Germany, meanwhile, operates with a much lower exchange rate than its productivity suggests, thanks to other euro members, resulting in the world's largest current account surplus, a vast 8.7 per cent of GDP in 2016. Having come under enormous pressure from Berlin to curtail spending, Italy now complains bitterly about Germany's trade surplus, calling for the Eurozone's economic powerhouse to fund an EU-wide fiscal expansion.

The European Commission agrees Germany's external imbalance is 'not healthy' for monetary union, creating 'very significant distortions both economically and politically'.[10] Even the US officials have said Germany 'continues to exploit other countries', while benefiting from a single currency that is kept artificially low by dint of less productive members.[11]

During the years after the single currency was launched in 1999, it held together quite well, amidst relatively buoyant growth and modest inflation. The southern European nations benefited as interest rates fell, converging with those of Germany, which spurred investment. But such borrowed credibility allowed the Club Med economies to take on far too much debt while avoiding measures to make themselves more competitive.

By the mid-2000s, though, the euro's key design fault had been exposed – the inherent impossibility of enforcing fiscal discipline in a currency union of sovereign states, each answerable to its own electorate. Politicians will inevitably meet short-term demands for more domestic spending, seeking popularity among their own voters, rather than heed strictures of restraint, however frequent, from the Frankfurt-based ECB or Brussels.

During this period, many argued that single currency membership guaranteed economic security. 'The euro area represents a pole of stability for those countries participating, by protecting them from speculation and financial turmoil,' claimed a report from the European Council in December 2001.[12] In the UK, politicians agitating for British membership derided those who urged caution. 'Opponents of the euro have been disheartened as their predictions of chaos and disaster have failed to materialise,' said former Chancellor Kenneth Clarke, in October 2002. 'The reality of the euro has exposed the absurdity of many anti-European scare stories.'[13]

Almost from the outset, though, the budget rules designed to keep the euro together – the Stability and Growth Pact – were ignored.[14] Among the first rule-breakers, ironically, was Germany – a breach that encouraged smaller nations to borrow beyond agreed limits as well. Despite the 'pole of stability' rhetoric, divergences in growth and indebtedness meant yields demanded by investors to lend to more profligate members rose sharply above those of the inherently more credit-worthy. The gap – or spread – between such yields and those of wealthier Eurozone nations then became even wider, as slower-growing indebted nations, which would ordinarily have adjusted in part via currency depreciation, had to live with a euro that was far too high given their relatively low competitiveness. That made recovery even less likely, resulting in still more borrowing.

As the global financial crisis struck in early 2008, a few lone voices warned that the euro 'was about to face its first serious test'.[15] The resulting pan-European slowdown did, indeed, expose vast holdings of systemically dangerous euro-denominated bank loans. The world's political and media classes, having dismissed the notion that monetary union could collapse as deranged and alarmist, were forced to face facts. During the previous decade, banks across the EU and elsewhere had bought billions of euros worth of high-yielding sovereign and corporate debt from various 'periphery' Eurozone members. As those economies continued to stagnate, locked into a cripplingly high exchange rate amidst a global slowdown, default dangers loomed – threatening a tumultuous 'euroquake' that would spread 'financial contagion' across the world.

CROSS-BORDER BAILOUTS

In early 2010, two years on from the implosion of Lehman Brothers, José Manuel Barroso was still referring to the euro as 'a protection shield against the crisis'.[16] Within a few months, the then European Commission President finally acknowledged the Eurozone's 'systemic' problems. As weaker, more indebted economies struggled to cope with the fallout from the biggest financial collapse since the Great Depression, denied the buffer of currency adjustment, their sovereign bonds came under intense speculative attack. World leaders were soon voicing concerns that, with the impact of the Lehman collapse still reverberating, the dysfunctional Eurozone was about to upend global markets once more.

As a result, in response to a fracturing monetary union, EU authorities have been forced into explicit taxpayer-funded bailouts. These have happened despite being illegal under the 1992 Treaty of Maastricht, the solemn agreement that is meant to underpin monetary union.[17] Throughout late 2008 and into 2009, as the market demanded ever higher yields to keep lending to flailing and increasingly cash-strapped nations across southern Europe, spreads between Eurozone members' debts grew even wider.

'The Treaties set out a "no bailout" clause, and the rules will be respected,' said ECB chief economist Jürgen Stark in January 2010, in a bid to stem speculation as the euro crisis grew more serious. 'Markets are deluding themselves if they think other member states will at a certain point dip their hands into their wallets to save Greece,' he said.[18] Stark was supported by Joaquín Almunia, EU Commissioner for Economic and Monetary Affairs. 'Solidarity is possible, [and] will exist,' said Almunia. 'A bailout is not possible and will not exist.'[19]

As the crisis grew deeper, the world looked to Germany to stop monetary union imploding. Berlin came under enormous pressure to prevent weaker Eurozone members from crashing, as that would impose big bond defaults on still under-capitalised banks, sparking a renewed global crisis. Chancellor Merkel remained defiant. 'We have a Treaty under which there is no possibility of paying to bailout states in difficulty,' she insisted in early March 2010.[20]

Amid intense speculation Greece was about to default, converting its euro-denominated liabilities into hugely devalued drachma, Germany's Economy Minister used the 'moral hazard' defence: 'Aid for Greece would be the wrong signal – we must not create a precedent other Eurozone countries can refer to,' argued Rainer Brüderle. 'It cannot be possible [that] German taxpayers must pick up the bill for mismanagement in Greece and elsewhere.'[21] By late April, though, it was clear the EU authorities, together with the IMF, had reluctantly concluded only a rescue plan would prevent market pressure forcing Greece out of the euro. While Greece represents just 2 per cent of Eurozone GDP, the big fear was that a small country departing would lead to speculation that a much larger member, like Spain or even Italy, could leave – involving defaults that extended to hundreds of billions of euros and calling into question the entire single currency construct.[22]

Once a Greek bailout became unavoidable, the Bundesbank, an institution viewed as the bedrock of Germany's post-war economic stability, attempted to rationalise a move perceived to stem from Greek profligacy and even corruption – albeit in rather technical language.[23] 'There is a grave threat of contagion effects for other member states in the monetary union and increasing negative feedback loop effects,' said Bundesbank President Axel Weber.[24] Finance Minister Wolfgang Schäuble also weighed in, trying to justify developments that much of the German and northern European public found shocking. 'We cannot allow the bankruptcy of a euro member like Greece to turn into a second Lehman Brothers,' he said. 'The consequences of a national bankruptcy would be incalculable – Greece is as systemically important as a major bank.'[25]

Once Merkel herself had finally relented, she also sought to explain to her compatriots that unless Germany acted, it risked being blamed, however unfairly, for failing to prevent havoc. 'The euro is in danger,' she said. 'If we do not avert this danger, the consequences for Europe are incalculable and the consequences beyond Europe are incalculable.'[26]

In early May 2010, the 'Troika' grouping of the ECB, the European Commission and the IMF launched the first Greek bailout. The €110 billion package, bigger than any rescue plan ever attempted, came with 'austerity' conditions and the forced sale of various state-owned Greek assets.

Since that package was agreed, the Eurozone has endured repeated crises, with Portugal, Spain, Cyprus and Ireland also being rescued from sovereign default. In all five countries, particularly those in southern Europe, the harsh bailout terms have negatively affected the popularity of the EU. The southern Eurozone members, in fact, have seen violent anti-EU riots against domestic budget cuts imposed by Brussels-appointed technocrats. And in Portugal, Spain, Cyprus and Greece, despite the bailouts, or perhaps because of them, domestic sovereign bond yields relative to Germany have remained alarmingly high, as has unemployment.

Once the Greek bailout had been unveiled, Karl Otto Pöhl, Bundesbank President during the 1980s, issued a warning. Attacking a rescue plan funded in large part by Germany, Pöhl argued the bailout was mainly about rescuing bank shareholders and wealthy Greek businessmen. 'The foundation of the single currency has fundamentally changed with the decision by Eurozone governments to transform themselves into a transfer union,' he boomed. 'In the treaties governing the EU, it's explicitly stated no country is liable for the debts of any other, yet we're doing exactly that, a violation of every rule.'[27]

In 2015, an unprecedented third Athens bailout was agreed, worth €86 billion – again, in a bid to stop Greece crashing out of the Eurozone. Over the summer of 2017, Greece has once again been embroiled in more bad-tempered high-stakes negotiations with the Troika, while on the brink of default – with considerable dispute breaking out within the Troika itself. The IMF insists that Greece – with a government debt burden approaching 200 per cent of GDP and unemployment above 20 per cent – simply must be granted significant debt relief, even if only in the form of extended loan duration, if the economy is to recover.[28]

Yet any move towards a debt write-off, as Berlin knows well, would stoke outrage across northern Europe, given residual public anger about the original bailout. Greek debt relief would be even more controversial among voters in other bailed-out Eurozone members, where the Troika's tough budgetary conditions have largely been met, but have caused considerable economic, financial and political pain. Future attempts to impose fiscal discipline on those countries would then be futile.

With bond yields suppressed only on the expectation of further bailouts, Greece remains locked in a cruel high-currency trap. Either Athens must leave the euro, reintroduce the drachma and benefit from devaluation, or Greek debts should be postponed until the economy has grown significantly bigger than it was before the Lehman collapse. The stability and even survival of any currency union where one member is locked in a deep, semi-permanent depression will always be in doubt.

The Eurozone, then, remains a highly precarious and potentially explosive arrangement. Monetary union has condemned millions of ordinary EU citizens to unemployment. Joblessness across the Eurozone remains around 10 per cent, with youth unemployment at a staggering 22 per cent, and this figure is far higher, of course, in Italy, Spain, Portugal and Greece. While much of the business and financial elite in these countries backs continued euro membership, many ordinary voters are suffering amidst sharp spending cuts and broader economic stagnation as their nations fail to recover.

Heated public negotiations and repeated standoffs between elected leaders of proud yet economically weak nations and faceless international bureaucrats do little to enhance European 'solidarity' – or democracy. Former Greek Finance Minister Yanis Varoufakis relays his experience of negotiating with the EU: 'It's the worst combination of authoritarianism, contempt for democracy and technical incompetence,' he wrote in mid-2017. 'But they don't care as it's all about the power.'[29]

UNFUNNY MONEY

As the fallout from the global financial crisis unfolded during 2009 and into 2010, it was clear that bailouts funded by EU taxpayers and multilateral organisations weren't enough to save the Eurozone. 'Extraordinary measures' were needed. During the immediate aftermath of the Lehman collapse, both the US Federal Reserve and the Bank of England used quantitative easing (QE) – a massive expansion of their balance sheets, employing tens of billions of 'virtually created' pounds and dollars to buy government bonds. In America and Britain, as well as China and Japan, QE has been used extensively to suppress government borrowing costs, so artificially bolstering state finances, while pumping up the price of other assets too – not least equity markets – in a bid to promote confidence.

While a detailed examination of QE is beyond the scope of this book, the extent of this expansion of Western central banks' balance sheets has no peacetime precedent.[30] From October 2008 to April 2017, the Federal Reserve increased US 'base money' more than fivefold – from around $800 billion to $4,400 billion – the Fed's balance sheet now equivalent to around 20 per cent of annual GDP. The Bank of Japan has also expanded aggressively, its balance sheet similar in absolute size to that of the Fed, but a massive 90 per cent of Japanese GDP.[31] The Bank of England, since starting QE in March 2009, has quadrupled its balance sheet to around £420 billion, 22 per cent of GDP.

By mid-2011, while other central banks were visibly undertaking dramatic monetary expansions, the ECB was seen as a laggard due to strong German opposition towards central bank bond-buying. The ECB came under increasing pressure, though, to backstop the finances of struggling Eurozone economies where governments were in danger of having to support troubled banks – amidst renewed fears that, despite fiscal bailouts, a systemic Eurozone failure could cause broader collateral damage on global markets. 'We need a concrete plan and structure that sends a clear signal to the markets that Europe is standing behind the euro, or we'll have continued market turmoil,' said US President Barack Obama in November 2011.[32]

As spreads between German bonds and those of Italy, Spain and especially Greece became even wider during early 2012, threatening to tear the Eurozone apart, such international warnings became increasingly shrill – just as they had in early 2010, ahead of the Greek bailout. In July 2012, amidst intense market volatility and without formal approval from Berlin, ECB President Mario Draghi famously committed to do 'whatever it takes' to hold the single curren-cy together.[33] Since then, the ECB has pledged to dowse the Eurozone bonds market with QE liquidity when required, a commitment which, to some extent and intermittently, has helped contain spreads, keeping market panic at bay.

The common impression that the ECB began QE later than other large cen-tral banks, and has used it far less, is mistaken. It is true the ECB's official QE programme was launched only in January 2015, years after the Fed and Bank of England, with Draghi announcing a €60 billion monthly bond-buying pro-gramme, later raised to €80 billion.[34] For a long time before that, though, even ahead of Draghi's July 2012 commitment, the ECB's balance sheet saw rapid expansion via a complex mechanism for settling payments between the cen-tral banks of individual Eurozone members known, rather euphemistically, as TARGET2.[35]

Explicit Eurozone QE was delayed for as long as possible so as not to aggra-vate extremely vociferous German opposition. On the latest figures, though, via overt and covert means, the ECB's balance sheet actually grew more than threefold between mid-2008 and March 2017 – from the equivalent of $1,500 billion to $4,400 billion. It is now a similar size to that of the Federal Reserve – and, in terms of Eurozone GDP, even bigger.[36]

Justified by the need to 'fight deflation' and fend off financial collapse, QE has caused considerable public discontent. Along with original public outrage at wealthy bankers being bailed out, dumping the implications of their mistakes onto taxpayers, the ultra-low interest rates related to QE have had a negative impact on individual savers and pension funds.[37]

The political fallout has been significantly aggravated within the Eurozone, though – with state bailouts becoming cross-border bailouts as we have described, adding an alarming nationalistic element to the anger such measures would anyway generate. Voters everywhere, particularly those across northern Europe, have also fretted over the impact on savings of QE – with the potentially inflationary fallout playing on painful German memories, when rapidly spiralling prices led to a disastrous radicalisation of domestic inter-war politics. And as with treaty-busting fiscal bailouts, the need for QE is widely seen to result from mismanagement and profligacy across the southern Eurozone.

For years, QE has been bitterly criticised by Germany's economic and political establishment. Finance Minister Schäuble has blamed QE for the electoral success of the right-wing nationalist party Alternative für Deutschland, while warning that Draghi's policies could 'ultimately end in disaster'.[38] In 2016, a group of academics and business leaders brought a case against the ECB's mass bond-buying programme to Germany's Constitutional Court, accusing Draghi of expropriating money from German savers. Germany's highest legal authority was also forced to consider if the ECB's Outright Monetary Transactions (OMT) scheme, which allows potentially limitless purchases of government bonds in the event of financial panic, exceeded the central bank's 'price stability' mandate. The case was eventually referred to the ECJ, which found in the ECB's favour.[39]

Further legal skirmishes are likely, though, as the German press becomes more vocal about Berlin's massive TARGET2 surplus. As of mid-2017, the ECB-held liability owed to Germany by the rest of the Eurozone, particularly Italy, Spain and Greece, is €843 billion, close to 30 per cent of annual German GDP.[40] If debtor countries crash out of the Eurozone, they would default on these huge liabilities.

For all of Germany's angst about euro-QE, though, the orderly functioning of the Eurozone bond market seems reliant on its continuation. When the ECB cut its monthly stimulus from €80 billion to €60 billion in early April 2017, the spread between yields of southern Eurozone members and their northern peers significantly widened. As this book goes to press, ECB policymakers are under pressure to implement more 'tapering' over the summer of 2017. Mindful of Germany's determination to rein in QE, the ECB, in its latest *Financial Stability Review*, repeatedly raises the danger of an 'abrupt' bond-market panic if the vast monthly monetary stimulus is reduced 'too quickly'.[41] Yet with German elections due in late September 2017, Merkel and Schäuble will press Draghi very hard – with the resulting rhetoric from Berlin likely to cause market angst.

BANKING ON A UNION

A monetary union ultimately requires a banking union. That entails pooling bank liabilities across all member states, with the ECB controlling a centralised bailout fund and acting as lender of last resort. The details of the Eurozone's banking union, under formal discussion for at least five years, remain the subject of much disagreement. Yet such a union is vital if the euro is to survive.

Within a pan-Eurozone banking union, Germany and other creditor nations – but mainly Germany – would need to agree to share the liabilities of other nations' banks, whatever the state of their balance sheets. Given the attitude of voters across northern Europe towards bailouts and QE so far, that could prove rather difficult, to say the least. Establishing a Eurozone banking union is made more complex still by the very high prevalence of non-performing loans (NPLs).

Having been hit by the prolonged slump, the Eurozone's banking sector remains weighed down by bad debts.[42] NPLs amounted to €866 billion as of December 2016 – some 9 per cent of GDP.[43] NPLs represent 6.4 per cent of gross loans outstanding across the Eurozone, well above the UK (1 per cent) or the US (1.5 per cent) where banks have raised more capital since the global financial crisis and acknowledged more write-offs.[44] High NPLs have kept fresh Eurozone bank lending subdued in recent years, helping to explain why private investment has yet to reach pre-crisis levels, stymying job creation and growth.[45]

Germany and France have reasonable NPL ratios of 3.2 per cent and 4.2 per cent of gross outstanding loans respectively. The figures for Greece and Cyprus are a shocking 43.5 per cent and 50 per cent.[46] The pooling of such deeply im-balanced Eurozone loan books would obviously provoke considerable anger in relatively wealthy countries, not least Germany. The biggest issue, though, is Italy's NPLs. Much of the massive $2,500 billion stock of Italian government debt – over 130 per cent of GDP – is held by a domestic banking system already swaying under the weight of bad corporate loans. Italian banks are shouldering an NPL ratio of 16.9 per cent, a massive €360 billion – up 80 per cent since 2010. Italy's NPLs, amounting to 20 per cent of GDP, account for a third of the Eurozone total.[47]

The Italians refer to NPLs as *le sofferenze* – the suffering. Italy's stock of bad loans is now so large that, with an economy 7 per cent smaller than before the 2008 collapse and still barely growing, the chances of a natural banking recovery look remote. Yet a systemic Italian bond crisis would shake the global financial system to its foundations. The sub-prime debacle was triggered by the build-up of bad housing loans that generated a 5 per cent NPL ratio among US banks. The bad loan share across Italian banks is over three times larger.

Were Beppe Grillo's Five Star Movement to prevail in Italian elections due before May 2018, and which could happen sooner, that would risk a bond crisis or even an Italian euro exit. Just the prospect of such a victory could push yields to crippling levels, with Rome unable to service its vast debt pile. At the time of writing, Five Star is at around 30 per cent in opinion polls, vying with the ruling Partito Democratico, on a platform of holding a referendum to leave the single currency. If Grillo's party gets close to power, Italy could emerge as the epicentre of Eurozone instability – an economy ten times the size of Greece.

At the height of the 2012 euro crisis, the average spread between German and Italian ten-year sovereign bond yields was a massive 5.15 percentage points. During the summer of 2017, the figure is still around 2 percentage points, much higher than it should be in a well-functioning currency union. The gap between Portugal's ten-year sovereign yield and that of Germany is close to 2.5 percent-age points, down from almost 4 percentage points several months before, but still considerable. The Greek–German spread remains extremely wide, at almost 5 percentage points, having been more than double that just few months ago. EU officials and politicians repeatedly state the 'euro crisis is over'. But it's clear that financial markets – which will ultimately decide the fate of the euro – think otherwise.[48]

Consider that in 2002, when the euro was working smoothly and markets assumed it was 'impossible' to leave, the average German–Italian spread was just 0.29 percentage points.[49] Given that the same gap, even outside of a 'crisis' period, is now almost seven times wider, such assumptions no longer apply. The likelihood must be that, short of full Eurozone banking and fiscal union, they never will again.

EVER CLOSER?

As the EU has grappled with the Eurozone crisis it has also, since 2015, faced the largest influx of people into Europe since World War Two. The arrival of millions of migrants and refugees, primarily from the Middle East and north and west Africa, has posed very serious challenges. The border-free Schengen Agreement has been suspended by several counties, amidst threats to political stability in several countries, particularly across southern Europe.

Since the 'big bang' enlargement of 2004, when eight Eastern European nations became EU members, some 20 million people have emigrated from central and south-eastern Europe. Around four fifths of them headed for richer EU nations – as we outlined in Chapter 1. An authoritative study released to mark the tenth anniversary of the 2004 'big bang' suggested some 'enlargement fatigue' by 2014, with the majority of the EU population against the admission of further members. Support for more enlargement in the countries that were originally the most opposed – France, Austria and Germany – had fallen even more a decade later.[50] Public expressions of concern were relatively infrequent, though, so were largely dismissed by mainstream politicians. There were certainly no serious protests against the EU's freedom of movement rules.

Since then, public opinion has changed markedly. The combination of Western intervention in Libya, followed by civil war and subsequent bombing in Syria, has seen a sharp influx in illegal immigration from outside the EU. The advent of widespread people smuggling, and its tragic consequences, have become all too clear from the heartbreaking television coverage of small boats, crammed impossibly full of people attempting to cross the Mediterranean Sea.

Asylum applications from outside the EU have risen from 250,000 in 2010 to more than 400,000 in 2013, almost 600,000 the year after and 1.3 million in 2015, as economic migrants and genuine refugees have taken advantage of the EU's relatively generous asylum rules. The numbers fell slightly to 1.2 million in 2016, after a deal was struck with Turkey to stop migrants entering Greece in exchange for cash payments to Ankara and the promise of visa-free travel for Turks and possible EU membership.[51] Efforts have also been made by European naval forces to intercept boats close to the north African coast, so they can be turned back without openly breaching the EU's human rights obligations.

Countless migrants, while arriving in southern EU nations, have been allowed to cross southern Europe illegally, in contravention of the Dublin Convention, travelling on to nations they see as more economically promising before registering.[52] In 2016, Germany registered no less than 722,000 asylum seekers, considerably up from 442,000 in 2015. Sweden, in contrast, registered 22,300 – sharply down from 156,000 the year before. Hungary processed 28,000 asylum seekers in 2016, also much fewer than the 174,000 it received a year earlier.

Germany recorded 60 per cent of all first-time EU asylum applicants in 2016, with Italy and France accounting for 10 per cent and 6 per cent respectively. In terms of registrations per head of domestic population, Germany outstripped Italy fourfold and France sevenfold. This has caused considerable bitterness in Germany towards other EU members, not least given Germany's role in bailing out other nations.[53]

It is telling that in 2016 the governments of five wealthy EU nations – Austria, Denmark, France, Germany and Sweden – 'temporarily' suspended the Schengen Agreement. Under intense domestic political pressure, the governments of these nations curtailed borderless, passport-free travel – one of the cardinal principles of the EU. None of these nations are on the frontier of the EU, yet they have lost trust in the ability, or even the inclination, of their southern and eastern EU neighbours to manage flows of people.

The migrant crisis has also generated anger across Western Europe towards Eastern European members. Having initially registered almost 175,000 asylum seekers in 2015, Hungary has since strengthened its borders and refused to accept its registrant quota required by Brussels. Poland, the Czech Republic, Romania, Slovakia and Slovenia, as of the end of 2016, have taken barely any asylum seekers – openly flouting EU rules, despite receiving billions of euros in EU structural funds.

Within the Eastern European member states themselves, the migration crisis has brought 'a significant reframing of the way the EU is debated' according to a detailed academic survey, leading to a 'sharpening' of euro scepticism 'among mainstream political actors'.[54] Having thrown off the Soviet yoke, the EU's Visegrád members – Poland, Hungary, the Czech Republic and Slovakia – won't be pushed around by Brussels. In November 2016, the four-strong group ratified its refusal to accept EU refugee quotas.

Once the star pupils of the EU's eastern enlargement, Poland and Hungary now face legal action for refusing to fulfil asylum seeker quotas, which they justify by citing terror attacks in France, the UK and elsewhere.[55] In response, French President Macron has called for sanctions on Poland.[56] The migrant crisis is not only exacerbating north–south EU tensions, adding to those generated by the single currency, but east–west divisions too.

If monetary union and related economic stagnation has generated an appetite for populist and nationalist parties since the 2008 financial collapse, the EU migrant crisis has sharpened such trends. In December 2016, an extensive poll of EU nationals found that 'growing support for populist movements' in Europe is linked to 'scepticism or hostility towards trade, immigration and European integration'. The same survey indicated a clear majority of EU citizens – 59 per cent – believe that 'refugees will increase the likelihood of terrorism in our country'.[57] According to Eurobarometer, immigration is now viewed among the public as the largest problem facing the EU.[58]

MULTI-SPEED EUROPE?

In mid-July 2017, the IMF provided their latest update on the global economic outlook.[59] Helped by cheap money policies in the West, and a recovery across emerging economies, the IMF reiterated its view of an upswing in global growth into 2018. Sharing in this recovery is the Eurozone. Following growth of 1.8 per cent in 2016, the Eurozone is expected to expand by 1.9 per cent in 2017 and 1.7 per cent the year after – with investment and employment both picking up, albeit from previously disappointing levels. Eurozone inflation rose in late 2016 and early 2017 as oil prices rose, just as in the UK, but has since started to ease. As such, the ECB is under no immediate pressure to raise interest rates. The debate has already begun to turn, though, towards when the ECB will be forced to tighten.

While German GDP expanded 0.6 per cent quarter on quarter during the first three months of 2017, the Greek economy shrank by 0.1 per cent, having contracted 1.2 per cent in the final three months of 2016. So Greece remains in recession. 'Europe is just sort of hanging on,' says Harvard Professor and former IMF chief economist Kenneth Rogoff. 'It's very much like Japan, where Japan chose not to grab the bulls by the horns.'[60]

One set of horns the Eurozone must grab, in common with other Western countries, is learning to live without QE, as the ECB comes under more pressure from Germany and other northern European nationals to rein in its balance sheet expansion. Eurozone members with high NPLs and heavy debt burdens like Italy would then fear having to handle higher sovereign yields – making it even harder to roll over existing loans.

This raises a paradox. If the political heat rises in Greece or Italy, with Beppe Grillo's party getting stronger for instance, Greek–German and Italian–German spreads will widen – putting additional stress on Greek and Italian finances. If, on the other hand, EU politics is less volatile than feared, Berlin may take the opportunity to attack QE head-on, calling for an end to 'emergency measures'. That would also widen spreads.

Draghi's term ends in November 2019. Yet, already, leading members of Merkel's CDU are laying claim to the nationality of the Italian's replacement. 'The next ECB chief must be German, bound to the Bundesbank's tradition of monetary stability,' Hans-Peter Friedrich, a former CDU Interior Minister, said in the German tabloid *Bild* in 2016. Markus Söder, Bavarian State Minister for Finance, told the same mass selling paper, 'it's time for a change of direction' and 'more German influence'.[61] The ongoing fight for ECB control is just one aspect of the broader battle over the future direction of 'Project Europe'.

Which brings us to the second, even bigger set of horns the EU must grab – how to square the opposing forces of divergence and convergence and, more specifically, make the single currency work. There has been much rhetoric since the UK's Brexit vote about pressing ahead with European integration. Could there be a new Franco-German initiative to relaunch the European project and push for full federalism? 'We have to reform so we have a real European government,' says Guy Verhofstadt, the former Belgian Prime Minister, now leader of the Liberal group in the European Parliament. 'Since Brexit, something has changed – the counter-revolution is already under way.'[62]

Following the UK's EU referendum, Verhofstadt wrote a book titled *Europe's Last Chance: Why the European States Must Form a More Perfect Union*, calling for the EU to reform along the lines of America's federal government.[63] 'Behind closed doors,' the book states, 'many politicians acknowledge the need for a United States of Europe, but claim their voters would not support this goal.' Since publishing this work, Verhofstadt has been named Chief Brexit Negotiator for the European Parliament.

During the early 1990s, across Germany, Italy, France and Spain, around 70–80 per cent of the public approved of EU membership. Such polls now regularly produce scores not much above 30 per cent.[64] Many voters strongly disagree, moreover, with Vefhofstadt's vision of a pan-European government – not just in the UK. Some 42 per cent of EU citizens feel 'some EU powers should be returned to national governments' according to a recent Pew survey, with another 27 per cent wanting the division of powers 'to remain the same' – a total of 69 per cent against 'ever closer union'.[65] When asked explicitly 'should national governments transfer more power to the EU?' in the same survey, only 19 per cent of EU voters agreed.[66]

Many EU governments are also uncomfortable with further integration. For years, and not only in response to the euro and migrant crises, a debate has swirled about the future model of the EU. What worked for six members in 1957, after all, is unlikely to work for almost thirty far more diverse members decades later – for all the European Commission's bluster about 'forging ahead' after Brexit.

The idea of a 'multi-speed' Europe, with different nations integrating at differing rates, has a long history. The Tindemans report, drawn up by a former Belgian Prime Minister in 1975, floated the concept of a two-speed Europe.[67] Some twenty years later, French Prime Minister Edouard Balladur suggested a Europe of three concentric circles: an outer circle of non-members with close links to the EU, a middle tier inside the EU but not the euro and an inner core of single currency members.[68]

Such ideas have lately seen renewed interest. In February 2017, Merkel used an EU summit in Malta to suggest 'a union of different speeds'.[69] A month later, that proposal was one of five scenarios laid out by President Juncker in his White Paper on the future of Europe, designed to provoke debate on how the EU might evolve after Brexit.[70] Far from imposing 'ever closer union', the scenarios ranged from 'nothing but the single market' to full-blown federalism. Acknowledging divisions across Europe, there were also indications that, under some proposals, EU members may not be subject to freedom of movement rules. Juncker is due to present these various scenarios to the European Parliament in September 2017. For such a committed and powerful EU federalist to even float such flexible scenarios marks a significant departure.

The Rome Declaration, too, signed in the Palazzo dei Conservatori just weeks after Juncker's White Paper, also contained a concession. EU leaders pledged member states could proceed at 'different paces' while 'moving in the same direction' – a subtly different message from 'ever closer union'. The declaration also vowed only to 'work towards' the 'completion of monetary union' – a tacit admission that Germany has very serious concerns about pooling bank liabilities with other Eurozone nations.

TEURER FREUND

There is much speculation that Macron's presidency will engender a 'rebirth' of the EU, with France and Germany coming together to drive the European project forward. In truth, Paris will find it extremely difficult to convince Berlin to back a more integrated Eurozone, with a communal budget and jointly issued 'eurobonds' – as that would entail regular transfers of wealth, on a far bigger scale than bailouts to date, from Germany to the rest of the Eurozone.

There are strong theoretical arguments for an EU 'fiscal union', of course. The Eurozone's successive debt crises starkly illustrate that a monetary union requires a 'joint Treasury', with a dedicated system of sizeable intra-region transfers. Without such a mechanism, the single currency – subject to periodic bond-market squalls and held together with printed money – will always be at risk of imploding.

In the US, for instance, taxes collected annually at the federal (national) level and redistributed across the various states have ranged between 14 per cent and 20 per cent of GDP over the last half a century, with an average of 17 per cent. The figures in more recent years for Canada and Australia are 12–16 per cent and 18–20 per cent respectively.[71] The EU, in contrast, collects less than 1 per cent of GDP – much of that going to farmers in relatively wealthy member states via the

CAP. Per capita transfers to poorer countries like Greece, Portugal and Hungary amount to a tiny proportion of comparable US inter-state transfers.

There are clearly huge discrepancies not just in per capita wealth but also competitiveness between Eurozone members. Germany, the Netherlands and Finland were all counted among the world's ten most competitive nations in 2016. Italy, meanwhile, ranked at forty-four, Greece at eighty-six.[72] The idea that these southern European countries can thrive with the same exchange rate and monetary policy as their north European counterparts, with no fiscal transfers to compensate, is absurd. Yet large, regular payments between Eurozone members would spark political outrage across creditor nations. With no transfers, but locked into a high currency, poorer Eurozone nations continue to stagnate, so generating political rancour.

None of this is a surprise. In 1977, the Scottish economist Donald MacDougall led an official EEC inquiry into the question of the fiscal transfers required to make a single currency feasible.[73] He concluded such payments would need to amount, 'at an earlier stage, to 7–10 per cent of GDP', eventually growing to '20–25 per cent of GDP, as in the USA and the Federal Republic of Germany'. At the time, the EEC's entire expenditure was 0.7 per cent of the bloc's GDP. The MacDougall Report, warning that monetary union was 'impracticable' and 'a long way off' was buried. The political hubris behind the move towards a single currency outweighed all economic logic.

The Eurozone remains hamstrung by the same problem MacDougall identified.[74] Yet Germany and other wealthier Eurozone nations clearly do not want to pay to fix it. Merkel's vision of a 'new' Europe is far less ambitious than that of the incoming French President. Macron warned in January 2017 that 'the euro may not exist in ten years' time' unless there are 'reforms'.[75] Berlin knows such reforms involve pooling risk, with a Eurozone Treasury and jointly issued eurobonds. Germany – Europe's dominant power – simply does not want this. Berlin is loath systematically to share its credit rating and accumulated wealth with other nations. That's why Finance Minister Wolfgang Schäuble told *Le Figaro* that the French president's plans were 'unrealistic' and *Der Spiegel* dubbed Macron '*Teurer Freund*' – our 'expensive friend'.[76]

At the time of writing, Chancellor Merkel looks likely to win the autumn 2017 German election, rather than the far more federalist SPD candidate Martin

Schultz, the former President of the European Parliament. That would give Macron almost no chance of getting his way. Berlin rhetorically backs 'Europe' and has spent tens of billions of euros on bailouts. But the German electorate looks extremely unlikely to accept a unified Eurozone finance ministry, with explicit fiscal pooling and mutually guaranteed banking sectors.

France and Germany seem irrevocably split on the future of Europe. Traditionally obedient Europhile nations like Finland and the Netherlands are complaining loudly about bailouts and QE. The Italians, Greeks and Spanish are angry. New members in Eastern Europe, particularly Hungary and Poland, are now openly chiding Brussels – cheered on by their increasingly Eurosceptic electorates.

The battle between opposing forces of EU integration and divergence has intensified, with north–south tensions accompanied by those between east and west. What political stability we have seen in mid-2017 rests in part on an increasingly authoritarian President Erdoğan, seemingly no longer interested in Turkey's EU membership. If Erdoğan were to renege on Turkey's deal to limit EU-bound migrants from the south, that could spark political turmoil anew.

What will the EU look like after Brexit? Will we see a multi-speed Europe? Might the Eurozone split into two – north and south? Devaluing the 'southern euro', though, would involve a massive soft default on loans owed to richer northern neighbours. The slightest hint of such plans would send bond markets haywire. The single currency, then, the heart of 'Project Europe', remains too dangerous to dismantle but too incoherent to fix.

'Europe will be made through a common currency or will not be made,' said the French economist Jacques Rueff, back in 1950.[77] Increasingly, though, mainstream politicians are starting to question if that makes sense. Across many Eurozone governments, the euro is tolerated mostly due to the perceived turmoil and difficulty associated with breaking it up.

As inflation rises towards the end of 2017, and northern European impatience with bailouts and QE grows, the choice between a return to national currencies and democratic control or the transfer of fiscal and political sovereignty to a European government will become even more stark. Whatever the fantasies of the federalists, though, the vast majority of European voters want power to reside with their nation states – which means more muddling through, with all the attendant pain across the 'periphery' and associated danger of a bond-market shock.

The single currency is a powder keg, posing in the minds of a large swathe of global investors an ever-present source of systemic risk. Attempting to make it work, while struggling with the migrant crisis, will be a major distraction for EU authorities and governments during the UK's Brexit talks. Ultimately, the Brussels institutions, in conjunction with the core EU governments, must decide, more than sixty years on from the Treaty of Rome, amidst ongoing crises and diverging economic fortunes, what the EU is to become. That is the backdrop against which the UK–EU Article 50 negotiations are taking place.

PART III

TAKING BACK CONTROL

CHAPTER 5

EARLY UK–EU SKIRMISHES

'When things get serious, you have to lie.'
Jean-Claude Juncker[1]

In early May 2017, Jean-Claude Juncker, the President of the European Commission, and his entourage spent an evening at Downing Street. After what had seemingly been a constructive working dinner, one of Juncker's aides then rang a German newspaper and said that Prime Minister Theresa May was 'deluded' for suggesting any UK 'divorce payment' relating to Brexit should be linked to a mutually beneficial UK–EU free trade agreement.[2]

The following day, the Commission helped to fuel speculation in the British press that the UK should pay €100 billion to leave the EU, up from the earlier €60 billion estimate. Anonymous 'Brussels sources' accused May of 'living in another galaxy', while speculating that 'more likely than not' the Brexit talks would fail.

Downing Street initially 'refused to comment on leaks' following the infamous Juncker dinner. As the press frenzy grew, though, the Prime Minister felt compelled to speak out: 'Events over the last few days have shown that some in Brussels don't want these talks to succeed and don't want Britain to prosper,' she said, accusing EU officials of seeking to influence the outcome of the June 2017 UK general election.[3]

What was striking about this episode was not so much the aggressive leaking sanctioned by Juncker – the European Commission President has a well-deserved reputation as a media streetfighter – but how quick much of the UK press corps was to accept briefings from the Juncker camp as an accurate analysis of the situation and, in particular, the relative bargaining power of the UK and EU.

It is never the job of the British press to blindly champion the government, of course. But serious newspapers and broadcasters should question and provide context. Juncker was clearly keen to put pressure on the UK ahead of high-stakes Article 50 negotiations. As Britain heads for the exit, the Commission is deeply concerned about losing the UK's annual contribution – some £13.1 billion in 2016, or £8.6 billion in net terms. So Juncker wanted to do everything he could to frustrate, delay and even help prevent that exit.

The ranks of bureaucrats that he leads are concerned that Brexit could threaten the broader European project that underpins their careers, generous per diems and pensions. Amidst breathless accounts of the Downing Street dinner, which apparently made Juncker 'ten times more sceptical' of reaching a mutually acceptable UK–EU deal, there was little mention of such background.

'NO NEED TO BE NASTY'

There is no doubting that these EU negotiations will be tough. It's also clear that, while many of those who voted Remain in June 2016 are reconciled to the UK leaving the EU, a minority of the electorate is still upset. There is a market, then, for doom-laden Brexit coverage. Yet Juncker not only has the motive to mislead, he also has form. The same German newspaper in which his leaked account of the Downing Street dinner appeared in May 2017 accused him, at the height of the 2011 euro crisis, of 'taking the lead on deception'.[4] When asked by a group of journalists at that time why he had been deliberately dishonest, he replied: 'When things get serious, you have to lie.'[5]

Jean-Claude Juncker represents the Commission – not the EU. It is the big EU nations, chiefly Germany, with whom the UK will ultimately negotiate during these Article 50 talks. Little of the analysis following the Downing Street dinner mentioned Juncker's very difficult relationship with German Chancellor Angela Merkel – a reality that undermines assumptions his views will significantly impact these negotiations.[6] Merkel fiercely opposed Juncker's initial 2014 appointment and, two days after the Downing Street leak, Stephan Mayer, her home affairs spokesman, weighed in. 'It is not good when negotiation details become public,' said Mayer. 'This situation is complicated enough.' A week later, *Der Spiegel* reported that Merkel herself was 'annoyed' with Juncker for trying to destabilise the Brexit negotiations.[7] It is unclear to what extent he will be involved in the Article 50 talks.

At stake during these negotiations are issues that go way beyond the question of how the UK and EU will continue to trade and collaborate after March 2019, important though that is. What will the EU itself look like one or two decades from now? Will the pursuit of 'ever closer union' continue, or will the nation state reassert itself, with some powers returning from Brussels back to member countries? In all the Article 50 dealings between the UK and EU, these much broader questions are also very much in play. Brexit is seen by those on both sides of the argument as a chance finally to set the EU on its chosen path – either attempting to forge ahead with an integrationist agenda, or rowing back on federalism instead.

On one side of the argument is Juncker and his close ally the former European Parliament President Martin Schulz – now leader of Germany's centre-left SPD party. Facing them are the majority of European governments, led by Merkel, but also including EU members in Western Europe, Scandinavia and Eastern Europe, too. Again, little of this context appeared in reports of the Downing Street dinner.

There is 'no need to be nasty' in negotiations with the UK, observed Merkel during the weekend after Britain voted for Brexit. 'It's important we work together to get the right outcome,' said Europe's most powerful politician.[8] Even before the UK's EU referendum, the BDI, the main German employers' organisation, was arguing that it would be 'very, very foolish' for the EU to impose high trade barriers against the UK.[9] Keeping trade as free as possible, after all, makes commercial sense for both sides.

Despite May's Conservative Party failing to win a parliamentary majority in the June 2017 election, Merkel has continued to make positive noises about the prospect of the UK and EU striking a free trade deal. 'I hope we will reach a good agreement, that will be in our mutual interest,' she said, a week or so after the poll. Powerful German business lobbies are urging negotiators on both sides quickly to agree new trading arrangements. 'The EU and Great Britain must absolutely avoid being left without an agreement in two years' time,' said VDMA, Germany's Engineering Industry Association, in response to the UK's hung parliament.[10] VDMA's member companies sold €7.3 billion worth of goods to customers in Britain during 2016.

As these Article 50 negotiations progress, much of the UK media establishment is likely to remain hostile towards the Brexit process. This engrained negativity, combined with the new fragility of the Conservatives' parliamentary majority, means numerous supporters of a Soft Brexit feel that this could be their moment, with Labour sensing it could even topple the government. Yet the 2017 general election did nothing to undermine support for the principle of Brexit – a case based on the decision of the last parliament, by a six-to-one majority, to hold a referendum on EU membership – a referendum in which the British public voted to leave.

A STRONG HAND

Despite widespread negativity, the UK has a rather strong hand to play in these Article 50 negotiations. The latest figures show that £384 billion of trade in goods took place between the UK and EU in 2016, with Britain chalking up a trade (goods) deficit of £96 billion.[11] Germany, Spain, Belgium and Luxembourg, the Netherlands, France, Poland, Italy, Sweden, Denmark, Portugal and Finland will all be keen that low- or even zero-tariff cross-Channel trade continues once Britain leaves the EU, seeing as they all sell considerably more to the UK than we sell to them. The annual German goods surplus with the UK was some £32 billion in 2016, based on heavy sales of cars, machinery and pharmaceuticals, totalling £65 billion of German goods exports.[12] Powerful business interests have much to lose if the UK imposes tariffs on such exports. French farmers and winemakers and Italian fashion houses and furniture producers may also have felt that Juncker's post-dinner comments were not particularly good for business.

France is sometimes portrayed as a country that wants to 'punish' the UK for leaving the EU. President Macron has described Brexit as a 'crime' and a 'tragedy', vowing to take an uncompromising approach to deter other member states from 'killing the European idea'.[13] Yet numerous French firms and even the French government itself have strong commercial interests in the UK, with investments across sectors including transport, automotive manufacturing and nuclear power.

The Netherlands, meanwhile, will want a zero-tariff deal with Britain so that Rotterdam, Europe's largest port, remains a UK trade hub. Again, while EU politicians and Brussels-based bureaucrats beat their chests and issue harsh rhetoric, influential business groups want trade restrictions between the UK and the Continent kept to a minimum.

EU members in central and Eastern Europe will want continued close political and commercial links with the UK during the Article 50 talks. There are around one million Polish people living in Britain, sending home remittances that inject over £1 billion into the Polish economy each year. Britain is the EU's second largest source of remittances after Germany, with cash sent from the UK accounting for between 3 per cent and 6 per cent of GDP in Hungary, Lithuania and Latvia.[14] The Baltic states are mindful, too, of Britain's role as Europe's most significant military power. Brexit does not alter the UK's pivotal role in terms of European security – with our position in NATO recently highlighted, at a time of heightened tension between the EU and Russia, by the deployment of 800 troops from 5th Battalion The Rifles to Estonia.

When it comes to details of trade negotiations during the Article 50 talks, one of the most important sectors under discussion is undoubtedly the UK car industry. Britain produces around 1.8 million cars annually, 1.2 million of those for export. The auto sector is, after agriculture, the most protected within the EU, with a 9.6 per cent tariff on cars exported from non-EU countries. Yet the case for a post-Brexit auto-sector trade agreement is strong, given the flow of car exports between the UK and EU – and the extent to which EU-based companies are themselves owners of UK-based car plants.

Britain is a key market for auto and car component makers based on the Continent, with countless manufacturing jobs in France and Germany dependent on the UK market, again pointing to mutual incentives to strike a low-tariff deal. Being outside the EU, though, could also see carmakers source more components from the UK, attracting investment, not least from the EU, which will boost the UK's domestic automotive supply chain. There are already signs of this happening.[15]

If the UK can secure trade deals with the world's leading economies that have eluded the EU, Britain could become a platform for EU carmakers to export high-margin upmarket cars to non-EU countries. At present, just over 40 per cent of the parts in British-built cars are made in the UK, less than the 50–55 per cent 'local content requirement' usually required for the purposes of bilateral trade deals. The prospect of trade agreements beyond the EU could provide a further incentive for the UK-based car industry to source more components at home – to get over the 'made in Britain' threshold allowing them to benefit from such trade deals.

Being outside the EU and free from Brussels regulations could also allow the UK to take a lead in new technologies such as hydrogen, electric and driverless cars – again a reason for EU carmakers to expand their UK-based operations. We discuss the UK's car industry in more detail in Chapter 8, but there is certainly scope for a deal on auto trade, either a sector-specific agreement or as part of a broader FTA. While there are clearly uncertainties, and Brexit is likely to slow investment for a period as carmakers ascertain likely outcomes, there are encouraging signs too. Domestic component makers are looking to expand and, as this book goes to press, BMW has just announced it will build the first electric Mini in the UK from 2019.[16]

Much concern has also been expressed regarding the financial services sector – which, post-Brexit, is seen as being vulnerable to EU diktat. The UK's financial services industry is obviously vital, employing around 1 million people directly, and another 1.2 million in allied professional services, generating around 11 per cent of GDP. But warnings that the City will be damaged by Brexit are mostly bluster from the European Commission or reflect pressure from large London-based financial services firms keen to highlight concerns so as to influence the UK government.

An OECD report released in the early summer of 2017 stated that EU nations have 'ample room' to keep trading in financial services with the UK after Brexit even within current international rules. The Paris-based think tank added that attempting to shut out the UK would risk starving the EU of capital vital to its economy.[17] 'Access' to the single market in this context essentially means non-EU countries having similar regulatory regimes for financial services, with rules in the US and Japan already deemed to be largely 'equivalent' by the EU. The same will surely apply to the UK, not least as, at the moment we leave the EU, there will by definition be full regulatory compliance. 'Unless UK and EU financial services regimes diverge significantly after Brexit, it can arguably be expected that the UK would benefit from selective recognition arrangements,' says the OECD.

London is, by most definitions, the world's financial capital.[18] The City acts as Europe's 'investment banker', where EU-based companies and governments come to place bonds and raise money, given the unmatched size and liquidity of the London markets. 'Erecting new barriers to financial services in the post-Brexit environment will not be in the collective interest of the global economy, where London plays such a key role in international banking, bonds and foreign exchange,' the OECD says.

These words echo the sentiments of Wolfgang Schäuble, Germany's highly influential finance minister. Schäuble wants the EU to offer Britain a 'reasonable deal' not least because of the City's status as a global hub for capital-raising, legal services and foreign exchange. 'The UK's financial centre serves the whole European economy,' said Schäuble in February 2017. 'London offers a quality of financial services that is not to be found on the Continent – we don't want to punish the British for their decision, we want to keep Britain close to us.'[19]

Like the automotive sector, the financial services industry is clearly of enormous importance to the UK economy. There is no doubt Brexit will cause some disruption, with certain product lines being impacted. The single market in services, though, is very limited – as discussed in Chapter 3 – while 'equivalence' rules suggest the UK will continue to sell all manner of financial services to the EU, as does the US. Every other major financial centre in the world has managed to thrive without EU passporting rights or membership of the single market. It may even be that, by cutting services-oriented trade deals across the world, something that EU membership has prevented, London will be able to build on its links with fast-growing emerging markets, enhancing its status as a global hub. We discuss the City's post-Brexit prospects in Chapter 9.

The rest of this chapter outlines the first two big themes of the Article 50 negotiation – starting with the 'divorce terms' cash settlement and citizens' rights. The third major topic of the first part of the negotiation – the border between the UK and the Irish Republic – we discuss in a later chapter on Ireland. The importance of establishing the UK's future relationship with various pan-European agencies – such as Euratom – is highlighted later in this chapter. We also discuss the prospect of the UK leaving the European Common Aviation Area (ECAA).

DIVORCE BILL

When the Article 50 talks began in June 2017, Brexit Secretary David Davis and EU Chief Negotiator Michel Barnier said ongoing discussions among UK and EU officials would be punctuated by monthly meetings between the two delegation leaders, each followed by a press conference. There have, at the time of writing, been two such meetings.

The formal Article 50 negotiations began with a concession on both sides. The EU has been determined to finalise the UK's 'divorce terms' before discussing any issues relating to future trade relations between the UK and EU. Britain, to some extent, accepted this approach – having previously wanted 'perfect sequencing', with negotiations over both issues taking place at the same time. Having said that, some simultaneous discussions on divorce and trade have been taking place. With some member states concerned that a 'cash-up-front' tactic might prove counter-productive, worsening the long-term outcome on trade, Barnier has agreed to dual discussions, provided there is 'sufficient progress' on other issues – particularly the question of cash.[20] This amounts to a softening of the EU's stance.

The EU's finances are set in a seven-year Multiannual Financial Framework (MFF), currently covering 2014–20. Once the MFF is settled, it is designed to roll out relatively smoothly. This makes sense as many EU programmes, principally those for research and regional policy, are enacted over a number of years. But it also means contracts signed at a point in time may not become due for several years. With the UK set to exit the EU in March 2019, this leaves seven financial quarters before the end of the current MFF – which has led to the notion of a 'divorce bill'.

Estimates of the UK's bill, unsurprisingly, spread across a wide range. The debate over the total amount burst into the public realm with the notorious €100 billion headline that appeared just after the May–Juncker Downing Street dinner.[21] Barnier later denied that was an official estimate, after the European Commission's own lawyers admitted such a total was 'legally impossible' to enforce.[22] Since then, a wide range of figures has been floated, taking into account the UK's outstanding budget commitments, loan guarantees and EC pension payments on the one hand, set against rebates and other UK assets on the other. The Bruegel think tank says the upfront gross payment could range between €54 billion and €109 billion, translating into a net payment of between €25 billion and €65 billion once the UK receives its share of EU spending, assets and repaid EU loans.[23]

A study by the Institute of Chartered Accountants in England and Wales (ICAEW) came up with three 'next exit charges' – a 'low scenario' of £5 billion, a 'central scenario' of £15 billion and a 'high scenario' of £30 billion.[24] Taking the central scenario, the ICAEW said 'the UK could be asked to contribute a gross amount of £55 billion, but the net cost would probably be closer to £15 billion after deducting rebates and the realisation of the UK's investment in the European Investment Bank (EIB)'. The Institute said this estimate 'excludes contributions to the EU 2019 and 2020 budgets after Britain leaves, as we believe the UK has a strong case for arguing that it should not be liable for authorised spending that will not be committed to until after its departure'.

During the initial divorce bill skirmishes, Theresa May has rejected arguments from some EU countries that the UK should not get back its proportion of EU assets. The Prime Minister has insisted the discussion over any settlement payment must 'look at both rights and obligations' while indicating that the UK may want to retain a share of the Luxembourg-based EIB. Britain's 16 per cent EIB stake was judged by a House of Lords report published in March 2017 to be worth around €10 billion.[25]

While the EU's demands for Britain to settle its outstanding MFF obligations may be justifiable in a narrow legal sense, the UK's liabilities are much less obvious with regard to bills not yet contracted and contingent liabilities for Eurozone loans. A different House of Lords Committee argued, also in March 2017, that the British government would be on strong legal ground if it chose to make no divorce payment whatsoever. Peers added, though, that if the government wants goodwill and a deal on access to EU markets, a budget agreement is important.[26]

The UK's strength in this part of the Article 50 negotiation reflects not only the strict legal position, but also the reality that our departure leaves a gaping hole in the EU budget. The UK is the EU's second largest financial contributor. Since 2000, the UK has paid €100 billion more into the EU than it has received – suggesting little public appetite for an additional, essentially voluntary payment. Two weeks after the June 2016 referendum, Standard & Poor's downgraded the bloc's credit rating from AAA to AA. 'After the decision by the UK electorate to leave the EU, we have reassessed our opinion of cohesion within the EU,' said the ratings agency. In April 2017, Standard & Poor's highlighted that the EU would 'come under pressure in an adverse scenario' if the UK did not meet a 'divorce bill' of up to €60 billion, indicating the importance to Brussels of Britain's annual contribution.

As political bargaining intensifies, the UK is in a strong position. British negotiators decided, correctly, not to publish an initial position paper on the Brexit bill but to criticise the EU's proposal instead. This reflected the reality that the strategic deployment of financial concessions as the talks progress is the best way to exert leverage over the EU. Just as it makes complete sense for Barnier to demand that payment is agreed up front, it also makes complete sense for the UK to resist such an agreement.

The European Commission itself has admitted to vulnerability if the UK does not make a large contribution. In June, a report entitled 'Future Financing of the EU' was published by a working group set up jointly by the European Commission, European Parliament and the Council of the EU. 'The gap in EU finances arising from the UK's withdrawal and from the financing needs of new priorities needs to be clearly acknowledged,' the report said. It pointed to various new joint revenue-raising measures across the EU, such as pooled corporation tax or common energy and environmental taxation – with some seeing an impending budget crunch as another opportunity to push for 'ever closer union'.[27]

Some UK politicians would refuse point-blank to pay anything to the EU. Certainly, the best way to secure favourable treatment for UK exports to the EU is to negotiate and lower our trade barriers in return. In theory, if this divorce payment is designed to 'buy' frictionless trade with the EU, then the net payment should be in the UK's favour, given that we buy more from the EU than we sell to it. While all this is true, the reality is that the UK has decided to leave and wants to depart on good terms – so should be prepared to discuss payment. The actual sum, though, in our view, should be finalised only at the end of the Article 50 period, then paid over a number of years, with the total reflecting the degree of goodwill and cooperation shown by the EU between now and March 2019.

In March 2017, a leak to a Dutch newspaper suggested the EU would take Britain to the International Court of Justice (ICJ) if the UK walked away without paying. That poses the threat of a long legal battle at The Hague.[28] The British government's legal advice is that the UK would not be liable. The difficulty of reaching an agreement on the divorce bill should not be a surprise. It is a highly visible, emotive issue that the public can fully grasp. Explicit sums of money can be translated into numbers of schools, hospitals or other public services foregone. One side's cash loss is, by definition, the other side's gain. Starting the Article 50 talks with this issue, when both sides are trying to score the first victory, was always going to lead to deadlock – which may be what Barnier wanted.

One way to resolve this issue would be to appoint an arbiter to determine the divorce bill, who could then take twelve to eighteen months to investigate – with the 'decision' emerging just ahead of March 2019. That would free negotiators from deadlock and save time. The Article 50 negotiations could then move on to matters more important than a one-off payment – albeit a potentially rather large one-off payment. There would, no doubt, be negotiation over the choice of arbitrator. Brussels would probably suggest the ECJ, to which the UK would object – as the ECJ is the EU's top court. The ICJ in The Hague, in contrast, is the principal judicial body of the UN and exists to settle legal disputes between states. The Permanent Court of Arbitration, also in The Hague but not linked to the ICJ, might be another candidate.

Taking the arbitration route could prevent any loss of face, with both sides effectively agreeing on the principles of how the divorce bill is to be worked out, with the actual amount emerging at the very end of the negotiation. The UK, though, would lose its ability incrementally to concede certain degrees of financial payment throughout the negotiations, in return for concessions elsewhere.

Far from opening the talks, settling on the divorce bill should be the final piece of the UK's Article 50 jigsaw. The UK should consider calling for arbitration – not least as our legal position is strong – but there is no guarantee it would turn out as expected. If Britain avoids arbitration, we should only gradually agree on the size of the ultimate cash settlement in return for permanent concessions from the EU on trade and other matters as the Article 50 talks progress. That would extract the most 'value' in terms of leverage in the broader negotiation process in return for the money eventually spent.

As this book goes to press during the summer of 2017, there is speculation the UK may agree to a payment of €36 billion. Any such agreement, while ensuring goodwill ahead of the trade talks, could form part of a stepping-stone process towards some sort of 'transition deal' to smooth the path of Brexit once the Article 50 period ends – which we discuss in the next chapter. In floating this amount, then knocking it down a few days later, unnamed Whitehall sources are stipulating that any UK payment should be linked to some form of trade agreement. The debate has come full circle, then, for the first of what could be several times, since Jean-Claude Juncker's aide called Theresa May 'deluded' for linking cash to a more favourable trading regime.[29]

CITIZENS' RIGHTS

In 2015 there were 3.1 million EU nationals living in the UK. Following the EU referendum in June 2016 there has been widespread concern about their status. 'Five out of six EU migrants who are here either have indefinite leave to remain or will have it by the time we depart,' said Brexit Secretary David Davis a few months after the vote, pointing to EU citizens being allowed to stay in the UK as part of a generally tolerant approach.[30]

Despite this, anxiety has understandably persisted, with the issue of 'citizens' rights' being raised in both Houses of Parliament on many occasions. There have been two Opposition Day Motions since June 2016 and three separate Select Committee reports as well as numerous speeches on the subject in the parliamentary debate on Article 50 itself.[31] This reflects a concern not only among UK-based EU citizens and often their employers, but also a more general unease across parts of the rest of the population that Britain may be giving the impression of intolerance.

There is a widespread desire to see the UK grant permanent residency rights to EU migrants who have moved to the UK and settled here in good faith under freedom of movement rules. It seems cruel to upend the plans of those who have built lives in Britain, often with children in school. The government, though, has been mindful of the equally important matter – less visible in the UK – of securing the rights of 1.2 million British citizens, some of them retirees, who have made their lives on the Continent.

Soon after the 2016 referendum, both authors argued the UK should unilaterally guarantee the rights of EU citizens, laying out a generous offer immediately, ahead of the Article 50 negotiations.[32] Our feeling was that once the UK had made such a bold statement, the European Commission would be forced by public outcry to reciprocate. There was little danger in this approach – not least as the settlement rights of EU-based UK nationals are guaranteed under other non-EU treaties such as the Vienna Convention.[33]

The benefits to the UK of providing a unilateral guarantee would have been considerable. Britain could have claimed the moral high ground, establishing itself – ahead of what will clearly be tough negotiations, fought out amidst the glare of publicity – as the constructive, open-minded party. A unilateral move, while pleasing the 3.1 million EU nationals themselves, would have reassured many Remain voters still angry about Brexit. Had the government taken this step, at a stroke, much of the negativism towards leaving the EU would have waned.

Taking the initiative on citizens' rights would, moreover, have taken an issue off the table that is far more sensitive for the UK than it is for the EU. Now the UK government is unfortunately in a position where EU negotiators can decide not to resolve 'citizens' rights', whatever the British side offers, while accusing the UK of 'using people as bargaining chips' – a narrative that will be gratefully reported by UK commentators who oppose Brexit. This is a problem made worse because Barnier has successfully linked migration rights to the red-line issue of ECJ jurisdiction. This could delay the resolution of the citizens' rights issue for some time.

Ministers have tried to provide reassurances over EU citizens' rights, as well as the rights of UK nationals abroad. Yet it was only in June 2017 – a full year on from the referendum – that the government's intentions were formally outlined in a White Paper.[34] The Prime Minister described the UK's proposals as a 'fair and serious' offer. In many respects, that is the case.

Currently, EU citizens can reside in the UK and after five years acquire the right to permanent residency. Under the White Paper proposals, a new 'settled status' will apply, akin to an indefinite leave to remain, for those who have been here for five years. Those not meeting the requirements for settled status can apply for 'temporary status', becoming 'settled' once they have resided for five continuous years. For EU citizens who arrive after the cut-off date there is a two-year 'grace period' before they can apply for residency. That date, yet to be determined, will be no earlier than 29 March 2017 and no later than the date the UK leaves the EU. For the purposes of state education, health care, benefits and pensions, migrants will be treated as if they are British.

During the referendum campaign, it was generally assumed that EU nationals living here would be treated the same as they are now, likewise those from Britain who live in the EU. The indications, as the negotiations progress, are slightly different. At the time of writing, EU citizens in the UK will lose some rights, including the ability to vote in local elections. When it comes to future migration issues, relating to bringing in spouses and dependents for instance, EU citizens are likely to be treated slightly less favourably than now – but in line with the UK's non-EU migrants. Equally, EU-based UK citizens look set to lose some rights. Brussels is proposing, for instance, that UK citizens may remain settled only in the EU country in which they currently reside.[35]

Aside from these details, the general impression at the time of writing is that the negotiations on citizens' rights have been going well. Position papers released by both sides in July 2017 pointed to agreement across many areas, with a subsequent joint technical paper suggesting that out of forty-four areas of debate, there was already agreement on twenty-two.[36] Yet while Michel Barnier suggested the two sides were 'now moving in a common direction', he insisted that there remains 'a fundamental divergence' on how to guarantee citizens' rights.[37] The EU has demanded that the rights of EU citizens in the UK are overseen by the ECJ, with the EU's court possibly also arbitrating on future trade disputes between the UK and EU.

Back in October 2016, as Barnier well knows, the UK declared that ending the jurisdiction of the ECJ within the UK was an absolute red line. 'Our laws will be made not in Brussels but in Westminster,' said Theresa May, in a speech to the Conservative Party conference. 'The judges interpreting those laws will sit not in Luxembourg but in courts in this country.' The Prime Minister added: 'The authority of EU law in Britain will end.'[38] These three sentences frame the issue of resolving citizens' rights in the UK and, indeed, the broader Article 50 negotiation.

It would be rather odd for the ECJ to oversee the rights of EU nationals who have settled in the UK, given that their rights will anyway be enshrined in British law. A former ECJ judge, the Belgian Franklin Dehousse, has described Barnier's demand for ongoing ECJ jurisdiction as 'drastic', suggesting it makes 'a final deal less likely'. Comparing EU proposals to retain ECJ jurisdiction in Britain to colonial 'Leonine treaties imposed by England on China in the nineteenth century', Dehousse said: 'Article 50 was invented, after all, to show that the EU was not a prison – we must apply it accordingly.'[39] Yet Guy Verhofstadt, the arch-federalist and chief Brexit negotiator for the European Parliament, was unrepentant: 'British and European citizens should be able to enforce their rights under a mechanism in which the ECJ plays a full role,' he insisted.[40]

It is rather unlikely Britain would, at some future date, renege on the rights of EU citizens who have settled in the UK. The British legal system is widely admired. Individuals and companies from across Europe, indeed from around the world, come to Britain to resolve complex legal disputes. As an EU member, the UK has applied EU law assiduously over the past four decades – to a greater extent, perhaps, than any other EU member state.

As such, and in light of Theresa May's October 2016 declaration, Barnier's ECJ proposal is a non-starter. David Davis has said, though, that he is open to setting up a new joint UK–EU arbitration body to resolve disputes over trade and the wider functioning of post-Brexit agreements – which could include citizens' rights. 'It may well be we have an arbitration arrangement over this,' he said, 'but it's not going to be the European Court of Justice.'[41]

Finding such a compromise could take a long time. Meanwhile, this highly sensitive issue remains up in the air. The delay resolving citizens' rights causes the UK a lot more political angst than it does the EU. As long as it remains outstanding, opponents of Brexit will use it in an attempt to suggest Brexit is causing dislocation and unhappiness as a result of UK intolerance. With a hung parliament at Westminster, and those calling for a second EU referendum becoming more vocal, the government cannot allow this problem to fester.

In Chapter 10, we address the question of the UK's post-Brexit immigration policy – which will need to be settled and prepared during the Article 50 period, ready for when we leave. In the meantime, by combining ECJ jurisdiction with citizens' rights, Barnier is exerting leverage over the UK. Just as Britain is refusing to agree a Brexit divorce bill – an issue of genuine importance to the EU – so Barnier is holding out on dropping ECJ jurisdiction over the high-profile and, for the UK, politically corrosive issue of citizens' rights.

One bold way to break the impasse would be to return to the idea of a unilateral approach. Two lobby groups for those affected by this protracted citizens' rights issue have sprung up – the3million and British in Europe (BiE) – who represent, respectively, UK-based EU citizens and British citizens in the EU. In a thoughtful joint paper, they recommended that the issue of citizens' rights be 'ring-fenced from the Article 50 negotiation', so that it can be settled as soon as possible, without having to wait for agreement on all other areas. 'The notion that "nothing is agreed until everything is agreed" is not a principle derived from Article 50 itself,' the lobby groups argued in July 2017. 'It is a requirement set out in the Negotiating Directives and is thus a political choice.'[42]

Might this be something the UK government could act on, if the EU insists on stringing out the issue of ECJ jurisdiction over citizens' rights? Why not publicly guarantee those rights, and be done with it? That would no doubt be enough to reassure the 3.1 million UK-based EU citizens – a guarantee of their rights under British law. The government could threaten to do this – privately or, if necessary, in public – to force Barnier's hand. The Vienna Convention remains in place, guaranteeing the rights of UK citizens on the Continent. And the EU can ill afford the public outrage that would follow if, having watched the UK move to prevent 'people from being used as bargaining chips', the European Commission refused then immediately to do the same.

NUCLEAR OPTIONS

Along with the divorce bill and citizens' rights, another early skirmish during the Article 50 talks concerned the UK's membership of Euratom (the European Atomic Energy Community). This has been less a UK–EU tussle than a domestic political row, an indication of parliamentary clashes no doubt to come.

Euratom is a Europe-wide body that oversees the international movement of nuclear goods and waste, people and services through a framework governing safety standards and research. Founded in 1957, at the dawn of the EEC, this nuclear body is legally distinct from the wider bloc, despite having the same membership. But it uses the same institutions as the EU and, crucially in this context, is under the legal jurisdiction of the ECJ.

Euratom is one of over fifty pan-European agencies, with varying degrees of affiliation with the EU, of which the UK is a member. Many resemble the UK's 'quangos' – quasi-autonomous non-governmental organisations – and, perhaps in this regard, it is surprising there are not more of them. The total annual budget of the European agencies is €10.1 billion and they cover a vast array of areas, from energy to the environment to aviation, research, fraud and even political funding.[43] These agencies vary in size and impact, so it is important not to group them all together. But the UK needs to work out which organisations it wishes to remain part of – with ongoing membership no doubt requiring an annual contribution – and which we should leave. In general, of course, there should be no objection to involvement with agencies promoting cross-border regulatory cooperation, as long as that does not result in ECJ jurisdiction.

There are three nuclear-related agencies – including Euratom – that are technically not part of the EU but are heavily interlinked.[44] Euratom creates a market in Europe for developing and distributing nuclear power technology as well as selling surplus power to other nations. It also administers funding for nuclear research. The government's February 2017 Brexit White Paper highlights that leaving the EU also means leaving Euratom.[45] But it says that Britain wants 'to collaborate with our EU partners on matters relating to science and research, and nuclear energy is a key part of this'. Signalling that the nuclear industry is of 'key strategic importance' to the UK, the White Paper states that 'our precise relationship … will be a matter for the [Article 50] negotiations'.

As such, 'leaving Euratom does not affect our clear aim of seeking to maintain close and effective arrangements for civil nuclear cooperation, safeguards, safety and trade with Europe and our international partners'. The UK could look further afield than Europe, though, when collaborating on future nuclear technology. Britain 'is a world leader in nuclear research and development and there is no intention to reduce our ambition,' the White Paper said. 'The UK fully recognises the importance of international collaboration in nuclear research and development and we will ensure this continues by seeking alternative arrangements.'

In April 2017, the House of Commons Business and Energy Select Committee warned of 'huge repercussions' on leaving Euratom. 'The continued operations of the UK nuclear industry are at risk,' the committee said, recommending that departure be delayed to allow the nuclear industry to set up 'safeguards and international nuclear cooperation agreements'.[46] There have, though, been very few amendments to the Euratom treaty since it was established in the late 1950s, partly because nuclear power is such a sensitive subject across Europe. This has led to criticism that the agency has become outdated and subject to little democratic oversight. As such, outside Euratom, Britain's nuclear industry could be better placed to pursue research and business opportunities, not least overseas.

The UK has an active nuclear power plant construction programme – including the Hinkley Point facility, which is being built by French power giant EDF. That gives Britain a strong negotiating position in terms of how it will leave Euratom and the nature of the UK's future relationship. With Chinese investment funding a large chunk of Hinkley, once free from Euratom restrictions, the UK could work on future nuclear developments with China and other increasingly wealthy and influential nations beyond Europe.

British companies such as Rolls-Royce are already exploring the development of 'small modular reactors' (SMRs) – mini nuclear power stations, the development of which would be possible outside Euratom. 'A UK SMR reactor programme will create vital British intellectual property and revitalise the UK's civil nuclear expertise and ability to deploy nuclear power,' said the company.[47] Rolls-Royce believes SMRs are the future of atomic power, with a global market worth up to £450 billion by 2035.

In a May 2017 report, the Institute of Mechanical Engineers said that while leaving Euratom is 'potentially complicated', it 'also presents the country with an opportunity to reshape its nuclear industry and once again become a world-leading innovator in nuclear technology'. Developing SMRs, said the Institute, could 'present the UK with key export opportunities and return the country to the international nuclear reactor supply arena'.[48] The report recommended the UK develop its own 'safeguarding office', to ensure the country conforms to international rules on safety and non-proliferation, while remaining an 'associate member' of Euratom for the specific purpose of research and development.

As the first country to develop a civilian nuclear power programme, the UK has a considerable heritage in terms of atomic energy. There is no reason a bespoke UK agency cannot adequately develop and regulate our nuclear industry – while providing greater scope to exploit international markets. Britain already has experience of operating multiple nuclear regulating systems and our safety record is among the best in the world. As a leader in this field, the UK will no doubt continue international collaboration. Certainly, the government confirmed in July 2017 that Britain will continue to pay its 'fair share' of the EU-funded Joint European Torus (JET) project 'until 2020'. Based in Culham, Oxfordshire, JET is the world's largest fusion reactor, exploring clean energy production.[49]

A row erupted in July 2017 over Euratom because nine Conservative MPs indicated that they disapproved of leaving the agency. That would be enough to negate the government's slim majority in the House of Commons, which itself relies on DUP support. Underpinning much of the government's future approach to these agencies is its view of the ECJ – and the extent to which the court intrudes into UK law.[50] During the passage of Brexit legislation through the Commons ahead of March 2019, any amendment attempting to keep the UK in Euratom, were that possible within the Article 50 process, could become a proxy battle over the broader ECJ dispute.

FLYING SOLO

Since the EU referendum, concerns have been expressed that all flights between the UK and EU could be 'grounded' as a result of Brexit.[51] While some of the stories have been alarmist, it is certainly true that flight clearance for the roughly 3,000 daily commercial departures from UK airports does form part of Britain's EU negotiations.

The UK possesses the world's third largest civil aviation network, handling 247 million passengers and 2.3 million tonnes of cargo annually, with 2.2 million flights going through UK airspace. The sector as a whole generated £52 billion in 2015 – over 3 per cent of GDP.[52] London's Heathrow is Europe's busiest airport in terms of passenger numbers, with Gatwick coming in at eighth.[53]

The EU operates a liberal aviation regime – based on the European Common Aviation Area (ECAA), which has existed since 2006 and is based on multiple bi-lateral agreements. After Brexit, the UK needs to negotiate equivalent operating rights across Europe. There is a lot of political momentum behind striking a deal, given the size of the UK aviation market and the extent to which EU airlines rely on access to the UK – Heathrow is by far the most important transatlantic hub. No EU politician wants needlessly to destroy air traffic with the UK.

With around 60 per cent of UK air passengers landing in the EU, a new deal is important. While there are off-the-shelf ways to replicate similar rights, it is not clear which route Britain will take or what pitfalls may arise. One possibility is for the UK to retain ECAA membership. That would provide unrestricted access to all EU destinations, but requires acceptance of EU aviation law. Having said that, some countries outside the EU and the single market are signatories to and beneficiaries of ECAA – including Albania, Bosnia and Herzegovina and Macedonia, Montenegro and Serbia.

Staying in the ECAA means the UK would need to sign up to common European technical rules. Much of Europe's safety and security regulation is pan-global, though, being determined by the International Civil Aviation Organization (ICAO), a UN body. So ICAO guidance applies whether the UK is in the EU or not. A greater obstacle may be that ECAA members establish a 'framework of close economic cooperation' with the EU – which is open to political interpretation. As such, aspects of the broader Article 50 negotiations – such as the UK's attitude to free movement – could impede on ECAA membership. The ECAA is also a multilateral agreement, so Britain could be blocked by another member seeking to gain political or commercial advantage.

Switzerland has its own bilateral open skies agreement with the EU. But this requires effective ECJ jurisdiction of aviation competition matters – which could be a red line for the UK. Another option is a more regular open skies agreement, which would allow UK planes to fly into and out of the EU as long as the routes start or end in Britain. For the UK's low-cost airlines, the stakes are high – with UK-based easyJet concerned it may not be able to fly from, say, Paris to Milan. Under certain forms of agreement, Ryanair, based in Ireland, may be unable to fly into London or other UK cities. EasyJet is setting up a mainland Europe base in a bid to circumvent any restrictions, but would still have to navigate EU ownership rules.

The UK's landing rights could also lapse on routes currently secured on agreements between third-party countries and the EU (such as the 2007 EU–US open skies deal).[54] Britain could seek to piggyback on EU agreements, as part of the broader negotiation. Then there is the question of airworthiness, which may mean the UK stays in EASA – Europe's airline safety regulator.

The UK, then, needs to seek ongoing membership of the ECAA, or strike a similar pan-EU agreement, along with a UK–US open skies agreement – or, again, a workaround such as adding itself to the EU–US deal. While the 'close economic cooperation' stipulation may prove troublesome, there is a precedent of countries joining from outside the single market.

This is clearly a complex situation – and global aviation is not covered by WTO rules, which we discuss in the next chapter. But the UK is a very big player in the aviation industry, with considerable bargaining power, and there are mutually compelling commercial imperatives to make the required arrangements. ECAA membership is reciprocal, so non-agreement would prevent EU-based airlines from flying to the UK. The combination of airline profits, landing fees and the revenues linked to UK business and tourist travel suggests the necessary agreements will be forged. Willie Walsh, the head of BA's parent company,

International Airlines Group, predicted in August 2017 that 'with policy support, it will be relatively straightforward' to agree a deal.[55] In the immediate term, if the details are not finalised ahead of March 2019, the UK would likely secure memorandums of understanding with various countries – extending current practice until new agreements are reached.

In general, the various EU agencies can be divided into those we no longer need to be a member of, those we wish to remain in and those we might still want to be in during a transition period, after which we will officially leave the EU.[56] Many will no longer apply to the UK – such as OLAF, the European Anti-Fraud Office, which deals with fraud in EU funds. There are some we may wish to leave even though their work is important, because we can do it better ourselves – such as the European Union Agency for Network and Information Security (ENISA), which deals with cyber security.

The UK may wish to remain a member of or have a strategic relationship with some economically important agencies, such as the Fisheries Control Agency (FCA) or the European Agency for the Cooperation of Energy Regulators (ACER). In the area of defence, policing and security, we may wish to share information with, if not remain full members of, the European Defence Agency and Europol. And we must certainly replace EU security policies such as the European Arrest Warrant and passenger data sharing with bilateral UK–EU arrangements.

When it comes to science and medicine, the UK will no longer host the European Medicines Agency – the body that regulates human and animal medicines across the EU. Many in the science community and across the UK's university sector have been very negative about Brexit, often due to concerns about EU funding. But the government, in many cases, will provide equivalent funding, with the UK continuing scientific collaboration after Brexit. After all, over a third of the countries in the EU's current funding network (sixteen out of forty-four) are not among the EU 27. As such, there are many avenues allowing for post-Brexit involvement in Horizon 2020, the EU's main funding body for collaboration on research and innovation.[57]

Some distinguished scientists point to advantages outside the EU. 'Being constrained by the EU's restrictive regulation in the future is a clear liability,' says Professor Sir John Bell, Regius Professor of Medicine at Oxford University. 'The cultural, ethical and philosophical environment that supports science is in many ways fundamentally different in the UK compared to many European countries,' he says. Bell points to 'needless regulatory hurdles' and 'huge inefficiencies and delays' connected with EU medical directives. The combination of lighter regulation and fewer 'constraints on state aid' means 'a future in which British scientists collaborate with their European counterparts but are not bound by EU regulation looks tempting'.[58]

Britain's heavy involvement in the European Space Agency (ESA) is also set to continue. The UK has played a major part in developing the main EU space programmes – Galileo and Copernicus. In December 2016, the government committed an additional €1.4 billion funding to ESA programmes over the next five years – including €670.5 million towards satellite technologies and services for UK industry and science.[59]

In the world of finance, the UK may want to retain membership of a number of agencies – such as the European Securities and Markets Authority (ESMA) – to help smooth the transition to a new post-Brexit regulatory framework. Depending upon the negotiations, there may be other financial agencies we remain in as well – perhaps keeping our stake in the EIB, as mentioned earlier. Given that London will remain the financial capital of Europe, the UK will also maintain a close relationship, if not full membership of, the European Systemic Risk Board (ESRB), which has macro prudential oversight of the EU's financial system.

While the early skirmishes of the Article 50 process have taken place within a hostile media environment, there has been some progress, with the broad outlines of the negotiations becoming clear. The divorce bill issue is clearly tricky, but the longer it remains unresolved, the more it may work to the UK's advantage. Having conceded 'obligations to the EU', the UK should seek to extend negotiations over cash, using incremental concessions to extract agreements in other areas.

The highly charged issue of citizens' rights has shown that the EU is fully prepared to use the UK's red line of ECJ jurisdiction to exert leverage. Barnier's insistence that the EU's top court, where the UK will have no judge, be the arbiter of citizens' rights and other judicial disputes – potentially including trade arbitration – is clearly designed to provoke the UK. With Theresa May having vowed to take the UK out of ECJ jurisdiction, the role of the Luxembourg-based court is likely to loom large throughout the entire Article 50 process.

There are signs, though, that EU demands relating to ECJ jurisdiction are softening. Keen to ensure that frictionless UK–EU trade continues, and that the negotiations in general run smoothly, Germany has indicated it would support a solution whereby a joint UK–EU panel serves as the ultimate judge of citizens' rights and related issues.[60] David Davis has likewise signalled that a judicial body with 'a mutually agreed chairman and somebody nominated from both sides' might be acceptable.[61] If such a solution is found with relation to citizens' rights, the resulting institution could develop into a broader non-ECJ dispute resolution mechanism applicable to a whole range of UK–EU issues. Were that to happen, and gain acceptance, it would lessen the potency of divisions over ECJ jurisdiction within the House of Commons, as the government seeks to pass Brexit-related legislation ahead of March 2019.

It is widely expected that the real meat of these Article 50 negotiations will involve discussions about trade – and, in particular, attempts by the UK and EU to strike and ratify a broad FTA ahead of March 2019. In our view, a Clean Brexit approach – maintaining that the UK is leaving both the single market and the customs union – maximises the chances of striking such a deal within this time frame. But we maintain there is a relatively high probability this will not be possible. Not agreeing an FTA with the EU during the Article 50 period is by no means a disaster, though – as we explain in the next chapter.

CHAPTER 6

WTO RULES AND TRANSITION

'Free trade is not based on utility but on justice.'
EDMUND BURKE[1]

'The first calling point of the UK's negotiator immediately after Brexit will not be Brussels, it will be Berlin, to strike a deal,' wrote David Davis on Twitter in May 2016.[2] This tweet is interesting on two levels. In the first instance, it suggests that Davis – who campaigned to leave the EU, but could have had no idea that he would later become Brexit Secretary – was confident ahead of the June 2016 referendum that the UK would vote to leave.

Secondly, and more importantly in this context, the tweet points to the over-riding feature of the Article 50 talks. It is with the governments of the EU's nation states, not Jean-Claude Juncker's European Commission, that Britain is negotiating. And of all those governments, it is Germany – by far the biggest economy, with the largest surplus on UK trade and the only country with the financial scope to rescue others in the event of another euro crisis – that ulti-mately calls the shots.

Berlin will not want to do anything that undermines the 'cohesion' of the Eurozone. So it is extremely unlikely the UK will be offered a continuation of its current EU trading arrangements, while absolving itself of obligations to make multi-billion-pound annual contributions and observe freedom of movement rules. But trade and jobs matter to Berlin far more than a perceived need to 'punish Britain'. This suggests that there is scope – as long as the UK does not push for an unobtainable, treaty-busting Messy Brexit – to keep these talks rea-sonably positive and constructive.

Wealth is created and people are lifted out of poverty when trade is as open as possible, markets operate relatively freely and property rights are protected.

Any country's trade policy should aim to limit the barriers faced by exporters while ensuring consumers benefit by being able to buy goods and services from overseas as cheaply as possible. The societal gains of an open trade policy are considerable, not least as they disproportionately benefit the poorest. This timeless reality was captured in the late eighteenth century by the Irish statesman and political theorist Edmund Burke in the quotation above. It was also expressed in the repeal of the Corn Laws in 1846 – which we discuss in a later chapter.

Political conflicts, though, and the influence of vested commercial interests, generally prevent free trade outcomes. These Article 50 negotiations – which could hardly be more high-profile, with the future of the entire European project at stake – are certainly full of political drama, with business lobbies attempting to pull strings at every turn.

The UK should aim at all times to keep our negotiating approach as simple as possible. That is not to diminish the difficulties facing Britain during the Article 50 talks. Trade technicalities can take many years to resolve, particularly in Brussels, and the UK's stated aim is to secure an FTA before March 2019. We would observe, though, that Britain is in a much better position than is commonly appreciated. And it is an entirely acceptable and satisfactory outcome for us to leave the EU without securing an FTA with the EU – for reasons we explain below.

This chapter outlines trading under WTO rules, expands on some negotiating principles outlined in the bullet points at the start of this book and describes the T-Tab transition arrangement the UK may need to adopt as we exit the EU. Sector-specific issues – relating to autos, the City, agriculture and so on – are covered in subsequent chapters.

CUT AND PASTE

In July 2017, the government laid the European Union (Withdrawal) Bill before Parliament. Having sent a letter triggering Article 50 of the Lisbon Treaty in late March, passing this legislation through Parliament represents the next major step towards Brexit. Designed to repeal the European Communities Act of 1972, which took Britain into what ultimately became the EU, the bill will also bring all EU law onto the UK statute books, while giving ministers the power to adapt and remove laws that are no longer relevant.

The Repeal Bill goes some way towards addressing cliff-edge issues by ensuring continuity after March 2019, when the Article 50 period expires and the UK legally leaves the EU.[3] But we would still argue some kind of transition period may be required – a Temporary Transition Agreement for Britain, or T-Tab. This is not necessarily because of the complexity of any deal that the UK strikes with the EU, but more because, by the very nature of politics and these highly charged EU negotiations in particular, the precise details of new arrangements between the EU and UK are unlikely to be known until just before the Article 50 period expires.

One of the main advantages of a Clean Brexit – keeping membership of the single market and customs union membership completely off the table – is that the outline of the UK's broad relationship with the EU and the rest of the world should be clear for some time ahead of March 2019. This allows the UK to make major preparations, such as expanding our customs clearance facilities to include UK–EU trade and preparing to re-impose cross-Channel immigration controls.

But a strictly time-limited T-Tab may still be needed given that many of the details of these negotiations are unlikely to emerge until the last moment. Acknowledging that early on will not only reassure businesses heavily impacted by Brexit, and help prepare public opinion, but will also strengthen the UK's bargaining hand during the Article 50 talks.

The Repeal Bill – to be debated in Parliament from the autumn of 2017 onwards – is the first of eight major pieces of Brexit legislation to be brought forward by the government. By bringing all EU law relating to the UK onto British statute books – in a sort of 'cut and paste' exercise – it ensures that on 'Brexit Day' nothing changes across a range of domestic sectors. This lessens cliff-edge dangers, reassuring both businesses and the public. Repatriating a vast body of legislation will also allow MPs of all parties to consider which aspects of EU law they may wish to alter – emphasising that Brexit, above all, is about re-empowering British democracy.

Clean Brexit rejects the idea of attempting a damaging and bad-tempered negotiation over the EU's 'four freedoms' that is almost certain to fail. Such a negotiation could only succeed by undermining the Eurozone, and possibly threatening the future of the EU itself. The EU's draft negation principles, issued before the Article 50 talks began, explicitly pointed out that 'the "four freedoms" are indivisible and there can be no cherry-picking'.[4]

In theory, these various treaty obligations 'are not inviolable and inextricably interdependent', as the former Treasury Select Committee Chairman Andrew Tyrie has highlighted.[5] In the end, if politics dictates it, rules and even treaties can be distorted or violated altogether – as we saw in Chapter 4, with the bending of Maastricht convergence criteria and widespread abuse of the Stability and Growth Pact.

It has been clear for some time, though, that Soft Brexit it not available. In August 2016, just two months after the UK's EU referendum, the Brussels think tank Bruegel published a paper entitled 'Europe after Brexit: A Proposal for a Continental Partnership'.[6] The purported model, aimed at the UK, offered non-EU countries partial membership of the single market without full 'free movement'. The paper suggested a system of decision-making that gave potential partial members a say (but no formal vote) in rule-making. The Bruegel scheme got a frosty reception all round. 'Both Brussels and national capitals dismissed the proposal,' reported *The Economist*, 'because it would have let Britain have its cake (barrier-free access to the single market) and eat it (limits on free movement).'[7]

Now the Article 50 negotiations have begun, there is no sign Soft Brexit is anywhere more likely to be acceptable. Some nation states are starting to rein in the EC's more federalist instincts – as discussed in the previous chapter. Germany is pushing for a joint UK–EU arbitration mechanism to try to ensure the issue of ECJ jurisdiction does not derail agreement on such vital issues as citizens' rights and trade arbitration. But when it comes to splitting the four freedoms, the entire EU remains petrified that 'cherry-picking' opens up 'the Pandora's box of disintegration', in the words of one very well-connected EU analyst.[8] We return to this subject in Chapter 14 – 'Respecting the Referendum Result' – which discusses the passage of Brexit-related legislation through Parliament, amidst growing clamour among some MPs for a Soft Brexit following the June 2017 general election.

WTO RULES OK

The Prime Minister has called for a 'bold and ambitious' UK–EU free trade agreement.[9] This is a laudable aim. But whether or not it is the best outcome for the UK depends on the precise details of that FTA. As such, the UK needs a well worked-out alternative. If we have an alternative, an advantageous FTA is more likely.

Unless the EU sees that we are prepared *not* to sign an FTA, we will only be offered a bad one. Signing a bad FTA because we are desperate to 'get a deal' would disadvantage UK exporters and consumers for a long time. That was David Cameron's mistake ahead of the June 2016 referendum. In trying to renegotiate the UK's relationship with the EU, he asked for very little and got even less. That's because he vowed to support ongoing EU membership whatever the terms.

Under a Clean Brexit, the UK government says it is fully prepared to trade with the EU 27 on the existing tariff-free basis from outside the single market and customs union. When such an arrangement is refused, we then state that the UK is happy to trade under WTO rules. We should also say that if the EU insists on imposing WTO tariffs on UK goods and services, then Britain will reciprocate.

To assume the UK must secure an FTA with the EU during the two-year Article 50 window would be a major strategic error. There is no need at all for the government to strike an FTA before March 2019, as long as we make the required preparations – such as setting tariff schedules and enhancing our customs infrastructure – to trade under WTO rules. All the UK should do is state, publicly and repeatedly, that we are ready and happy to negotiate an FTA with the EU – either during the Article 50 window or beyond.

WTO rules are often presented as 'a disaster' or 'irresponsible' by those who are determined to keep the UK within the single market. This is alarmist and wrong. Over half the UK's trade is with countries outside the EU – largely under WTO rules. The US and China conduct extensive trade with the EU under WTO rules – Britain can do the same. As part of the EU, the UK already trades under WTO rules with over 100 countries around the world, including the US (our largest single export market), as well as China, India, Brazil and Singapore.

Access to the single market is not granted by the EU, but is available to all nations, as we established in Chapter 3, provided regulatory standards are met and on payment of generally low tariffs. This is why countries across the world that are not members of the single market export successfully to the EU. The UK is well placed to trade with the EU on WTO terms – not least as we start from a position of full regulatory compliance.

The rules of the WTO require each member to levy consistent tariffs on all its trade partners. Positive exceptions – lowering or eliminating tariffs for particular countries – must be made through specific bilateral agreements. A country specifies its tariffs in a 'WTO schedule' – with the UK currently levying the EU's tariff schedule, as Brussels represents all twenty-eight member states at the WTO. It makes sense, in the period immediately following Brexit, for the UK to apply the same tariffs as the EU. For all the scare stories regarding WTO rules, this would not be complicated. The Repeal Bill copies over the EU's existing classifications and rules, so it is relatively straightforward for the UK to adopt the EU's tariff schedule – with HMRC applying the same rates as now. This was confirmed by the UK's ambassador to the WTO in January 2017.[10]

There has been much confusion about the UK's ability to reoccupy its own individual WTO seat. During the referendum campaign, WTO Director General Roberto Azevêdo warned that Brexit would spark 'tortuous negotiations' between the UK and all 161 WTO members.[11] Following the vote, Azevêdo changed his tone. 'The UK is a member of the WTO today, it will continue to be a member tomorrow,' he said. 'Trade will not stop – there will be no discontinuity and I will work very intensely to ensure this transition is fast and smooth.'[12]

Agreeing our WTO schedules with other members should be straightforward. As long as the UK adopts the EU's schedules, or others that make no other WTO country worse off, there should be no problem.[13] Were there some kind of challenge, UK trade would continue. The EU's schedules from 2004, when it expanded to twenty-five members, were only accepted by the WTO in late 2016. That twelve-year hiatus did not stop trade.[14] Complaints to the WTO are not uncommon and take time to be settled. But they do not prevent trade in the interim.

As well as agreeing WTO schedules, there is the issue of mutual recognition agreements (MRAs). These mostly cover technical rules that might prevent a product from entering a particular country. The US and China both trade with the EU under WTO rules, but have MRAs in specific areas. The EU has such agreements with virtually all countries around the world, including those that are neither members of the single market nor have an FTA in place.

As all EU regulations will be transferred into UK law under the Repeal Bill, most of the EU's MRAs should 'port over' to the UK. If the EU itself refused to agree MRAs with us, this would count as discrimination under WTO rules, resulting in fines. It would also be commercially counterproductive, incensing EU exporters to the UK, while breaching the EU's own treaties.

Under a Clean Brexit, then, Whitehall assumes and prepares to trade under WTO rules with the EU. This involves reoccupying the UK's WTO seat and adopting our own tariff schedules. We also need to prepare alterations to UK–EU and cross-Channel trade facilitation. Some claim that UK–EU customs clearance could bring 'gridlock to the south-east of England' with 'lorries queueing for up to 30 miles in Kent to get across the Channel'.[15] Yet both the UK and the broader EU are already introducing new streamlined customs procedures to handle third-party imports – from which the UK will benefit once we leave. Under simplified procedures for freight, the electronic registration of consignments will allow clearance at importers' premises once the goods have been successfully delivered. Despite threats to 'punish' Britain, the EU has every interest in rapid clearance procedures on both sides of the Channel, given its huge exports to the UK, not least of perishable agricultural products.[16]

These improvements to customs procedures reflect the WTO Agreement on Trade Facilitation, which took effect in February 2017. Described by the European Commission as 'the most significant trade deal since the establishment of the WTO', Brussels has pledged that 'EU customs authorities will play a leading role in the implementation of this agreement', becoming 'an example to follow' and 'an engine for further progress in trade facilitation within the EU and at international level'.[17]

With this in mind, given the quarter of a century the UK has spent in the single market, NTBs on goods should not prove too troublesome when we leave. These non-tariff barriers to trade are created via regulations of 'quality' and anti-dumping duties and, at present, do not exist between the UK and EU 27 by definition. As such, any attempt to create new NTBs after Brexit, by either side, could be challenged in WTO courts, where all countries desire to maintain good reputations because of continuing WTO disputes in many areas.

NO DEAL, NO DISASTER

While trading under WTO rules is fine, the UK would clearly prefer an FTA with the EU – but only if that FTA is favourable. Such a deal can be agreed after Article 50 expires. With WTO rules as a solid platform, there is no pressing need to strike a UK–EU FTA by March 2019. The UK should remain open to negotiation, of course – and that includes negotiating on sector-based deals, in automobiles or financial services, for instance. But agreeing a complex, multi-sector deal with twenty-seven governments, who each want to protect their own conflicting interests, plus ratification by national Parliaments and the European Parliament, could be tough during the time frame.

There are enormous mutual incentives for the UK and EU eventually to strike an FTA. While UK exports to Germany are estimated to support some 752,000 British jobs, around 1.3 million German jobs depend upon exports to the UK. This pattern is repeated across other EU countries.[18] Once outside the EU, the UK will be the bloc's biggest non-EU market – accounting for 17 per cent of the EU's exports of goods and services to non-EU countries.[19] Again, though, we should not become fixated on securing an FTA before March 2019. No deal really is better than a bad deal. The UK should state this clearly and often.

Under 'no deal', relatively low WTO tariffs will apply to UK exports to the EU, and we should reciprocate those tariffs. The EU is surrounded by a tariff wall – the common external tariff – for those outside the customs union, as the UK will be after Brexit. The CET rates are low, averaging 2.3 per cent, as we explained in Chapter 3. On some products they are higher – 9.6 per cent for autos and above 20 per cent on some agricultural products.

These tariffs are a legacy of the EU's origins, reflecting a desire to protect French farmers and German carmakers. Over time, though, globalisation has driven tariffs down – and, on balance, this looks set to continue. WTO rules is also just a starting point, providing a base, with the UK free of Article 50 time pressure, to negotiate a 'bold and ambitious' FTA that, by definition, will lead to lower tariffs.

In the meantime, the tariffs our exporters will incur under WTO rules are generally far less than the depreciation of sterling since mid-2016. For most exporters, such tariffs will be a manageable business cost. While there are concerns about 'complex supply chains' across the EU, most components are zero-rated for tariffs, even if the goods attract a tariff on final sale. And if parts are subject to tariffs and travel backwards and forwards into and out of the EU, the tariff is only charged once.

Given Britain's trade deficit with the EU, mutually imposed WTO tariffs will raise revenue, which the government can use to compensate exporters, as part of a transition arrangement for specific sectors like agriculture that currently receive sizeable EU-administered support. We discuss the automotive sector and agriculture, and their response to EU tariffs, in Chapter 8.

The necessary preparations for the UK to trade under WTO rules, while far from insurmountable, are significant and must be made. Customs facilities do need expanding and technological upgrades must be in place – for which funding must be made available. To facilitate the UK's preparation for WTO rules, while highlighting our willingness to leave the EU with no FTA, the government should set a 'no deal' deadline, and make it public.

If an FTA looks impossible during the Article 50 window, this should be acknowledged early enough so that more attention can be focused on getting ready to trade under WTO rules. After a certain pre-announced cut-off point – perhaps sometime in the autumn of 2018 – the priority would shift from active FTA negotiations to preparing for WTO rules instead.

Trading with no FTA, then, does not amount to 'crashing out of the EU' – as opponents of Brexit so often claim. While it is not our preferred option, it is, nevertheless, an entirely coherent position, in terms of both the UK's Article 50 negotiation and as an outcome in itself. Not securing an FTA is by no means the same as failing to settle issues of mutual interest such as customs recognition, common standards and other agreements that facilitate trade. These are existing and entirely uncontroversial administrative protocols granted by the EU to countless non-EU members. For Brussels to deny them to Britain would breach both WTO and EU law, while threatening billions of euros of profit and tens of thousands of EU jobs.

In some senses, it should be relatively simple for the UK and EU to strike an FTA, not least as they are currently part of the same customs union. Trade negotiations generally involve haggling over phasing out tariffs on thousands of products, while 'harmonising' complex product regulations. The UK and EU, though, start with zero tariffs and identical rules. Any UK–EU trade agreement would be the first negotiated between nations that already have something close to free trade. 'This is the only free trade deal in the history of the world where the countries are already in a deal and have identical product standards,' said David Davis in March 2017. 'We are in exactly the same place.'[20]

An FTA between the UK and EU needs to include a 'divergence' process – which oversees what happens if either side alters its regulations. This is a feature of any trade deal. The agreement would also have to cover so-called rules of origin. These prevent third-party countries from avoiding the EU's CET by routing goods through the UK to take advantage of any bilateral tariff reductions agreed between Britain and the EU. Again, this is standard procedure in any trade deal – with such rules already applying to Norwegian and Swiss exports to the EU.

Yet the complications should not be dismissed, particularly as the UK begins to consider FTAs beyond the EU. Across the automotive industry, for instance, there is pressure to maintain current UK–EU trade arrangements. Yet tariff-free cross-Channel trade in autos would be difficult to square with the EU's customs union charging a 9.6 per cent tariff on US cars, particularly if the UK then does an FTA with the US. The British pharmaceutical industry, similarly, is heavily integrated into that of the broader EU – and there is a strong desire within the industry to maintain common regulatory arrangements. But that could prevent the UK from cutting an FTA elsewhere, seeing as pharmaceuticals are often a major part of any free trade negotiation.

As such, even though a UK–EU FTA looks simple on one level, securing a deal becomes more complex once Britain begins to size up FTAs elsewhere. This is another reason that the most likely outcome by March 2019 will be 'no deal'. This makes it all the more important that preparations are made to trade under WTO rules.

Yet the commercial pressure to strike a UK–EU FTA remains considerable. By declaring Clean Brexit, the UK benefits from powerful EU business lobbies urging their governments to strike favourable trading terms with Britain, knowing they will otherwise face reciprocated WTO tariffs. And once an unobtainable Soft Brexit is off the table, can the UK not be treated like other third-party nations with which the EU has struck FTAs, without insisting on freedom of movement, annual payments or ECJ jurisdiction?

The answer, unfortunately, is probably not. There is a strong political imperative for the UK to be seen not to benefit from Brexit, so as to avoid encouraging populist parties in nations such as France, Italy and Greece to push harder for their own EU membership referenda. Throughout the EU today, the political establishment is threatened by the rise of anti-establishment parties ... which, it is believed, would gain strength from anything that could be remotely construed as giving a Brexit benefit to the UK,' says former Chancellor Lord (Nigel) Lawson. 'This is the overriding political context in which the Article 50 talks will take place.'[21]

As such, says Lord Lawson, 'no remotely acceptable post-Brexit trade agreement between the UK and the EU is negotiable'. This may indeed be the case – with commercial pressure to maintain relatively friction-free UK–EU trade being trumped by political considerations, at least during the highly charged atmosphere of negotiations ahead of March 2019. That is yet another reason why the UK must prepare now to trade under WTO rules.

TRADING NATION

Trading under WTO rules not only provides a foundation from which the UK can negotiate a future FTA with the EU, but also with other non-EU countries. Some EU officials have claimed that the UK cannot negotiate FTAs with the rest of the world during the Article 50 window. Yet Britain is fully entitled to discuss and even formalise an FTA with another nation, as long as it does not come into force until we have left the EU. Any future FTAs should focus on access for the UK's services sector and investment flows, the safeguarding of intellectual property rights and a commitment to remove tariff and NTBs – as we discuss in the next chapter.

The UK should be clear, though, that non-EU FTAs need not be in place or 'signature ready' before March 2019. It would be helpful if the EU saw Britain making progress with FTAs with other countries during the Article 50 talks – and, as described earlier, major third-party agreements could impact the shape of any UK–EU FTA. But such non-EU deals are not vital and rushing into them could, once again, result in unattractive terms. The UK already sells 56 per cent of its exports outside the EU, largely under WTO rules with no FTA. The notion we must have a string of trade deals in place before the Article 50 window closes, or our trade will collapse, is nonsense.

Having said that, Britain should work with nations with which the EU has existing FTAs and other trade facilitation arrangements to arrange an 'exchange of notes', so such deals apply to the UK after Brexit. While these 'legacy' agreements will not always be immediately transferable, they provide a significant head start on cutting deals from scratch.

Outside the EU, the UK should adopt, as a point of principle, the promotion of free trade around the world, with the aim of eradicating both tariffs and NTBs. As such, Britain needs to ensure it has the knowledge base and capability to conduct trade deals, building a secretariat with detailed knowledge of the overarching trade and legal agreements. These include the General Agreement on Trade in Services (GATS), the Agreement on Trade-Related Aspects of Intellectual Property Rights (TRIPS) and the Agreement on Trade-Related Investment Measures (TRIMS).

There are encouraging signs that Whitehall is gearing up, recruiting widely, including from nations such as Canada, Australia and New Zealand. After Brexit, the civil service will need some restructuring to reflect the return of competencies from Brussels. The Department for International Trade should become permanent – allowing the UK to manage and constantly seek to widen the scope of our FTAs around the world.

Some liberal economists argue the UK should grant the EU tariff-free access after Brexit, even if the EU imposes WTO tariffs upon us. Although sympathetic to this view, on balance we disagree. A policy of unilateral free trade (UFT) is attractive in theory, and would lead to lower prices for UK consumers and intermediate goods via cheaper imports. In our view, though, this should be a destination that Britain moves towards, rather than a one-off change linked to Brexit. Once outside the EU, trading under WTO rules, the UK will be well placed to negotiate a UK–EU FTA, as we have said – which will, by definition, reduce import tariffs. But having WTO tariffs we can offer to remove will strengthen our hand in future negotiations, encouraging the EU to lower tariffs in response.

Detailed modelling work by the economists Patrick Minford and Edgar Miller suggests that adopting UFT, eliminating protection in favour of free trade and full competition in one swoop, would raise UK productivity and lower the cost of living – leading to a 'long-term GDP gain of 4 per cent and an 8 per cent fall in consumer prices'.[22] The economist Roger Bootle has also pointed out that UFT would 'reduce prices and intensify competition in the UK market'.[23]

While accepting these arguments, it is important, during the early post-Brexit years, to consider the economic dislocation to UK sectors currently behind the EU's tariff wall – such as agriculture and some parts of manufacturing.[24] We do not favour subsidising producers at the expense of consumers, but are

conscious of the regional impact from exposing some domestic sectors immediately to global competition – as we discuss in Chapter 8. Tariffs, in our view,
should be reduced steadily alongside temporary 'transition' payments within
certain sectors.

Even with such measures, there is much scope once outside the EU for the
UK to return to the forefront of worldwide efforts to secure free trade among
major economies, just as it has been at the forefront of reducing corporation tax
whilst preserving workers' rights. Keeping some tariffs, as we have suggested, will
help to negotiate away trade barriers maintained by other countries.

Our approach, then, is to trade with the EU under WTO rules, offering a
free trade policy while reserving the right to impose reciprocal tariffs. In due
course, we may negotiate a UK–EU FTA, but the timing of that is not under UK
control – and it could well be impossible during the Article 50 window for both
political and practical reasons. While we would not move immediately to UFT,
we believe the UK should, in certain sectors, offer a 'sequenced' reduction of
WTO tariffs, as transitory government support is reduced, as part of our broader
attempt to strike an FTA with the EU during the post-Brexit years.

UFT should, then, be a scheduled destination, rather than an immediate
post-Brexit policy. We believe this approach combines recognition of the benefits of free trade with a pragmatic grasp of domestic and international political
realities. Rather than a straight abolition of import tariffs, we advocate a more
gradual approach, tied to the domestic policy agenda.

Ahead of March 2019, as the UK seeks to cut an FTA with the EU, there
will no doubt be cries of doom from those trying to stop Brexit, foreseeing
disaster if a deal is not struck before the end of the Article 50 window. Yet, as we
have explained, trading under WTO rules with no FTA in place is an entirely
reasonable position. Imports and exports worth $686 billion flowed between
the US and EU in 2016 – with no FTA, under WTO rules. The US and China
similarly chalked up $649 billion of trade, the EU and China $613 billion – all
under WTO rules.[25] The world's three largest economies, then, have no FTA
between them. Trade generally happens not because politicians sign trade deals
but because private firms and individuals see mutually beneficial opportunities.

It is of cardinal importance that the UK's senior politicians, as well as the
broader population, understand and acknowledge that it is perfectly acceptable

for the UK to leave the EU in March 2019 with no FTA in place. No deal really is better than a bad deal. This is, to anyone with even a passing knowledge of international trade law, a statement of the obvious.

With this knowledge, the UK is in a strong position to refuse a disadvantageous FTA – meaning that, as and when we do strike a UK–EU trade deal, it will be on far better terms, even if this happens after March 2019.

BRIDGE TO THE FUTURE

In early January 2017, the authors of this book suggested a transition agreement would be necessary to make Brexit smoother, not least given the complications of getting any UK–EU deal ratified by twenty-seven nations and the European Parliament ahead of March 2019.[26] Theresa May highlighted the same possibility in her Lancaster House speech later that same month. The final point of the Prime Minister's twelve-point Brexit plan expressed the government's belief that 'a phased process of implementation, in which both Britain and the EU institutions and member states prepare for the new arrangements that will exist between us, will be in our mutual self-interest'.[27]

Some politicians and analysts who supported Brexit feel that a transition amounts to some kind of 'betrayal'. We support a transition arrangement as long as it is carefully designed and cannot be used to keep the UK in the EU beyond a pre-agreed period. The nature of the Article 50 negotiation is such that the precise details of new arrangements between the EU and UK are unlikely to be fully known until just before March 2019 – which makes a transition necessary. Following Brexit, certain sectors of the UK economy will also need time and support while adjusting to a new tariff and trading regime. So a transition plan involves both our interaction with the EU and a programme to assist with domestic adjustment.

We propose a 'temporary transition agreement for Britain' – T-Tab. Relatively early in the Article 50 process, the UK and EU should agree on interim measures – ideally, a strictly time-limited 'zero-for-zero' tariff deal, along with transitional customs arrangements and mutual recognition of financial services. This would minimise any disruption to businesses on both sides, with the UK legally leaving the EU in March 2019. Far from being used to keep the UK in the EU by the back door, T-Tab would be specifically designed to ensure that the mandate from the referendum is respected – taking back control of our laws, borders, money and trade.

Any transition period must be time-limited, with the end goals clearly defined. So T-Tab must only come into force once the new deal on long-term arrangements with the EU has been struck. We are pleased that, as this book goes to press, there are signs of emerging agreement across government and among political parties that a transition is needed – to give businesses and the government more time to plan for and then adjust to future arrangements.[28] While the Single European Act came into force in 1987, the single market itself was launched in 1993, providing all member states with a five-year transition. A similar amount of time from the June 2016 referendum should be more than enough to leave the EU.

The UK's 'transition' – or 'implementation phase' – is about taking us from existing arrangements to new ones. Rather than a cliff edge, T-Tab would act as a bridge. Before stepping onto a bridge, we generally know how long it is and where it is taking us. The Article 50 negotiations are unlikely to produce much in the way of detailed outcomes until late 2018 or even early March 2019, when we are scheduled legally to leave the EU. So businesses with long planning horizons should feel reassured by a transition. Companies about to face even moderate WTO tariffs, and/or with integrated supply chains, should not have to wait for a deal to be agreed in the small hours, one morning in Brussels, shortly before it takes effect. Having a deadline to finalise any agreement in March 2019, then knowing the details of that agreement, ahead of a one- or at most two-year period before the negotiated changes take full effect, helps everyone.

The auto sector, given the prospect of relatively high tariffs under WTO rules, would likely benefit from a transition. The government may also decide to help some carmakers adjust to the new tariff regime, using revenues raised from the imposition of reciprocal WTO tariffs. The UK's world-class aerospace industry, also with integrated supply chains and long planning horizons, might benefit from T-Tab, as could Britain's space sector.[29]

The City, too, has called for a transition deal. For the financial services industry, T-Tab would in our view be a bonus, rather than a necessity. The MiFID II regulations allow so-called regulatory equivalence, which should alleviate many of the concerns raised about Brexit. The biggest City worries relate to access to highly skilled EU migrants and passporting for wholesale financial activities – as we will discuss in Chapter 9. A twelve-month or 24-month transition deal for the City would help what is already a highly adaptable and innovative sector, but is not essential.

It makes sense for the government to compile a sector-by-sector menu to guide both the Article 50 negotiations and planning for T-Tab – including farming, fisheries, pharmaceuticals, universities and the creative industries, as well as the sectors mentioned above. There should be close consultations with industry leaders within each sector, particularly those with deep experience of exporting to the EU.

Since the 2017 general election, there has been greater engagement regarding the UK's Brexit plans between the government and the business community.[30] Having said that, some British businesses are short-termist, have failed to invest enough over many years, and are less interested in adapting to Brexit than in attempting to preserve the status quo.

The leaders of some large multinational corporations, sensing the government's legislative programme is vulnerable amidst the vagaries of a hung parliament, are trying to frustrate the Brexit process. In July 2017, Carolyn Fairbairn, the current director general of the Confederation of British Industry (CBI), called for continuing membership of the single market and customs union as part of a transition agreement which she referred to as the 'maximum continuity' option.[31]

While we recognise the need for a transition, we view this CBI proposal as a ploy to reverse Brexit. The CBI is dominated by large corporations that view EU regulations as barriers to entry against smaller competitors. EU membership gives firms access to unlimited flows of low-wage unskilled migrants – who are then subsidised by the state via tax credits – benefitting big businesses disproportionately. The EU's single market allows some large, multinational firms to engage in legal but aggressive cross-border tax avoidance, as we will discuss in Chapter 8. It is also in the interests of some large firms to stay in the customs union – with the EU's tariff barriers providing protection from global competition – at the expense of consumers who end up paying higher prices.

The EU itself has a long and, in our view, somewhat dishonourable history of frustrating democracy. Over the past fifteen years, numerous referenda – in member states ranging from France to the Netherlands to the Republic of Ireland

– have been reversed or ignored, as discussed in Chapter 1. This helps explain suspicions that a 'transition deal' out of the EU could become permanent, with the UK never achieving full Brexit.

Some have advocated the use of the 'Norway Option' as a transition. This involves the UK staying in the EEA, which, as we outlined in Chapter 3, means remaining a member of the single market while continuing to make annual EU contributions and accepting freedom of movement. The UK would still be subject to ECJ jurisdiction during the transition, but without any representation at the ECJ.

Former Conservative Leader Iain Duncan Smith has criticised this plan, pointing out that legislation to repeal the 1972 European Communities Act – already presented to Parliament – ends the supremacy of EU law. 'We must specify that any interim arrangement is agreed between two sovereign legal entities, which precludes the Norway option,' he said in July 2017.[32] As a long-standing Brexit advocate, Duncan Smith is concerned that ongoing ECJ jurisdiction breaches the Prime Minister's red line set in October 2016, with the UK having only truly left the EU once it is free of ECJ jurisdiction.

Other leading Brexit campaigners, though, feel the EEA model could work, albeit with complications. Former Foreign Secretary Lord Owen played a high-profile role during the EU referendum and, as an Independent Social Democrat peer, remains an influential figure at Westminster. He agrees that EEA membership for anything longer than the 'implementation period' highlighted by the Prime Minister 'would not fulfil the referendum result'. But he thinks being in the EEA is the 'best option during any transition'.

One attraction of the EEA, Owen says, is that while keeping the UK in the single market after March 2019, allowing a smooth transition for UK exporters, Britain will then be able to choose when it leaves. Owen has drawn attention to a clause in the EEA Agreement (EEAA) that allows the UK to exit at any time – as long as the government gives one year's notice. So the EEA route avoids any nervousness about a cliff edge, while providing more time for the UK to negotiate an FTA with the EU, says Owen. The EEA could then be used 'on a strictly time-limited basis', providing what Owen describes as 'a flexible full exit timetable, under UK control'.[33]

There is, at the time of writing, much confusion regarding the constitutional basis of any transition period. The UK, as an EU member, is a member of the

EEA. But the European Commission has argued that the UK's Article 50 letter provides no legal basis for staying in the EEA after March 2019, and there is no formal provision for this to happen under EU law.[34]

The UK may be able to negotiate a continuation of the economic and commercial status quo for twelve or twenty-four months after March 2019, while having no political representation at EU institutions. Article 50 could itself be construed as a legal basis for that – but possibly only outside the EEA. The precise legal framework of T-Tab will clearly itself be subject to debate and negotiation between politicians and lawyers. It seems clear, though, that the British government will not accept ongoing ECJ jurisdiction during the transition – at least not on an open-ended basis. There is also scope, at least from the perspective of the British side, to consider any EU contributions during the transition period as part of the divorce bill discussed in Chapter 5.

During early August 2017, the Institute of Directors said there is 'an urgent need' for the government to address 'the most imminent risk to business from Brexit: what happens, or doesn't, on Brexit day'. In a report assessing transition period options, the Institute of Directors (IoD) highlighted the 'unprecedented nature' of the Article 50 talks while pointing to 'increasing scepticism' that a future trade agreement can be reached before the Article 50 window expires in March 2019.[35]

In this context, the signs of broad political agreement over the summer of 2017 that something like T-Tab is required is good news, even if the precise constitutional mechanism to provide 'the economic bridge' has yet to be agreed between the UK, EU and other counterparties. We are also reassured that business leaders are now starting to accept WTO rules as an acceptable and even strategically astute post-Brexit scenario, and by government announcements on assistance to critical domestic sectors of the UK economy during the transition period.

ON ALL FRONTS

There are many strategic areas where the EU would benefit from future close ties with the UK, whether in defence, security, environmental protection, scientific research, or educational and cultural exchange. Britain has a leadership role, of value to EU members, across numerous strategic headings. Such realities are significant to these Article 50 negotiations.

Theresa May explicitly linked economic relations and security cooperation in the Article 50 letter she sent in March 2017. 'In security terms, a failure to reach agreement would mean our cooperation in the fight against crime and terrorism would be weakened,' the Prime Minister wrote. Home Secretary Amber Rudd said that, while trade and security talks were 'separate', security cooperation was a reality of EU membership and would need to be negotiated after Brexit. 'The UK is the largest contributor to Europol and if we left Europol, we would take our information with us – this is in the legislation,' she said. 'Our European partners want us to keep our information there, because we keep other European countries safe as well.'[36]

In terms of defence and security, the EU without its largest military power is a very different body. How Britain positions itself with France with regard to defence is important, not just for these Article 50 negotiations but future European cooperation and security. Since signing a defence treaty in November 2010, the UK and France have become more militarily intertwined than at any time since the Second World War.[37] The two countries, collaborating on a range of defence projects, have set up a 5,000-strong Combined Joint Expeditionary Force. This is a bilateral agreement, which exists entirely separately from the EU. The UK's 'hard power' strengthens its negotiating hand in these Article 50 negotiations. While the government will be sensitive about stressing this, it is a reality.

The government's Brexit policy was clearly laid out at Lancaster House in January 2017 and in the subsequent White Paper. It was repeated in the Article 50 letter of March 2017 and the supporting Act of Parliament – and is now embodied in the EU Withdrawal Bill. During the Article 50 negotiation, with regard to both the early skirmishes described in Chapter 5 and the broader negotiation issues outlined here, we believe that the UK has a strong hand to play.

The EU cannot punish Britain without going against its own principles. Presenting itself as a champion of free trade, the EU will not look good if it is seen to complicate and generally frustrate an FTA with the world's fifth largest economy. The US and Japan, during trade negotiations with the EU, are not asked to make multi-billion-pound payments for access to EU markets, or accept freedom of movement rules. Countries that have already signed an FTA with the EU, such as Mexico, do not meet such conditions. Making such demands of the UK, a nation that has voted to leave the EU but wants the most open trading relationship possible, looks absurd to the wider world.

A project whose founding purpose was to bind nations together through trade should surely be doing all it can to ensure an amicable split with Britain, so trade might continue smoothly. Yet federalist politicians across the EU – and particularly at the European Commission – are nervous that if the UK is successful after Brexit, that would encourage others to leave the club. The EU's supposed ideals of cooperation and openness are about to be tested. Will the UK be able to achieve a Brexit that promotes openness and cooperation? Or will the EU gainsay its supposed founding principles?

Britain must avoid attempting a Soft Brexit – which will simply become a Messy Brexit. The Article 50 agreement should be kept as simple as possible. A drawn-out, acrimonious negotiation over 'the four freedoms' would do serious damage to UK–EU relations, business sentiment, investment and jobs – and would likely end in stalemate. Better for the UK to offer a UK–EU FTA, while being fully prepared to trade under WTO rules.

In December 2016, Theresa May stood alone for a few seconds at an EU summit in Brussels. It was described as 'Brexit in a single shot'.[38] The footage was promoted heavily by UK media outlets determined to portray Britain as isolated. Yet the Brexit vote has resonated across the Continent. The EU is unpopular, increasingly so, as it does not speak for the people it purports to represent.

The EU 27 is, in fact, deeply divided. The Eurozone remains one political event or economic downturn away from another serious crisis – which will, once again, bring the divisions outlined in Chapter 4 to the fore. While weighed down by the trappings of federalism, the EU is made up of nation states, each with its own electorate. The leaders of those countries will complain loudly during these Article 50 negotiations, making outlandish demands as happens in high-stakes negotiations. But they have everything to gain from preserving good relations and open trade with Britain.

What matters to voters are jobs, trade, growth and prosperity. While there will be grandstanding and political drama, neither the UK nor the EU 27 will want to do anything that sacrifices the huge trade volumes, stacked in the EU's favour no less, that flow across the Channel.

CHAPTER 7

GLOBAL NEGOTIATIONS

'Imagination is more important than knowledge. For knowledge is limited to all we now know and understand, while imagination embraces the entire world, and all there ever will be to know and understand.'

ALBERT EINSTEIN[1]

Imagine being at Southampton harbour the day the RMS *Titanic* set sail. Its size gave the impression of invincibility, safety and security. Despite receiving warnings of impending danger, this 'unsinkable ship' famously didn't change course, hit trouble and sank.

The EU can be compared to the *Titanic*. Because it is huge, some in the UK feel we would be safer and economically stronger if we remained 'inside Europe'. But Britain has seized the opportunity to board a different ship, allowing us to chart our own course. This is not a 'leap into the dark', as then Prime Minister David Cameron claimed ahead of the EU referendum. For those able to look ahead, it could be viewed instead as a move to safety.

Having chosen to leave the EU, the UK can better position itself to be outward-looking and adaptable. Instead of remaining on the *Titanic*, we can picture ourselves aboard a medium-sized ship leaving Southampton harbour at the same time. The crossing may have been choppy to begin with, but the smaller ship reached the new world safely.

When the *Titanic* set sail in 1912, that new world was America. Today, the new world represents a global economy changing as never before, due to population dynamics, innovation, urbanisation and technological change. The UK needs to play to its strengths, be flexible, steer its own course and learn to thrive amidst an ever-changing global seascape. It can do this far better under its own control. The EU, for its part, also needs to adapt – given the concerns raised in Chapter 4.

But it is by no means doomed. To avoid the fate of the *Titanic*, though, the EU must change course.

The UK is leaving the EU at a time in history when the combination of globalisation, instant mass communication and broader technological change is transforming the shape of the global economy at an unprecedented pace. The extent of the shift is brought home by Professor Danny Quah at the National University of Singapore, who has carried out a series of calculations to determine the world's 'centre of economic gravity' based on the changing GDP of various countries. As recently as 1980, the 'mid-point' of the world economy was out in the Atlantic Ocean, reflecting the importance of both the US and Western Europe. By 2008, when the global financial crisis hit, that centre had shifted to a longitudinal mid-point between İzmir in Turkey and Minsk in Belarus, reflecting the relentless pull away from Western Europe and towards Asia. Quah calculates that by 2050, the economic centre of gravity will have shifted eastwards even more, to between Ürümqi in China and Calcutta in India, towards the heart of the Indo-Pacific region.[2]

Calcutta, or Kolkata as it is known locally, is a dynamic, pulsating city, with a thriving port. Once visited, it is never forgotten. In the past, Calcutta was associated with Mother Teresa, grinding poverty and backwardness. Now it is the spearhead of an economic renaissance evident across the east of India. Just as the scale and pace of change in China over the last quarter of a century has taken many by surprise, the same could apply to India over the coming decades: if India really succeeds economically, then just as with China, the entire world will notice. Uttar Pradesh, India's most populous state, has a population as big as Brazil. The second most populous state, Maharashtra, is home to as many people as Mexico. The population dynamics of south Asia, and the growth of domestic markets across the region, are truly breathtaking: one in six of the people alive today live in India. Half of those – one in twelve of the world's population – are under the age of twenty-six.[3]

In November 2016, on a visit to India, Secretary of State for International Trade Liam Fox pointed out that the UK is the largest G20 investor in India, accounting for 8 per cent of its inward investment. Moreover, he highlighted that the British government wants the local catchphrase 'Make in India' to be 'synonymous with "Finance in the UK"'.[4] That sounds sensible, given the potential for the City of London to capitalise on its expertise and reputation to become a centre of finance for fast-growing markets across the globe. The City has in recent years already become a place where numerous overseas-based companies list their shares, not least companies from large emerging markets. London has also begun to position itself as a trading hub for the Chinese yuan – set to become a leading reserve currency – and as a market for Islamic finance.

Ürümqi in north-west China is the largest city in central Asia and has already been earmarked as one of the main 'nodes' on China's 'Belt Road' – which is set to open up new trade ties for a multitude of countries. Britain is trying to benefit commercially with firms winning contracts across the Belt Road and working with China on joint projects in other countries on the route. The economist John Ross estimates that China and the economies associated with the Belt Road will account for a massive 46 per cent of global growth over the next five years, versus 24 per cent from North America and just 10 per cent from the EU.[5]

In Chapter 2, we outlined how the shape of the global economy has already shifted. The combined GDP of the six countries of the EEC, when the UK joined in 1973, made up around a quarter of the global economy. Today, the twenty-eight countries of the EU account for just a fifth. In 1980, the emerging markets were 30 per cent of the global GDP. Now, their share is 54 per cent and rising. By 2030, the biggest four emerging markets alone – China, India, Russia and Brazil – will be home to 80 per cent of the world's middle classes.[6]

Most growth and consumption in the world, then, is already happening beyond the West. That relentless trend, driven by demography and economic 'catch-up', will continue during the decades to come. The kind of imagination that underpins China's Belt Road project is exactly the sort that Britain needs to show as it reaches out to global markets after Brexit. It is vital that the UK's political and business classes fully recognise and act on this reality. It is time to reallocate our political, diplomatic and commercial resources away from the EU and towards the rest of the world. This is by no means a call to ignore Western Europe, but we must make sure we seize opportunities and stake the UK's claim to a share of the growth markets upon which the prosperity of future generations will depend.

AVOID GROUPTHINK

Economists, unfortunately, are known less for their imagination than for a tendency towards 'groupthink'. This is also reinforced by a bias towards the status quo. Almost all professional and academic economists who publicly expressed a view were wrong about an immediate economic collapse following the UK's Leave vote, particularly regarding job losses. 'Most economists' still argue Britain will lose out due to Brexit – even though all the world's major economies trade extensively with the EU from outside and despite the growth potential across the rest of the world. The economic consensus continues to be that the UK will look less attractive in trade and investment terms after Brexit, and higher exports to non-EU markets will not make up for that loss.

The performance of the British economy since the June 2016 referendum should have triggered some collective humility among the economics profession. In contrast to firms fleeing the country, as many economists predicted, large numbers of domestic and overseas businesses have either recommitted to previous UK investments or announced additional projects. Foreign Direct Investment (FDI) rose from \$33 billion in 2015 to no less than \$254 billion in 2016 according to the OECD, with more than 70 per cent of that total coming after the June vote.[7] While inward investment can change sharply from year to year, these are impressive figures demonstrating confidence in the UK economy. Britain remains Europe's No. 1 destination for inward investment, and that seems unlikely to change once we have left the EU, with the UK building on its reputation as a global hub.[8]

More generally, there should also be a wider acknowledgement among economists of the disappointing performance of the UK in the single market over the last ten to twenty years and the constraining influence it has had on our domestic economy. There is a huge disconnect between the bulk of the economics profession suggesting that four decades of EU membership has been great for the UK, then highlighting all the economic problems that we still have!

Misplaced fears about trading with the EU from outside the Union should dissipate over time. The core idea of the 'gravity models' used by HM Treasury and many other public sector forecasters is that we trade more with larger economies that are geographically near than with smaller ones far away. Yet, as the economist Ryan Bourne notes, 'gravity models … are backward-looking and may simply not be well suited to analysing large long-term regime changes'.[9] Since the referendum, genuine concerns about the underlying economic methodology of 'gravity models' have emerged. 'The Treasury do admit that the data is troublesome,' says the Cambridge economist Graham Gudgin. 'It is not obvious that these results can be applied to a well-developed open economy like the UK.'[10]

The think tank Open Europe has carried out analysis suggesting many reasons for the UK to be optimistic if we pursue a truly global trading strategy, cutting trade deals with the world's largest economies, not least the emerging markets. While Germany's GDP is expected to grow 14 per cent by 2030, Open Europe expects India's economy to more than double over the same time period.[11] Examining the impact of trade deals based on the size of India today, rather than in 2030 – as some analysts did ahead of the referendum – will underplay the potential benefits of enhanced trade with this huge market, while overstating the relative merits of being part of the EU. The same applies to other fast-growing markets where the UK has scope to develop a much deeper trading relationship – such as Canada, Pakistan, Israel and Nigeria.

Economists are right that any UK–EU deal over 'access' to the single market will – in trade terms – not be as favourable as the unlimited tariff-free access of membership. Yet, as we have noted, other aspects of single market membership are not necessarily good for the UK – such as the imposing of EU regulation on all firms, not just exporters, and the inability to cut services-oriented trade deals. For sectors where single market membership matters more than others, the UK will seek a favourable deal that closely reflects current terms, as noted in Theresa May's Article 50 letter. While the uncertainty ahead of a deal will deter some firms from investing, the scale of investment since the referendum suggests this impact may be relatively small.

Membership of the single market has not worked well for a services-oriented economy like the UK. It is no surprise we have a large EU trade imbalance that has increased significantly since the mid-1980s. The latest figures put our trade deficit in goods and services at £37 billion, with a surplus in services of £97 billion outweighed by a deficit in goods of £134.1 billion.[12] Britain's biggest export markets for goods are, in order: the US, then Germany, France and the Netherlands, followed by Ireland. Our largest goods imports are from Germany and China, then the USA. As a country, the UK needs to invest and export more – and Brexit must act as a catalyst for policies to help make that happen.

Liam Fox has outlined some ambitious aims. In July 2017, the International Trade Secretary launched a report in Washington detailing the UK's trade and investment relationship with each of the 435 congressional districts of the US. Speaking in Geneva that same month, he outlined how the UK is keen to take a lead at the WTO's eleventh ministerial conference in Buenos Aires in December 2017.[13] One area the UK wants to focus on is the WTO's Treaty in Services Agreement (TiSA) – as Britain looks to combine with the US to lower global barriers to trade for the services in which both economies specialise.

The pace and scale of change represented by the fourth industrial revolution will overtake many economic projections. Central to this revolution are emerging technological breakthroughs in fields such as robotics, artificial intelligence, 3D printing, quantum computing and nanotechnology.[14] An excellent debate on this subject took place in the House of Commons in September 2016. 'There is one aspect of this revolution that should have every decision-maker in our economy on high alert: the rapidity with which it is occurring,' said one of the debate's co-sponsors, Labour MP Peter Kyle. 'The fourth industrial revolution will sweep through our economy in a matter of years, rather than the centuries it took the previous industrial revolutions to unfold.'[15]

Change is not new, it is constant. Veteran newspaper columnist Anthony Hilton recently made a telling observation about the FTSE 100 index that charts the fortunes of the largest London-listed companies. 'Fewer than ten of its original list from 1984 make the cut today,' says Hilton. 'Think about it: 90 per cent of our biggest companies have gone within a generation.'[16] The UK's departure from the EU is indeed happening in complex, fast-moving times. 'Britain is in a global race for success, and if we don't act now, we will be left behind,' says Conservative MP Alan Mak, in his report on the fourth industrial revolution. 'In the future, every sector of our economy will be a tech sector, so only by taking action now to back innovation, train our workforce and boost our digital infrastructure, can we reap the benefits just as we did in the First Industrial Revolution two hundred years ago.'[17]

The UK needs to export more into the big emerging markets and rapidly growing economies across the 'new, new world' of technology and change. Out of global financial centres such as London, finance for new trade corridors connecting goods, services, people and intellectual property is emerging. Reinforcing this trend is the growing importance of the economies and markets into which the UK's services, goods and ideas will flow.

Demographics are key. Africa's working age population will increase by twice that of India and China combined over the next fifteen years.[18] China, meanwhile, with its 1.4 billion people, is seeing a switch from export-led to domestic-led growth. Germany benefited initially from China's expansion, as it exported capital goods, albeit with the advantage of a currency kept artificially low from a German perspective, given the nature of monetary union. The UK should be determined to thrive during the next phase, as our service-sector exports find a home in China's growing domestic market. The same should be true for the UK in many other economies, too.

The fast development of the emerging markets points to tremendous opportunities, but caution is needed. While bureaucrats and politicians have an influence, it is entrepreneurs and firms that trade. You need to have products and services that people want to buy. It is vital that the UK is at the forefront of innovation and new products for this new industrial age – issues we explore in Chapter 8, when discussing the post-Brexit UK economy.

While UK goods and services need to be attractive and competitive, we must avoid a race to the bottom on price. There are different facets to this, not least the need to safeguard workers' rights. Some fear these will be eroded outside of the EU. Having been set in Brussels, such rights will now be determined by politicians in Westminster, responsive to the wishes of the UK electorate. Despite much scaremongering, there is no reason to believe Brexit will lead to a diminution of those rights, given that many UK labour market regulations are actually more progressive than those emanating from the EU.

The right to holiday pay in the UK, for instance, was introduced in the 1938 Holiday Pay Act, with UK workers now entitled to 5.6 weeks of paid holiday, compared to four weeks under EU rules. The UK has one of the highest minimum wages in the world, while there is no minimum wage law across the EU, and only eighteen out of twenty-eight EU nations have a minimum wage. EU law requires a minimum of fourteen weeks' maternity pay, with no minimum pay level, while UK law provides fifty-two weeks, on 90 per cent pay for six weeks and £140 a week thereafter.

Consider, also, that the UK legislated for equal pay between men and women in 1970, before we joined the EEC. It is by no means the case, as many opponents of Brexit argue, that the development of trade links with the rest of the world means a race to the bottom on workers' rights. In fact, based on the past, Britain will likely be at the forefront of a progressive attitude towards workers' pay and conditions, driven in the future by decisions made in Westminster. After Brexit, the UK is to compete outside the EU's protectionist wall. As such, we must look to cut FTAs with some of the world's most dynamic economies. But our competitiveness must come from our intelligence, imagination and creative abilities rather than attempts to drive down labour costs and conditions.

STRIKING DEALS

At the time of our 1975 referendum, the British public saw 'Europe' as 'the future'. The UK's eyes are now set wider. Leaving the EU allows Britain to position itself far better in a changing global economy, maximising its trading opportunities with the wider world. Outside the EU, of course, Britain will once again have 'competency' to negotiate our own free trade agreements. Striking such deals should ensure more of our future growth derives from trading with the four fifths of the world economy that is outside the EU.

Much has been made of the EU's negotiating 'clout' and the large number of FTAs the EU has cut over recent decades. In reality, as discussed in Chapter 3, the complexity of negotiating as a large bloc of countries, often with conflicting interests, means most of the EU's trade deals are with relatively insignificant economies. The combined GDP of nations covered by the EU's FTAs is less than 10 per cent of the world economy. Britain's demands are just one of twenty-eight, often way down the list.

Countries negotiating on their own behalf often do far better – and the UK has a great deal to learn from their example. A relatively small economy like Switzerland, for instance, operating alone, has signed trade deals with nations boasting a combined GDP of $39,800 billion. That's more than five times the $7,700 billion value of the economies covered by EU trade deals – despite, or perhaps because of, the sprawling Brussels trade bureaucracy, employing count-less consultants and full-time staff.[19] If Switzerland can strike an FTA with China, as it did in 2013 after a three-year negotiation, why can't the UK – an economy four times the size?[20]

Chile, South Korea and Singapore have also struck extensive trade agreements with partner economies, their trade deals covering markets worth a combined

GDP of $58,300 billion, $40,800 billion and $38,700 billion respectively. Again, these are all significant multiples of the total size of the EU's signed-up trade partners. The FTAs secured by Switzerland, Chile, South Korea and Singapore, moreover, unlike those signed by the EU, emphasise trade in services. The EU's FTAs have opened up services trade in combined markets worth just $4,800 billion. Trade deals including services struck by Switzerland and Singapore cover markets of $35,800 billion and $37,200 billion respectively. The equivalent numbers for South Korea and Chile are $40,000 billion and $55,400 billion.[21]

Several much smaller economies than the UK, then, with far less commercial and diplomatic influence, have signed a range of FTAs dwarfing those struck by the EU in terms of their size and scope. Exporters from Switzerland to South Korea, and service-sector exporters in particular, enjoy more preferential access to far bigger markets than those based in the UK – despite the EU's 'clout', to say nothing of the financial and political costs of our membership.

Negotiating FTAs can be a long, drawn-out process. But there are encouraging signs the UK is well placed to strike deals with countries all over the world. While the EU has no operating trade deal with any leading world economies, Britain could quickly succeed in striking such an FTA. Far from being 'at the back of the queue' to agree a trade deal with the US, for instance, the UK now has 'a front seat'.[22]

Other nations have shown a willingness to cut trade agreements with the world's fifth largest economy. 'An FTA with the UK will be no problem,' said the Australian High Commissioner to the UK in June 2017. 'It would not take very long because we would not want to put a lot of obstacles in the way of British exports.' Canada's High Commissioner to the UK said something very similar: 'We'll be able to arrive at something as quickly as the political leadership in both countries want it to happen … a trade agreement will be easy to reach.'[23]

Such comments are no surprise. When one looks at goods exports to the EU, Britain is the primary market for Australia, Canada, India, New Zealand, South Africa, Pakistan, Sri Lanka and Jamaica. The UK is the second biggest EU market for Bangladesh, Kenya and Papa New Guinea and the third largest for Singapore, Malaysia and Malawi.[24] We need to ensure that there is more two-way trade between these nations and Britain, as we look to broaden UK exporters' horizons. For now, such countries are not huge markets for the UK. We should maintain good ties with the EU, then, and there is no reason we cannot do that, enjoying the same 'access' to the single market as every other major economy.

Many of the issues linked to the stalled EU–India talks 'will instantly go away between India and the UK,' says the Confederation of Indian Industry. 'It would be an agreement that would almost be made in heaven.'[25] Of course, there are areas – notably the 'mode four issue' regarding migration of skilled workers – that need to be resolved for the UK to make real progress in striking an FTA with India. But this is clearly achievable.

China, too, offers great potential in terms of UK trade. President Xi talks of a 'golden age' in terms of Sino-UK relations, following his successful state visit in 2015.[26] It would be wrong to suggest that there has not been some uncertainty following the UK's change of government in 2016 and the initial delay over proceeding with Chinese involvement in Hinkley Point. The UK needs to show positive intentions, then – and it was welcome that Chancellor Philip Hammond attended the Belt and Road Summit in Beijing in May 2017. One idea might be to form a high-level task force between the UK and China to work on specific projects linked to the Belt and Road Initiative. The authors believe such an initiative would be welcomed by the Chinese.

'Free trade agreements are not the panacea for increased trade,' as the Free Enterprise Group (FEG) of MPs has pointed out. With or without government involvement, exchange between people and firms takes place across international borders anyway. But, as the FEG notes, FTAs can help reduce not only tariffs but also the so-called non-tariff barriers that can prove problematic in particular for service-sector trade, in which the UK excels.[27]

There is much willingness being shown outside of the EU to embrace a post-Brexit Britain. 'Brexit means the UK is back,' says former Australian Prime Minister Tony Abbott. 'The country that gave the world the English language, common law and the Mother of Parliaments is once more to seize its destiny as a global leader.'[28]

SELLING OURSELVES

It was in February 2011 that the British government last produced a White Paper on trade and investment. The Labour Party called for a new one in its manifesto published ahead of the June 2017 general election – and was right to do so.[29] One issue such a White Paper should urgently address is the UK's export promotion operations. While the existing export agency UK Trade and Industry does good work, the extent of support provided to potential UK exporters must be significantly increased, not least for small and medium-sized firms. SMEs often only start exporting after receiving uninitiated enquiries or orders from overseas. That needs to change.

Naturally, many SMEs have tighter margins and limited resources compared to their larger counterparts. 'Small firms trade with countries based on ease, cost and value,' says Mike Cherry, chairman of the Federation of Small Businesses (FSB). An FSB survey suggests that 63 per cent of SME exporters see the EU as their key market, 49 per cent name America, 29 per cent Australia, 28 per cent China and 23 per cent Canada. It is encouraging that no less than 78 per cent of SME exporters are already selling to non-EU markets. Having said that, only one in five small businesses is an exporter. In its 'Keep Trade Easy' report, the FSB says that 'with the right support there is potential to double this figure'.[30]

Achieving a more balanced economy certainly requires the UK to export more. Our exports amount to just 27.6 per cent of GDP, according to the World Bank, compared to a 28.6 per cent OECD average, 30 per cent in France and 46.8 per cent in Germany. During the 2017 election campaign, the Conservatives proposed to resurrect the UK's 'Board of Trade', an idea that has worked well in the past but has long been abandoned. This would bring together senior business figures and politicians to help lead trade delegations, boost exports and 'make sure the benefits and prosperity of Brexit are spread equally across the country'.

UK trade commissioners would be based 'overseas in nine different regions, determined by markets rather than national borders, to ensure UK trade policy is guided by local experience and expertise'. This kind of proactive approach, actively seeking to attract FDI to the UK as well as boost UK overseas trade, would be most welcome, particularly if supported by Britain's network of embassies. 'While one in five UK small businesses is an exporter, that compares with one in four in Germany,' says Tom Thackray, head of enterprise at the CBI.[31] Germany has clearly developed an effective network of Chambers of Commerce across the world, which has helped enhance the country's export performance, not least among SMEs. British officials and business leaders can learn from this example.

Part of the UK's net annual contribution to the EU could be diverted into the creation of a major new body focused on export promotion. There are examples from around the world – not least Australia's 'Austrade' program and Enterprise Ireland – both of which have helped increase their nation's export share, including among small firms. Again, as we seek to raise exports as a share of GDP, the UK can benefit from studying international best practice.

As already highlighted, it is not governments and bureaucrats that trade, but businesspeople who, between them, and across international borders, identify commercial opportunities of mutual benefit. In that respect, government must ensure an enabling environment in which trade can occur – and FTAs can help do that, as can domestic economic and regulatory policy.

In this regard, UK regions should be focused on improving global connectivity, so they can achieve increased trade penetration.[32] Taking a regional, bottom-up approach will help unlock opportunities in terms of attracting global trade and investment. While there are 3,500 free trade zones across the world, including 250 in America, in the UK there are none – as EU state aid laws and our customs union membership prevent us from setting up such zones. That can now change.

A study by Rishi Sunak MP argued the case for UK free ports, suggesting they would help Britain 'recapture our buccaneering free trade spirit'.[33] Free ports would be outside the UK customs authority, allowing goods to be imported, manufactured or re-exported inside the free trade zone without incurring domestic customs duties or taxes. The introduction of free ports could be supported by financial incentives like research and development grants, other tax credits and regulatory flexibility. This would boost Britain's ports sector, already the second largest in Europe, while also having a positive regional impact – as many ports are 'in areas of high deprivation'.

While bilateral trade deals are important, and can encourage and facilitate cross-border commerce, most international trade happens outside of formal free trade agreements. The UK already trades heavily with the US and other markets without an FTA being in place. Even operating under the WTO's most favoured nation rules, there will be many opportunities to enhance UK trade beyond the EU. Non-tariff barriers rather than tariffs are often the biggest obstacle and these are best addressed, if not through specific trade deals, then by working with others at the WTO to eradicate NTBs.[34]

Outside the EU's customs union, the UK will be able to determine its own tariff structure on imports, as part of the country's new WTO schedules. Britain can learn from the likes of Singapore and South Korea, who have struck FTAs that are iterative in the sense of being easy to replicate, playing to their strengths and with large or fast-growing markets. Underpinning our FTAs should be access for the services sector, access for investment flows, intellectual property rights and a commitment to remove tariffs and NTBs.

Britain needs to continue rebuilding the required skill set across Whitehall to carry out complex future trade negotiations – as we mentioned in the previous chapter. And although the UK cannot enter into trade deals until formally leaving the EU, that does not prevent preparatory work now, including negotiations, to ensure progress is made by the time we leave. The UK should be using this Article 50 window to establish networks, and deepen bilateral ties, taking future FTAs as far as possible before March 2019.

POLYAMOROUS RELATIONSHIPS

Since the EU referendum, there has been much discussion of the UK's 'divorce bill' – as outlined in Chapter 5. Yet in the modern era, talk of marriage and divorce is often wide of the mark. Whether Brexit amounts to a conscious uncoupling or an amicable split, the UK should strive to maintain an open relationship with the EU, while developing 'polyamorous' relations with other countries across the world.

The Special Trade Commission, set up by the London-based think tank the Legatum Institute, recommends that the UK attempt to lead 'a plurilateral FTA process – a prosperity zone'. This would be a group of countries committed to the key areas of open trade, competition and the merits and protection of property rights. Shanker Singham, a British trade expert based at Legatum, proposes an existing trade network to which the UK could accede, such as the Pacific Four (P4) Trade Agreement including Singapore, New Zealand, Brunei and Chile. This could then be used as a platform agreement others could join – initially Australia.[35]

While some of these countries are rather small, it is important to appreciate the need to develop a multitude of networks, including ties with large markets as well as those that are growing particularly quickly. The UK should be open-minded about where opportunities may arise. In her 2009 Christmas message, the Queen said that the Commonwealth 'is, in lots of ways, the face of the future'. While some may dismiss this as harking back to a colonial past, there is a great deal of truth in this remark.[36]

'The Commonwealth is, to the surprise of some, one of the fastest developing associations of nations in the world,' observes former Secretary of State and foreign affairs expert Lord David Howell. 'It contains at least seven of the world's most dynamic, knowledge-driven economies.' Howell identifies these nations as India, Canada, Nigeria, New Zealand, Malaysia, South Africa and Australia – 'countries with like-minded values and principles'.[37]

Stressing the importance of the 52-nation Commonwealth should not be seen as nostalgia.[38] Many of these countries are geographically remote from the UK, but that ignores the extent to which global trade has changed. The spread of almost total and continuous connectivity and the plummeting cost of communications and information transfer inside global value chains have utterly altered world trade patterns, producing a new wave of globalisation which makes old, trade-bloc thinking increasingly irrelevant.

Production has become largely internationalised, with the separate stages and processes spread between different countries. Gone are the days when one country made a product from start to finish and exported it to another. A study by McKinsey Global Institute calculates that soaring trade flows of data and information connecting the new world of fragmented and dispersed production generates more economic value than the whole of global goods trade – a crucial shift to understand for a service-oriented economy such as the UK.[39] In this context, countries that share a language, legal codes and cultural affinities can thrive when they trade. As such, the Commonwealth, by a quirk of history, provides a very useful network for the UK, but it need not be the only one.

At the very least, Britain should reach out to Commonwealth nations, identifying opportunities and issues. For some, agriculture may be their sticking point, as it often has been in their dealings with the EU. After Brexit, released from the CAP and CET, the UK could cut agricultural import tariffs if we wish – providing scope to do broader trade deals with Commonwealth members and other emerging markets. For a nation like India, on the other hand, migration might be a potential hurdle given the importance of future two-way services trade. But again, outside the EU, Britain has the freedom to negotiate and overcome such issues, to mutual advantage.

Brexit also allows the UK to further enhance its commercial relationship with the US – already the biggest single-country destination for UK exports. There is clearly scope, as mentioned, for a UK–US trade deal. It is also not impossible that Britain may want to associate itself with NAFTA. While that may sound like a long shot, it is certainly the case that the US and UK together, the world's two largest service-sector economies, can now push for reductions in the NTBs that continue to be such a hindrance to services trade. The EU, reflecting its protectionist DNA, has singularly failed to ensure that the 'single market' extends to services, as discussed in Chapter 3. This is true across much of the rest of the world, a reality that Britain and the US can now jointly tackle, within the WTO and beyond.

PROTECTIONIST PRESSURE?

In the wake of President Trump's accession to the White House, and following some strong 'America first' rhetoric, there have been fears about a potential rise in protectionism. That could set back globalisation, making it harder for Britain to secure new trade opportunities as we leave the EU. It has also been suggested that Brexit will make the UK itself more 'isolationist'. We reject this analysis. While a balance needs to be struck between promoting the domestic economy and positioning the UK globally, the government has signalled a clear intention to push for fewer, not more, restrictions on UK trade.[40]

Worries about protectionism have not emerged simply as a result of Trump's election victory. According to the OECD, there has been a steady stream of protectionist measures since the 2008 financial crisis.[41] That being said, Global Trade Alert (GTA), an agency that measures protectionism, says the number of restrictive measures fell to 358 in 2016, the lowest in any year since 2008, when the GTA database began.[42]

Some measures deemed 'protectionist' might be justified. For instance, there have been 1,664 bailout or state-aid measures on the GTA database since 2008 – at least some of which will not be blatantly designed to protect. It is also worth noting that, at the time of writing, there are signs of a pick-up in global trade. During the years before the 2008 financial crisis, trade flows typically grew at twice the rate of world GDP growth. But in recent years, trade has been much less buoyant, with the growth of cross-border commerce only matching global GDP growth of 2.7 per cent and 2.4 per cent in 2015 and 2016 respectively.

In 2017, though, while the World Bank foresees world GDP growth of 2.7 per cent, it is forecasting a 4 per cent rise in global trade flows, up from a post-crisis low of 2.5 per cent the year before. A similar, positive pattern is predicted in 2018 and 2019, with global growth of 2.9 per cent in both years, but world trade growth of 3.8 per cent, with trade continuing to increase faster than the size of the overall global economy. As we leave the EU, the UK has an opportunity to tap into this increase in global trade.[43]

An extremely important bulwark against protectionism is the WTO itself – with its 164 member states and another twenty-two in the process of joining.[44] The WTO is central to international trade, operating a system of rules while providing a Geneva-based forum for governments to strike deals and settle disputes. At its core are WTO agreements negotiated and signed by the bulk of the world's trading nations and ratified in their Parliaments. Their aim is to ensure that trade flows as predictably, smoothly and freely as possible. Formed after World War Two as the General Agreement on Tariffs and Trade, the WTO has helped liberate global trade by keeping the short-term, protectionist instincts of politicians in check. The result has been a thirteenfold expansion in global trade between 1950 and 2015 – a huge increase in worldwide prosperity and, compared to the first half of the twentieth century, relative peace.

Former director general of the WTO Pascal Lamy calls this most important of multilateral bodies 'the world's insurance policy against rising protectionism'.[45] The prominent British economist Tim Congdon similarly describes the WTO as 'the institutional impediment to a global resort to protectionism'. While it has 'become fashionable to opine that the era of globalisation is ending and a retreat to protectionism looms,' Congdon points out that 'all major economies are locked into legally binding commitments not to raise tariffs and can only reverse these measures by compensating other WTO members – so the worst that can occur is that further liberalisation stalls.'[46]

Although the WTO has much going for it, it has suffered dents in its credibility. The inability to complete the 'Doha Round' of trade liberalisation talks, launched in 2001, amounts to the first failure of a multilateral trade negotiation since the 1930s. Back in 1998, when addressing the WTO, President Clinton proposed members explore alternatives to multi-year, multi-issue rounds as the principal model for multilateral trade negotiations.[47] Clinton may be right.

Once the UK has left the EU, it has every chance of striking meaningful FTAs in its own right, suited to the needs of our economy. It is also no exaggeration to say that Britain has, in addition, the opportunity to forge an influential, independent and proactive leadership role in helping revitalise the WTO itself. Luis de la Calle, Mexico's former trade negotiator, has been upbeat about Britain's ability to cut beneficial trade deals outside the EU. The UK has 'strong historic relationships' and a 'world-class services sector that doesn't benefit much from many of the EU's trade agreements', observes de la Calle. This combination, he says, means 'Britain is probably the only country on earth that can realistically cut trade deals with the US, China and India as well as the EU'.[48] Such deals, if they happened, would cover two thirds of the global economy – more than six times the coverage of the EU's free trade deals.

Crawford Falconer, New Zealand's former trade ambassador, sees the WTO as 'fundamental to the stability and growth of the post-war world and vital to our future'. In his view, the UK 'has a massive opportunity to provide global economic leadership' by acting independently within the WTO, rather than as just one of twenty-eight EU countries.[49] The UK should indeed speak up for the free movement of goods and services, for international cooperation and, above all, for the continuation of healthy trade and dialogue between West and East – particularly at a time when the US is perceived to be veering towards more protectionism. Britain has a record in such matters that, while historically complex, is second to none.

One area where the UK could set an example once we have left the EU is agriculture. For decades, global trade talks have stalled, or failed altogether, due to the unwillingness of large developed nations – particularly the EU and US – to open up their agricultural markets to global competition. With its relatively small and efficient agricultural sector, the UK could help to change that by offering various nations 'agriculture for services' trade agreements. These would benefit UK consumers via lower food prices, while securing trade ties with many poor but fast-growing and populous nations across the developing world. Breaking the logjam on agriculture, while providing suitable support for UK farmers, would show that the UK means business in terms of trade expansion. Leaving the EU, far from isolating the UK, makes our advocacy of global free trade increasingly credible.

Britain already sends more than 56 per cent of its exports of goods and services beyond the EU – the only EU member to trade more with the rest of the world than with the bloc itself. Our non-EU trade not only accounts for the majority of our overseas commerce but is also fast-growing and generates a surplus. The UK's ability to negotiate FTAs with the rest of the world, further expanding our trade beyond the EU, depends not only on our economic and financial capacity but also Britain's widely admired institutions and our enviable cultural reach.

Outside the EU and its protectionist customs union, the UK has much to offer as it negotiates trade deals with the rest of the world, rediscovering its global vocation. The British economy, while facing structural issues that must be addressed, remains an attractive and resilient trading partner, with many innovative firms and a large and sophisticated domestic market. The central place of British law and the English language across world markets, along with the financial might of the City and the ability to settle disputes in London, bodes well for the UK's ability to strike deals and claim a larger share of international commerce.

The UK's defence capabilities and broader diplomatic influence will help as we look to establish polyamorous trading relationships after Brexit. Britain has unrivalled 'soft power' too. The strong reputation of our leading universities, already well known to numerous international business leaders who attended them, is another major cultural asset. They are the source of much potential future innovation. The scope for both academic and commercial collaboration between British universities and firms overseas is vast.

GLOBAL NATION

Some say that the UK will 'lack influence' outside the EU. Yet Britain will remain a key member of the G7 and G20, important groups of nations that cooperate on geopolitical and economic issues. The UK will be in the 34-member Paris-based OECD, a group of 'advanced' nations that aims to share best economic practice. Britain will retain membership of the IMF and World Bank, remain on the Financial Stability Board that coordinates and influences global financial policy, while regaining its own seat at the WTO, instead of being represented as just one of twenty-eight EU members.

Beyond economics and commerce, the UK is central to the 28-member North

Atlantic Treaty Organization (NATO) and one of the five permanent members of the UN Security Council along with the USA, Russia, France and China. Britain is also at the heart of the 'Five Eyes' group, the world's leading defence and security intelligence network, sharing sensitive information with the US, Canada, Australia and New Zealand.

When one considers this list it is hard to argue that the UK would suddenly lose influence outside of the EU. It is certainly not as if the EU has been able to cut FTAs better than nations acting alone – as has been shown. Free from the collective responsibility of EU membership, Britain can also play a major role in helping to strengthen vital existing bodies such as the UN and WTO so they are fit for the future, as well as helping shape institutions such as the Asian Infrastructure Investment Bank, which will play a leading role in decades to come.[50]

A fully sovereign UK, exploiting its links with Europe but not bound by them, while harnessing its influence across the rest of the world, will be well placed to influence the direction of global governance: far from being 'isolated', we will have more ability to influence the global standards increasingly governing cross-border commerce.

The reality is that a large and growing part of the law that governs international commerce, even within the EU, is made by global institutions, then handed to Brussels and transferred to member states.[51] Food standards, for instance, are determined by the UN and the WHO. Numerous energy-related regulations have their origins in the Kyoto Accord on climate change and subsequent international agreements – such as the Paris Climate Conference (COP21) in December 2015.[52] Financial services, particularly since the 2008 collapse, are overseen at a global level, via the Basel Committee on Banking Supervision and the G20 Financial Stability Board. Safety standards across numerous other sectors, such as autos, are also determined by global groups.

The UK's elected politicians and the officials answerable to them are currently not always able to play their natural roles at such global forums, often hamstrung by common EU positions not reflecting British interests. Ongoing membership of the single market, and related ECJ authority, would mean such constraints continue, preventing the UK from fulfilling the global governance role that the nation's history and ongoing commercial and military prowess suggest we should.

Brexit, more generally, allows Britain to distance itself from the future challenges confronting the EU. Like those on the *Titanic* sitting in privileged first-class seats, oblivious to what was going on down below, the EU has failed to confront many of the serious issues it faces, including the deeply dysfunctional single currency and chronic youth unemployment.

Jumping ship and acting under our own steam allows the UK to address directly issues such as trade, immigration and broader sovereignty where we have, in recent years, come adrift. In an era of globalisation, technical change and innovation, Britain needs to send a clear and bold signal – that it is moving beyond the centralising, controlling and regulating environment that comes with EU membership. We need to leave the protectionist customs union and reject the onerous, anti-democratic conditions of single market membership. The economies that succeed over the coming decades will need to be global in their outlooks, adaptable and flexible, controlling their own destinies to the greatest possible extent. Brexit then starts to become a sizeable opportunity.

Outside the EU, then, Britain needs to move decisively towards free trade across the world, focus on pro-growth policies driven by increased investment, enhanced infrastructure and innovation. And we need to do this while protecting and upholding workers' rights. The UK's future lies in building a competitive economy based on high value-added services and manufacturing, with media, artistic and cultural exports also playing an important part. Well placed to achieve that, we need significantly to 'up-skill' our workforce, emphasising vocational education, training and retraining, while doing everything possible to encourage our small and medium-sized firms.

Having executed a successful Clean Brexit, having left the single market and the customs union, while undertaking to secure FTAs across the world, it is vital that the UK then forges ahead and builds an economy fit for the high seas of the twenty-first century and beyond. That is the subject of the second half of this book.

PART IV

THE UK AFTER BREXIT

CHAPTER 8

ECONOMIC AND INDUSTRIAL LANDSCAPE

'The economy, stupid.'
JAMES CARVILLE, 1991[1]

A vision is needed; leaving the EU will not, by itself, transform the UK economy. The policies we adopt during the Article 50 period, and once the UK has left, are of vital importance. Crucially, outside the EU, we will have a greater ability to set our own policies – to the extent an individual country can, within the context of a fast-globalising world economy.

Brexit should empower the government to devise and implement measures that can help truly to transform the UK economy. Before that, though, there are many areas of policy where Britain will reclaim 'competencies' from Brussels. These range from regional policy to state aid. Also, as Britain leaves the EU, we should sharpen our focus in many areas where attention has sometimes been lacking – on things that we should have been doing anyway, and for whatever reason did not. A good example is infrastructure spending, which is vital both to raising productivity and spreading growth across the regions. After March 2019, our politicians will no longer be able to blame Brussels for any problems. Gone will be those tabloid headlines telling us it is all Europe's fault.

During the exit negotiations, it is quite possible the Eurozone and the broader EU 27 could grow at a faster pace than in recent years, helped by the easy money policy of the ECB and a pick-up in the world economy. This should not make us doubt the benefits of leaving. A cyclical upturn across the Eurozone is long overdue. And while such an improvement would help UK exports, it won't solve the deep-rooted structural issues facing monetary union.

Both Brexit and the June 2017 general election should be triggers for a fundamental rethink of domestic economic policy-making. Since the 2008 financial crisis, the UK, and much of the Western world, has shown a rather mixed policy record. While more investment is necessary, and there are areas where the state could perhaps play a more active role, there is also a need to restate the case for the market economy.

History has shown, again and again and throughout the world, that the market economy – suitably regulated and tempered – is the only sure route to economic success and rising living standards. The 2008 Lehman Brothers collapse, far from undermining the case for broadly free markets, actually served to strengthen it. When banks are allowed to get so large and complex, in cahoots with captured regulators, that they are too big to fail, that shows market discipline has gone. The global financial crisis happened not because there was too much capitalism, but too little. The UK must fall back on its free-market instincts – making sure markets operate free of 'cronyist' restrictions – while maintaining good-quality, comprehensive public services.

Outside the EU, the UK must aspire to be one of the best-performing Western economies – a nation that succeeds on the global stage in both economic and diplomatic terms. To do that Britain must position itself for the future, while addressing immediate domestic challenges, such as low wages, sluggish investment and weak productivity. Following the release of the August 2017 Inflation Report, Governor Mark Carney acknowledged that the Bank of England had continuously been reducing their view of the economy's potential growth rate since before the financial crisis, from around 2.4 per cent to just under 1.75 per cent.[2]

The UK also has a triple problem of a large current account deficit, a still-high budget deficit and economic recoveries that are often associated with rising household debt. All these challenges pre-date Brexit and have not been solved by our membership of the EU. Yet, despite these problems, there is reason to think the UK is already among Europe's most adaptable and agile economies, well suited to economic change.

In 2005, the OECD identified a list of five key responses for an economy to cope well with change and shocks – macroeconomic policies; labour market policies; regulatory framework; institutional and governance structure; and liberal trade and investment policies. Brexit leaves the UK far better able to cope with all of these. And in 2016, the ECB already judged the UK to be among the EU's most flexible economies, based on the quality of our institutions and the efficiency of the UK's labour and product markets.[3]

In the wake of the global financial crisis, while there have been a host of policies designed to make the financial sector more resilient, in terms of the overall economy much still needs to be done.

The main focus of the UK's post-Brexit economic policy should be the promotion of stability and the creation of an 'enabling environment' for strong, sustainable economic growth. Policy needs to be focused on ensuring there is sufficient demand in the economy, as well as learning from the past, where supply-side reform, highlighted by labour mobility and low income taxes, had a positive impact.

After Brexit, we need to look for quick wins, while taking measures aimed at the longer term too. The quick wins include liberal trade and investment policies and steps to unblock domestic finance, ensuring SMEs in particular have greater access to capital. The long-term measures must have at their heart the enhancement of 'human capital' – skills and education – and enhanced investment in 'physical capital' too.

Competition and innovation are key factors that we need to get right if the UK is to benefit from the fourth industrial revolution. We need to encourage both. While keen on post-Brexit regional policy, we also believe that the wider UK has much to learn from London. The capital is outward-looking and open to innovation, while benefiting from labour mobility and the strength of its service sector. A recent London success story has been the capital's new technology cluster, which has blossomed into a hub that, on some measures, can challenge Silicon Valley. This growth in technology was not a direct consequence of government policy, reflecting instead a combination of factors including low costs and the magnetic pull of London. With a sensible migration policy, the capital's ability to attract skilled people should not suffer. And with a sensible housing policy, the cost of living across London and the south-east need not be prohibitive. We address these concerns in future chapters.

Creating the right environment for clusters to develop depends on ensuring SMEs can grow. For these, particularly those focused on the domestic market, it is important to ease the regulatory burden and keep taxes low. During the referendum campaign, neither author based the case for leaving the EU on lower regulation. That being said, there is a potential regulatory benefit outside the single market, as we have discussed. Exporting firms, though, do need to adhere to global regulatory standards, so policymakers must tread carefully.

Outside the EU, the UK government has greater policy leeway. Some policies may be partly interventionist but, in most instances, what is important is getting the incentives right so that the market works properly. The main point is that decisions will be made by the UK electorate and the government they choose – not based on trade-offs between twenty-eight countries or the outcome of lobbying in the corridors of Brussels. Alongside this, the UK must play to its strengths, across its service and creative sectors and other successful areas of the economy – from high-end manufacturing to universities and health care; from professional and financial services to pharmaceuticals and biomedical sciences; from technology, including fintech, to tourism, culture and the arts.

The British economy is now overwhelmingly a services-based economy. Knowledge-intensive services account for around 30 per cent of our gross value added (GVA), with financial services alone accounting for 9 per cent. Other services make up 47 per cent of GDP.[4] Having said that, despite declining since the 1970s, when manufacturing contributed 25 per cent of GDP, the UK remains the ninth largest manufacturing nation in the world. Manufacturing accounts for almost 10 per cent of GDP and 45 per cent of all exports, employing 2.7 million people and driving 68 per cent of business research and development spending. The UK needs to excel and raise its ambitions across manufacturing as well as services – an effort underpinned by technology and innovation. This means being at the forefront of the fourth industrial revolution, mentioned in the previous chapter.

Above all, we need to be positive, as well as realistic, about what we can achieve. Too often it has seemed that the UK needs a long-term strategic vision. One approach would be for Britain to identify where it wants to be in a decade, then for it to determine what this would mean for policy now; we do not want, for instance, to concede to maintaining EU rules on state aid that might constrain us. Setting out a credible and upbeat vision is important to help businesses and investors see beyond the near-term uncertainty associated with a minority government and Brexit, as the Article 50 negotiations intensify.

THE THREE 'I'S

The UK government must put investment, innovation and infrastructure at the centre of its economic thinking. Macro-economic policy also needs to ensure that there is effective demand in the economy. That requires effective future coordination between fiscal and monetary policy, including steady monetary growth. We need supply-side reforms that cut taxes on income and ease the burden on SMEs. Britain must upskill its workforce to cope with the digital age. We should also rethink the role of the public sector, moving away from an obsession with size, focusing instead on what the state does well and what delivers what might be called 'taxpayer value for money'.

In many respects this has already begun, as shown by the intense debate about the NHS, social care and the ageing population during the June 2017 general election. Such discussions have a long way to go, though, and must include debate about the future affordability of the UK's long-standing Beveridge approach to welfare.[5] While continuing both to fund and reform public services, the UK needs to conduct a measured and honest exploration of whether welfare access should be based more on contributions – including the role social insurance could play in providing public services, while preserving the principle of 'free at the point of use'.

Then there is the overwhelming need to uphold workers' rights. Some might view leaving the EU as an opportunity to pursue a race to the bottom on labour standards. This is precisely the kind of Brexit that, overwhelmingly, voters do not want. It is not highlighted often enough that by returning sovereignty to Parliament, we empower the UK public to get the policies it chooses. Moreover, as we highlighted in Chapter 7, Britain has a track record on working conditions and labour standards that, in many respects, is more progressive than much of the EU.

Brexit will force us to address domestic issues that, at some stage, must also be tackled by other European economies. There is a fundamental shift in the world economy as we have stressed – not just from West to East, but also in terms of technology. Given these long-term global trends, it makes sense to leave a protectionist, inward-looking trade bloc that too often seems reluctant to adapt and change. Competing with the rest of the world means being competitive both in terms of price and quality. Relying too heavily on price competition risks poor working and living standards and, in many cases, would ultimately be futile in the face of much cheaper overseas labour. Britain must focus instead more on quality, becoming a high-skilled, high-wage, high-productivity economy.

Leaving the EU affords some tremendous opportunities, including returning 'competencies', or decision-making abilities, from Brussels to Westminster across a range of areas. One of the most pro-EU British governments in recent history was the Conservative–Liberal Democrat coalition of 2010–15. This government released more than thirty competency reports that constituted 'the most extensive analysis ever undertaken of the UK's relationship with the EU' in the words of the Foreign Office, drawing on 'nearly 2,300 pieces of written evidence'.[6] While these reports highlighted the need for the EU to reform, now that the UK is leaving the same studies can be used to examine the extent of the powers returning from Brussels to Westminster.[7]

The UK may not have been an original signatory of the 1957 Treaty of Rome, but we obviously accepted its implications when we joined the EEC in 1973.[8] The ceding of competencies from the UK then continued with successive post-1973 treaties introducing the single market, common foreign and security policy, joint employment law and competition and social policy.[9] And while the UK secured opt-outs from the border-free Schengen area, justice and home affairs legislation and monetary union, we still ended up contributing to successive Eurozone bailouts.[10]

The tight-knit and multifaceted nature of this UK–EU legal interaction helps explain why the government has opted to do a one-off Repeal Bill – bringing all EU law into the UK statute book, in a bid to avoid a cliff edge. It still makes sense, though, as discussed in Chapter 6, to smooth the process by negotiating a temporary and possibly sector-specific transition period. This is particularly true in industries where there are long planning horizons and long supply chains. One such industry is the auto sector, which will be discussed in more detail below.

Regardless of the future UK–EU relationship, ahead of the 2017 general election there was considerable focus on industrial policy, with both the Conservative and Labour manifestos emphasising the need for greater government involvement. For several years, such ideas have been under discussion, heralding in the minds of some a move back to the 1960s and 1970s. In those days, industrial policy was about the state picking winners, intervening in certain sectors, attempting industrial consolidation and promoting certain technologies.

As the UK attempts to position itself for the digital age and the growing impact of robotics, we should recall that discussions about appropriate government action under such circumstances are not new. Back in 1963, Harold Wilson, in his famous 'white heat of technology' speech, talked about the state helping to boost scientific progress, while preparing society for dramatic changes that would stem from automation and computerisation.[11]

Today, technology is driving the UK in a new direction, as in the early 1960s. There are positive aspects to many different approaches, and much of what Wilson outlined over half a century ago seems prescient today. 'Britain's future,' as Wilson said, 'depends to a unique extent on the speed with which we come to terms with the world of change' – presaging similar contemporary concerns about the impact of digital technologies and robotics on living standards and jobs. While Wilson's statist solutions were not always effective, being very much a product of their time, he was surely right to warn that the UK's response to looming seismic change could not be left solely to the private sector.

The idea of the state explicitly picking winners was unsuccessful in Wilson's time. It makes even less sense in today's age of globalisation. The UK's shift away from such policies during the 1980s, towards competition and more liberalised markets, certainly encouraged foreign investment and ultimately boosted growth. Yet the state clearly has a role to play as we face this fourth industrial revolution – in bridging the skills gap, in encouraging the uptake of science and technological subjects in schools and universities, in backing certain forms of research and helping incentivise our brightest minds towards careers in engineering, technology and other scientific pursuits.

Since Theresa May became Prime Minister following the June 2016 EU referendum, she has emphasised the need for 'a UK industrial strategy'. Given the mixed track record of such policies, this shift has been met with some scepticism. Yet the initial signs appear positive – with an emphasis on addressing the UK's regional divide and productivity gap, while boosting transport, broadband connectivity and helping to ensure cheaper energy.

During the election campaign there were a range of suggestions. Some, like the Conservative's manifesto pledge of an energy price cap, were too intrusive.

Others, such as free ports, made total sense. An Industrial Strategy Challenge Fund that earmarks state funding for certain types of research and development also sounds promising. Six areas have been outlined, including healthcare and medicine; robotics and artificial intelligence; batteries for clean energy and flexible energy storage; autonomous cars; manufacturing and materials for the future such as supporting civil aerospace to develop the next generation of affordable lightweight composite materials; as well as satellites and space technology.

We should also take note of successful polices from elsewhere. Professor Robert Wade of the London School of Economics has pointed out how the US has 'encouraged state level agencies to foster domestic high-end innovation and production'.[12] Instead of contracting large firms who may then subcontract to more innovative smaller firms, state agencies – including the military – have in Wades's words 'created venture capital funds' to invest directly in the small firms themselves. This has boosted the economy's innovation stream, 'creating a form of state venture capitalism' that has worked. Such ideas could help ensure sufficient capital finds its way to the very best SMEs – something that is often lacking in the UK. While private capital provision is generally preferable, this US approach merits attention – as a modern-day version of 'picking winners'. While today's digital revolution in no way warrants a 1960s top-down approach, something more than laissez-faire is needed. As is often the case, good policy is about getting the balance right. The government needs to create the right business environment, along with infrastructure that boosts productivity, while promoting competition and further investment. This should be market-friendly and not be confused with heavy-handed intervention.

SECTOR SPECIFICS

Industry leaders have given Brexit-related advice to the government, both publicly and in private, ahead of the Article 50 process. The businesses that get their message widely heard tend to be the large ones – or those doing well. Such companies are often in favour of the status quo, meaning ongoing membership of the single market and the customs union, going against a Clean Brexit.

Having determined to leave both the single market and the customs union, though, there are certain key sectors the UK government must consider particularly carefully during these Brexit negotiations. Below, we consider three in turn.

THE AUTO SECTOR

When declaring her desire to see a 'bold and ambitious' UK–EU trade agreement in her March 2017 Article 50 letter, Theresa May said that any such deal 'should cover sectors crucial to our linked economies such as financial services and network industries'.[13] In terms of the UK's network industries, the automotive sector is the most important. Employing over 800,000 people, some 170,000 in manufacturing roles, the automotive industry is a key aspect of how Brexit will impact British industry.

The UK is headquarters for seven main car manufacturers, eight premium manufacturers, seven Formula One teams, six design studios, thirteen research and development centres and over 100 specialist brands. The UK currently produces 1.8 million vehicles annually, below the peak of 1.9 million reached in 1972 but still representing a steady rise in recent years. Britain has a sizeable domestic car market, which attracts considerable imports, not least from Germany. The UK has also proved a good base from which to export elsewhere, particularly to the EU. Around two thirds of vehicles produced in the UK are exported and, of those, over half are EU-bound.

After agriculture, the auto industry is the most protected sector within the EU. The tariff wall around the customs union places a 9.6 per cent tariff on cars exported from non-EU countries. Auto parts attract a lower tariff, with the Society of Motor Manufacturers and Traders citing 2.5 per cent to 4.5 per cent.[14] Many in the industry would like to retain the present set-up, with the UK enjoying frictionless trade with the EU and the auto sector cushioned behind a tariff wall.

Outside the customs union, we calculate that the likely total tariff the auto sector would pay on exports to the EU is about £1.9 billion, based on 2015's full-year motor vehicle exports of £25.6 billion.[15] Although there are exports and imports as part of the supply chain, and hence parts may flow back and forth, the tariff is not paid twice on the same component or other car parts.

Though the case for a post-Brexit auto sector trade agreement is strong, given the two-way flow of car exports between the UK and EU – and the extent to which EU-based companies are themselves owners of UK car plants – this could result in much lower, or even zero tariffs. One possibility to explore would be a special FTA in which, across all industries, the UK keeps the same external tariffs as now (the EU's Common External Tariff), with 'rules of origin' not being an issue. Such a deal makes sense for the auto sector as both the UK and EU want to keep value chains going and, considering all components, the EU still runs an auto sector surplus with the UK.[16]

Those sceptical about the prospects for an auto trade deal should remember the UK is a key market for the EU – not least for Germany, as outlined in Chapter 5. A report authored by Deloitte in June 2017 said Germany's auto sector faces significant downsides if the exit negotiations fail to produce a trade agreement, with 18,000 jobs being at risk during the first year.[17]

If we left the EU with no FTA, UK car exports to the EU would face a 9.6 per cent tariff. While this could be considered a manageable expense for those facing it, the industry cites tight margins. Tariffs could be set against the gain from sterling's devaluation, but there is a difference between a continuous cost in the form of a tariff and an exchange rate gain that could be reversed. The auto sector tariff cost could be covered, to a degree, by some of the UK's current EU contribution, if the government so wished.

It is the UK's potential use of import tariffs, though, that gives Britain an added degree of bargaining power during any negotiation. Tariffs are effectively a tax. Whenever an EU politician threatens tariffs, the UK media's response is often that we should hit them with tariffs too, without acknowledging that UK consumers pay tariffs imposed on imports. An imported car is made less attractive because of the additional 9.6 per cent tariff the consumer must pay.

Imagine if we left the EU without a deal, and decided to keep tariffs at 9.6 per cent. Outside the EU we would be trading under the WTO's 'most favoured nation' rules, so 9.6 per cent would apply to all imports – unless we have agreed a trade deal with a particular non-EU country. This would immediately add to the retail price for cars imported from the EU – although the exact increase would depend on the extent to which a particular auto producer decided to alter its margins.

So EU cars would be on the same tariff as those imported from the rest of the world. To UK buyers, German vehicles, for instance, would therefore be less attractive than before, while the price of American cars would be the same. But, if there was no deal and the UK decided to cut car import tariffs to zero, regardless of the fact that the EU was charging us a 9.6 per cent tariff, what would happen?

At first, this might seem like a strange strategy, until you consider that zero tariffs benefit UK consumers. Under WTO rules, zero tariffs must apply to all future car imports into the UK, regardless of where they come from. Suddenly cars we are importing from the rest of the world would be 9.6 per cent more competitive than they are now, whereas imports from Germany and the rest of the EU would be the same. The gainers would be UK consumers and automobile manufacturers selling to Britain from outside the EU.

It is this fear of their prices becoming relatively less attractive and losing a share of the big UK market that most worries EU car exporters, and augurs well for a post-Brexit auto sector UK–EU trade deal. At the same time, of course, the UK needs to ensure it remains an attractive location from where to build and export cars. We would not advocate a policy of unilateral free trade (UFT) in general, as we explained in Chapter 6. If we trade with the EU under WTO rules, maintaining tariffs on UK imports will give us bargaining power to negotiate lower EU tariffs in the future. There are certainly some sectors, though, such as autos, where both domestic production and domestic demand are strong enough that a zero-tariff strategy may be warranted from the outset, or soon after we leave the EU.

AGRICULTURE

One of the most exciting, but potentially problematic, sectors where Brexit will have an impact is agriculture. While accounting for less than 1 per cent of UK GDP, agriculture is symbolically important, not only due to the precious nature of food, but also the role farmers play in maintaining our 'green and pleasant land'. While Blake's 'Jerusalem' was England, the same aesthetic applies, if not more so, to the devolved regions of Scotland, Northern Ireland and Wales. While the UK as a whole is a net contributor to the EU, when it comes to CAP payments to farmers, Scotland, Wales and Northern Ireland all receive more than double the figure for England in per capita terms.[18]

With the EU, large tariffs on agricultural imports from outside the customs union are combined with payments via the CAP – which accounts for almost 40 per cent of annual EU spending. Pillar 1 payments are based on the amount of land held by each farmer, while Pillar 2 subsidies are linked to rural development. As such, the largest UK landowners receive huge CAP payments, with millions of pounds of taxpayers' money going to British aristocrats, Arab princes, large agribusinesses and offshore landholding trusts.

Meanwhile owners of smaller farms, many of them struggling to survive, are granted far lower subsidies. The UK's top 100 CAP recipients received £49.9 million in 2016, more than was paid out to the bottom 35,000 farmers combined.[19] Overall, Pillar 1 payments account for around 56 per cent of farmers' income, with Pillar 2 allocations providing another 16 per cent.[20] In 2015, UK farmers received almost £2.4 billion in direct payments, according to the National Farmers' Union (NFU).

These figures highlight the dependency of many UK farmers on such subsidies.[21] Yet the evidence suggests that a majority of farmers voted for Brexit, despite the NFU campaigning for Remain.[22] It seems that many farmers want to be rid of overly bureaucratic EU rules, with the UK government better able to target financial help to farmers who need it most, via a simpler, more direct payments system. Brexit will also allow the government to regain power to establish regulation in areas such as plant and animal health and GM foods.

Soon after the Brexit vote, ministers pledged to continue the subsidies UK farmers receive under the CAP until 2020.[23] That promise was extended to 2022 in the May 2017 Conservative election manifesto.[24] The long-term vision, though, should be a British farming sector dependent on neither subsidies nor protection. If the City, which can adjust quickly, is arguing for a transition period, there are far stronger grounds for agriculture, with many farmers extremely vulnerable to dramatic change. The Landworkers' Alliance points out that between 2005 and 2015, nine farms were 'lost' each day, suffering from low or non-existent margins.[25] But, overall, the subsidies inherent in the CAP system reduce competition, deter farmers from making the best use of their land and support inefficient farming. Cutting subsidies, in a phased and gradual way, could be a positive catalyst.

New Zealand took a radical approach to reforming agriculture in the mid-1980s, cutting subsidies overnight. The long-term impact on farming has been positive, but there was a considerable initial shock.[26] Some UK farming sub-sectors, such as upland livestock, are clearly much more dependent upon subsidies than others. If UK farm subsidies are maintained for a limited transition period, it makes sense to cap them, as the present approach favours big farms, big business and large landowners.

For environment and conservation purposes, rural development, as captured under Pillar 2 payments, is important. With cities accounting for an ever-increasing share of economic growth, while housing a larger proportion of the population, Brexit provides an opportunity to radically rethink the environmental and tourism opportunities across the countryside, developing a long-term strategy to boost the rural economy and village life.

Many farmers and other agricultural specialists accept that, with suitable transition payments, Brexit offers the best opportunity in a generation to replace the CAP with a progressive British agricultural policy that will allow farmers to succeed while the sector as a whole produces more and better-quality food. Any change from the status quo will be painful for those who benefit from it, but is necessary to improve competitiveness and productivity. We believe that capped, time-limited transition payments should be used to encourage a move towards a 'whole farm management' system. State payments would then be targeted towards the provision of environmental, social and economic public goods – such as land management practices that would improve water and air quality, or reduce flood risk, and enhancing the natural environment – rather than at food produced for commercial consumption.

Tariffs are the other big issue. And, like subsidies, a careful approach is needed. Over many decades, global trade negotiations have repeatedly failed because advanced economies – led by the EU, US and Japan – have protected domestic farmers by refusing to allow developing economies freely to export food products where they have a comparative advantage. CAP subsidies and high EU tariffs also protect inefficient European farmers from more efficient counterparts in countries like Australia and New Zealand. This results in a large bill for UK taxpayers and higher prices in the shops for UK consumers.

Within the EU, protectionism has driven food prices above world prices. Outside the customs union, prices could fall significantly if Britain decides to cut existing tariffs on agricultural imports. Some estimates suggest UK food prices are about 17 per cent higher than they would be due to the CAP and the EU's Common External Tariff as huge expense is added onto consumers who wish to buy products from outside the bloc.[27] Leaving the EU gives Britain the opportunity to reduce food prices to the benefit of all consumers, especially those on lower incomes who spend a higher share of their wages on food.

After Brexit, the UK's agricultural exports to the EU would potentially face a high tariff wall, with estimates 'ranging between 18 per cent and 28 per cent'.[28] When it comes to negotiating a deal over agriculture, we believe that the UK's £16.7 billion annual deficit in food and drink with the EU means we have a strong hand to play.[29] With over 70 per cent of our agricultural imports sourced from the EU, the UK is in a good position to negotiate an FTA that includes agriculture. The EU has much to lose if Britain's food trade with Europe moves away from the current existing regime.

Given that the EU is already so protectionist, it is unlikely the UK would want to raise import tariffs further on food – not least as that would increase consumer prices. There is a strong case, in fact, to eradicate import tariffs completely. 'The UK should unilaterally phase out tariffs,' recommends the economist Warwick Lightfoot, in a post-Brexit study on farming.[30] Certainly, farm import tariffs makes food more expensive and complicate new trade deals for the UK.[31]

Again, we would recommend a gradual approach, with tariffs being reduced alongside temporary support for farmers exposed to global competition.[31] The UK should, though, remove tariffs on agricultural sub-sectors where there is no domestic production – given that such measures were introduced to protect farmers elsewhere in the EU. The aim should be eventually to cut tariffs on all food imports – putting the consumer first. And cutting tariffs is separate from altering standards on food quality, whether at home or from overseas.

FISHERIES

The UK fishing industry is currently small. Made up of around only 6,000 vessels, the UK fishing fleet landed 708,000 tonnes of fish in 2015, worth around £775 million. Fishing was once a large employer, though, and the decline of fishing communities since the early 1970s has generated much antipathy towards the EU in certain parts of the UK. Before we joined the EEC, Britain had the largest living marine resource of all member states. In the hours before 1 January 1973, when the UK assumed membership along with Denmark and Ireland, the six pre-existing EEC members created Fisheries Regulation 2140/70, the effect of which was to allow access for all members to UK waters.

The then Prime Minister Edward Heath obtained a transitional derogation, that has to be unanimously agreed every ten years by the EU, allowing UK fishermen exclusive fishing rights up to six miles from shore and partial rights between six to twelve miles. Subsequently, international law established a 200-mile fisheries zone worldwide in 1994. That meant UK waters could be fished by all EU countries, and effectively have been, using a quota system. There is a vivid description by the campaigning author John Ashworth of how the town of Peterhead in Aberdeenshire, once a premier fishing port, is now largely run-down. While there are 'hardly any Scottish vessels', says Ashworth, the town is deepening its ports 'to accommodate Spanish and French vessels using it as a transit point'.[32]

Fishing, along with many other areas of our economy, illustrates the need to replace poorly designed EU policies with a better, domestically oriented legal framework. The EU's Common Fisheries Policy (CFP) that currently oversees fishing is a bloated bureaucratic mess that has taken decades to reform in the face of withering criticism from both the UK fishing industry and environmentalists concerned about over-fishing.[33]

As with many post-Brexit policies, the government and Parliament need to be clear about what they want and then consider the best way to proceed. The UK will be able to regain control over its own territorial waters – provided we do not for any reason give this away during the Article 50 negotiations. Many EU 27 nations, not least Spain, which possesses one of the world's largest fishing fleets, will be keen for the EU to retain access. It is arguable that current Spanish overtures towards the sovereignty of Gibraltar are a possible future bargaining chip to retain access to UK fishing waters.[34]

While allowing EU fleets access to UK fishing grounds, the present system is run by bureaucrats and is unresponsive to changing sea temperatures and the movement of fish. Marine life, as Ashworth informs us, is 'fast, furious and cruel'.[35] The food chain is critical and the CFP is not suitable. 'When you have a rigid system like the CFP, you might go several years in your area catching species for which you have a quota and then, suddenly, they disappear and in comes a species for which you have little or no quota. What do you do? Answer: you have to cheat to survive.'[36]

There are different routes the UK could take. One suggestion is to differentiate between the inshore industry that operates out to twelve miles, and an offshore industry operating from twelve to 200 miles. Another approach is to look at best practice elsewhere, such as the system operated by the Faroe Islands, where licences are allocated based on a number of 'days at sea' system. The tiny Faroe Islands have no problem deciding what is best for their fishing industry and determining who may fish in their waters. Having their own system also gives them the scope and flexibility to negotiate reciprocal fisheries agreements with their neighbours. The Queen's Speech of June 2017 made provision for post-Brexit fisheries legislation. It is vital the options are debated in Parliament, restoring the loss of faith in British democracy understandably felt by fishing communities the length and breadth of the UK, while recognising the opportunity afforded by regaining control over our fishing policy. In July, the government announced the triggering of a two-year leaving period relating to the London Fisheries Convention (LFC) – a reciprocal fishing agreement signed in the 1960s, before we were members of the EEC.[37] While separate from EU legislation, and covering different waters, withdrawing from the LFC is an important symbolic step, ahead of Article 50 negotiations, towards reclaiming the UK's sovereign fishing rights.

The benefits to the UK of effective post-Brexit fishing policies are potentially substantial and wide-ranging. Fishing ports could be revitalised, as small family-run fleets are once again able to thrive. A new approach also allows a wider group of stakeholders to be considered, as government money saved from administering the CFP is spent instead on British fishing. There needs to be a strong social and environmental dimension that reinforces the economic benefits. A British Fishing Policy should aim to reinvigorate both the commercial and recreational side of the industry, with the abolition of the quota system helping us move, in UK waters at least, from overfishing to sustainable fishing.

One of the surest ways to help coastal villages and towns to recover is to adopt an approach that benefits small businesses, not least fishing. That in turn will boost local spending and encourage people to stay and raise families, thus rebuilding what were once economically and cultural vibrant local communities. In time, tourists will be attracted to such towns. As some of the most deprived rural areas are adjacent to the coastline, they should benefit too.

REGULATION AND PRODUCTIVITY

Businesses often complain about the regulatory burden, but when it comes to individual pieces of regulation it can be difficult to determine which should go.

In isolation, individual regulations may make sense. The problem often seems to be the overall scale, and the scale of EU-derived regulations is vast.

In March 2015, the Open Europe think tank produced a detailed report examining 'the 100 most burdensome EU regulations'.[38] It found that 95 per cent of the benefits of such regulations, as identified by a prior independent assessment exercise conducted by HM Treasury, 'failed to materialise' in practice. In addition, these regulations imposed net compliance costs estimated at over £33 billion. Open Europe identified the most costly as the renewable energy strategy, the capital requirements directive, the EU climate and energy package, as well as the temporary agency workers directive. Within specific sectors, the UK insurance sector found the cost of Solvency II directive prohibitive – as will be discussed in Chapter 9 – while in the chemicals industry, the EU's REACH regulatory program attracted stern criticism, even though it deals with safety as well as single market access.

In a globalised world economy, there is a pressing need to compete. It must make sense that the UK is able to set its own regulations which, while compliant with standards that are increasingly set globally, allow our companies to compete as effectively as possible. And it is surely right that the vast majority of UK firms that do not export should not, as they do now, have to absorb the trouble and cost of complying with all the regulations relating to membership of the single market.

While encouraging more spending on innovation, investment and infrastructure, the government needs to set the right economic incentives by creating an enabling environment in which firms can grow, helped by low taxes for small firms. As well as sensible regulation, this also requires a suitable macroeconomic policy. There is an argument for the government to take advantage of unusually low long-term interest rates to raise finance for infrastructure projects that generate revenue streams and future growth.

The list could include a new national airport (outside the south-east) and national toll roads, as well as the improved rail links (including HS3, connecting our great northern cities, so that together they form an alternative growth centre to London). For many years, UK infrastructure has generally taken much longer to build, and at higher cost, than in comparable nations such as France and Japan. That assumption, and the procurement culture that seems to drive it, must change.

Building better infrastructure in strategic locations should be seen as the key component of the UK's post-Brexit regional policy, as improved transport connects economic clusters and cities, encouraging new investment in businesses and housing. Once the UK is rid of an antagonistic European state aid regime, it should be easier to plan and approve the enhanced infrastructure spending we need. Digital connectivity, too, must be improved, in part by directly confronting the quasi-monopoly position of British Telecom.

The UK has, traditionally, been a low-investment economy. The short-termism of British firms is often cited. The difficulty of raising long-term finance – particularly for SMEs – is a significant problem. While helping SMEs grow into major, world-beating companies, we also need more emphasis on commercialising the ideas that come out of UK universities. This combination, in particular, will help push the UK to the forefront of the technology revolution.

More innovation, investment and infrastructure will help raise UK productivity, bridging the gap that has emerged between Britain and other leading economies in North America and Western Europe. While the UK has recovered since the global financial crisis, productivity has remained low. Given how many jobs have been created, this may not be as big a puzzle as some have suggested – seeing as countries with apparently higher productivity, like France, often have much higher unemployment. Low UK productivity may also be partly explained by firms holding onto staff in the hope of demand increasing in the future, along with the misallocation of capital based on ultra-low interest rates and the reluctance of banks to pull the plug on 'zombie' firms. But the deep-rooted nature of low UK productivity clearly means the supply side of the British economy needs to improve – with an emphasis on skills and infrastructure provision above everything else.

Governments can't micromanage economies. The emergence of east London as a global tech hub had little to do with direct government policy.[39] Again, instead of attempting to pick winners, the government should create the enabling environment that allows such clusters to develop. This requires a policy focus on low taxes, good infrastructure, great digital connectivity, a skilled workforce and trade deals that provide access to growth markets. An enabling environment also means access to adequate and affordable housing – an issue we cover in Chapter 11.

TAX AND SPEND

A final part of the overall industrial and economic policy relates to fiscal policy and tax. For many years, it has been hard for the UK's tax take to rise much above 38 per cent of GDP. Yet public spending is way above this, hovering around 44 per cent, which raises serious problems – including a spiralling national debt. It is only when the annual deficit between spending and taxation is eliminated, and the budget records an annual surplus, that the UK can start to reduce its national debt.

The message gleaned by some from the June 2017 general election was that the public is tired of austerity. But given that the UK must broadly live within its means, how then do we deliver better public services? Part of the answer, of course, is economic growth, which creates the wealth needed to pay for the public sector, while making debt more manageable. The message from the election, though, at least from Labour voters, was that we need higher levels of taxation. This raises the inherent difficulty of increasing the tax take, not least in the context of a globalising economy where it is not always easy to tax highly skilled and mobile workers and multinational companies. It may be that the government needs to explore effective ways of capping government spending, in line with the tax take – if this can be done without undermining activist fiscal policy when needed.

Although taxation is seen as a national competency within the EU, there have been some areas where membership has had an impact – including constraints on VAT and the extent to which multinational companies (MNCs) use the EU to avoid paying tax.[40] Outside the EU, we certainly have the scope to alter VAT rates, whether for cyclical purposes or more specific reasons. In terms of MNCs, globalisation has provided opportunities for firms to practice tax avoidance – across the EU and beyond. Yet it is not always appreciated that Britain's membership of the single market has contributed to this problem, limiting our room for manoeuvre.

According to fascinating research from Global Britain, MNCs have been taking advantage of, or legally abusing, the EU's 'freedom of establishment'.[41] This is the corporate version of the freedom of movement of people and is a vital component of the single market. Smaller EU nations also use aggressive tax policies to attract MNCs, hosting European headquarters of such companies,

creating local graduate jobs, payroll taxes and local spending. The MNCs, meanwhile, benefit from the tax advantages – whether it be accelerated depreciation
schedules, low corporation tax, specific local tax regimes or even favourable
asymmetric treatment of revenues that can be derived from specific costs. The
biggest culprits in this regard are Ireland, Luxembourg and, to a lesser extent,
the Netherlands.

The MNCs then exploit their freedom of establishment to trade within the
single market out of these companies incorporated within the EU state with favourable tax regimes. Various business models are adopted – such as having a UK
salesforce on behalf of a sister company in Ireland – be it in sectors ranging from
coffee to fast food to information technology. The UK Exchequer suffers, it is
argued that as our ability to address this tax loss is constrained by our EU membership. The sums involved are huge, with some £10 billion of taxes lost annually. We
could also lose an equivalent amount in spending by these firms if, in seeking to
access the UK market, they were incorporated onshore. Instead, some MNCs steer
their UK-derived income away from HMRC, equating it to tax-deductible costs
of a separate company, so minimal tax is paid. While entirely legal, this amounts to
aggressive tax avoidance facilitated by UK single market membership.

It is vital the UK recognises this phenomenon and does not allow it to continue as a result of the Article 50 negotiations. Admittedly, offshore taxes of
MNCs are a concern in the US, too, although there the issue is about reducing
tax rates to encourage firms to repatriate income. If the UK government can
address this issue once outside single market membership, the result could be
more higher-value jobs and higher payroll taxes, as well as more money spent by
the relevant MNCs and employees in the UK. It could also mean higher indirect
taxes and a fairer share of the corporate taxes that MNCs should be paying to
access UK consumers.

When it comes to assessing the UK's post-Brexit economy, two key phras-
es help describe the current challenge facing politicians and economic policy
makers. These are 'hypernormalisation' and 'policy normalisation'. How they are
resolved will have a big impact on economies and markets in the years ahead.
Hypernormalisation is the acceptance of the current situation even though we
know it could and should be better. Originally applied to the demise of the
Soviet Union, it is now a relevant concept when analysing Western economies.[42]

In the UK and elsewhere, there is a widespread assumption that growth will be modest and wages will, for most people, remain relatively low. In some respects, this realisation and the visceral response provoked by it have fuelled Donald Trump's ascent to the White House as well as gains by populist parties in recent elections across Europe – including the unexpected advance of Jeremy Corbyn's Labour Party in the UK.

As society lives with hypernormalisation, the related concept of policy normalisation threatens to be a constraint on our ambitions. The markets and international investors assume the hands of politicians are tied. In the UK, for instance, the budget deficit persists, and nine years after the banking crisis the national debt continues to rise. The market view is that there is not much room for fiscal manoeuvre: it is only if you are in a cash-strapped situation that you borrow to pay your current bills. But most people understand and would accept the good sense of borrowing to invest. If we are to avoid a slowdown now, while positioning the UK for the opportunities presented by Brexit, we should use fiscal policy more proactively. The fact that the UK ill-advisedly ran budget deficits in years of strong growth does not mean we should necessarily cut spending in a downturn.

Higher growth in nominal GDP helps reduce the annual deficit, along with the overall stock of debt, provided bond yields and related borrowing costs stay low. For the latter, markets must not lose faith in the long-term budgetary outlook. The UK's debt-to-GDP levels have spiralled from 35 per cent just before the global financial crisis to a peacetime record of almost 90 per cent. After the Second World War, this ratio was 240 per cent but then fell sharply – during a period of high nominal GDP growth but also growth-friendly demography.

In the 2009 Budget, a year after the banking crisis, UK government spending was £671 billion. In the 2017/18 Spring Budget, the same figure was £802 billion. During that period, welfare spending rose from £189 billion to £245 billion, health from £119 billion to £149 billion and education from £88 billion to £102 billion. Some smaller departments that were not ring-fenced, though, endured absolute spending cuts.[43] This, along with sluggish public-sector wage growth, has created an aura of austerity, even though, over the last decade, the national debt has ballooned – from £557 billion in 2007/08 to £1,726 billion in 2016/17.

The UK needs to debate radical fiscal change. Many people want

Scandinavian-style public services. But this would require a significantly higher tax take, which could see growth and business investment suffer. If Britain can continue to grow, and the public finances strengthen, then creative ways need to be sought to finance long-term investment, not least infrastructure bonds. These can divert the UK's very substantial pension and life industry savings away from low-yielding gilts and towards more productive use.

Equally, 'policy normalisation' affects central banking too. UK interest rates have remained at ultra-low levels for almost a decade. Extremely loose monetary policy, combined with QE, has propped up equity markets and kept gilt yields low. But it has warped returns on regular financial instruments and hammered ordinary savers, while fuelling asset inequality. The economist William White, formerly of the Basel-based Bank for International Settlements and now at the OECD, suggests that the problem isn't that rates fell sharply in difficult times, but that they did not rise enough following an emergency situation.[44] 'Disinflationary pressures ought not to have been interpreted as indicating the need for ever increasing domestic credit expansion,' says White. Just because inflation was quite low, it does not mean monetary policy needs to remain loose. While the US Federal Reserve has begun raising rates, the Bank of England has not yet followed suit.

One option, if current global reflation continues, is that leading Western central banks – the Fed, the ECB, the Bank of England and the Bank of Japan – embark upon a series of coordinated rate rises to signal a degree of policy normalisation. Such joint action would draw a line in the sand, demonstrating that emergency conditions are over, while also removing concerns about the loss of currency competitiveness associated with unilateral rate increases.

If we are to address hypernormalisation while accepting policy normalisation, then we require courageous leadership. We need infrastructure spending – while also enabling the private sector to generate the innovation, investment and growth that will drive the economy forward outside the EU.

Caution is necessary, of course; if rate rises happen too quickly then financial markets could panic. But as the Bank for International Settlements said in its latest annual report: 'Keeping interest rates too low for long could raise financial stability and macroeconomic risks further down the road, as debt continues to pile up and risk-taking in financial markets gathers steam.'[45]

Caution is also needed on the fiscal side. If the UK is to explore the use of a more activist fiscal policy then extreme care must be taken to ensure that borrowing is channelled into growth-enhancing projects, with an identifiable revenue stream, rather than current spending. If not, Britain's still-fragile public finances could unnerve financial markets, causing a hike in market interest rates or an inflation spike courtesy of a sharp dip in sterling. This risks triggering a decline in business confidence that could seriously undermine the post-Brexit investment climate.

It really is 'the economy, stupid' that determines the broader well-being of a nation, and the success or otherwise of any incumbent government, as James Carville so memorably pointed out in 1991. But Carville, a senior advisor to Bill Clinton, also made another, less well-known contribution to the political lexicon. 'I used to think if there was reincarnation, I'd come back as the President or the Pope,' Carville quipped. 'But now I want to come back as the bond market. You can intimidate everybody.'[46]

Carville's observation remains relevant today. If the UK takes too many fiscal liberties and coherent fiscal activism turns into renewed profligacy – the cultivation of a cross-party magic money tree – then the bond markets will punish UK gilts and in turn the pound.

CHAPTER 9

WHY THE CITY WILL THRIVE

*'It is a disadvantage of "the long run" that in the long run we are all dead. But I
could have said equally well that it is a great advantage of "the short run" that in
the short run we are all alive. Life and history are made up of short runs.'*
JOHN MAYNARD KEYNES[1]

In the wake of the 2008 global financial crisis, the City of London, and the
UK's financial services industry more broadly, were widely viewed with disdain by the European Commission and various EU governments. Anglo-Saxon
capitalism was seen as a source of instability and problems, as something to be
controlled, not encouraged. How times change.

Now, the City is eyed with envy from the Continent. It provides many of the
things that the EU would like – not least access to capital, well-paid jobs and a
source of future income, growth and tax. Brexit is seen by the likes of Frankfurt
and Paris as an opportunity to take business from London and to reshape the
future for European financial markets.

The financial services industry employs just over 1 million people in the UK,
including some 421,000 in banking, 315,000 in insurance and 41,000 in fund
management.[2] The professional services sector, with which finance has many
ties, employs another 1.2 million – with 477,000 in management consultancy,
382,000 in accountancy and 311,000 in legal services.

As such, around 2.2 million work in the UK's financial services industry.
London has 751,000 such employees, Birmingham and Edinburgh have 49,800
each, Manchester 45,500 and Leeds 37,000. Many of these may be working in
areas and on projects related to the UK economy, while some clusters of finance
industry workers, such as the 11,560 employees in Bournemouth, run so-called
back-office facilities, often supporting the financial activities of international

firms. But London and Edinburgh remain the only two UK financial services centres with truly global reach.

Finance is a vital part of the British economy. It accounts for 10.7 per cent of the UK economy's GVA, employs 7.3 per cent of the working population and generates 11.5 per cent of the country's tax receipts. Yet it is the international, rather than the domestic, side of our financial services industry that we think of as 'the City' – with its state-of-the-art skyscrapers, largely concentrated in the Square Mile around the Bank of England, and also nowadays in sprawling Canary Wharf, servicing companies and clients across the globe. There is little doubt that the City is world-class: London accounts for 16 per cent of cross-border lending, 23 per cent of insurance premium incomes and 37 per cent of global foreign exchange transactions worldwide. Also, the UK is the leading exporter of financial services across the world, with a larger finance sector trade surplus than those of the next four leading countries (USA, Switzerland, Luxembourg and Singapore) combined. These are impressive figures. It is a high-tech, creative and fast-moving sector. While the City plays to its strengths, it is also extremely good at adapting and changing as the need arises.

Brexit is just one of many issues impacting financial firms in the UK. Others include the high cost of living in London, the risk of overzealous regulation by the UK authorities and the challenges and opportunities arising from robotics and financial technology. When it comes to the future of the City, it is rarely one issue that dominates. Much of the City's appeal, though, is 'Brexit-proof'. Of vital importance are the UK's time zone and the dominance of English as the global language of business, as well as the major role played by English common law and the intoxicating atmosphere of activity and energy that is London in all aspects of life. Furthermore, it will not be easy to replicate London's scale, skills, knowledge and deep-rooted infrastructure, spanning legal, consulting services and technology, all unmatched anywhere else in the EU.

We should not lose sight of domestic financial services, though. Calls for the UK finance industry to do more to help the broader British economy are long-standing and will need to be addressed post Brexit. In 1931, the Committee on Finance and Industry, more popularly known as the Macmillan Committee, examined the role the City played in financing local businesses and, in words that resonate today, concluded that banks needed to play a greater part in aiding small and medium-sized firms. The 'Macmillan Gap' was the name given to the difference between the finance that UK industry needed and the amount banks provided. Twenty-two general elections later, and eighty-six years on, this gap has not yet been closed.[3]

The role of the financial sector is one of the vital issues confronting the UK in a post-Brexit world. In the wake of the 2008 global financial crisis, which saw taxpayers bail out bankers, many feel the UK remains overly dependent on financial services.[4] Also, in the aftermath of that crisis, there seemed to be a lack of leadership in the City. By the 2016 referendum, however, there was little doubt the UK financial services establishment was speaking with a common voice as bodies like the British Bankers Association and TheCityUK pushed the case to remain in the EU.

It was clear, though, that many individuals working in financial services – whether in insurance, asset management or trading activities – were in favour of Brexit. Although their voices were not always heard when the main finance industry lobby groups spoke, key individuals, such as Dame Helena Morrissey, then chief executive of Newton Investment Management, advocated the benefits of leaving the EU.

GLOBAL COMPETITION

Following the June 2017 election, there has been a renewed effort by many senior figures in the City to put forward their viewpoints to the government. Naturally, it makes sense for ministers to consider the City's concerns, which include wanting a transition deal both to help planning and avoid a cliff edge, preserving the 'passporting' regime that helps sell financial services across the EU, safeguarding euro clearing and retaining the ability to hire the best talent from around the world.

Like many others with experience in financial services, the authors believe London will retain its status after Brexit as Europe's leading financial centre. Some businesses might move to stay within the EU but, while it is hard to quantify, such movement is not expected to be drastic. Some people think Brexit will undermine London in the longer term, but this is not a common view or one that we share.

There are only a handful of global financial centres: London and New York are the leading two, followed by Singapore, Hong Kong and Tokyo. Shanghai may join this list at some stage. Europe has no global competitor of the same calibre as London. Instead, there are a number of niche financial centres, such as Zurich, Geneva, Frankfurt, Paris, Dublin and Luxembourg.[5] In the City, Frankfurt is regarded as the strongest possible challenger, but it does not have the critical mass of expertise, nor the attraction and quality of life of a global city like London – ranking just twenty-third in the world. Paris, meanwhile, is not trusted in terms of regulation and labour market regimes – and ranks twenty-ninth. If business was to move from London, though, it is likely to be due to regulatory changes that force some euro clearing businesses, to move – probably to Paris – or because of a loss of passporting, thus denying direct access to the EU market for some UK-based firms.

In terms of passporting, there are many places of possible relocation away from the UK, depending on where any business might already have existing EU operations and where its customers are based. In September 2016, though, Moody's downplayed the extent of such relocation. 'The direct impact of a loss of passporting is likely to be modest,' said the international credit ratings agency. 'The greater impact will be felt through higher costs and diversion of management attention, as the companies concerned restructure, reducing profitability for a time.'[6]

In 1992, the German authorities changed the minimum reserve requirements for repos and other instruments deliberately to force business from London to Frankfurt. Many firms obliged, moving trading desks to Germany. Within a couple of years the same firms were back in London. The reasons included greater liquidity, major counter parties and clients. All these issues matter now, arguably more than before. Likewise, in recent years, some hedge funds have relocated to Switzerland to avoid paying tax but are now back in London – and, hopefully, paying the taxes they owe.

London's major competitor is New York and its future competition is global. Amsterdam was the original global financial centre around the turn of the eighteenth century, when Holland was enjoying its golden age. But it was usurped by London, with its expertise in trade, the British Empire and related wealth. London stole a march on the global competition in the 1960s, benefiting from US credit controls that held back New York and had the unintended consequence of allowing London to become the offshore destination for US borrowing. The accumulation of dollars in London acquired the name 'eurodollars' and the markets in which they traded became known as the 'euromarkets'. By the mid-1980s, London needed to adapt and change to regain its competitive position against a resurgent New York and this it did through the 'big bang' in October 1986. This led to new working practices on the London Stock Exchange, ushering in a period of deregulation and dominance for the City as it attracted much international capital.

During the three decades since, while London has always been a global financial powerhouse, the extent of the City's role on the world stage has expanded further. This has happened alongside growth in the foreign-born population of London, which has risen significantly, from 1.2 million or 18 per cent in the 1981 census, to 3 million or 37 per cent in the census of 2011. It has likely risen further since. Thus the benefits and challenges of migration, as well as its scale, are very apparent.

Over this period, the UK's relationship with Europe has been a constant talking point in the financial sector, highlighted at the end of the last century by the debate over whether the UK should join the euro. At the time, the fear was that if the UK did not adopt the single currency, London would lose out to Amsterdam, Frankfurt and Paris – but such fears were wholly misplaced.

The City benefits from agglomeration effects, as it has everything needed for a global financial centre, with high numbers of skilled workers, the market and customers, as well as an infrastructure of banks, legal firms, consultants and technology experts that is hard to rival. While politicians and bureaucrats can clearly have a bearing on the outcome, ultimately, London must be competitive in order to grow: it needs to be a place people want to do business 'in' as well as 'from'. The offshore renminbi, Islamic finance and 'green bond' markets are examples of the latest important forms of financial activity that are growing and where London has positioned itself to be in a strong global position, highlighting its innovative zeal.

The City has the ability to be a major beneficiary of leaving the EU, making gains that could bolster the UK economy. But as in much of the post-referendum debate, there are still far too many who are looking to block change and keep things as they are, rather than looking ahead to exploit the opportunity that leaving presents. Hence there is a danger that we fail to seize this seismic moment.

STRONG POSITION

Watch what they do, don't just listen to what they say, may be the best way to view City financial institutions regarding Brexit. During these Article 50 negotiations, there is an incentive for leading financial firms to threaten that the world will cave in, largely to pressurise politicians to leave things as they are. Ministers and officials always fear the downside risks, just as they did after the global financial crisis and rushed to bail out the banks, at huge cost to UK taxpayers. But while the negative aspects of leaving the EU are emphasised, the real message from the City since the June 2016 Brexit referendum is that profits and recruitment are up.[7]

The City is in a very favourable position post Brexit, despite the current barrage of media stories to the contrary. The last thing it should be wanting is to burden itself with expensive and constraining EU rules and regulations. In contrast to the UK government, the EU does not appear to want to encourage financial services. Take Solvency II, the EU directive aimed at the insurance industry. This was described in 2016 by the former head of the UK civil service Lord Turnbull as 'absolutely dreadful'.[8] He is quite right. Expensive and burdensome, Solvency II, which began in January 2016, will certainly constrain the insurance industry's ability to expand, particularly in Asia and the US. 'Solvency II was meant to create a pan-European harmonisation of regulation, but it absolutely hasn't,' said Nigel Wilson, chief executive of Legal & General, reflecting the view of many that EU rules requiring UK insurers to hold two or three times more capital than their French or German rivals have hamstrung the industry. 'We have sold our Irish, French, Dutch, German and Italian businesses over the past two or three years and there is a greater chance of us entering the EU market in a post-Brexit world where, bizarrely, we will have much more of a level playing field than we have pre-Brexit,' he added.[9]

Then there is MiFID II, the EU's Markets in Financial Instruments Directive II, which comes into effect in 2018. The first version, MiFID I, introduced in 2004, allowed new competitors to take on national stock exchanges – and had the unintended consequence of dark trading.[10] Many fear that MiFID II – a huge, complex piece of costly legislation already delayed by a year – is an ill-thought-out scheme, reflecting interfering bureaucrats at their worst.

As a result, the City should be careful what it wishes for. A Brexit deal that implies little change or that ties the UK's financial services industry into the EU could seriously undermine the City's global competitiveness and may result in longer-term pain – particularly as the UK would be unable directly to influence that regulation. This would be the case if, for instance, Britain remained a member of the EEA. Just when London needs to compete, then, with New York and Asian financial centres on the front foot and positioning themselves for growth, it is vital the City and the UK's broader financial services industry are not constrained by EU-derived regulations that may be wholly inappropriate for a global financial capital.

'Everyone in the City is a Eurosceptic except that some want to remain in the EU while others want to leave,' said one former Lord Mayor of London, speaking on the basis of anonymity. This sums up the mood in the City quite well. Even those leading bankers and financiers who wanted to remain in the EU were not always happy about the direction of travel, and most agreed the EU needs reform.

This was captured well by the previous coalition government's Competency Reports released in 2013 and 2014, focusing on important areas of the UK's relationship with the EU, which we mentioned in the last chapter. The reports covering financial services reminded us that Britain has a 'disproportionately low level of influence considering the national importance of the UK's financial sector', our ability to influence the EU's financial regulatory agenda declining long before the referendum on EU membership had even been announced.[11]

Given the importance of finance and the City to the UK, this ebbing British influence stood in sharp contrast to France's control over all things agricultural within the EU. The UK was not able to resist the financial transactions tax that, while not yet introduced, looks set to impact us in the future. The same is true of the bankers' bonus tax, which drove up base salaries and the ban on short selling, which will do nothing to help markets operate properly. The UK did ensure the decision on euro clearing went its way in early 2015, but that was only because of an unprecedented and concerted political effort that would be extremely hard to replicate. Indeed, that very victory exposed the City's Achilles heel: had the

UK voted to remain in the EU, the ECJ would continue to adjudicate on future controversial areas.

This was not the only area about which the coalition government's report expressed concern. 'Over the last ten years, there has been a roughly ten-fold increase in the volume of EU law on financial services,' the report said.[12] That same 2014 competency review also highlighted the extent of unhelpful EU intrusion into retail markets. Consider that around 61 per cent of defined benefit pension schemes in the EU are in the UK and 24 per cent in the Netherlands. 'It seems wholly inappropriate', said the UK's National Association of Pension Funds, 'that the 20-plus member states with less than 1 per cent of defined benefit liabilities should, collectively, have a greater say in relation to supervision and funding requirements for those liabilities than the UK and Netherlands.'

In case we decide to align ourselves more closely with the EU in future, let us not forget that during David Cameron's pre-referendum negotiations in 2015 and 2016, the UK failed to secure a veto between the Eurozone and the non-Eurozone countries.[13] If we failed to secure that veto when we were in the EU, there is no way we are going to be able to stand in the way of the EU as it makes future regulatory policy as friendly to the Eurozone as possible.

CITY CENTRAL

The City is central to our Brexit negotiations, as the Prime Minister made clear in her March 2017 Article 50 letter. Since then, the general election outcome has strengthened the City's position, giving it more scope to lobby a weaker, more precarious government.

Like so many economic and financial issues, the debate about the importance of the City is by no means clear-cut. The City's success has created some challenges for the UK. Since the mid-1980s there has been a constant argument that the UK economy is too skewed towards finance. The City attracts many of the best graduates, be they engineers from Cambridge or mathematicians from Warwick, employing them in highly paid positions. It is argued that many such roles ultimately add little value to the economy compared to what such talented individuals might otherwise do in terms of industry, medicine or commerce. But the lure of high salaries for young graduates is too strong for many to resist, especially when student loans need to be repaid.

To compound this, in 2008 the City almost brought the economy to its knees. Many taxpayers rightly feel the country has paid a high price for bankers to survive.[14] 'Heads we win, tails you lose' is a phrase that, for much of the general public, captures the position of the UK's largest banks. The EU referendum brought two issues about the City to the fore: the need to help fix a broken domestic economic model that does not deliver for all; and ensuring the UK remains outward-looking and able to compete in a fast-changing global economy. Project Fear was not only wrong to predict economic collapse immediately after the Leave vote but was also wrong to expect financial Armageddon. For the most part, markets have remained relatively calm since June 2016.

The hope is that there will be a smooth transition through the exit process. In April 2017, the Bank of England's Deputy Governor for Prudential Regulation, Sam Woods, wrote to the CEOs and branch managers of all financial institutions with operations in the City. 'We expect all firms with cross-border activities between the UK and the rest of the EU to undertake appropriate contingency planning for the UK's withdrawal from the EU, in light of the UK Government's decision to trigger Article 50,' the letter said.[15]

This makes sense and is welcome. For many firms, such contingency planning should mean little or no change, while for others Brexit could cause some operations to move out of London to the EU, although in the scheme of things this should not be a large exodus. While it makes sense for firms to be prepared, there is a danger that the pessimistic and wrong economic thinking we witnessed before the referendum may be repeated now, only this time forcing financial firms to make misjudged decisions about their business.

One of the most important issues for the City since the referendum is having clarity about the role of EU citizens. This matters for current staff, as one in eight who work in the City is an EU national from outside the UK. It also matters for the City's ability to attract talent in the future from anywhere in the world. An important part of leaving the EU is that the UK will be able to adopt a migration system that suits its domestic interests, allowing access to those people we need, not just those who want to be here. As this system evolves, it will likely favour skilled workers, not least those vital to financial services.

Another issue, given a renewed lease of life in the wake of the election, has been the City's demands for a transition agreement. The argument is that this would minimise disruption and allow firms to plan and adapt to the new, future environment. In early January 2017, a letter from the Chief Executive of the Financial Conduct Authrority to the Treasury Select Committee outlined some of the issues linked to transitional deals. The letter highlighted the need for legal certainty, that any transition should allow the FCA an effective and clear rulebook, allowing mitigation against future risks and a continuous and effective working relationship.[16]

While a transition period makes sense, this must be kept to a sensible length, perhaps two years at most. For as long as the UK stays in the EU, we will have to continue to adopt and implement EU regulations, which might be expensive and burdensome – and in all likelihood ones we cannot influence. In the fast-moving world of finance it is hard to justify a very long transition.

PASSPORTING AND EQUIVALENCE

The possible loss of passporting rights for financial services is a major concern cited about Brexit. Just as a passport allows you to travel across borders, passporting rights allow UK and EU firms to conduct business across EU borders. Specifically, they allow a firm based in one member state of the EEA to do business in another.[17] Although passporting may be important for the business models of some firms, we should remember that it came into effect only in 2007 – and long before that the City was already well established as a global financial centre. As stated earlier, fears about the impact a loss of passporting may have on the City need to be kept in context.

Likewise, passporting is a two-way issue. According to the FCA, as of August 2016 there were 5,476 financial services firms based in the UK holding a total of 336,421 'outbound' passports allowing them to operate across the rest of the EEA. But some 8,008 non-UK EEA-based firms held 23,532 'inbound' passports enabling them to trade in the UK. There were more firms in Europe than UK-based firms holding passports, then, but those based in Britain held multiple numbers of passports – as one would expect given the City's role as a financial hub.[18]

Concerns about passporting rights are far less pressing in the retail sector than among firms operating in wholesale markets that deal with other financial institutions or companies. With wholesale markets the impact very much depends upon the business model of the firm. Some firms that sell across the EU solely from London may also need to set up a future base in another EU market. This might include some of the American and Japanese investment banks. Even so, they are likely to retain the bulk of their operations in London and only move specific business units. Within the asset management industry, many firms already run their assets under management out of London, with operations in Dublin and Luxembourg. It has been suggested that the centre of gravity for retail funds could move to these two centres, while for institutional funds, Frankfurt and Paris could gain.

When it comes to cross-border retail financial services – financial services in one EU country aimed at people living in another – it is interesting to note how poorly things work across the EU despite the headline figures appearing good. According to the European Commission, some '80 per cent of funds from undertakings for collective investment in transferable securities (UCITS) and 40 per cent of alternative investment funds (AIFs)' are marketed cross-border and thus 'the EU marketing passport has contributed to creating a successful cross-border market'.[19]

Yet, as the Commission itself acknowledges, 'the distribution of funds remains geographically limited'. One third of funds marketed cross-border are sold in only one other EU country and another third in no more than four. There are many reasons for this, including cultural preferences, but primarily it is the difficulty for any retail market in financial services to work properly across borders. Hence firms in the retail space, if they want to be successful, must be based in the country to which they are selling. For them, then, passporting is less of an issue, mattering much more for wholesale financial services firms.

If the UK were to stay within the EEA, passporting rights do not change. This might be relevant if there was a transition deal involving EEA membership as a stepping stone towards leaving the EU fully, as we discussed in Chapter 6. Leaving both the EU and the EEA, though, which is the government's current intention, means either the passport is lost, or something needs to be put in place to compensate.

Lloyds of London has already opened a Brussels office. That makes sense, given that 4 per cent of its overall business is with the rest of the EU and it feels it must make plans now to service those clients. But the numbers of people involved in any such move is small compared to those in London. The firms that have been most outspoken about the loss of passports are those that have predicated their business models on using London as the base for their European business.

If there is a deal on financial services as part of the Article 50 negotiation, as the Prime Minister wishes, there will be no need to change. Perhaps the City needs to readjust its thinking. As pointed out by Barney Reynolds, a lawyer who has produced much excellent work in this area, 'passporting is the harmonised application of identical rules, effectively by the same people'.[20] So it is not necessarily the route all the City will want to go down. One option might be a tiered system, with those firms that want to passport into the EU adopting a different approach from those aiming to deal with the rest of the world outside the EU, and those that want to service UK clients.

Better still, 'equivalence' should be the new focus, rather than 'passporting'. In January 2018, when MiFID II is due to come into effect, a 'third country' firm operating outside the EU will be allowed to operate fully in the EU if that country's regulatory system is deemed 'equivalent'. There is no doubt that, at the moment we leave the EU, the UK's regulatory system and hence London would be viewed as such. Following this, each bank or broker in any third country that wanted to do business in the EU would then be considered for recognition. Again, for most firms, this should be straightforward. And, as MiFID II states, EU members 'shall not impose any additional requirements' on such third countries. This treatment will be symmetrical. Failing this, the firms that depend upon passports may consider setting up subsidiaries in those EU counties in which they plan to operate and seek regulatory approval. And vice versa.[21]

Equivalent regulation does not mean identical regulation. Furthermore, while it covers the vast bulk of the financial markets, there will be the opportunity to cover the gaps for areas where equivalence does not currently apply, primary insurance being one of them.

EURO CLEARING

Alongside passporting, the other hotly disputed topic is the clearing of euro-denominated derivatives. Companies, banks and financial institutions have exposures or the need to hedge their exposures to a multitude of currencies and interest rates.

In the days when bank cheques were ubiquitous, people were used to the concept that cheques needed to clear, allowing the process of writing or receiving a cheque to be treated, for the most part, as actual payment. Clearing covers the process from the initial commitment to the eventual settlement and is important in many areas of finance, including currencies and rates.

About three quarters of euro clearing takes place in London; Paris is next with about one tenth. The US is important too. It has become known that the EU would like the euro-clearing business that takes place in London to move to the EU area. But it is not as simple as that.

Since the Brexit vote, the media has been full of stories that this business will move from London, with wild and misplaced predications of huge job losses. Because the UK is not going to remain in the EU, one might ask why we should be surprised if euro clearing moves from London. The reality is that clearing is no different to many other things: it takes place where it is most competitive for it to do so.

Currency-denominated instruments can be cleared outside the country to which they relate. For instance, euro, sterling and yen instruments are routinely cleared in the US, a long way from the EU, UK or Japan. Such clearing takes place within highly regulated clearing houses that allow banks and others to set out their positions and reduce their overall costs. This also helps attract the volume of business needed to ensure markets are deep and liquid enough to operate efficiently, with costs and spreads low.

As in many other areas, London has the combination of factors that gives it a cutting edge. Economic and commercial realities determine where the market goes, not pen-pushers in Brussels. The media often gives the misleading impression that the EU could decide if the market will move. It cannot. But what the EU can do is change regulations and rules to force EU banks to conduct their business in the EU, not outside. This might be seen as protectionist by, for instance, Washington – creating a threat of retaliatory action by the US. Such a move by the EU would also make no economic sense. If the EU wanted, it could issue a ruling – but whether euro operations would actually move is a different matter. London is where the liquidity is, where multiple global currencies are cleared and where banks can make more effective use of their capital. In Paris, or Frankfurt, liquidity would be lower and bid-ask spreads subsequently higher

– which would result in a forced fragmentation of the financial industry, leaving everyone worse off.

Such a move by the EU would be 'incoherent, protectionist and damaging', said the City titan Michael Spencer, speaking in April 2017.[22] 'It would be nationalistic madness to do so,' Spencer subsequently wrote. 'And any demand by the EU that transactions in euro-related instruments have to be executed exclusively within Europe would by definition mean that this could no longer happen in Asia or North America.'[23]

Spencer speculated that Jean-Claude Juncker may have trouble telling President Trump that he wanted to ban the clearing of euro swaps in Chicago. The EU could only effectively impose such regulation on EU banks, forcing them to settle and clear their trades in Paris or Frankfurt, while the remaining UK, US, and Asian banks could carry on as before. 'This would force the EU banks to clear in a smaller liquidity pool and endure higher costs than their global rivals, disadvantaging them,' observed Spencer. The OECD echoes such thinking, as we mentioned in Chapter 5, commenting that raising barriers between Europe and the UK's financial services would 'not be in the collective interest of the global economy' because London 'plays such a key role in international banking, bonds and foreign exchange'.[24]

The EU would really need to get the exchange itself to move from London, and that shows no sign of happening. Speaking in April 2017, Jeff Sprecher, Chair and CEO of Intercontinental Exchange (ICE), said London was uniquely placed, and that Europe overall would benefit from the ability to bring risk into one place. But he also outlined how he had been wooed by Germany, France and Holland, in what he described as a 'holistic approach' involving taxation and schooling, to move his business.[25] While Sprecher said he did not want to move, there is a sense that the UK is not doing enough to encourage businesses to take advantage of post-Brexit opportunities in London. It raises the risk that between them, various British regulatory and commercial bodies may yet snatch defeat from the jaws of victory for the City. Thankfully, though, the overwhelming impression since the EU referendum is that, despite the UK authorities, the market and business looks set to stay.

How will the debate over euro clearing play out? Despite warnings from experts about likely damage, Brussels has called for the EU to have more powers over clearing. The ECB, which calculates that over 90 per cent of daily euro-clearing business happens in London, has set out proposals to give it more regulatory oversight.[26] The UK is clearly facing pressure over its dominance of what amounts to a €1,000 billion-a-day market, with the ECB's move following a European Commission report calling for more EU powers over clearing euro-denominated financial products after Brexit.[27]

Brussels has so far held off trying to force relocation, though, presumably because, for the reasons outlined above, it will not work. And while there is likely to be a lot of rhetoric relating to this prized, high-profile market during the Article 50 talks, the weight of practical and logistical evidence suggests London will retain its grip on this lucrative activity after the UK has left the EU.

MANY SHORT RUNS

What else might change? One area of business that would certainly have come to London had the UK voted to stay in the EU would have been the benefits of the European capital markets union. The need for this has been driven by the high dependence of EU companies on bank lending – certainly compared to the US, where firms raise a significant share of their funding from capital markets instead, issuing debt or equity. Also important for the EU is the need to have deeper, integrated capital markets across Europe – and, to a lesser extent, the desire to reduce barriers to cross-border investment within the EU.

The question now is where will this business locate? London still has the deep pools of liquidity and capital that make it central for the whole of the EU. If 'no deal' on financial services is seen as likely, this may encourage the EU 27 to proceed more quickly with capital markets union, which would include the EU building up its own capabilities. One such area is the 'prospectus directive' – aimed at making it easier for smaller firms to access capital markets with reduced regulation surrounding the formal prospectus. Another such area is securitisation – the creation of liquid, tradable instruments from illiquid or semi-liquid underlying assets. Beyond that, much will depend then on the route London takes as to how well placed the City will be to fulfil European needs.

The City also needs to watch out for developments in other global centres. Just as it is possible for one financial centre to burden itself with rules that hold it back, others can seize the moment and take the opportunity to grab market share, realising their ambition to grow. In this context, President Trump's 'America First' approach to financial regulation could have profound implications.[28]

While the City will want to remain the financial centre of Europe, the UK must be mindful not to be just a recipient of the EU's rules and regulations. For while we are leaving the EU, there is a danger that, during the Article 50 negotiations, Britain ends up agreeing to be bound by the EU – which must be avoided. We should be reassured that more and more of the regulations governing finance are set at the global level. In the wake of the 2008 banking crisis, the Financial Stability Board (FSB), based in Basel, Switzerland, became the ultimate authority regarding financial regulation. It is vital that the UK, home to arguably the world's most important financial capital, can influence the FSB in its own right, rather than having to calibrate its position, negotiating as just one member of the broader EU.

Will Brexit provide a regulatory dividend for the City? It is premature to suggest it will. There is no doubting the UK has pushed for some of the regulations that have subsequently been adopted by the EU. Once outside, there should be a comprehensive debate about the future regulatory agenda and where and whether there is the need and scope for change. As we have stressed, the UK must avoid a race to the bottom on regulations, and in many areas, both in finance and beyond, future global trade will be set more by the global coordination of rules and regulations, limiting the scope to deviate.

One area where change clearly is needed is competition law – with application across the whole economy. Here the UK has adopted EU thinking that is not always economically rational or market-friendly. Competition law should work in response to problems arising. What we have instead is the opposite approach, where *a priori* the desirable market outcome appears to be picked. This is not efficient, and does not necessarily reduce costs or improve choice for customers.

At the same time, we should not lose sight of the dramatic economic changes that are already underway. Technology, innovation and the digital economy are revolutionising how finance is conducted, and will continue to do so. Consider the revolution over recent years in mobile personal banking. Finance is becoming borderless at a time when politicians and bureaucrats in Brussels seem to think they control all the levers. They don't. Their interventions are more likely to distort markets; fragment them, raise costs and lower consumer choice. It is not just the practitioners in the financial industry who are changing their ways, but customers too, seeking out new ways of doing things. Bureaucrats and politicians are often the last to change their thinking.

Already a global hub, London is also rapidly becoming the financial technology – 'fintech' – capital of the world. Jes Staley, CEO of Barclays, has cited the decision by Google to increase its investment in London as a clear sign that the City will continue to succeed. Digitalisation and 'big data' mean that finance will continue to change in dramatic ways and London is well placed to respond – as long as it remains global in its outlook, attracting skilled workers while remaining attractive to inward investment. We need an enabling environment – one that encourages both invention and innovation.

This sentiment takes us back to the quotation that began this chapter – from John Maynard Keynes, undoubtedly Britain's greatest economist. Many are aware of the famous Keynes utterance that, 'in the long run, we are all dead'. But as Keynes also said, 'life and history are made up of short runs' in which 'we are all alive'. This conveys an important notion for the UK, its approach to Brexit and how the City attempts to position itself – that Britain must seize control of its destiny. The government, and the country as a whole, should be on the front foot, as we attempt to drive the agenda and deliver an outcome in the best interests of the British people. When it comes to the City – and financial services more generally – the UK has a very strong hand to play.

CHAPTER 10

IMMIGRATION

'We can be pro-immigration and champion immigrants as part of a non-racist and open society, while recognising we have to manage immigration so those values aren't threatened.'
STEPHEN KINNOCK MP[1]

During the 2016 referendum campaign, and since, many of the leading politicians who backed Remain claimed that Brexit would make the UK more 'insular' and 'inward-looking'.[2] We believe, on the contrary, that being outside the EU provides the UK with an opportunity to reaffirm our status as one of the world's most open, globally minded and tolerant societies. This will be in addition to, and not at the expense of, boosting our domestic economy.

Focusing more of our diplomatic and commercial efforts on increasing trade with the four fifths of the world economy beyond the EU is a good start in terms of enhancing the UK's global credentials.[3] Disassociating ourselves from the Common External Tariff, the EU's blanket protectionist measure against all non-EU derived goods and services, a tariff regime that penalises some of the world's poorest nations, will also help.[4]

A policy of sensibly managed immigration is important too, including treating potential immigrants to the UK on their individual merits, whether they come from the EU or not. Brexit provides Britain with the opportunity to do all of the above – enhancing our trade with the wider world, moving away from the EU's protectionist mindset and ending discrimination against non-EU immigrants, not least those from parts of the world where the UK already has deep cultural and familial ties, such as the US, India, Anglophone Africa and Australasia.

Taking back control of our borders allows Britain to establish clearer and fairer rules, while restoring the democratic accountability of our immigration process.

Designing, legislating for and implementing a modern system of managed immigration that provides the labour required, while restoring public confidence in our border policies, is a very significant part of achieving a Clean Brexit and, in turn, making a success of leaving the EU.

Immigration has long been a net positive for the UK, as we outlined in the introduction to this book. The British economy and our broader cultural life have benefited enormously, over many centuries, from successive waves of immigration from continental Europe, Ireland, the West Indies, Africa, Asia and elsewhere. Immigration has brought numerous talented and hard-working people to the UK – and Britain, for the most part, has strong interracial and multicultural relations.

The reality is, though, that sharp increases in annual net immigration over recent years have raised questions that no longer can be ignored. For far too long it has been fashionable to dismiss or deny concerns related to soaring immigration numbers. While mass immigration may be favoured by some employers for example, as an easy way to recruit staff, a rapid influx of migrants has suppressed the wages of many low-income workers, making their financial insecurity more acute. Large-scale immigration has also deterred some firms from investing in staff training, while creating local tensions by further stretching the public services upon which poorer citizens disproportionately rely – not least the NHS, social housing and other low-cost accommodation. In this chapter, we highlight the need for a sensible, autonomous post-Brexit immigration system. It is vital that the UK reintroduces effective border controls that will allow migrants to come to Britain at a pace that benefits our economy but also restores widespread confidence in the country's immigration policy.

IMMIGRATION NATION

While immigration has benefits, both economic and cultural, the scale of UK immigration in recent years has become a legitimate and contentious concern for millions of British voters. Net migration was 48,000 in 1997, rising to 177,000 in 2012 and then 333,000 in 2015, the year before the EU referendum, a figure equal to the population of Cardiff. So net immigration has almost doubled since 2012 and has increased sevenfold since 1997.[5] The 2015 total doubles again if you include those granted a national insurance number who stayed in the

UK less than twelve months. Even if such workers make lengthy visits to the UK for many successive years, they are currently not included in the headline immigration numbers. Including new national insurance numbers granted to non-UK nationals, annual net UK migration in 2015 was close to the population of Leeds.

Low-skilled work accounts for 13 million jobs in the UK – 43 per cent of those in employment. Just over 2 million of those low-skilled jobs, around 16 per cent, are performed by migrant workers.[6] For workers in low-skilled trades – including food processing, hospitality, business service outsourcing, construction and non-unionised transport – wages have been suppressed in some localities due to immigration, even if the impact on national average wages appears not to have been large.[7] Increased immigration has also clearly added to pressure on public services and housing costs.[8]

While many incoming UK migrants are highly skilled, many more, particularly from relatively new EU member states, are competing for low-skilled employment – undermining wage levels for financially insecure UK voters already working in such sectors. Many of these migrants may be in vocational roles, which in itself exposes an additional challenge, namely that the UK needs to ensure that these vocational skills are created here at home in future – through vocational training.

There is little doubt that Britain needs to return to a system of managed immigration – designed by UK ministers, with the legislation passing through Parliament in the normal way. This will allow us to access the overseas labour the economy needs, while retaining broad public support for immigration. As the rest of the EU struggles with a Schengen arrangement that is sapping confidence, fuelling intolerance and nationalism, the UK has a chance to put its immigration policy, and the nation's inherently positive and generous attitude to migrants, back on a stable footing. Negotiations over single market membership must not stop that from happening – which is one reason we advocate a Clean Brexit.

During the 1950s, net immigration into the UK averaged less than 10,000 per year. It then became negative during the 1960s and 1970s, as emigration from the UK rose, outweighing the number of arrivals. During the 1980s, net immigration became positive again, averaging 7,500 people per annum. Between 1990 and 1999, though, after freedom of movement was enshrined in EU law as part of the Maastricht Treaty in 1992, average net UK immigration shot up to 62,500 people per year, an eightfold increase on the decade before.[9] An even more dramatic rise occurred after the 2004 'big bang' enlargement, as we outlined in Chapter 4, when eight Eastern European states became EU members – with Britain a strong advocate of enlargement.

Unlike most existing EU states, the UK (along with the Republic of Ireland and Sweden) decided not to impose temporary labour market restrictions on workers from these new members. A study commissioned by the Home Office predicted in 2003 that average annual net immigration from the so-called A8 new members would be 'relatively small, at between 5,000 and 13,000 immigrants per year up to 2010'.[10] The actual outcome was, to say the least, rather different. In March 2008, a House of Lords inquiry reported that 'more than 765,000 A8 workers … have registered for employment in the UK since gaining free access to the UK's labour market when their countries joined the EU in May 2004'.[11]

By 2010, the Conservative Party manifesto was promising to 'take steps to get net migration back to the levels of the 1990s – tens of thousands a year, not hundreds of thousands', a message that David Cameron reiterated in several subsequent speeches.[12] The manifesto failed to mention that the UK has no control over immigration from other EU countries, a lack of clarity some of Cameron's political opponents quickly exploited. In 2014, as immigration continued to rise, UKIP won the European parliamentary elections – securing 27 per cent of the vote, the first time a party other than the Conservatives or Labour had topped a national election since 1906. The following year, UKIP polled 13 per cent in the 2015 general election, up from 3 per cent five years earlier.[13]

The Leave majority in the June 2016 referendum undoubtedly represented, in part, a vote of no confidence in the handling of immigration by successive governments. Between 2004 and 2016, UK net immigration has totalled no fewer than 3,277,000 on official figures, a yearly average of over 252,000.[14] This represents a migration-driven population increase, in each of the last thirteen years, equivalent to a city the size of Newcastle upon Tyne.

Immigration into the UK from outside the EU has been on a declining trend in recent years but remains substantial. For over a decade, though, generally falling non-EU net immigration has been more than offset by the rise in immigration from the rest of the EU – leading to higher immigration overall. The core question for those, like the authors, who believe Britain benefits from immigration, economically and otherwise, is how to lower both EU and non-EU numbers to levels that make more economic sense and are acceptable to the majority of the electorate, while rebuilding public trust.

One reason many large employers are keen to retain the EU's freedom of movement rules is that a virtually limitless, low-cost workforce is clearly attractive to well-established commercial interests. The CBI continues to support UK membership of the single market – which implies something close to freedom of movement – even though this is entirely incompatible with Brexit. The public voted for, among other things, a more accountable immigration system managed by the UK government – which is what must now be introduced. Such controls should allow for an inflow of skilled and unskilled labour based on domestic economic needs. A new immigration system needs to admit such overseas labour in manageable numbers. Of course, the UK should continue, as it does now, to accept refugees from across the world, and that is a separate issue to the immigration debate.

It is vital that, during these Article 50 negotiations, preparations are made to reintroduce a system of managed immigration. Demonstrating the UK government is in charge of our borders once again, as it was until relatively recently, with immigration fairly but firmly managed, will send a message of reassurance to the population. Conversely, settling on a system that is business-friendly, with provision for all types of labour and no change to the UK's commendable asylum policies, will reassure many who voted Remain.

This new system should be agreed as quickly as possible, so it is ready to be introduced when we leave the EU. Showing that immigration is once again under the jurisdiction of the British government should allow MPs and the country as a whole to move on from the divisiveness of the referendum campaign and begin to recognise the opportunities presented by Brexit. There is, indeed, no time to waste – the UK's new arrangement must be in place by March 2019, or by the end of any transition period that might follow.

POINTS, PLACES, PRIZES

A credible migration policy, that serves domestic, economic and social needs, by no means amounts to 'pulling up the drawbridge' – a phrase often used by those determined to shut down any reasonable debate regarding managed UK immigration. Under any feasible post-Brexit scenario, net immigration will continue – and in numbers that will be viewed as sizeable by some. Rather than the EU's freedom of movement, though, or something close, the UK must identify the sectors where labour and skills gaps hold back progress, tailoring our immigration policies largely to that end. Passing such legislation and preparing for implementation should be manageable within the Article 50 window – not least as the UK had a managed immigration system in the relatively recent past.

One option is that Britain adopts a points-based system (PBS), used in Australia and elsewhere. Introduced in the late 1980s, Australia's PBS selects migrants on the basis of their likely contribution to society, awarding points for factors including age, recognised qualifications and previous experience abroad, with skilled workers in their late twenties and early thirties usually scoring most highly.

One issue with PBS is that the nations using it – which include Canada and New Zealand, as well as Australia – are trying to raise the share of skilled migrants while expanding their relatively small populations. Britain, in contrast, is more concerned about reducing immigration. Under the PBS, if you score an adequate number of points, you are generally allowed to migrate, with the system acting more as a filter on quality, rather than a control on quantity. The UK, with its relatively small landmass, housing challenges and stretched public services, may instead require a work permit system (WPS) that includes skills quotas and a cap on overall immigration. Such limits, though, could be altered from year to year, contingent on particular skills gaps and the state of the economy.

The UK currently operates a partial PBS, but only for those looking to move to the UK from outside the EU. Introduced by Gordon Brown's government in February 2008, this classifies potential migrants into four broad 'tiers', based on their potential contribution to the economy.[15] It is worth nothing that the Tier 3 migrant applicant category, which covers low-skilled workers, was scrapped in 2010, after the coalition government decided that no more low-skilled non-EU labour was required – not least as so many were arriving from the EU in search of low-skilled jobs.

One possible post-Brexit outcome is that the current PBS that applies to non-EU migrants is extended to EU migrants as well, with the Tier 3 category being reinstated across the board, but subject to an annual limit. A work-permit system of immigration (WPS), in contrast, would require potential migrants to have an identified job, with the employer rather than employee submitting the application and the government deciding on the individual merits of each case. Adopting a WPS is certainly more labour-intensive and costly to administer, but would impose the most demonstrable control – which may be seen as a political priority over the next few years. Using a WPS also provides the best way to secure overseas talent – which, as long as the system is targeted on the skills lacking among domestic workers, could boost the productivity of the broader UK economy.

Much has been made of the problems certain industries may face when re-cruiting low-skilled labour once the UK has left the EU. Some fear that if the non-EU PBS is extended, many EU migrants who are currently in low-skilled jobs would fail to qualify, damaging UK businesses that are reliant on such labour. Yet Sir David Metcalf, head of the government's independent Migra-tion Advisory Committee (MAC) from 2007 to 2016, has argued that both the number of low-skilled migrants and the amount of time they spend in the UK could be controlled under a WPS. Such a scheme would be 'pretty straightfor-ward' to run, says Metcalf, and could be 'time-limited and capped', as was the UK's previous WPS for seasonal agricultural workers.[16] This would allow certain sectors of the UK economy to access low-skilled labour without imposing undue additional long-term strain on UK public services.

Another possible post-Brexit option, apart from PBS or WPS, is an emergen-cy brake that would trigger a temporary halt in EU migration in certain sectors or even locations where wages are being undercut or public services are under particular pressure. Some say this would allow the UK to keep adhering to EU rules – which, in principle, permit freedom of movement to be suspended for a number of years. That would then help Britain during the Article 50 talks, the argument goes, allowing us to strike a better deal on single market access.

Such an outcome is politically highly unlikely – given that, following the UK's EU referendum, any decision to apply an emergency brake would have to be at the British government's discretion. This is not an outcome the EU would accept, as it would then be demanded by other member states. Certainly, when David Cameron negotiated an 'emergency brake' ahead of the June 2016 ref-erendum, on benefit payments to EU nationals migrating to the UK rather than migration itself, even that was subject to approval by all other EU governments and then the European Parliament.

The conditions imposed on an EU-approved brake on actual migration could be even more onerous. And after any brake period, the UK would once again be subject to the EU's freedom of movement rules. For all these reasons, neither the UK government nor the EU 27 are likely to agree on an emergency brake on migration. We would advise against such an approach, as it would likely result in the kind of Messy Brexit stalemate we described in Chapter 3. It makes far more sense to go for a clean break from the EU's immigration rules and put time and energy into setting up our own immigration system, while attempting to negotiate an FTA with the EU as we would with any other counterparty.

Having said that, the idea of the UK adopting regional immigration controls – sometimes discussed in the context of an emergency brake – is interesting. We hope the possibility of a 'devolved' immigration policy, entirely free of EU rules, will be seriously explored by the government and Parliament, as the UK moves towards a new system of post-Brexit border controls. The EU referendum demonstrated, after all, that different parts of the country have markedly different interests and concerns when it comes to immigration. The costs and benefits of the recent migration influx have certainly been unevenly distributed.

Some areas with high levels of immigration, such as London, voted Remain. But such areas have often absorbed and assimilated migrant communities over many years or even generations. It is the pace of immigration that tends to determine local opinions, not the overall total. That is why some semi-rural, rather disadvantaged localities strongly voted to leave. In these areas, where immigration has gone up most sharply in proportionate terms over recent years, even if the overall numbers remain low by national standards, concerns about immigration have been most acute.[17]

There are signs the Labour Party is considering such a 'devolved' immigration policy. The UK's main opposition party has floated the idea of allowing higher immigration to London while imposing tighter restrictions on moving to other parts of the country. This approach could help Labour maintain the support of both its liberal metropolitan voters, some of whom reject all migration controls, while accommodating more traditional supporters in former industrial areas, where immigration is of greater concern.[18] This idea would likely require some kind of employment or housing permit system, allowing migrants with regional visas to work, live and buy property only in certain localities, given that the UK obviously has no internal border controls. Ensuring it could be executed properly in the UK would be a key consideration, but there are international precedents where regional immigration policy has been used successfully, such as Canada.

Devolving immigration decisions allows different parts of the country to act according to their own specific interests. A system could be developed under which region-specific work visa quotas, broken down by sector, would be filled by applicant employers. The size and composition of each quota could be decided at the regional level – by forming committees comprised of local council leaders, the new 'metro mayors' and local MPs.[19] In the case of Scotland, Wales and Northern Ireland, the respective existing devolved assemblies would be used. This would help to accommodate the differing results in the EU referendum between Scotland and Northern Ireland on the one hand, which voted Remain, and England and Wales, which backed Leave.

Each part of the country could decide what kind of migrants it needs each year in terms of skills and overall numbers – taking into account not just labour requirements, but also considerations such as public services and housing. This exercise, conducted annually, would also generate extremely detailed regional data regarding the gaps in the skills profile of the UK's domestic workforce – information that could be used to develop future training programmes.

Settling on a post-Brexit immigration policy is seen as a serious challenge for the UK government – and the broader body politic. The relevant parliamentary debates between now and March 2019 will no doubt be contentious – not least given the government's slim Commons majority. If such a policy is designed carefully, though, leaving the EU could help the UK to strike a better balance between economic need and democratic accountability when it comes to immigration. It could also provoke a meaningful and ongoing discussion between employers and politicians at the grass-roots level regarding skills and related investment in training, while providing a major boost to local democracy – features that should appeal to politicians across all parties.

Such a regional approach would lead to some labour force rigidity – as migrant workers with regional visas could not be redeployed from one part of the country to another without affecting each region's quota. If such a system was made too complex, it could also become overly bureaucratic. There is surely some logic, though, after a regionally divisive Brexit referendum, a vote that has since threatened to split up the UK, in devolving migration decisions so they are made by the communities directly impacted.

Immigration policy would not be devolved in its entirety. Regional visas would still be cleared centrally, by the Home Office, when it comes to criminal and security checks. Our approach to asylum and refugee resettlement would also still be set at the national level. And the system could be designed so there was a cap on immigration overall – with the total number of permits being reduced pro rata if the sum of all local immigration 'bids' is greater than a national limit set by ministers. That UK-wide immigration limit could, in turn, be set by a revamped MAC, accountable to ministers and Parliament, with reference to broader macroeconomic forecasts.

We feel that devolved immigration is an idea worth consideration. It is noteworthy that the City of London Corporation, the governing body overseeing the historic centre of London, the home of the UK's financial services industry, has floated the idea of a regional visa system. The Corporation's aim, it says, is to lessen the danger of post-Brexit staff shortages – and not just in financial services. 'A regional visa could present an opportunity for the UK to have a nuanced immigration system that successfully meets the requirements of UK business and economy,' argues the Corporation in a recent report, which examines visa systems used by Canada and Australia. 'A regional visa system could facilitate and promote economic development outside of London,' the Corporation concludes.[20]

The Corporation is also interested in some form of 'London visa' – one which would give preferential treatment to EU nationals within the capital. In 2015, around 850,000 Londoners were born in another EU country – almost one in ten – with EU workers filling many more highly skilled managerial and technical jobs in the capital than they do across the rest of the UK.

It seems feasible to us that regional visas could help local governments and the 'metro mayors' conceive and implement ambitious and highly desirable development plans not only for the capital, but equally for alternative growth centres such as Manchester, Birmingham, Newcastle and Bristol, attracting international labour to help them do so. It could also help the City of London maintain its international competitiveness. The reality is that the labour needs of Yorkshire, the Highlands of Scotland and the UK's capital city differ dramatically. A devolved migration policy helps to recognise this and tries to address the issues.

BUILDING CONSENT

With Theresa May seemingly supporting a WPS – while some other Cabinet ministers argued for a PBS during the Brexit referendum campaign – agreeing a new immigration system, and then getting the legislation through Parliament, will not be straightforward. The new system, though, must clearly be credible and legally robust. As such, it should be subject to consultation and introduced not using statutory instruments but full Acts of Parliament that come into effect when the Article 50 window expires in March 2019, or after any ensuing transition.

While the timetable is tough, polling research suggests that 68 per cent of the population want the EU's freedom of movement rules to end, including almost 80 per cent of Leave voters and 58 per cent of those who backed Remain.[21] While the government has only a small Commons majority, Parliament seems unlikely to deny those wishes. Although there is a vociferous Soft Brexit lobby among moderate Labour MPs, some of whom want to maintain freedom of movement, others have broken ranks. In a thoughtful post-referendum intervention, Labour's Stephen Kinnock recognised that current levels of immigration are 'not socially or politically acceptable'. Arguing for a WPS, Kinnock made clear that 'opposing freedom of movement isn't the same as opposing immigration'.[22] It is also significant that another leading progressive voice in Parliament, the new Liberal Democrat leader Vince Cable, has admitted to 'serious doubts that EU free movement is tenable or even desirable'.[23]

Having implemented a UK-controlled immigration system during the Article 50 process, that system must be managed carefully to provide the economy with the labour it needs. It is high-skilled migration, rather than unlimited low-skilled migration, that brings economic benefits. Low-skilled migration should be kept to a minimum, while monitoring the impact of all immigration on capacity across our public services. The government should communicate clearly the scale of immigration and broader population growth and the provisions it is making to expand public services accordingly. This is an important part of ensuring our post-Brexit immigration system commands broad public consent.

Since the June 2017 election, the government has focused more attention on the needs of business. Home Secretary Amber Rudd announced in late July that she had commissioned MAC experts to carry out a detailed study of the role EU nationals play in the economy and society. More information is always welcome, of course, but reports that this group will not publish its findings until September 2018 are a surprise, as much of the analysis is surely already available.

The aim of the study is to highlight the role EU migrants play in certain sectors – such as the City, where one in eight workers is from the EU.[24] The health sector will also be a focus – given that 10 per cent of doctors and 7 per cent of nurses are EU nationals.[25] The aim of the UK's post-Brexit immigration system, as stated, is not to restrict the skilled workers the economy needs – although again it begs the question whether better training at home would allow more of these roles to be filled domestically.

International students should not be included in the UK's immigration figures, in our view. Such migrants are not permanent residents and attracting them delivers significant immediate and future gains for the economy. Overseas students generated almost £11 billion of export earnings in 2015, adding more than £25 billion a year to UK GDP, according to a recent study. The consultancy Oxford Economics estimates that international students supported 206,600 jobs in the UK's university towns and cities, providing a significant boost to local businesses.[26]

Low-skilled workers are not affected if foreign students study at UK universities. Students should only count as migrants if, having completed their degrees, they then stay. While that right should by no means be guaranteed, when considering any such application, a recently awarded UK degree should be looked upon favourably – especially if it is in a subject such as IT, engineering or medicine on the government's 'shortage occupation list'.

Some, including the Prime Minister, are reluctant to take overseas students out of immigration numbers. When she was Home Secretary, Theresa May repeatedly dealt with the issue of 'students' on 'fake courses' – and is rightly concerned that the system is open to fraud. Under the coalition government, over 700 colleges were banned from bringing students into the UK from outside the

EU. New tests, including English language and means testing, have since been introduced in a bid to stop bogus students coming to Britain to work.

The student visa system needs to be tightened further, with greater sanctions on degree-granting bodies. Visa fraud is a criminal offence, and should be treated as such. Universities and colleges should pay hefty fines, as well as the 'students' themselves, in cases of fraud or an overstayed visa.[27] The immediate economic benefits of the overseas students coming to the UK are enormous. The long-term 'soft power' gains in terms of future business and political leaders being educated in Britain, forming contacts and hopefully a positive opinion of the country, are also huge. At a time when we are trying to boost regional growth and win more international trade, it makes no sense to limit numbers of overseas students in a bid to hit a much broader immigration target.

In attempting to tackle student visa fraud, there is a strong case for the further use of biometric and other forms of electronic identification, not only for those taking language tests and other aspects of any student visa application, but for migrants more generally. While some may baulk at this on civil liberties grounds, regular reports that the Home Office has 'lost track' of 'tens of thousands' of migrants – including asylum seekers and 'students' – seriously undermine confidence in our immigration system, among both law-abiding migrants and the broader British public.

Britain has been issuing so-called e-passports to its own citizens since 2006 – and all new passports are now biometric. The Home Office has used biometric residence permits since 2015. The government is also proposing to issue 'online ID cards' – which may or may not exist in physical form – to EU citizens and their families who take permanent UK residency after Brexit. Electronic identification has become more prevalent and acceptable over recent years, in fields from online banking to the use of voice recognition software across a range of applications. It surely makes sense for the UK government to be at the forefront of this trend, given the challenges of managing the borders of one of the world's most attractive and popular migrant destinations.[28] In the battle to win back public confidence in our immigration system, technology has a huge role to play.

The scale of immigration from the Middle East and North Africa into Europe has now reached crisis levels. The European Commission managed to partially close one route for refugees across the Balkans in 2016 by striking a deal with

Turkey. But Ankara's agreement is increasingly in question and other routes are taking over. Ahead of elections in Germany in the autumn of 2017, and Italy early in 2018, Brussels has been scrambling to prevent another migrant crisis.

At the time of writing, though, such a crisis is unfortunately coming into view. During the first half of 2017, about 85,000 people landed on the shores of Italy after illegally crossing the Mediterranean. This compares with 71,000 during the same period the year before, according to the International Organization for Migration, a UN body. This is causing severe tension between Brussels and some EU members in Eastern Europe that are refusing to accept refugees allocated under an EU relocation programme, which is designed to take some pressure off Italy and Greece. Another looming crisis is also generating angst in France, Germany and Scandinavia, considering that migrants from North Africa and the Middle East often head north and west.

It is vital that, once Britain has left the EU, we continue to work with the EU 27 to address the 'push' factors encouraging people to leave these regions. Some of the UK's overseas aid budget could help prevent such nations losing so many of their talented and motivated people through emigration to the West, for instance. Aid could be aligned in part to the export of UK university courses, helping developing nations gain human capital and international contacts that will help drive future growth.

Once we have left the Common Agricultural Policy and our non-EU imports are no longer hamstrung by the EU's Common External Tariff, the UK should also remove all barriers to farm exports from north and west Africa, while encouraging the EU to do the same. For many years, the rich world's agricultural subsidies have penalised some of the most economically precarious developing countries. By encouraging overproduction in both the EU and US, such assistance has long distorted world prices, making it impossible for hundreds of millions of peasant farmers to earn a decent living.

Such policies – implicitly, if unintentionally, supported by those calling for the UK to stay in the EU – are a major cause of chronic poverty and economic marginalisation. Western agricultural subsidies and protection lock African nations that are close to Europe into a cycle of depravation, which not only contributes to radicalisation but also causes many families to travel to Europe in search of a better life. The EU's CAP and customs union, and the global trading system more generally, work against developing countries – not least those in north and west Africa. By helping to change that, and urging the EU to do the same, the UK will be helping to tackle Europe's migrant crisis.

'This migration issue will not go away,' said European Commission First Vice-President Frans Timmermans in July 2017, while contemplating the latest numbers on migrant Mediterranean crossings. 'Not today. Not tomorrow. Not next year. Not for a decade, not for two decades. This is a global phenomenon that will be with us for generations.'[29]

HONEST CONVERSATION

The government has no time to waste when it comes to implementing an immigration system that is ready for when the UK leaves the EU. We would have liked to see Britain make a much earlier and bolder move in terms of resolving the post-Brexit status of the 3.1 million EU nationals living in the UK, as we wrote in Chapter 5. We still believe that a generous unilateral gesture, immediately after our EU referendum in June 2016, would have done much to improve the atmosphere of post-Brexit Britain, while winning the UK much goodwill across the EU.

In June 2017, though, the government finally did indicate it would grant UK-based EU citizens the right to apply for inclusion on a 'settled status' register, giving them the same 'indefinite leave to remain' status as many non-EU nationals who have also lived in Britain for five years. While this came late, allowing the EU to get the upper hand in this aspect of the negotiations, it is a generous set of proposals. The UK offer includes guarantees on UK state pensions, together with uprating and paying out on aggregated rights if the recipient later lives abroad.

This raises another issue, linked to immigration but broader. The UK needs seriously to consider the question of whether our welfare system should become more 'contributory' – moving from a 'Beveridge' approach where everyone qualifies for various 'universal benefits', to a 'Bismarck' approach where an individual's history of contributions plays a greater role in determining their level of entitlement. We raised this possibility in Chapter 8. Such an inquiry should be conducted with an open mind and with any recommendation in no way detracting from the provision of minimum subsistence-level benefits, regardless of contributions.

Such a fundamental shift would take considerable time. It strikes us, though, that the upcoming flurry of legislation and reorganisation, when the UK will be rethinking everything from border controls to our international trading patterns, is a good time to at least begin this discussion. Certainly, a more contributory benefits system, combined with the use of technology to deliver less illegal immigration, would help rebuild public confidence.

Migration into the UK will, of course, continue after Brexit – including from the EU. There will always be a demand in the UK for highly skilled workers from France, Germany, Italy and elsewhere across the EU 27. And given that the UK's minimum wage in 2016 was four times the average wage in Bulgaria, three times the average wage in Romania and twice the average wage in Poland, there will continue to be a flow of ready workers from the EU prepared to do unskilled work – a flow that can continue to some extent, to the benefit of both countries, but which needs to be managed.[30]

The British people voted to take back control of our borders in June 2016. While a national immigration limit should be set, we believe the Prime Minister's current insistence on 'tens of thousands' – a repeat of the Conservatives' 2010 manifesto pledge – will likely take some years. What matters is that the limit each year should be set after close consultation with business and political leaders from across the UK – as would happen under the model of devolved immigration we outlined above – and with reference to broader macroeconomic forecasts. For much of the population, regaining control of our borders is more important than meeting any particular net migration figure, as long as the inflows are significantly lower than the historically very high numbers seen over the last twenty years.

It is vital that, as a nation, we engage in a mature and open discussion about immigration. It is not right to respond to those who have legitimate concerns about immigration with a 'like it or lump it' approach. This is not only complacent but potentially inflammatory and counterproductive. It also risks squandering an important opportunity to create a UK immigration system that is backed by genuine political consent.

We should not be afraid of implementing immigration controls. They are used by practically every other advanced country across the world. The exception is the EU – and within the EU, of course, the lack of border control is fuelling

rising nationalism, with the Schengen Agreement breaking down, while arguably encouraging people smuggling across the Mediterranean, with all its ghastly
and tragic consequences.

Immigration is highly beneficial – both economically and culturally. But we
must be mindful that if immigration proceeds too quickly, or the number of
immigrants is sizeable, then low-income communities suffer disproportionately,
which can lead to social tensions. The UK can continue to be pro-immigration,
championing our diversity and tolerance. But we must recognise that immigration needs to be managed, or our tolerance will be gravely threatened.

Our recent history has been marred by a disgraceful lack of regard for the
worries and concerns of a broad swathe of the population. It is time for an
honest discussion that results in a system of managed migration that promotes
economic growth but also commands public respect. While the arithmetic in the
Commons will be tight, and there will no doubt be diehard Remainers in the
Lords, we are optimistic that Westminster will deliver.

CHAPTER 11

HOUSING AND YOUNG PEOPLE

'The big developers must release their stranglehold on supply. It's time to stop sitting on landbanks and delaying build-out – the homebuyers must come first.'

Sajid Javid MP[1]

This chapter outlines policies designed to spark a significant and sustained rise in UK house-building – improving not only social mobility and wealth distribution, but boosting the economy and living standards more generally. We then briefly cover the UK's post-Brexit university sector and other issues of particular interest to younger voters.

Britain is in the midst of a housing crisis – in terms of affordability, quality of new homes and reflected in a serious shortage of homes. For the last four decades, the rate of house-building has fallen well behind the UK's demographic requirements. Professor Paul Cheshire of the London School of Economics, an eminent housing expert who has advised successive governments, says the 'chronic' and 'acute' lack of homes has caused prices to spiral. 'Over the last twenty years, the UK house-building industry has built 2.3 million too few homes,' says Professor Cheshire. 'We have not been building nearly enough since the 1960s – and a growing supply gap over recent years has seen prices become more and more unaffordable.'[2]

The seminal Barker Review of 2004, written for HM Treasury, established beyond doubt that there was 'considerable evidence' of a shortage of homes in the UK, pointing to 'significant benefits from a higher rate of house building'.[3] Barker suggested around 240,000 new homes needed to be built each year to meet population growth and household formation. Yet house-building had failed to reach that level since the late 1970s. A later government report, published in

2011, estimated that the number of households in England alone was growing by 232,000 a year. Yet by then, house-building had fallen even further.[4]

During the Thatcher era, as fewer council houses were built, an average of 190,900 new homes were constructed each year. That figure fell to 160,800 while John Major was Prime Minister as we came to rely ever more on private-sector house-builders, before falling to 156,000 under Tony Blair. Gordon Brown's short premiership saw annual house-building fall further to 143,400, in the aftermath of the 2008 credit crunch, which wiped out many small and medium-sized builders. There was then another sharp drop under the coalition government of 2010–15, as new homes per annum fell to just 123,560 on average, the lowest peacetime level since the 1926 General Strike. This fundamental lack of supply, coupled with the Bank of England's ultra-loose monetary policies since 2009, has seen house prices spiral.

It is wrong to blame immigration for the UK's housing crisis. The large number of new arrivals in recent years has certainly added to the pressure on our housing supply. But it pales into insignificance when compared to our abject failure to build enough homes. Britain has roughly double the population of Canada and yet builds just one third of the new homes that Canada builds each year. The solution to the lack of affordable housing has little to do with reducing immigration. The solution is to build more homes.

HOME TRUTHS

Back in the early 1990s, low- and middle-income workers needed to save 5 per cent of their wages for three years on average to build a deposit for a first-time property. Today, they need twenty-four years of such savings. That's why home-ownership has dropped sharply, particularly among youngsters. Ten years ago, 64 per cent of 25–34-year-olds, the crucial family-forming age group, owned their own home. Now that figure is 39 per cent. Well over half of a generation of young adults is locked out of the property market – an economic and social disaster.

As house prices spiral way ahead of wages, more and more youngsters – even those holding down professional jobs – are being priced out. Over half of the first-time buyers in 2015 had assistance from 'the Bank of Mum and Dad', rising to two thirds in London and the south-east. Such realities lay bare the uncomfortable truth – the growing gulf between 'property haves' and 'property have-nots'. The UK housing market, traditionally a source of social mobility and security for millions, is now fuelling social immobility and resentment.

If the UK is to thrive during the decade after Brexit, with a relatively buoyant economy, it is vital that the government puts house-building at the heart of its economic strategy. A significant feature of the 'enabling environment' for growth we outlined in Chapter 8 is access for the workforce to adequate and affordable housing. A major programme of house-building won't only bring benefits in terms of future labour market flexibility, but also a more immediate economic boost. Every UK recovery from recession over the last century has been associated with a sharp rise in house-building – with the exception of the post-2008 recovery. It is no coincidence, given the slow pace of house-building, that we have just lived through the longest and slowest economic recovery in British history.

The government has accused the UK's large house-builders of deliberately restricting the supply of new homes to keep prices rising, so pushing up profits. The 'big developers [have] a stranglehold on supply', said Communities Secretary Sajid Javid in October 2016. They are 'sitting on landbanks', while 'delaying build-out'.[5] The idea of 'land-banking' – with the biggest house-builders remaining on go-slow, the resulting shortage of homes pushing up prices, so raising their profit on each unit – used to be dismissed as a conspiracy theory. As housing affordability has become more acute in recent years, this view has changed.

A quarter of all new homes in the UK are built by the biggest three providers, with over 50 per cent provided by the top eight. A recent report from the House of Lords Economic Affairs Select Committee described Britain's house-building industry as having 'all the characteristics of an oligopoly'.[6] During the 1980s, small and medium-sized builders, keen to build fast to aid cash flow, accounted for two thirds of all new homes built each year. In 2015, their share was just a fifth.

Lobbyists for the large house-builders deny deliberate delays, blaming restrictions imposed by the UK's planning system instead. There is evidence, though, that while the planning system remains cumbersome, more and more approvals are now being given, yet the homes are not being built. In 2015, the big three house-builders – Barratt, Taylor Wimpey and Persimmon – completed 44,000 homes, but they had planning permission to build another 200,000. They also owned combined 'strategic land holdings' that could accommodate well over a quarter of a million more homes.

Internal government figures show that, in England alone, there is planning permission outstanding for over 476,000 homes that remain unbuilt – a record high. Across the UK, a 28 per cent rise in planning permissions granted between 2012 and 2014 led to just a 10 per cent rise in completed homes – with the entire increase in planning approvals being absorbed by alleged 'land-banking'. That may help explain why, since 2008, the average delay of twenty-one months between planning permission being granted and the completion of a new home has risen to thirty-two months.

The campaign group Shelter estimates that nearly one in three homes granted planning permission between 2012 and 2016 has not been built – amounting to 320,000 units. In London, the share of so-called phantom homes is one in two. Over the same period, the profits of the UK's five largest house-builders soared by 388 per cent, reaching £3.3 billion in 2016.[7]

There seems to be evidence that the current house-building system encourages large developers to sit on land and drip-feed new homes onto the market in order to keep prices high. Excess demand, which in turn drives prices even higher, diverts disproportionate shares of post-tax incomes into mortgage and rental payments, damping down broader consumer spending, while wiping out savings. As people move further away from their place of work, so they can afford to buy, the resulting longer commutes not only lower productivity but also negatively impact family life and general well-being.[8]

TARGET 2022

The Queen's Speech of June 2017 was dominated by Brexit – with the government scheduling a Repeal Bill, new immigration legislation and other measures related to leaving the EU. But the speech also included a pledge to 'promote fairness and transparency in the housing market, and help ensure more homes are built', following the Housing White Paper published in February 2017.[9] We believe that tackling the UK's housing crisis should be the government's absolute priority, second only to steering the UK through the complex Brexit process. The housing shortage is now so serious and causing such economic and social damage it is no longer feasible to hope that the situation will change without radical reform.

The government must take immediate and bold steps to facilitate the building of 300,000 new homes each year over the next five years – roughly double the current rate of construction. While this will involve granting additional planning permission, the pressing need is to ensure that large builders implement approvals that have already been granted. Ministers must get tough on developers, giving councils the power to tax those who refuse to build fast enough, while granting planning permission to developers based on their track record of delivery.

The government should boost the UK's post-Brexit economy by creating powerful Housing Development Corporations (HDCs) – bodies that acquire land, grant themselves planning permission, then sell on the land in parcels to private developers. The HDCs would use the 'planning gain' from the sharp rise in land values to fund new schools, hospitals, roads and so on. If new housing means local public services are significantly enhanced, there would be far fewer objections from existing residents. Variations of this model have been successfully used in countries from Germany and Holland to Singapore and South Korea.[10]

It is ridiculous that no new town has been successfully developed in the last thirty years, despite rapid population growth. The 'garden city' movement must be revived, building attractive new towns that combine private residences with high-quality social housing, rather than relying on tower blocks. Since the February 2017 Housing White Paper, the government has altered legislation so local authorities can set up 'new town corporations' without having to wait for Whitehall to take the initiative, with local government able to retain the proceeds of land sales, ensuring they are channelled into local infrastructure. The use of these new powers should be encouraged.

Building new towns may limit the need to use greenbelt land and other highly sensitive sites. Yet some greenbelts may still need to be shifted, recognising that our big cities have expanded since greenbelts were first designated in the 1950s. The government, in addition, should sell many of the small sites it owns for housing, reserving plots for SME builders, so homes are built quickly.

The Grenfell Tower tragedy highlighted the poor quality of much of the UK's social housing. Over the past two decades, under governments of various parties, only a few thousand council houses have been built each year, falling to just a few hundred for several years under Tony Blair. There is further scope for the government to offer large developers land with planning permission at relatively low cost, on condition it is used to build social housing that generates a return for developers in the form of low, regulated but steady rental payments. While the bulk of the solution to the UK's housing shortage lies with the private sector, Britain is always going to need a significant and regularly replenished stock of social housing.

Not only do more homes need to be built for purchase and rental, but the taxation of housing must change – starting with a sharp reduction of stamp duty, to boost turnover in the secondary market, along with a comprehensive assessment of the alternatives.[11] Once we have left the EU, perhaps coinciding with a move towards greater devolution, local councils could be empowered to decide whether limits should apply to the buying of homes within certain geographies by overseas investors.

In 2015, ministers publicly set a target that 1 million new homes would be built in the UK within five years – amounting to 200,000 per year. That target was dropped in the 2017 White Paper but should now be reinstated and enhanced, aiming for 300,000 houses per year until 2022. In 2016, while the number of new homes started by house-builders was up 5 per cent, the number completed fell. Just 168,000 new builds came to market across the UK, way below the 250,000 needed annually to meet demand, let alone addressing the huge supply deficit.

We've been here before. In the face of an acute housing shortage after Second World War, an outgoing Labour government oversaw the building of 200,000 homes in a year. The Conservatives were then elected on a promise, largely met, to build 300,000 annually. We need to invoke the 1950s sense of emergency and social justice to help overcome remaining planning restrictions, vested interests and housing industry torpor.

YOUNG AT HEART

It is often claimed that Brexit is bad for young people, and that the June 2016 referendum result has somehow 'stolen their future'.[12] That is based more on propaganda than fact. Brexit is positive for the country's long-term future. It is also the case that the vast majority of young adults care far more about the UK's broken housing market and student debt than they do about Brexit. The reason so many young voters backed Labour in the June 2017 general election was that the party's campaign was issue-driven, barely featuring Brexit – and when Jeremy

Corbyn did speak about leaving the EU, he stressed that he was in favour.[13] The Liberal Democrat campaign, on the other hand, focused heavily on the party's desire to stay in the EU and ultimately failed to engage young adults, with the party enduring a falling share of the vote and its worst ever general election result.

Young British people will still be able to travel across Europe after Brexit, as they can now across most of the globe. The Article 50 negotiations could well produce a deal that relates visas to 'work' rather than 'visits', allowing all of us the freedom to travel for pleasure in the EU 27, unencumbered by red tape. When it comes to young adults taking 'working holidays', again, there is every incentive for the EU to make this as easy as possible. Over recent years, far higher numbers of EU-based young adults have come to live and work in the UK rather than the other way around – not least due to extremely high levels of EU youth unemployment. Countless young Britons also choose to study or work in America and Australia – and do so successfully – even though neither country is in the EU.

It is important that the UK maintains its leading role in educational exchange programmes, some of which predate the EU. The UK may remain part of the Erasmus scheme and other European youth and student exchange programmes such as Horizon 2020 and the Marie Curie scholarship. Since it was established, more than 200,000 British students have been directly funded by Erasmus grants to study in EU countries, with Horizon 2020 channelling around £2 billion of EU funds to British universities. The government has agreed to support these programmes until the UK's EU withdrawal – so little will change until 2019 at the earliest. But even after that, one should expect continued UK involvement in international research and exchange programmes.

It is worth noting that a number of non-EU countries – Liechtenstein, Norway, Russia, Turkey, Egypt, Israel and Jordan – already collaborate with the Erasmus Plus programme. In addition, academics are exploring the possibility of the UK adopting a version of the Swiss–European Mobility Programme – which guarantees Switzerland an association agreement with the EU for research projects in exchange for academic free movement. The attraction of the UK's university sector, which is world-class across a range of disciplines, gives Britain a strong hand in negotiating such an agreement.

Another proposal under discussion would extend Erasmus to facilitate a global network of scholars and students, going beyond the EU. British universities would then be in a position to attract even greater numbers of students and researchers from the US and leading growth markets such as India and China. These leading emerging markets are attractive not only as Britain is keen to foster non-EU trade ties, but also because they are, in certain fields, now at the forefront of technological and scientific research. Such an arrangement would be far more likely to prosper if there was academic free movement and students were excluded from immigration numbers – another reason we suggest this happens.

In Chapter 8, we outlined the importance of soft infrastructure – at the heart of which is the UK's university sector. While the numbers attending university have soared in recent years, the share of young adults in vocational training has fallen. These trends should be reversed, with vocational training given more priority and greater status. The current student loan system should be replaced with a 'graduate tax' – while providing free university education for high-achieving students in key subjects important for the economy (ranging from STEM to certain languages). If Brexit brings renewed focus on skills training, and the importance of extending educational exchanges beyond Europe and to the wider world, it will have served young adults well.

It is perplexing that the science community and many working across the university sector have been so negative about the prospect of Brexit. Their analysis seems driven largely by concerns over their current EU funding – and a determination, in this context, to secure replacement funds from the UK. The government should reassure universities of ongoing funding, but also use Brexit as an opportunity to make state funding of research more efficient. Soon after the referendum, the government announced that all research spending that currently comes via the EU would be maintained for now, prior to evaluation in terms of value for money. When such an evaluation takes place, it will provide an opportunity to streamline state funding of research, strip out duplication and ensure better taxpayer value.

In her Lancaster House speech in January 2017, the tenth point in Theresa May's twelve-point speech was her desire to make the UK the best place for science and investment. We should continue to collaborate with our European partners on major science, research and technology initiatives. But, with Asian universities soaring up the research rankings, there is no reason at all to single out EU universities for special treatment. UK universities, of world renown for centuries, should be collaborating with centres of learning across the entire globe.

Some academics feel that EU freedom of movement has undermined academic exchange programmes with the US and Australasia. If British universities can maintain our recently enhanced academic links with the EU, while restoring our historic ties with scholars in Anglo-Saxon nations, we can have the best of both worlds. The current scope for global collaboration should not be underestimated.

The UK has some of the best universities in the world. London has four: Imperial, the LSE, UCL and King's. Britain has some of the best medical schools too. While many people are concerned the UK will somehow lose out by not being in certain international research groups, or will fail to attract skilled staff, we feel these fears are misplaced. Indeed, of the forty-four countries that take part in the EU's Horizon and scientific groups, one third are already from outside the EU – as we mentioned in Chapter 5. This reinforces the case of the second half of this book – that the success of Brexit will depend heavily on our domestic economic agenda. Outside the EU, the British government will be more empowered to help set the rules and influence the policies that ensure that science is funded, and innovation continues, across UK universities.

These last two chapters have ranged across immigration, housing and universities. One common underlying theme in our recommendations across all three headings is the importance, post-Brexit, of central government continuing to devolve power. In the next chapter, we tackle devolution head-on, examining specific aspects of Brexit that impact Scotland, Northern Ireland and Wales. We then discuss how Brexit could affect the extremely important relationship between the UK and the Republic of Ireland.

CHAPTER 12

NATIONS AND REGIONS

'Leave came top in nine of the UK's nations and regions, with Remain coming top in just three. The West Midlands had the highest vote share for Leave, with Scotland highest for Remain.'

BBC, EU REFERENDUM: THE RESULT[1]

On 23 June 2016, more people in the UK voted to leave the EU than have ever voted for anything in the history of this country. A total of 17,410,742 supported Brexit, some 51.9 per cent of all votes cast. Meanwhile, 48.1 per cent – 16,141,241 voters – backed staying in the EU. The winning majority for the Leave side was 1,269,501.

Three parts of the UK voted Remain. Some 60 per cent of London supported staying in the EU, a majority of 750,287. Of the capital's thirty-three boroughs, twenty-eight wanted to keep EU membership.[2] Scotland voted Remain by 62 per cent to 38 per cent, a majority of 642,869. Nicola Sturgeon, the Scottish National Party leader, described this as a 'strong, unequivocal vote'.

Northern Ireland was the third area to back Remain, with a vote share of 56 per cent to 44 per cent and a majority of 91,265. Across the other nine UK regions, the respective majorities favouring Brexit ranged from 82,225 in Wales, where 52.5 per cent voted to exit the EU, to 548,512 in the West Midlands, where 59 per cent wanted to leave.

While Brexit opens up many opportunities, it uncovers some controversial issues in the UK regarding regional policy and devolution of power. The referendum result also raises broader constitutional questions, having triggered renewed debate over another Scottish referendum, for instance. The SNP, though, endured a sizeable loss of support in the general election of June 2017, the Scottish electorate seemingly keen to avoid the acrimonious divisions of yet another independence campaign. We do not expect there to be another Scottish referendum any time soon.

The focus of attention, instead, has been on Ireland, particularly the possibility of a hard border between Northern Ireland and the Republic of Ireland. This issue is seen as so important by both the UK and EU that it was one of the three topics chosen for the very first phase of the Article 50 discussions – along with the size of Britain's 'divorce bill' and the rights of UK citizens living in the EU and their British EU-based counterparts. We consider relations between Northern Ireland and the Irish Republic in the next chapter, which is devoted to the island of Ireland. This chapter, alongside Scottish devolution and potential post-Brexit independence, tackles constitutional, economic and financial issues relating to Wales and the English regions.

DEVOLUTION EVOLUTION

Leaving the EU allows the UK to return competencies from Brussels in areas such as state aid and the distribution of cohesion funds, the latter being key for regional policy. In a detailed report in 2012, the think tank Open Europe raised serious questions about the benefits of the existing EU structural funds for the UK.[3] Of the UK's contribution, 'around 70 per cent goes to other member states and only 5 per cent is redistributed across the regions', said Open Europe, 'with the remaining 25 per cent being redistributed within the same region in which the funds were raised'. So most of the money the UK receives from EU structural funds ends up 'round-tripping', going back to the same region from where it came in the first place.

Only two regions in the UK were net beneficiaries of the EU's structural funds: namely Cornwall and the Isles of Scilly and West Wales and the Valleys. Meanwhile, thirty-five UK regions were net contributors. This means that some relatively poor areas have been losing out as a result of EU membership. Open Europe estimates that in 2012, the West Midlands, which has the UK's lowest disposable income per capita, paid £3.55 to the structural funds for every £1 received. The equivalent figure for Merseyside, with a disposable income that is just 88 per cent of the UK average, was £2.88. 'The North East paid in more than it got back, as did Northern Ireland – £1.58 for every £1 received,' says Open Europe. 'And all sub-regions in Scotland are likewise net losers from the EU's structural funds.'

The previous coalition government, in one of its Competency Reports cited earlier, indicated there was probably not much difference in value for money between structural funds spent by Brussels and regional assistance provided by the UK government.[4] But the report acknowledged there would be greater flexibility in determining priorities if the funds were allocated from Britain. It should be noted, also, that making such payments via the EU involves bearing the cost of several extra layers of bureaucracy – from both Whitehall and Brussels – before the efficacy of the actual spending delivered can be judged. And it is surely better that UK taxpayers' money spent on regional assistance in Britain is overseen by ministers and officials directly accountable to UK voters.

The importance of returning regional policy 'competencies' to the UK should not be understated. It ties in with economic issues we highlighted in Chapter 8 concerning the need for regional infrastructure spending and fiscal devolution. Three of the five most competitive regions in the EU are in the south of England, according to the European Commission, with another in the top ten.[5] Out of 263 sub-regions analysed across the EU, London was the most competitive and Berkshire, Buckinghamshire and Oxfordshire was second. Utrecht in the Netherlands was third, Stockholm was fourth and Surrey, East and West Sussex was fifth. Hampshire and the Isle of Wight was judged the tenth most competitive EU region out of 263. The bottom ten regions included five from Greece, three in Romania, one in Bulgaria and one in France.

London clearly dominates the UK economy, but not, based on competitiveness measures, to an extent that is particularly unusual. Across the twenty-eight current EU members, the capital region is the most competitive in all but three countries – Italy, Germany and the Netherlands. The gap in competitiveness between the capital and the next region is relatively small in the UK, but that is probably because the reach of London in terms of productivity stretches a long way across southern England.

The EC also notes that the UK has 'heterogeneous scores', reflecting a wide distribution of competitiveness across the whole country – pointing to the need, once again, for a concerted post-Brexit regional strategy. The least competitive UK regions are Northern Ireland (145th of the 263), West Wales and the Valleys (134th) and Cornwall and the Isles of Scilly (133rd). In terms of GDP per head, meanwhile, the highest UK region was North East Scotland (tenth of 263), followed by London (thirteenth). There were a number of low GDP per head scores for the UK, including South Yorkshire (182nd) and Cornwall and the Scilly Isles (179th).

Some interesting contrasts between neighbouring UK regions were noted by the EC. West Wales and the Valleys came 204th for income per head while East Wales was much higher at 127th. Merseyside was the seventy-sixth most competitive region and 166th in terms of GDP per head, while Greater Manchester was forty-forth in terms of competitiveness and 125th in per capita income. This should be a wake-up call to those proclaiming that EU membership has been good for the UK's regional economy. For large parts of the country, it clearly has not.

Recent years have been challenging not just for various parts of the British economy, but for our constitution too. The long-standing stability and success of the UK's unwritten constitution has generally been achieved by observing the maxim 'if it ain't broke, don't fix it'. Over the last quarter of a century, though, that cautious approach has changed. First, there was devolution of powers to the various national assemblies in Holyrood, Stormont and Cardiff in the late 1990s. Then we had the Scottish and EU referendums in 2014 and 2016 respectively, which prompted the question of whether the UK itself would survive. Some Eurosceptics, such as former Conservative leader William Hague, argued ahead of the 2016 referendum that they were supporting Remain, largely because of the fear of a UK break-up if Brexit provoked another referendum on Scottish independence.[6]

Now, as we consider the UK after Brexit, there is an opportunity – and perhaps a necessity – to take steps to shore up the Union. Certainly, we need to maintain and improve this enduring and largely successful constitutional arrangement by allowing and facilitating its many very different and disparate communities to feel engaged. The constitutional construct that is the UK, above all, needs to become once again a source of stability, rather than an institution that seems on the verge of collapse.

The Constitutional Reform Group, an influential cross-party body of peers, has reasserted some important basic principles.[7] Each part of the UK should be entitled to determine how it governs and arranges its own affairs. At the same time, certain areas are best governed from the centre – such as defence, foreign affairs, immigration, civil service and macroeconomic policy including monetary policy. We do not necessarily need to reinvent the UK's constitutional wheel, but rather clarify areas of confusion and identify the need for reform. When it comes to neutralising the risk of separation, though, following a clearly divisive Brexit vote, it certainly makes sense to move towards a more federal UK structure.

The EU itself has deep-rooted regional problems. These are seen most clearly in the vast disparity between the core economies, such as Germany, the Netherlands and Finland, and those on the periphery, including Portugal, Ireland, Italy, Greece and Spain. Over the last few years, Ireland and Spain have enjoyed a cyclical rebound in their economies, while Greece, in particular, remains mired in depression. This has led to renewed debate about a multi-speed Europe, as discussed in Chapter 4.

In this context, any decisions made within the UK relating to Scotland or Northern Ireland could have wider implications across the EU. The possibility of Scottish independence, for instance, has previously attracted the attention of Spain. If an independent Scotland can stay in the EU, Madrid is concerned that it could encourage Catalan separatists to go down the same route. Any decision regarding the Irish border, similarly, will be of interest to Greece – given the possible implications for Cyprus.

SCOTLAND THE BRAVE?

The case for the UK to leave the EU is by no means the same as the case for Scotland leaving the UK. In fact, the two could hardly be more different. In democratic terms, the UK has been ceding more power to Brussels, losing sovereignty over the last four decades. In contrast, with the 1998 devolution and in the wake of the 2014 independence referendum, Edinburgh has been gaining power from London. That is only right in the case of Scotland – and these transfers of power have been implemented, for the most part, without rancour. On top of that, Scotland is a net recipient of funding from the rest of the UK, while the UK is a large net contributor to the rest of the EU. The relationship between Holyrood and London, then, stands in stark contrast to that between London and Brussels.

The Scottish independence referendum was far closer than many had expected. In response to the question 'Should Scotland be an independent country?'

44.7 per cent voted 'Yes' and 55.3 per cent backed 'No'. During the last few weeks of that referendum campaign, moving to protect the Union, then Prime Minister David Cameron and other party leaders offered Scotland more powers. As the SNP made clear in their independence campaign, the Scottish Parliament controlled only 7 per cent of public expenditure within Scotland at that time – an illustration of the extent of the UK's centralisation, and the case for further fiscal devolution.

The 2014 vote was followed by an impressive SNP performance in the 2015 general election – in which the party won fifty-six of the fifty-nine Scottish constituencies, securing a 50 per cent share of the Scottish vote and 4.7 per cent of the nationwide total. That put the possibility of another independence referendum centre stage during the EU campaign in 2016. The fear that a vote to leave the EU might well trigger another referendum in Scotland – and independence – was clearly a focus for many. After the 2017 snap election, though – in which the SNP lost twenty-one Westminster seats, the party's vote share falling sharply to 36.9 per cent in Scotland and 3 per cent nationwide – calls for a second Scottish referendum were put on hold, the SNP backing down on previous demands.

The message from Scotland seemed to be that the public did not want another divisive independence vote. That holds lessons for the broader UK, as we discuss in Chapter 14, with an extremely vocal and well-funded part of the political establishment continuing to call for a second EU referendum, despite little appetite for a repeat vote among the broader population.

One of the major issues during the 2014 independence referendum was whether an independent Scotland could continue to use the pound. Mark Carney, the Governor of the Bank of England, made two important interventions on this – one in a balanced speech months before the political campaign began; the second, closer to the day of the vote, when he answered a question after speaking at the TUC conference in Liverpool.[8] Carney made clear that a currency union was incompatible with Scottish sovereignty, undermining SNP claims that an independent Scotland could keep the pound – a position the party had been forced to take amid heightened speculation from 2010 onwards that the Eurozone could collapse, with some nations reverting to their legacy currencies.

History shows that currency unions of sizeable sovereign nations must become political unions if they are to survive.[9] This has certainly been evident in terms of Scotland and England, joined together by the Act of Union of 1707. This is also the clear direction of travel for the Eurozone, a philosophy encapsulated in the EU's push for 'ever closer union'. This is a view of Europe that the UK has never been close to accepting, and which is fast losing popularity across the rest of the EU too.

While there are many small, independent countries successfully running their own affairs, the challenge for Scotland would have been the initial dislocation of leaving the UK, not only due to currency issues but also the removal of long-standing financial support from the rest of the UK under the Barnett formula.[10] While the location of the UK's offshore oil industry was a rallying call for the SNP in 2014, the subsequent volatility of the oil price highlighted the need for Scotland to diversify its economy. The collapse in oil prices, from an average of $86 a barrel in 2014 to $41 the year after, blew a hole in the SNP's oil-based case for financial independence. 'Official Scottish government statistics show we spent £14.8 billion more in 2015–16 than we raised in taxes,' noted the influential journalist Bill Jamieson, 'equivalent to 9.5 per cent of Scotland's GDP'.[11] The reason for such a large Scottish budget deficit was falling crude prices – which saw Scotland's share of North Sea revenues plummet from a peak of £11 billion in 2011/12 to £1.8 billion in 2014/15 before crashing to just £60 million the year after. This was somewhat short of the £7 billion the SNP had 'conservatively' estimated for 2015/16.

Every August, Edinburgh hosts one of the world's most important cultural festivals – an impressive performance by any standards, highlighting Scotland and the UK's role as a global leader in the creative industries. The Scottish capital, moreover, occupies an important position as one of Europe's niche financial centres. Scotland's food and drinks industry saw its total turnover rise from £10 billion to £14.4 billion between 2010 and 2015, with its exports rising 40 per cent between 2007 and 2016, reaching £5.5 billion.[12] There is a growing Scottish life sciences industry, too.

With Brexit, the fiscal devolution issue becomes important for Scotland. Regional growth also comes to the fore, given the importance of ensuring that more economic success is felt across the whole of Scotland. There is an initial temptation to link such success to regional aid – particularly in any transition phase. The long-term aim, though, must be for various parts of the UK, to the greatest extent possible, to stand on their own two feet – fostering dynamic domestic economies which are also globally competitive. While this should be relatively easy for Edinburgh, Brexit can also revitalise the Scottish fishing industry, as we outlined in Chapter 8. Rethinking our agricultural and environmental policy outside the EU could also have a transformational impact on the Scottish countryside, boosting the tourism industry.[13]

We also believe that Scotland is a prime candidate to introduce the free ports we advocated in Chapter 7. Outside the UK's customs authority, free ports allow goods to be imported, manufactured or re-exported without incurring domestic customs duties or taxes. They can be supported by research and development grants, as well as regulatory flexibility. Scotland has the industrial heritage, global connections and entrepreneurial zeal to be at the forefront of the UK's free ports movement, igniting prosperity in Clydebank, for instance, or Dundee. The EU, with its instinct always to 'harmonise', seems determined to clamp down on areas keen to introduce lighter taxes or fewer regulations in the name of sparking innovation and growth. After Brexit, the UK would be in the position to encourage new free ports, with Scotland well positioned to take full advantage.

Further economic independence makes sense for Scotland. Brexit further encourages the current trend towards greater devolution from Westminster, facilitating a regulatory environment that allows Scotland itself to grow. But first, perhaps, there is a need for a change of mindset, away from the idea that Scotland would somehow do better tied to the EU, as opposed to embracing Brexit.

In general, it is strange that those in favour of full Scottish independence want to continue ceding power to Brussels. If an independent Scotland was ultimately able to join the EU – and Spain and Greece may object, as mentioned earlier – it could be forced eventually to join the single currency, which remains technically an EU entry condition. Unlike other new entrants, though, Scotland's income per head is relatively high. So it would receive little in the way of structural funds and may even be classed as a net contributor – on the basis of income levels based on previous transfers from Westminster that would stop once independence took effect. So, in fiscal terms, Scotland would lose out twice.

Beyond sovereignty issues, former Prime Minister Gordon Brown has made a compelling case against post-Brexit Scottish independence, pointing out that the country's exports to the UK's single market were £48.5 billion in 2015, four times those to the EU's single market.[14] The importance to Scotland of British defence spending should also not be dismissed. Scotland currently has 14,000 military regular and reserve personnel and 3,930 Ministry of Defence civilian staff. The Faslane naval base on the Clyde is Scotland's second biggest single-site employer, providing 6,800 jobs directly, with around 11,000 industry jobs supported by related Scottish supply chains.

While the UK's military is currently subject to personnel cutbacks, and Scotland is not immune, it is noteworthy that all eleven Royal Navy submarines will be based at Faslane from 2020, seeing the number of people directly employed at the base rising to 8,200.[15] And in July 2016, it was confirmed that the Ministry of Defence will purchase nine new Boeing P-8A Poseidon maritime patrol aircraft, to be based at RAF Lossiemouth in Moray, north-east Scotland, providing 400 extra jobs.[16] The government has also identified Lossiemouth as the preferred location for an additional squadron of Typhoon fighter planes, requiring 400 more on-site staff.[17]

While regional policy and fiscal devolution will provide opportunities, another necessary mindset change is for Scotland to move away from an over-reliance on the public sector and to boost private-sector growth. The dynamics of the Scottish economy are changing – as global trends are becoming more evident, and given the impact of new technology and the emerging 'gig economy'. One interesting development is the 26 per cent rise in the number of self-employed people across Scotland since 2006, almost three quarters of that increase accounted for by women. Overall Scottish employment is up 5.6 per cent over the last decade, with 45 per cent of that rise accounted for by self-employment.[18]

'We need to develop diverse local economies,' says Andy Willox, the Scottish policy convener of the Federation of Small Businesses, 'so a single local closure or industry challenge doesn't hit a community, or the entire country, for six.'[19] We would agree that diversifying the economic base and boosting the private sector has to be Scotland's Brexit dividend.

DESTINATION WALES

On a high turnout of 71 per cent, the Welsh voted to leave the EU by 52.5 per cent to 47.5 per cent. Some were surprised by this result, given that Wales has

attracted sizeable EU grants and subsidies over the years, be they structural funds
or related specifically to agriculture or education. As Brexit takes place, Wales
will certainly be one of the regions where transitional assistance from Westminster is most likely to be needed. This surely, though, cannot be the long-term
goal for Wales – a reliance on aid from London as opposed to Brussels.

The history of Wales is one of industrial strength, blighted by over-reliance
on certain activities. The principality's clear ability to attract FDI, despite economic difficulties, reflects positively on the available skill sets. The value of FDI
projects into the Welsh economy during 2015/16 'totalled £681 million', according to the Welsh government, with investment coming 'from twenty-three
different countries'.[20]

Such FDI derived from eighty-five overseas companies, creating and safeguarding 11,546 jobs in 2016/17, despite concerns the Brexit referendum would
deter overseas investors. Wales won 11 per cent of all jobs secured by FDI flows
into the UK, despite accounting for under 4 per cent of the overall economy.[21]

Manufacturing accounts for 16 per cent of the Welsh economy, up from
14 per cent in 2008, and above the 11 per cent share across the UK as a whole.
Hosting aerospace and defence companies such as GE Aviation Wales, Airbus
UK and Raytheon, along with carmakers and suppliers including TVR, Aston
Martin, Toyota and Calsonic Kansei, Wales has seen something of a manufacturing renaissance since the global financial crisis. From 2008 to 2015, the
Welsh manufacturing sector expanded by 27 per cent, driving a quarter of
all Welsh economic growth over this period. That amounted to the third best
regional manufacturing performance in the UK, after the East Midlands and
West Midlands – one reason Welsh unemployment was at a ten-year low of 4.8
per cent in mid-2017, only slightly above 4.6 per cent for the UK as a whole.

Wales could benefit as the government seeks to promote opportunities for
manufacturing companies. Farming and fisheries should also gain, as in Scotland, with the creation of a post-Brexit regulatory structure favouring UK
fishing and smaller farmers. The biggest challenge for Wales is to stimulate domestic demand while ensuring its young people are qualified for skilled work
and then choose to remain and build families.

Wales is a direct recipient of EU funding, often matched by UK spending. It
receives for instance £680 million annually, consisting largely of structural funds

and £295 million of CAP remittances.[22] Unlike the UK as a whole, though, Wales is a net exporter to the EU, with Germany the biggest export market. It is also an agricultural exporter and so its EU exports could possibly be hit by high tariffs, if no FTA is reached or Wales fails to diversify its agricultural export markets beyond the EU.

Over the medium term, the Welsh economy tends to track closely that of the UK. That being said, the Welsh government has expressed concern that because of low incomes and higher levels of deprivation, Wales is vulnerable to economic shocks. While the principality has attracted considerable FDI, one implication is that workers are disproportionately reliant on large-scale employers. Clearly, the picture is mixed.

The EU divides Wales into two regions: 'West Wales and the Valleys', where income per head is below 75 per cent of the EU average; and 'East Wales', where GDP per capita is above 90 per cent of the average across the EU. Given that West Wales and the Valleys receives considerable EU funding, it will need direct economic assistance after Brexit.

In 2014, when the coalition government's Competency Reports examined various aspects of the UK's relationship with the EU, such spending coincided with a worsening of the situation. '[In] west Wales and the Valleys ... GDP per capita had fallen from 74.1 per cent of the EU 25 average in 2000 to 64 per cent of the EU 28 average in 2011,' concluded the report.[23] Correlation is not causation, of course, but the record suggests that the structural funds were not well targeted. Various parts of Wales clearly need to become more competitive – and there is a requirement to boost the economy in a more general sense.

In that respect, regional funds may be needed as part of a Brexit transition programme, only this time from London, and targeted more effectively. It would be wrong, though, to think of this as a permanent process. The Welsh Local Government Association noted in its evidence to the competency review that EU funds had helped in the absence of a more robust redistributive UK regional policy. External assistance has a role to play, but what is ideally needed is for the private sector to engage to a greater degree.

There are many issues at play, not linked to the EU, explaining the vulnerability of certain Welsh regions – one of which may be public-sector pay. As in other UK regions, the lack of local public-sector wage variation forces up wage scales in a manner that appears to 'crowd out' private-sector employment. The Welsh median wage for a private-sector worker, for instance, was £23,390 in 2016, while for a public-sector worker it was £28,489.[24] National public-sector wage bargaining across the entire UK (despite relatively small London weighting adjustments) fails to recognise huge variations in living standards, while making regions such as Wales far too reliant on the state.

Wales also lags in terms of education. The OECD's Programme for International Student Assessment (PISA) results for 2016 show Welsh fifteen-year-olds behind those of England, Scotland and Northern Ireland in literacy, maths and science.[25] Wales has fewer high-performing and more low-performing students in science, reading and mathematics. 'Alarmingly 21 per cent of students tested in Wales cannot read well enough to participate effectively and productively in life', says the PISA report. Having said that, the figures for the rest of the UK – 18 per cent in England and Scotland and 15 per cent in Northern Ireland – were only slightly less concerning.

In their post-referendum analysis, the Welsh government made, among other things, a strong call for the UK 'to negotiate to continue as a subscribing partner of the European Investment Bank (EIB)'. As an EU member, Britain is a 16 per cent shareholder in the EIB and, under current rules, only EU member states can own EIB stakes. But the EIB does not just invest in EU countries, 'being active in over 160 countries' as its own website makes clear.[26] 'There is no equivalent body in the UK providing the same sort of investment funds at equivalent cost,' says the Welsh government.[27] This is a valid point, particularly as the EIB has provided commercial expertise as well as funding for a number of projects, such as the South Wales Metro.[28] In our economic recommendations, we support the idea of a long-term infrastructure fund, an idea outlined in the 2017 Labour Party manifesto – and a policy that, we believe, would benefit Wales.[29]

Exports from Wales to the EU are significant, across a wide range of goods sectors – including agriculture, steel, automotive, chemicals, electronics, aerospace, pharmaceutical, transport equipment and petroleum. This highlights the fact that Wales has much to gain from an FTA with the EU, while demonstrating that the principality has many economic strengths to build on. Also, Welsh service exports globally include insurance and pension services, manufacturing services such as repairs and financial services. The key has to be reinvigorating the domestic economy and attracting investment for the UK-wide market, as well as internationally. It was pleasing that, as this book was going to press, the Spanish train maker CAF announced it was opening a new factory in south Wales, creating 300 jobs.[30] The success of Wales in attracting such inward investment must continue.

REGIONS, COUNCILS, CITIES

In terms of UK government spending, Northern Ireland is the highest recipient region with £14,018 per head. That was before the DUP secured an extra £1 billion for Northern Ireland, following the June 2017 general election, in return for pledging to support the Conservative government in a hung parliament. The next biggest recipient is Scotland, with £13,054 of government spending per head, followed by London on £12,686 and Wales on £12,531. The bottom two regions are the East of England, on £10,591, and the South East (excluding London), which receives £10,582 – the lowest amount of all.[31] Too often the South East is mentioned in the same breath as London without an appreciation of the low government spending that takes place there, despite its proximity to the capital.

Only three UK regions are generally net contributors to the HM Revenue and Customs – providing more in taxation than they receive in government spending. These are, in order, London, followed by the South East and the East of England. Given that they are net contributors, while also being the lowest recipients, the South East (excluding London) and the East of England arguably get the worst deal in terms of the UK's public finances.

Northern Ireland, in contrast, receives by far the highest amount of net government spending – although this in part reflects efforts being made to cope with the aftermath of decades of sectarian violence. It is also worth noting that, like a number of other farming areas, Northern Ireland receives a large amount of EU funding. Direct CAP payments represent around 80 per cent of farmers' incomes across Northern Ireland. While the government has pledged to maintain CAP payments until 2022, replacing funds previously received from Brussels during the first few post-Brexit years, Northern Ireland will clearly need careful consideration as Britain reorganises its system of farming support outside the EU. We return to Northern Ireland in the next chapter.

There is a tendency in the UK not to see ourselves as a large economy. Compared with the US or China, we are not, but beyond the world's two economic superpowers the UK is definitely a major economic player. Britain ranks fifth, after Japan and Germany, and is on a par with France. According to Eurostat, using data from 2013, London alone would be the eighth biggest economy in Western Europe, larger than the whole of Sweden. The UK capital accounts for a quarter of national income – not unusual in general, but this is a relatively large share for a single city to command in a world-ranking economy like the UK.[32]

The constitutional challenges and regional economic policy issues discussed in this chapter feed into a debate on the future role of cities. How far should the UK pursue fiscal devolution – should it give more power to regional mayors and to local representatives? Even though the role of regional mayors and local politicians are not impacted by our EU membership, they become more relevant in a post-Brexit environment, given that regional policy will be central to the government's response.

The 'London effect' spreads productivity gains across much of the South East, as noted above, even if parts of the region do not share in London's wealth. Yet the capital's productivity still outperforms that of the UK as a whole by no less than 72 per cent. This picture is seen in some other large cities too, with Paris outperforming France by 67 per cent in terms of competitiveness and New York beating the US as a whole by 36 per cent. This perhaps reflects the tendency for large cities to attract clusters of high value-added sectors.

'The bad news is that the productivity gap between our capital and our second, third and fourth cities is greater than in any other major economy in the world,' said Chancellor Philip Hammond in October 2016. 'Closing that gap is key to Britain's future outside the EU – and that's why we are doing regional devolution deals, and why tackling those regional differences will be one of the key drivers for our industrial strategy.'[33]

It is appropriate that, following a Brexit vote that exposed clear divisions and income disparities across the UK, regional policy is now taking a more central role in the UK's political discourse. There are lessons to be learned from the past. When hit by the deindustrialisation of the 1980s, some parts of the country did not recover. The same applies to areas impacted by the miners' strike of 1984–85 – when the pits shut, a number of economically undiversified areas suffered significant decline. The same can be said, too, of many fishing and coastal areas following the UK's loss of control over fishing rights when we joined the EEC in 1973.

Regional policy links directly into the issue of clusters across the UK. Often these are centred around universities, which play an important role. There is also a wider issue of ensuring that regions and provincial cities are attractive enough to retain qualified young people; they need to be places where people want to raise families. Many cities across the UK see net outward migration of young qualified people to London – a trend that is inevitable to some extent but which could be slowed to the benefit of regional cities.

Urbanisation is one of the big global growth drivers in the UK, as mentioned in Chapter 2.[34] London is the only British city that figures on most measures in the top cities of the world. It is a global city and there is a need to ensure it continues to succeed. Crucially, though, we must ensure our mid-tier cities can also compete globally. That is why we would argue that airports in Birmingham and Manchester should be expanded. The HS3 train link connecting north-western and northern cities should be prioritised too, as well as better motorway connections to, for instance, Newcastle and the north-east.

While the public sector can play a role, there is a danger of the government overstepping the mark. Politicians keen to appease local electorates or bureaucrats in Whitehall – like those in Brussels – are not necessarily able to pick winners. There will be times when protecting a firm may work but generally speaking it fails.[35] Outcomes may be better served by focusing on removing barriers that add to the cost base for small firms without any noticeable benefit, while advisedly backing UK firms when procurement contracts come up for renewal.

Creating an 'enabling environment', as we described in Chapter 8, is ultimately the best route to growth, with more effective 'hard' and 'soft' infrastructure, such as physical and digital connectivity and better skilled workforces. Some of these measures, like removing regulations where it is possible to do so, produce quick wins, while others, like skills improvement, are obviously longer-term projects.

MUNICIPAL MARKETS?

Devolution of power is an important component of the UK's post-Brexit growth plan. We are starting to see this with the creation of metro mayors. In Chapter 10, we suggested that regional visas could help boost growth, with local council officials, mayors and local MPs liaising with business in an attempt to set immigration targets, while attracting international labour and talent as part of a regional development plan.

While devolving power to the regional and local level can boost openness and transparency, it is important that the local decision-making units make economic as well as political sense. The London Finance Commission, for instance, has argued for greater powers for London, including retaining money raised from property stamp duty, in order to channel this revenue back into local house-building.[36]

Devolution should also not only be about tax-raising powers. Increased competition between regions would help, with certain localities offering lower tax rates, perhaps around examples of the free ports we advocated earlier, to boost growth and drive a higher tax take overall. The ability to set business rates at a local level would certainly be one way to encourage local tax competition.

The municipal bond market is also a potentially useful option, allowing cities to borrow for their own needs, albeit under careful monitoring and regulation. Such bonds could force market discipline on local authorities, with short-termist and poor outcomes penalised by higher borrowing rates. There are concerns about what economists call 'moral hazard', of course, with local councils gambling that Westminster will not let them go bust. The so-called Orange County problem will always loom, named after the district in California forced to declare itself bankrupt in 1994 after losing $1.6 billion on derivatives trading. With certain investment safeguards, though, 'munibonds' could raise finance for local-level projects, providing investors with a more attractive alternative to central government bonds, while providing localities with access to funding they otherwise would not have.

We are by no means encouraging local authorities to borrow in order to pile into vast commercial property investments, engaging in hedge fund-style activities. This has clearly become a problem in recent years, as highlighted by the financial journalist John Plender, with UK local councils engaging in 'carry trades' – borrowing at rates lower than the private sector to fund apparently high-yielding property deals. Some of that funding has been provided by the Public Works Loan Board, a part of the Treasury that has been helping finance capital spending by local government for more than 200 years, its borrowing rates linked to gilts. We would agree with Lord (Matthew) Oakeshott, a highly experienced institutional property investor, when he says that 'councils punting on property is an accident waiting to happen'.[37]

Certainly, during the 1980s, Japanese cities suffered huge losses after speculative property investments went wrong, doing serious damage to the country's public finances. There are signs that such a bubble is brewing in Britain. The property consultant Savills suggests that local councils accounted for 2.5 per cent of all UK commercial property deals in 2016 – up from 0.2 per cent in 2015. Gerald Eve, another consultancy, reported that local authorities bought 25 per cent of all office investments in the south-east of England during the first three months of 2017.

It is clear that many local councils are cash-strapped – caught between rising health- and care-related expenditures and government funding cuts – and looking for alternative sources of income. If they are to issue municipal bonds, such borrowing should be on the state ledger – avoiding the incredulous ownership transfer and often scandalously high service charges associated with the private finance initiative. We would also argue that local councils should avoid investing in commercial real estate – a sector particularly prone to speculative instability.

With such restrictions, local and national government should be able to collectively raise private funds for specific infrastructure projects, such as toll roads and other transport facilities with a demonstrable income stream. As such, municipal bonds could be sold to investors on the basis that the money will be used to build a tangible income-generating asset in a certain locality.

The UK seems on the verge of a municipal bond revival. A new quasi-government entity, the UK Municipal Bonds Agency (UKMBA), has been set up to help councils issue bonds with maturities of between ten and twenty years. There is no reason why a more fiscally devolved UK should not build a successful market in municipal bonds, as already exists in Australia, New Zealand and, for the most part, the US. But, in our view, the UKMBA should only be promoting municipal bonds sold to complete infrastructure projects, not to invest in shopping centres or office blocks.

We could also encourage the UKMBA to strike deals with the EIB, mentioned earlier in a Welsh context, to help channel credit to smaller local authorities for infrastructure purposes. While the UK's relationship with the EIB is in flux due to the Article 50 talks, the prospect of a collaboration that gives the bank an opportunity to gain more exposure to local government in Britain might incentivise politicians on both sides to ensure the EIB and the UK maintain close links once we have left the EU.

Another idea to consider, as the UK looks to develop regional growth centres after Brexit, is whether universities could also issue their own debt. That may be a more effective and inexpensive way of raising funding not only for the very best British universities, but also for first-class departments in some second-tier institutions. Such bodies certainly have identifiable affinity groups that might want to invest in the form of alumni, and often tangible assets that could act as collateral. There are many possible options here, but given the desire to both reward good universities and courses, and to reduce the number of poor-quality courses, some external market discipline may be useful.

Regional policy, in general, is one of many areas where the UK will regain competency on leaving the EU. This is important, given the income discrepancies between the various parts of the UK. How we fare after March 2019 is not only about Brexit, but about what domestic and international policies we implement amidst the freedoms that being outside the EU provides.

Economic policy must recognise that the bulk of workers are involved in areas remote from the global economy and focused on the UK market – such as retail, the health system and social care, the public sector, the maintenance sector and vocational roles, as well as services. An important part of the financial sector is also domestically focused. This all argues for a dynamic and innovative domestic economic agenda, addressing all the nations and regions of the country as we have outlined.

Alongside this, more regions of the UK need to pay their way in the world as the country seeks to reduce its still-large current account deficit. This points to ensuring, post Brexit, a competitive and outward-looking economy, across all sectors – including manufacturing, the arts, technology and services, as well as international finance.

CHAPTER 13

IRELAND

*'Simply sitting on the sidelines and allowing the EU to negotiate
for Ireland is essentially untenable.'*

RAY BASSETT, FORMER IRISH AMBASSADOR[1]

The result of the UK's EU referendum was the latest twist in the deep and complex history of the relationship between the UK and Ireland. The good news is that Brexit is happening at a time when such relations – between Ireland and the UK, and between the six counties that form Northern Ireland and the twenty-six that make up the Irish Republic – are perhaps warmer and more stable than they have ever been.

During Prime Minister Theresa May's Lancaster House speech of January 2017, the safeguarding of joint UK–Irish interests was as high as fourth in a list of twelve Brexit objectives. 'The family ties and bonds of affection that unite our two countries mean that there will always be a special relationship between us,' said May, words unthinkable from a Conservative leader until relatively recently. 'Maintaining that common travel area with the Republic of Ireland' will be 'an important priority', said the Prime Minister.

The multi-faceted impact of Brexit on Ireland includes issues relating to the border between the North and the Republic, the post-Brexit future of Northern Ireland itself, and how the Republic responds during the ongoing Article 50 talks between the UK and the EU.

BORDERLANDS

The 310-mile land border between the North and the Republic has changed dramatically in a relatively short space of time. It is hard to imagine it ever reverting to its form of only a couple of decades ago. During the Troubles, the border was marred by watchtowers, heavily fortified army checkpoints, patrols and armoured personnel carriers, as well as troops inspecting lorries and queues of cars waiting to be either quizzed or waved on.

All that is now thankfully gone, a positive legacy of the peace process and the 1998 Belfast Good Friday Agreement. Now, the border exists in name only. There is free movement of both people and goods, with the North and the Republic rebuilding deep, intertwined local and national economic relations, as conflict has been replaced by peace.

It is of enormous significance that all the main political players are determined to avoid any return to a hard border – including the leading political parties of Northern Ireland and the governments of both the UK and the Irish Republic, to say nothing of the populations of both the North and the Republic. Yet the EU's chief Brexit negotiator Michel Barnier, addressing both Houses of the Irish Parliament in Dublin in May 2017, said that keeping the border control-free might be complicated, as 'customs controls are part of EU border management'.[2] So where, for practical purposes, will the border between the EU and the UK actually lie?

Unionist politicians in the North are uncomfortable in principle about passport and customs controls at airports and seaports linking Northern Ireland with the British mainland. Some politicians in the Republic, meanwhile, have expressed concern about the logistic complexity of hosting British border authorities in Dublin, Shannon and elsewhere. Something will have to give – but, in our view, technology will play a vital role in easing logistical and, in turn, symbolic concerns. As long as the UK invests heavily in new technology and border staff, there is no reason why goods and people should not continue to flow freely.

As we have noted elsewhere, a 'frictionless' border exists between the US and Canada, despite there being no customs union between them. And the extra 'dwell time' for non-EU goods coming into French ports, over and above that for EU goods, averages around six minutes. Goods should continue to flow freely and efficiently across the border, with minimal delay, given the overwhelming political will in the UK and the Republic that they should do so – as long as sufficient investment is made in the required technology and border personnel.

It is telling that Niall Cody, chairman of the Irish Republic's Revenue Authority, does not envisage customs posts along the Irish border after Brexit. 'I'm practically 100 per cent certain we will not be providing new trade facilitation bays in whatever parts of Donegal, Monaghan or Cavan,' he told an Irish parliamentary committee in May 2017, referring to a number of the border counties.[3] Cody has confirmed that an ongoing analysis of cross-border trade along Ireland's internal border shows that most goods are related to the food and construction industries and can be documented online and cleared via an automated e-border.

There is also a need to handle the flow of people to and from the rest of the EU, and beyond, into Ireland in a manner that satisfies both the UK and the Republic. While Dublin must adhere to the EU's freedom of movement rules, London is concerned about the Republic becoming a backdoor into the UK for anyone from the EU.

All travel from the Republic to the UK mainland and EU is, for obvious reasons, by boat or plane. Passenger information is already collected – given that the Republic, while subject to EU freedom of movement, is not part of the Schengen passport-free zone. As such, border checks can be carried out electronically, with staff intervention where required, before boats sail or planes take off. All that is needed is proper information-sharing between the UK and Ireland and close cooperation between each country's respective border forces. Such cooperation is already strong.

Brexit clearly impacts Northern Ireland, particularly in political terms. As the Article 50 negotiations began, Brussels was quick to suggest that the UK's departure from the EU, and the required adjustment to arrangements between the UK and the Republic, could lead to a united Ireland. A statement in the minutes of the EU's first official Brexit summit stated that if Northern Ireland voted in favour of a united Ireland then 'the entire territory of such a united Ireland would thus be part of the European Union'. As such, EU negotiators were accused by UKIP leader Nigel Farage of 'stoking Irish nationalism and all that could come with that' in a bid to make the UK's 'Brexit negotiations more difficult'.[4]

While the possibility of a 'border poll' is certainly outlined in the Good Friday Agreement, it is clearly vital to ensure the peace established in Northern Ireland over recent years is not undermined. Former Taoiseach Bertie Ahern also acknowledges that UK–EU negotiations have 'stoked up the debate about a united Ireland and having a border poll'. A key architect of the Good Friday Agreement, Ahern insists now is not the time. 'This is still a divided society and the institutions are not operational,' he said in May 2017. 'Brexit is creating problems, but we are realists – the British people have voted for this and we have to come up with solutions.'[5]

As these Article 50 talks continue, it is worth noting that free movement between the UK and the Republic of Ireland dates back to the formation of the Irish Free State in 1922, many years before the EU existed. Governments in Dublin and London – to say nothing of the vast majority of voters in both countries – adamantly want a continuation of the long-standing 'free-trade, free-movement' arrangement between Ireland and the UK. While there is enormous public will for this to prevail, there will no doubt be some political complications. If the UK and Ireland have completely open borders, Brussels may argue, why not the UK and France?

Solving these border issues will test the nerves of both the UK and the Republic, and relations between their governments and broader populations. Squaring this circle will mean compromise not just between London and Dublin, which should be relatively straightforward, but also between both governments and the EU – which Brussels has every interest in making as difficult as possible.

There is much to be gained, though, from both Irish nations, despite their historic differences, considering what is in their collective interests. 'People talk about a special relationship with the EU for Northern Ireland,' says Professor James Anderson of Queen's University Belfast. 'What they should be thinking about is a special relationship with the whole island, north and south, that protects Irish markets in Britain and the North's markets on the Continent, and makes it unnecessary to even begin to think about a hard border.'[6]

The 2017 general election saw the Democratic Unionist Party (DUP) win ten of Northern Ireland's eighteen Westminster seats, with Sinn Féin taking seven and one going to an independent. The hung parliament has given the DUP considerable power, of course, the party securing a financial windfall of an extra £1 billion of UK government spending in Northern Ireland in return for a confidence and supply agreement with the Conservatives.[7]

It is precisely because the UK government is reliant on the main unionist party for its House of Commons majority that Brussels has every incentive to make negotiations over Ireland's land border – an issue of acute sensitivity not just in Northern Ireland but across the entire UK – as difficult as possible.

IRISH SPRING?

What then of the Republic? The Irish authorities were deeply shocked by the UK referendum result. Their immediate reaction was to ensure that there was no speculation as to their future intent. The message, loud and clear, from the political and diplomatic establishment was that Ireland was sticking with 'Team EU'. This is not a surprise. Ireland, like many member states, has viewed EU membership largely as a political project. Joining what was then the EEC on the same day as the UK in 1973 made sense economically, not least given the importance of the Republic's trade with Britain, but it was far more significant as a political statement.

When the Republic of Ireland 'went into Europe', the country was not yet twenty-five years old, having been granted formal independence in 1949. This marked the moment when Irish people were finally able to represent themselves diplomatically on the world stage. Brussels-backed motorways and other structural fund spending have been important in terms of cementing the Republic's relationship with the EU. But the political aspects of membership, above all the escape from British dominance, have made the EU central to the identity of modern Ireland. Still, though, the UK remains hugely important – both economically and culturally – a reality brought into sharp focus by Brexit.

Since 1973, Ireland has been, for the most part, an enthusiastic EU member, joining the single currency, while serving as an important example of 'small country success' for new Eastern European member states. There have been signs of discontent, though. The Republic voted against both the Nice and Lisbon Treaties in 2001 and 2007 respectively, as outlined in Chapter 1, before being forced by Brussels on both occasions to vote again. Then a bailout was forced upon Ireland at a time when the country, while weak, was not technically bankrupt. Badly regulated Irish banks borrowed and lent with abandon ahead of 2008, causing a large property bubble, but the economy overheated in part because of the single currency – which resulted in Ireland having to live with interest rates far lower than its economy needed. The Republic then had EU finance effectively foisted upon it in 2010, in a bid to calm financial markets and prevent a break-up of the broader Eurozone.[8] The Irish state ended up burdened with huge debts as a result, leading to widespread public discontent.

Ireland has since staged an economic recovery, largely due to its strong trading links with the US and UK, which have grown faster than the Eurozone since 2010. Yet the financial crisis saw net emigration turn positive once again, as numerous well-qualified young adults strove to find success abroad. In an important paper published in June 2017, Ray Bassett, an experienced Irish diplomat, who retired as an ambassador the year before, observed that, in response to recession, Irish people 'headed for the old emigrant destinations – Britain, USA, Canada, Australia and New Zealand'. This was, Bassett proclaimed, 'a formidable demonstration of where the Irish felt culturally more at home'.[9]

Economically, the Republic of Ireland is still tied quite heavily to the UK, with British trade accounting for around €1 billion of trade each week and one in ten jobs across the country. The German–Irish Chamber of Industry and Commerce (AHK) has warned that Brexit means Irish exporters need to diversify beyond the UK.[10] Some business leaders in the Republic, though, while aware that Brexit will bring disruption, are seeing opportunities. Ireland boasts a relatively young, well-trained pool of labour, and is set to become the only native English-speaking economy in the EU.

The Irish financial services industry, for instance, which accounts for a significant 8 per cent of GDP, is already starting to benefit. London-based international banks and asset-management companies are looking to open Dublin offices, to stay within EU jurisdiction. As this book goes to press, in fact, the Bank of America has just picked Dublin as the base for its post-Brexit EU operations, moving its investment banking and market operations to the Irish capital – even though London will remain the lender's headquarters for Europe as a whole, Africa and the Middle East.[11]

The reality is that Ireland has diversified away from Britain, but not in a manner that is commonly understood. Back in the mid-1970s, around 50 per cent of all Irish trade was with the UK. Since then, that share has fallen to 14 per cent as Ireland has traded more with the EU. But much of the diversification away from Britain has headed across the Atlantic, with the US now accounting for a quarter of Irish trade. Add in the rest of the world and, after Brexit, almost two thirds of Irish goods and services exports will be destined for non-EU markets.

It should be remembered, also, that while overall reliance on UK trade has fallen markedly over recent decades, there are sectors that remain heavily dependent. Some 55 per cent of Irish exports in the timber and construction sectors go to the UK, for instance, along with 50 per cent of beef exports, almost half of Irish clean technology and electronics exports and 42 per cent of food and drink exports.[12]

In purely practical terms, Ireland's location on the western side of Europe also raises Brexit-related issues. A large share of the country's goods exports pass through western British ports, then travel by road across the UK, before leaving southern and eastern British ports, headed for the EU and global markets. The UK's decision to leave both the single market and the customs union could cause administrative barriers even to Irish exports not ultimately bound for the UK.

It is also noteworthy that, having been a net recipient of EU funding for many years, the Republic became a net contributor in 2014, the €168 million deficit between its EU contributions and receipts now likely to grow, not least as Brexit means Brussels is losing its second-biggest net contributor. That financial reality has started to play on minds in Dublin, as has the EU's repeated challenge of Ireland's decision to charge low rates of corporation tax in a bid to win more FDI from large multinationals – a strategy central to the country's economic success, not least its recovery from the most recent financial crisis.

The pressure on 'official Ireland' to shift its mindset will become immense, though, as and when the UK concludes a free trade deal with the US. The Republic will end up geographically in the middle of a UK–US FTA, which it will be forbidden to join due to its membership of the EU customs union. The Republic of Ireland will find itself unable to join a trade bloc tailor-made for the country, economically, geographically and culturally – an absurdity that will be exposed for all to see. The idea of leaving the EU could rapidly shift from the fringes of Irish politics.

COMMON PURPOSE?

Ray Bassett's paper states that the Irish Diplomatic Service has, for decades, been guilty of 'excessive Europhilia in the face of economic reality'. This is man who helped negotiate the Good Friday Agreement and who was Ireland's ambassador to Canada – one of the country's most important postings. Other diplomats, in the face of increased hostility from Brussels, are privately questioning this most fundamental principle of the last forty years of Irish foreign policy. The financial crisis of 2008 confirmed, in the eyes of many Irish people, that a small country on the western periphery of Europe will always be subservient to the bigger European project. Having been understandably angry after the June 2016 referendum, and deaf to any notion that the Republic might benefit from Brexit, parts of 'official Ireland' are starting to realise that most of Ireland's external trade is actually in currencies other than the euro.

Bassett warns that 'there will be a price to pay' whatever the outcome of the Brexit negotiations. He points out that in the UK–EU Article 50 talks, Ireland is just one voice among the twenty-seven EU members looking for an agreement. If there is no trade deal keeping tariffs and regulations at bay, as there is now, Ireland will face very particular difficulties given its UK exports and the role Britain plays in funnelling Irish exports to other markets.

'Sitting on the sidelines', Bassett argues, 'with the EU negotiating for Ireland, is essentially untenable'. The first duty of the EU negotiators is to act on behalf of the EU as an institution. The deal that Ireland requires, including an FTA with the UK, directly contradicts the EU negotiators' mandate that anything relating to Ireland and her border must 'maintain the integrity of the EU's legal order' – with no exceptions to the customs union. That's why, Bassett concludes, Ireland must 'seriously consider' leaving the EU. Immediately after his paper was published in June 2017, 'Irexit' entered the lexicon of the Irish media.

Politicians in the Republic of Ireland are, by nature, transactional. For now, the Irish political establishment is extremely wary of Irexit and will want to see signs first that Britain has made a success of Brexit. But the question 'could become mainstream quite quickly', according to the influential Irish economist David McWilliams. 'There is simply too much at stake for Ireland to outsource this nego-tiation to a French federalist in the pay of the EU Commission,' says McWilliams, whose columns and broadcasts enjoy an avid following in Ireland. There is certainly a risk that, in attempting to 'punish' the UK, the EU also punishes Ireland. There is also a risk, as McWilliams observes, 'that [Irish] negotiators will want to be seen as "good Europeans", leading them to sign a deal that is damaging to Ireland'.[13]

For decades, Irish politicians and diplomats have been extremely keen to side with Brussels – not least as a way of remaining independent of the UK. Such fear and insecurity now seems misplaced. The Republic has a higher GDP per capita than the UK and is one of the world's most widely admired nations – not just for its high standard of living and vibrant culture, but for its diplomatic acumen too.[14] The reality, anyway, is that when it comes to these Article 50 talks, London and Dublin, culturally entwined and fiercely determined to maintain open borders, are on the same side.

Brussels should be careful not to overplay its hand. Yes, the Republic of Ireland values EU membership. But the UK and the Republic are uncannily close. The contemporary family and cultural ties are extremely strong, to say nothing of the historical shared experiences and ongoing economic links. If Ireland faces a choice between free trade with the UK, America and potentially the rest of the world on the one hand, or the EU on the other, the EU could eventually lose.

It seems probable that, as these UK–EU talks progress, Ireland will demand to play a role that goes beyond the EU 27. If Brussels refuses, Irish public opinion towards the EU – still smarting from the 2010 bailout and previous 're-referendums' – would rapidly deteriorate. That would be noticed in Eastern Europe and elsewhere, should the EU's star pupil start openly berating Brussels.

'We should be talking to the British officially and openly at the highest level, not hiding behind the EU,' says David McWilliams. 'Brussels is demanding that only the EU can talk to the UK – this is nonsense from an Irish perspective.' It seems inevitable that the Republic of Ireland will play a big role in these Article 50 talks. And, for all the efforts of the Irish diplomatic class to prevent it, at least the threat of Irexit could soon be very much on the table.

We do not expect a hard border to be put in place, then, between Northern Ireland and the Republic. With customs pre-clearance and information-sharing between the UK and Irish border authorities, the logistical issues relating to the movement of goods and people can be solved. On top of that, there is overwhelming backing among politicians and the broader population, across the island of Ireland and indeed across the entire UK, for a 'frictionless' Irish border. This is unlikely to change.

The EU may try to scupper this outcome, attempting to use the Republic of Ireland as a pawn in these UK–EU negotiations. What happens during these Article 50 talks, after all, carries an economic and political significance that goes way beyond Ireland – and even beyond the UK. Such attempts by Brussels to gain an advantage over Britain, though, harming the Republic at the same time, are likely to bring Britain and Ireland closer together.

Raising the spectre of hard borders, while stirring up ancient enmities, however delicately, is likely to be counterproductive. The current strength of UK–Ireland relations, the work it took to create them and the determination of both countries to keep them that way, is likely to increase their joint resolve to maintain open borders – securing a free flow of goods, services, people and cultures that has existed for so long.

The authors do not advocate Irexit. We believe that, on balance, EU membership is good for the Republic of Ireland. The situation is changing fast, though, as Irish entrepreneurs and companies forge links across Asia, Latin America and Africa, and international investment pours into the Republic, much of it from the US. Certainly, a UK–US trade deal could change Irish priorities significantly. For now though, we believe the best strategy for Ireland – a strategy that happens to coincide with what is also best for the UK – is to put Irexit on the table and to leave it there, in full view, for EU negotiators to see.

PART V

MOVING ON

CHAPTER 14

RESPECTING THE REFERENDUM

'Believe me, Brexit can be stopped, it can.'
ALASTAIR CAMPBELL[1]

'You are voting on whether we leave or remain in the European Union ... the government will implement your decision.'[2] That was the message printed in an 'information booklet' produced by Whitehall ahead of the June 2016 referendum. Sent to all 27 million UK households, the document was covered in HM Government heraldry, including numerous coats of arms. The official leaflet, in large 38-point font, described the referendum as 'a once in a generation decision'. Throughout the referendum campaign, too, the public was told by Prime Minister David Cameron, repeatedly, that this was a 'once in a lifetime vote'.

Despite all that, a core of Remain campaigners – in the House of Commons, the House of Lords and the broader political and media classes – have continued to argue that the EU referendum was 'advisory' and 'non-binding'. While claiming they 'accept the will of the people', they are demanding a second referendum, sometimes adding, depending on their audience, that those who voted Leave were 'misguided', 'stupid' or worse.

The House of Commons voted in June 2015 for a bill to allow a UK referendum on EU membership – by a huge majority of 554 MPs to fifty-three. As such, the decision on whether or not Britain should stay in the EU was emphatically delegated to the people. The electorate subsequently voted by a relatively slim but clear majority – almost 1.3 million votes – to leave. Most observers within the UK and across the world judge that Parliament has given its consent for the UK to exit the EU.

During the referendum campaign, it was clear that staying in the EU was

the preferred choice of the establishment. David Cameron staunchly supported Remain, as did his Chancellor George Osborne and almost all the Cabinet.
The pro-EU side, more generally, was backed by the machinery of government.
Supposedly neutral Whitehall departments became a key part of the campaign,
producing Brexit-related 'studies' and 'forecasts' that were uniformly and omi-
nously pessimistic.

The Labour Party leadership campaigned on the Remain side, along with the
leadership of the Liberal Democrats, the Greens, the SNP and Plaid Cymru. The
Bank of England warned of 'recession risks' if voters supported Brexit, as did a
host of international economic bodies, such as the IMF and the OECD. Remain
was also the choice of the CBI and the TUC.

There were, of course, a handful of Cabinet ministers who urged voters to
gainsay the government. The Leave camp also raised a similar amount of money
to the Remain side – around £15 million – from a combination of state and
private donations, subject to a cap. The government, however, spent an additional £9 million producing, posting and digitally promoting the leaflet quoted
in the opening paragraph of this chapter. Entitled 'Why the government believes
that voting to remain in the EU is the best decision for the UK', it presented a
one-sided and, in some places, misleading case.[3]

The leaflet was, in addition, sent with cynical timing, just days before the
government's pre-referendum 'purdah' period began. As such, the cost of producing and distributing a wholly pro-Remain mailshot was met from general
taxation, not counting as part of the specific and equal state funding earmarked
for both sides. That meant campaigners backing Brexit began with a huge financial disadvantage.

RESPECTING THE VOTE

It is the view of the authors, and much of the British public, that the June 2016
referendum outcome must be respected. The UK needs to implement Brexit and
move on.[4] Parliament passed a law twelve months before the EU vote, delegating
the decision on whether or not the UK remains a member to the electorate.
In February 2017, when a legal challenge determined that Parliament should
be consulted again on implementing Article 50, MPs voted by 494 to 122 to
proceed.[5] Then, in the June 2017 general election, both the Conservatives and

the Labour Party stood on a platform of leaving the EU, including the single market – and between them secured 82 per cent of all votes cast.

There was another parliamentary vote in June 2017, after the general election, on an amendment to the Queen's Speech, in which eight of the twenty-seven bills related to Brexit. MPs again voted down proposals to stay in the single market and customs union, by 322 votes to 101.[6] This was the so-called Soft Brexit amendment, supported by parliamentarians who appear to believe that ongoing membership of the EU's two most fundamental legal constructs – each with extensive conditions, responsibilities and restrictions on UK sovereignty – is compatible with 'leaving the EU' and 'respecting the will of the people'.

With these Commons votes, then – in June 2015, February 2017 and June 2017 – MPs first backed a referendum and then voted unequivocally to quit the EU. In the June 2016 EU referendum, and again in the June 2017 general election, the public supported the decision to leave. As the Brexit process takes place, all the related bills – on the UK's new immigration system, on trade, on sectors such as fishing and farming – will similarly be subject to intense parliamentary scrutiny, just like any other legislation.[7] As such, Brexit empowers the UK Parliament, as we argued in Chapter 3. But before this can happen, Parliament needs to refrain from blocking that very return of sovereignty it previously offered to the British public – and which the British people accepted.

In the wake of the June 2017 general election, there has been much comment on the implications of the resulting hung parliament for the UK's Article 50 negotiations. A common suggestion, particularly among MPs and media outlets opposed to Brexit, has been that the government no longer has a mandate to leave the EU. Yet nothing in the latest election changes the referendum result, or the previous votes in the Commons to facilitate leaving the EU. Also, the two major parties that opposed Brexit during the June 2017 election campaign, supporting attempts to reverse the referendum result, both did poorly.

The SNP lost twenty-one seats, the party's vote share falling from 50 per cent to 36.9 per cent of the Scottish electorate, as we noted in Chapter 12. The Liberal Democrats' national vote share, meanwhile, fell to 7.4 per cent after a campaign focused heavily on 'fighting every step of the way' against 'an extreme and divisive Brexit'.[8] This was the worst general election showing in the party's history.

Over four fifths of the vote in the June 2017 general election went to the

Conservative and Labour parties combined, both of which campaigned on 'implementing Brexit' and being 'outside the single market'. It was the authors' impression during the campaign that the voting public felt Brexit was a done deal – and the government should just get on and leave the EU. That explains the wholesale rejection of the Liberal Democrats' repeated calls for a second referendum. The bulk of campaign attention certainly seemed to be focused on domestic factors such as education, social care and other public services. But by the very nature of a general election, it is impossible to know precisely why people voted the way they did.

'It is never wise to use election results to make claims on any particular issue,' said Professor John Curtice, the highly respected psephologist, one month after the election. Despite that, the result 'has inevitably led some to claim the outcome … is indicative of a change of public mood on Brexit,' he observed. 'Voters vote the way they do for a wide variety of reasons, while their judgements are distorted by the prism of a non-proportional electoral system,' Curtice added.[9] Quite. Which is why, from time to time, under very particular circumstances, when significant constitutional issues are at stake, Parliament passes legislation for the public to vote in a referendum.

The June 2017 election, though, has clearly re-energised those in Parliament and across Whitehall who remain determined to scupper Brexit – not least as Theresa May's position as Prime Minister is now much weaker. There has been speculation of a shift in the UK government's approach, with some suggesting staying in the single market but leaving the customs union, or even vice versa. These options, while superficially appealing as political compromises, make little legal, logistical or diplomatic sense.

Some business interests want to see the UK remain in the EU – as we discussed in Chapter 6. They are hopeful the hung parliament means Brexit could yet be reversed. As this book goes to press, the Labour Party's position is in flux – as various factions in the party attempt to take advantage of shifting opinions, looking for a way to use the passage of Brexit-related legislation through Parliament to topple the government, their own party leader, or both.

Jeremy Corbyn, a lifelong advocate of leaving the EU, was persuaded by 'moderate' Labour MPs to campaign for Remain in the 2016 referendum – which he did, albeit in a rather half-hearted fashion. At the time, Corbyn's leadership was under challenge, and he was too weak to ignore the demands of the pro-EU Blairite wing of his parliamentary party.

After the EU referendum, the result of which was swung to a large extent by Labour voters in 'traditional' working-class areas backing Brexit, Corbyn became more openly supportive of leaving the EU. The party's subsequent 2017 manifesto said: 'Labour supports the referendum result' and 'freedom of movement will end when we leave the European Union'.[10] The party's stronger than expected performance in the June 2017 general election – with its vote share rising to 40 per cent, up from 30.4 per cent two years earlier – has seen Corbyn become more assertive within his party, not least on Brexit.

At the time of writing, the Labour leader is still insisting membership of the single market is 'inextricably linked' to EU membership.[11] Labour's international trade spokesman Barry Gardiner agrees, arguing that the UK should also rule out remaining in the customs union beyond any transitional period.[12] Yet senior colleagues are breaking ranks. Shadow Brexit Secretary Sir Keir Starmer says that while it is 'vital' to obtain the benefits of the single market and the customs union, 'how we achieve that is secondary to the outcome'. Directly contradicting Corbyn, Starmer argues that 'no options for Brexit should be swept off the table' – which throws Labour's plans into confusion.[13] Shadow Chancellor John McDonnell has also said he does not rule out staying in the single market.[14]

The parliamentary Labour Party is deeply split over Brexit, with that split now out in the open. This could result in various parliamentary groups coming together to somehow block the government's stated aim of leaving both the single market and the customs union. While the 2017 general election result does not change the fact that the UK electorate voted to leave the EU, it certainly makes the process of achieving Brexit more complicated. The cold reality of the parliamentary arithmetic means the government is now vulnerable to attacks from Remain supporters in all parties, not only in the Commons but also in the Lords.

SOFT-HEADED

When challenged on the importance of respecting the democratic outcome of the EU referendum, many implacable Remainers retort that the country 'did not vote for a Hard Brexit'. We reject such a partisan and misleading term, as noted earlier in this book. The repeated use of 'Hard Brexit' – which has become ubiquitous, used freely by broadcast news media – makes leaving the EU seem like an extreme, ideological and damaging position. Hard Brexit suggests isolation and a bleak economic future. Soft Brexit, conversely, conveys a comfortable, ongoing relationship with the EU, one where Britain remains 'part of the club'.

With the debate framed in this way, a political narrative has developed that the UK would be better off economically staying inside the single market and the customs union. The corollary is that those who want to leave are driven by an obsession with UK sovereignty, immigration controls, or both – and are prepared for the economy to be damaged, as long as they get what they want.

As such, remaining a member of one or other of the single market or customs union is presented as some kind of concession to Remain supporters – a civilised compromise that 'respects the wishes of the 48 per cent', a balance between ideology on the one hand, which the public was hoodwinked into supporting, and enlightened common sense on the other. These are the ubiquitous and widely accepted terms of the UK's Brexit debate, going into the autumn of 2017, as the Article 50 talks heat up. Yet they are wrong on every level.

Leaving the EU, but retaining membership of the single market and/or customs union would leave the UK in a dangerous halfway house. Our laws would remain subject to rulings by the EFTA court or the ECJ, as explained in Chapter 3. Britain would become a 'rule-taker', bound by huge restrictions on our economic and political freedom, but no longer able to vote on or influence those rules, even if they were changed to Britain's disadvantage. We would still have to make multi-billion-pound annual payments to Brussels and the EU's freedom of movement rules would almost certainly still apply.

Since 1999, as mentioned in an earlier chapter, the share of UK trade with the EU has fallen from 61 per cent to 44 per cent.[15] The single market barely covers services, in which the UK excels and which make up more than three quarters of our economy. Politicians can cite slogans about a 'jobs-first Brexit', insisting that means ongoing single market membership. But if the single market is so good for the UK, why do we trade less with the EU than with the rest of the world? Why is our EU trade shrinking as our non-EU trade expands? Why do we have a large deficit on our EU trade, but a sizeable surplus on our trade outside the EU?

Staying in the customs union, meanwhile, means the UK must charge high import tariffs on goods where there is often no UK industry to protect. British consumers are paying more, on a range of imports from outside the EU, to shield uncompetitive producers in other EU states from cheaper global prices. Because 80 per cent of all revenues from the Common External Tariff are paid to Brussels, and the UK does more non-EU trade than any other EU member, Britain accounts for a disproportionately high share of the EU's combined tariff revenues. Again, this burden is shouldered by consumers. And, as is now well known, inside the customs union we are forbidden from cutting trade deals with nations outside the EU – countries that account for four fifths of the global economy and are the world's fastest-growing markets. This is no way amounts to a 'jobs-first Brexit'.

The rest of the world, as we have established, trades quite happily with the EU from outside the single market. America conducted almost a quarter of a trillion dollars' worth of trade with the EU in 2016, without accepting ECJ jurisdiction, freedom of movement rules or making large annual payments. Tariff-free trade between the UK and the EU can continue after Brexit under an FTA that preserves our ability to reach trade agreements across other parts of the world.

If no FTA with the EU is possible before March 2019, the UK can trade with the EU 27 under WTO rules, with the mutual recognition of standards made relatively simple given a starting point where there is, by definition, full compliance. The US and Canada, meanwhile, share 'friction-free' customs arrangements, with no customs union. More goods cross this North American 'virtual border' each year than enter the entire EU.

Under Soft Brexit, the UK would be subject to EU rules while having no say in making them. We would endure all the restrictions and costs of EU membership, with none of the advantages of shaping our own laws or grasping better trading opportunities elsewhere. While Soft Brexit is often the preference of politicians who see themselves as liberal and progressive, we wonder if they understand how the EU works. Staying in the single market promotes the interests of producers over consumers while entrenching the advantages of large corporations over small firms. Staying in the single market suppresses the wages of the UK's most financially insecure workers, while helping numerous multinationals dodge tax.

An additional problem for those aggressively selling Soft Brexit to the British public is that it looks to be wholly unobtainable. Ever since the EU referendum, various UK political parties and groups have furiously debated the intricacies of what kind of 'deal' they might accept. Yet nothing can be settled with regard to Brexit except in agreement with the EU and, in particular, the twenty-seven national governments and the European Parliament. British politicians are making demands and suggestions that strike the rest of Europe as absurd – above all, those so earnestly advocating Soft Brexit.

We began Chapter 3 with a statement made by Michel Barnier in December 2016. 'The single market and its four freedoms are indivisible,' said the EU's Chief Negotiator. 'Cherry-picking is not an option.' Yet such cherry-picking is precisely what the Soft Brexiteers think they can achieve, attempting to break apart the EU's four freedoms by seeking single market membership along with a special dispensation from freedom of movement rules and other related conditions.[16]

Advocates of Soft Brexit on both the Labour and Conservative sides of the Commons demand such an outcome, even though it ignores the 2016 referendum result and the June 2017 manifesto pledges of both respective parties. They insist the UK can 'leave the EU but stay in the single market' while 'getting a deal on free movement', even though trying to secure such an outcome would almost guarantee gridlock during the Article 50 talks. Yet Soft Brexit, as we have argued, will end up being Messy Brexit – causing a diplomatic stand-off, along with chronic uncertainty for citizens, investors and businesses, risking serious economic and damage. Soft Brexit puts the UK in direct and absolute conflict with the EU's core principles – principles which, if seriously breached, could tear the bloc apart.

In late July 2017, this point was made with devastating clarity by Fabian Zuleeg, the chief executive of the European Policy Centre – a think tank with very close links to the European Commission. Referring to voices 'outside government demanding that the UK reconsider its position', Zuleeg described as 'misguided' any notion the EU 27 would accept a treaty-busting Soft Brexit deal. 'What is missing in these discussions is a real appreciation of the view from the other side of the Channel,' said Zuleeg. 'Allowing cherry-picking of benefits would act as a signal to others inside the EU that a Europe à la carte is obtainable, opening the Pandora's box of disintegration.'[17]

In July 2017, Tony Blair, the erstwhile spiritual leader of Labour MPs advocating Soft Brexit, said that Europe is willing to 'consider changes to accommodate Britain, including around freedom of movement'. The former Prime Minister's statement, seemingly based on inside knowledge, electrified the Westminster village. Yet it was soon dismantled by Zuleeg.

'The Tony Blair suggestion is unworkable,' he said, because 'the EU is a community of law, underpinned by EU treaties'. Such a deal would 'be struck down in court', Zuleeg continued, referring to the ECJ. The day his article was posted online, it was retweeted by Sabine Weyand, the EU's Deputy Chief Negotiator who works directly alongside Barnier – confirming it as official EU policy.

This illustrates the precise reason why the authors have been advocating Clean Brexit since before Theresa May's Lancaster House speech – declaring up front that the UK will be outside both the single market and the customs union. Not only does this respect the referendum outcome, it also makes diplomatic sense. Eschewing a long-drawn-out negotiation in favour of an FTA, or using WTO rules as a platform to strike future trade deals, Clean Brexit is a practical, transparent, democratically mandated position. We believe it limits the inevitable uncertainty surrounding the Brexit process as much as is possible, while minimising the damage done to the UK, the EU and their important continued relationship.

Clean Brexit means taking back full control of our laws and borders, leaving the EU in a pre-announced, planned manner – allowing for proper preparation, knowing that we are going to be outside both the single market and customs union. The alternative is a Messy Brexit – which would damage business confidence, maximise cliff-edge dangers and risk a disastrous UK–EU stalemate. Zuleeg is exactly right. Pushing for a Messy Brexit does indeed threaten to 'open the Pandora's box of disintegration'.

When it comes to getting Brexit legislation through Parliament, most Conservatives proposing Soft Brexit are, in the end, likely to vote with the government. It is 'moderate' Labour MPs, those trying to use Brexit to destabilise both the Prime Minister and their own leader, who are most likely to derail the government's plans – as long as they can attract some Tory rebels. This is despite the Labour manifesto pledging to accept the referendum result while ending free movement. Many in the Labour heartlands voted for Brexit as they want to stop unlimited unskilled immigration undercutting local wages, while preventing further billions of pounds going to Brussels. Both changes are only possible if we leave the single market.

NOT *ANOTHER ONE*?

'Not *another one*?' This was the response of one pensioner when told by BBC TV reporter Jon Kay, out canvassing opinion on the streets of Bristol, that Theresa May had just called an election for June 2017. 'Honestly, I can't stand this – there's too much politics going on at the moment,' said 'Brenda from Bristol'.[18] The clip went viral, seen by millions of people via social media, with many commenting that this charming, highly articulate pensioner spoke for the nation.

Within a three-year period, the UK has experienced the 2014 referendum on Scottish independence, a general election in 2015, the highly divisive EU referendum in 2016 and then another general election in 2017. Brenda from Bristol had a point. Despite that, the increased confidence of those trying to block Brexit means there are growing calls for a second EU referendum.

The authors take the view that the result of the 2016 vote must be implemented and, as such, another referendum on EU membership is wrong in principle. There have been a number of occasions when apparently sovereign nations have been pressured to vote again when an EU-related referendum has failed to produce the 'correct result' – as outlined in Chapter 1. Examples include Denmark in 1993 and Ireland in 2001. And when voters in France and the Netherlands rejected the EU constitution in 2005, scheduled referenda in other countries, including the UK, were cancelled. The centralising measures in the constitution, drawing more power away from individual EU nations, were repackaged as the Lisbon Treaty – which almost every government then decided did not require a vote because the word 'constitution' had been removed.

Such practices are not just undemocratic, but anti-democratic. The fact that the European Commission acts in this way, and EU governments allow it to do so, with the national politicians involved often getting well-paid jobs in Brussels after the event, is one reason support for the EU has plummeted in recent years. To the authors, the idea that the UK, arguably the most vibrant democracy in Europe, could be asked to vote again on an issue of major constitutional significance because the first vote was at odds with 'Project Europe' is scandalous.

A few months after the 2016 referendum, apparently sharing the same fundamental concern about talk of a repeat vote, then Liberal Democrat Business Secretary Sir Vince Cable spoke out. 'There are people in the party who don't accept the outcome, who feel incredibly angry and feel it's reversible, that somehow we can undo it,' Cable told a fringe meeting at the Liberal Democrat annual conference, contradicting his own party's policy. 'The public have voted and I do think it's seriously disrespectful and politically utterly counterproductive to say "sorry guys, you've got it wrong, we're going to try again" – I don't think we can do that.'[19]

Yet Cable has now changed his mind.

When the Liberal Democrats campaigned on a 'second referendum' platform during the June 2017 general election, the party's vote share slumped to an all-time low. Yet in July 2017, when Cable became party leader, he promptly adopted the same second-referendum policy, despite previously stating that it would be 'seriously disrespectful' to the electorate.[20] He also asserted that 'Brexit may not happen'.[21] Before the June 2017 general election, Cable had argued against the EU's freedom of movement rules, as we mentioned in Chapter 10. 'I have serious doubts that EU free movement is tenable or even desirable,' he wrote.[22] Ending free movement, though, means leaving the EU – a policy the party that Cable leads now wants to reverse.

This multiple volte-face by one of the UK's most respected and thoughtful parliamentarians is indicative of the febrile mood at Westminster, given the uncertainties raised by a hung parliament. Not only in the Commons, but also the Lords, the anti-Brexit lobby is mobilising – with opposition parties sensing an opportunity. Cable's actions illustrate that, when it comes to base politics, carefully reasoned positions and instinctive principals go out of the window. If you can damage your political opponents to the benefit of your party, you adopt the policy position required to do so. The close parliamentary arithmetic means rational debate has given way almost entirely to blatant opportunism.

If the prospect of a second referendum 'on the deal' gains serious ground, then that would seriously undermine the UK's ongoing Article 50 negotiations. The EU – keen to retain the UK's multi-billion-pound annual budget contribution, while discouraging other member states from leaving – would have every incentive to offer the UK the worst deal imaginable, while making the two-year process as uncomfortable as possible. This would make it more likely, in turn, that the terms were rejected when the second referendum was held, with the UK then remaining in the EU – precisely the outcome that Brussels wants.

If, in contrast, the UK maintains the position that we are definitely leaving the EU's single market and customs union, with no question of any second referendum, there is a clear incentive for the EU to strike agreeable terms with us, given the value of British markets to many EU companies. That's because under WTO rules (the outcome if no FTA is agreed) EU exporters face tariffs when selling into the UK. As long as Britain's clear and unequivocal destination is a Clean Brexit, commercial interests across Europe who export heavily to Britain will push EU politicians to strike an FTA with Britain. There are already signs of this happening.

If there is absolutely no possibility of the UK staying in the single market, or reversing the entire Brexit process with a second referendum, powerful commercial interests across leading EU member states will press their politicians about the countless jobs and billions of euros of UK-trade-related profit at stake, doing much of our lobbying for us. The prospect of the UK staying in the single market, or holding a second referendum, stops that key political dynamic from happening, much to the detriment of the UK's economic and political interests.

Any second referendum also poses more general economic and financial dangers, prolonging business uncertainty to the detriment of investment and jobs. If the UK electorate rejected 'the deal' the UK strikes with the EU, what would happen? Would there be another negotiation process and yet another referendum? The best of three, perhaps, or even five? The British political system would become paralysed by splits and confusion. Financial markets would, at the very least, factor in ongoing uncertainty and instability, seriously undermining sterling, equities and the broader business environment. The fall in the pound since the June 2016 EU referendum has been largely beneficial to the economy – a depreciation long overdue. But a sharp future drop, reflecting a chronic loss of confidence in political decision-making, would be counterproductive, causing inflation to spike.

Under these circumstances, the UK could lose its hard-won reputation as a relative haven of stability with a predictable political environment. At a time when the sustainability of the Western world's 'extraordinary monetary measures' is being questioned, with sovereign yields having already risen from all-time lows as QE is withdrawn, a British 'neverendum' would weigh heavily on UK bond prices – pushing up government, corporate and personal borrowing costs and risking a sovereign downgrade.

The political, and therefore the economic and business, risks of a second referendum are significant. A damaging political risk premium would be added to the UK. Financial markets understand that political instability is a fact of life – even in advanced economies like Britain. Since June 2016, though, investors have come to terms with the fact that Brexit means Brexit, recognising there is now an overwhelming desire for the political classes to implement the verdict of the British people.

Those agitating for a second referendum need to be called out and exposed. Despite endlessly claiming to 'recognise the June 2016 referendum result', they are simply trying to secure a different outcome. Many of those advocating a Soft Brexit also want to subvert democracy – again, despite endless airy claims that they 'respect the will of the British people' – as even their most ardent media cheerleaders have the decency, on occasion, to admit.[23] Reversing the Brexit vote would not only risk serious public discontent and disillusion with the political process, it would also trigger genuine alarm among investors both in the UK and abroad.

The government should press ahead, then, sticking to its plan to achieve Clean Brexit, on the basis not only of economic advantage but also democratic principles. The idea of a referendum on 'the deal' is disingenuous nonsense. Following the Repeal Bill, the deal will be whatever successive British governments and parliaments, elected by UK voters over many years, decide we want to do with our inherited EU legislation.

Outside the single market and customs union, existing and future laws relating to our labour market, financial services, immigration system, farming and fisheries and a host of other areas will, once again, be scrutinised and determined by elected politicians. This is what was requested by voters in an EU referendum granted to them by Parliament, a verdict Parliament has since repeatedly endorsed. What could be more democratic than that?

UPPER HOUSE, UPPER HAND?

Since the June 2017 election, when it comes to gauging the prospects for Brexit, all eyes have been on the Commons. This is unsurprising, given the dramatic election result and precarious parliamentary arithmetic. Yet there is also, in our view, a danger Brexit could be derailed by the Lords. In her January 2017 Lancaster House speech, the Prime Minister confirmed there would be a parliamentary vote at the end of the Article 50 process. 'I can confirm today that the government will put the final deal that is agreed between the UK and the EU to a vote in both Houses of Parliament,' she said.[24]

A strong Remain-supporting lobby in the Lords made a concerted attempt to alter the vote to be offered by May on any UK–EU agreement, by amending the legislation to trigger Article 50. Under the government's proposal, if Parliament voted against the deal, the UK would revert to a default option of trading with the EU under WTO rules, the process by which most UK trade is conducted with the rest of the world. The Lords amendment proposed a default option that was somewhat different, with the UK staying in the EU, despite the referendum result, should Parliament choose to reject any UK–EU deal.

Just as with a second referendum, or the prospect of a Soft Brexit, such a 'default EU membership' parliamentary vote would seriously undermine the UK's negotiating position. If Parliament had an effective veto on Brexit, EU negotiators – mindful of Britain's large financial contribution and the need to discourage other nations from seeking to leave – would once again ensure any deal was so bad as to guarantee public outcry and parliamentary rejection.

A vote that reverts to WTO rules, in contrast, gives the EU an incentive to make the trade aspects of any UK–EU deal beneficial to both sides, mindful that imposing unfair conditions on the UK could result in WTO rules, including tariffs on EU exporters. Powerful European commercial interests would once again be incentivised to push for a constructive UK–EU trade deal, with ongoing cooperation across a range of headings.

The highly contentious amendment on a vote defaulting to EU membership was debated in the Lords in early March 2017. It was tabled by the crossbench peer Lord Pannick – the barrister behind the high-profile Supreme Court case brought by fund manager Gina Miller, which originally forced Theresa May to seek parliamentary approval for triggering Article 50.

Pannick was accused of having a 'hidden agenda' by former Conservative Cabinet minister Lord (Michael) Forsyth. 'I have to say to the noble Lord, we know what he's up to, we know what is going on here,' said Forsyth. 'This House is absolutely full of people who still haven't come to terms with the result of the referendum and this is a clever lawyers' confection in order to reverse the referendum result.'[25]

In the end, despite more than seventy hours of parliamentary debate, the 137-word bill triggering Article 50 was passed without amendment. Yet the combination of a hung parliament and the ongoing determination of the Lords' pro-Remain lobby suggests the government's plans face significant hurdles. Peers could once again amend a future Brexit-related bill with a 'binding vote' amendment, including a 'revert to EU membership' clause – not least given the result of the June 2017 general election.

The Salisbury Convention is an arrangement that forms part of the UK's unwritten constitution. Adopted just after the Second World War, it has since governed the relationship between the Commons and the Lords.[26] The convention says that if a party pledges a certain measure in its election manifesto, then wins office, the Lords will not table a 'wrecking amendment' altering the intent of any bill implementing that measure. The Salisbury Convention, then, ensures the supremacy of the elected chamber. The Lords can scrutinise a bill implementing a manifesto pledge, passing 'reasoned amendments', but cannot prevent the thrust of any policy promised in the winning party's manifesto.

Had the government won a clear majority in June 2017, the Salisbury Convention would clearly apply. The Conservative manifesto stated the UK would leave the EU, including the single market and the customs union.[27] When Theresa May called the election in April 2017, a major part of her rationale for doing so was to win on a manifesto stating the UK would be outside both.[28] With Labour and Liberal Democrat peers outnumbering the Conservatives by 305 to 254, to say nothing of the 180 or so fiercely independent crossbenchers, many of them Remainers, the Prime Minister knew she needed to neutralise the Lords as a potential block on Brexit. She intended to do so using to the Salisbury Convention.

The election outcome, of course, was not the one she planned. And it is not at all clear that the Salisbury Convention holds in a hung parliament. Under a 'confidence and supply agreement', which the Tories have with the DUP, one could argue the combined Tory/DUP majority means the convention does hold, not least when it comes to Brexit, given that the DUP also campaigned to leave the EU.[29]

'This House recognises the primacy of the Commons, and that is how we have always conducted ourselves,' said Baroness (Angela) Smith of Basildon, Labour's leader in the Lords. She was speaking in late June 2017, just after the Conservatives had concluded their agreement with the DUP. This initial statement suggested Labour will adhere to the Salisbury Convention. 'What is also clear,' Smith then added, 'is that the House of Commons has primacy, not the executive or government.'[30] What this indicates is that Labour peers could act to block Downing Street's Brexit plans, if the Soft Brexiteers can persuade Corbyn to change his mind and enough Tory MPs rebel in the Commons.

The Liberal Democrats could certainly attempt to stop Brexit in the Lords – not least as their new party leader has now changed his mind on the need for a second referendum. Lord (Richard) Newby, Liberal Democrat leader in the Lords, is a very committed supporter of continued EU membership. 'This is not the end, it's just the beginning,' he declared after the Lords' failure to amend legislation triggering Article 50.[31] 'People here, like me, have had Europe as one of the central themes of our entire political lives.'

When asked if he feared the government would abolish the House of Lords if it tried to stop Brexit, sparking a constitutional crisis, Newby was unapologetic. 'If I thought the option was that we could stop Brexit or that I'd be booted out of Parliament, I'd be booted out tomorrow.' Perhaps it is worth noting that, after the Labour Party's 2005 general election victory, the Liberal Democrats openly questioned the Salisbury Convention, saying they did not feel bound by it, given that is was originally an agreement between Labour and the Conservatives.[32]

After the 2010 election, which also produced a hung parliament, the Conservatives and Liberal Democrats formed the first coalition government since 1931 – before the Salisbury Convention was introduced. A parliamentary inquiry into the formation of the 2010 coalition took evidence on how the Salisbury Convention should work from the highly respected Hansard Society. 'Whether or not this constitutional convention unravels will ultimately be a matter of peers' political judgement,' the Society said.[33] The approach of peers to particular pieces of legislation will 'depend on the circumstances of the moment and the application of acute political judgment as to the attitude and reaction of the general public on the issue'.

A great deal, then, will depend on how the ongoing Brexit process is perceived by the general public. The hung parliament, and the uncertainty it has generated, means politicians on either side of the still-entrenched divide will likely continue to present every piece of economic data and every legislative skirmish as either wholly positive or wholly negative for Brexit in principle, or for the government's plans to leave the EU. As such, the public debate is likely to continue to generate a lot more heat than light.

1975 AND ALL THAT

The authors have, since June 2016, been rather shocked by the quite extraordinary negativity of much of the British establishment towards Brexit. Since the referendum result, many in the public eye have been doing their best to talk down Britain in every way possible. Scrutiny and criticism are obviously entirely justified and vital. But there is a big difference between robust democratic debate and putting a deeply negative skew on every development – with the ultimate intention of trying to reverse a referendum result which represented, in terms of votes cast for Brexit, the biggest act of democracy in British history.

The group of people doing this is small and London-centric, but extremely vocal and well-funded. Their Unite for Europe March on 25 March 2017, celebrating the sixtieth anniversary of the signing of the Treaty of Rome, attracted around 20,000 people. That is not a large number. The 1998 Countryside Alliance March against the foxhunting ban drew over half a million people. In 2003, at least a million marched against the war in Iraq – fifty times as many as Unite for Europe. But those 20,000 included a lot of people who write newspaper articles and blogs and appear on television. That does not make them representative of the British people.

The government has made some mistakes so far in its handling of Brexit. There should have been a much earlier, unilateral move to recognise the rights of the 3.1 million EU citizens living in the UK, as we have said. That would have been the right decision for the people who have come to live and work in the UK in good faith, and also for the firms employing them. It would have sent a positive signal to the world, while helping to reassure many Remain voters that Brexit was a process they could ultimately support.

There have also been mistakes in terms of messaging and advocacy. During the June 2017 election campaign, the Conservatives made almost no attempt to explain the government's Brexit policy – not least the many downsides of staying in the single market and customs union and the upsides of leaving. The January 2017 Lancaster House speech laid out exactly the right Brexit policy framework. But there has since been very little effort to explain why these policies make economic and diplomatic sense – and, above all, why they represent the only genuine method of delivering on the referendum result and actually leaving the EU.

There was no vision, during the election, of how the UK could remake domestic policy once it has left the EU, to tackle the issues and divisions the referendum campaign so clearly exposed, improving the lives of ordinary voters. There was no attempt to paint a justifiably positive picture of the UK's prospects of increased trade with the rest of the world. Brexit was, instead, presented by the Prime Minister as a burden she must carry, a cross that she must bear. This is not the case. Yes, leaving the EU presents us with complex issues that must be resolved. But it is, and should also be presented as, a major and unique opportunity.

Ministers must relentlessly advocate their approach to Brexit, explaining what they are doing and why, while challenging Remain's well-choreographed scare stories. No one is suggesting the government should reveal its entire Article 50 negotiation strategy, but it makes complete sense to explain why trading under WTO rules, for instance, does not amount to 'crashing out of the EU'. We already do more than half of all our trade under WTO rules, such trade is fast-growing and generates a large surplus – yet operating under WTO rules is often described as 'a disaster'.

'No deal' similarly will not mean 'queues of lorries at Dover' and 'planes falling out of the sky' – as those attempting to stop Brexit like to claim. These stories are nonsense, yet the government is not systematically and effectively challenging them. There is much talk of a cliff edge – yet such issues will be largely addressed by a combination of the Repeal Bill and ongoing Mutual Recognition Agreements, as we explained in Chapter 6.

The way to maximise the chance of cliff-edge dangers – in fact, to almost guarantee we leave the EU wholly and dangerously unprepared – is to go through the Article 50 negotiations unsure if we are leaving the single market and uncertain if we are reinstating our EU borders. If Soft Brexit comes to the fore, though – or if the government is forced to accept a second referendum or the Lords secures a 'Remain default' amendment on any of the numerous upcoming pieces of Brexit-related legislation – that is exactly what will happen.

The EU referendum is over. The hung parliament, though, means ministers must engage in sustained advocacy. Some worry about explaining the intricacies of these issues to a broad audience. Yet the public is far more sophisticated than much of the political class understands. If those supporting Brexit think general arguments on leaving the single market and customs union are too complicated for public consumption, they are guilty of the same prejudices towards their fellow citizens as many of those looking to overturn the referendum result.

Had the 2017 general election resulted in a large government majority, that would have settled the Commons and neutralised the Lords. The process of Brexit, while still complex, would have been somewhat more straightforward. Now the government must negotiate with the EU against a more precarious and unpredictable domestic political backdrop.

Brexit is not just a government issue. There is a cross-party responsibility to ensure the referendum result is implemented. At the time of writing, public discussion of the actual issues surrounding Brexit has given way almost entirely to political infighting – both within and between parties – and naked opportunism. Yet if leaving the EU results in parliamentary gridlock, or some other kind of constitutional crisis, causing economic turmoil and financial instability, bringing chronic uncertainty to thousands of businesses and millions of lives, it is the political class as a whole – 'the system' – that the public will blame.

There has always been, at critical moments, a defeatist streak in the British establishment. Britain remains one of the strongest, most capable and widely admired nations in the world. The general public seems to understand that better than some of our political class. As such, there is now a huge gulf between the pitched, self-indulgent Brexit battles in Parliament and the media, which amount to party leadership battles by proxy, remote from the realities of life elsewhere.

'While Westminster laments, people and businesses across Britain are getting on with meeting the new challenges,' writes investment manager Paul Marshall. 'By focusing all their energies on resistance and delay,' he says, 'those opposing Brexit are writing themselves out of the essential debate about how Britain forges a strategy to deliver prosperity for future generations.'[34]

'Can we not change our minds?' asked Alastair Campbell in March. 'Didn't you fight after 1975?'[35] A new EU referendum was warranted in 2016 because more than forty years had passed since the British people had been asked about the UK's relationship with Europe. During that period, the common market we joined has changed, to say the least. Successive treaties and numerous other centralising measures had altered significantly our relationship with Europe since the last referendum was held.

The 2016 referendum on the UK's EU membership was entirely justified and, when it finally arrived, long overdue. It took place just over a year ago, as this book goes to press. It has yet to be legislated for, let alone implemented. Attempting to reverse the referendum result because of perceived practical difficulties, barbed rhetoric from a Brussels bureaucratic class worried about cash, or an economic downturn the Remain camp so desperately hopes will arrive, can only be described as an act of democratic sabotage.

Many at Westminster are still fighting the referendum. Yet the result of the June 2016 referendum is clear: the British people want the UK Parliament to have the final say over their country's laws, its immigration policy, its taxes and its trade negotiations. That is simply impossible if we remain inside the single market and inside the customs union. Some powerful people, unused to not getting their own way and who have still not comes to terms with the outcome of the referendum, now talk of fighting 'Chaotic Brexit'. This is sophistry. If Parliament fails to implement the referendum decision, it will have failed in its basic function as a democratically representative body that reflects the will of the people.

CHAPTER 15

REMAKING GLOBAL BRITAIN

'Should the United Kingdom remain a member of the
European Union or leave the European Union?'
REFERENDUM BALLOT PAPER, JUNE 2016

We reject the common and often unchallenged assertion that Britain will be poorer outside the EU. This notion was expressed forcefully in the Treasury's 'Project Fear' document, produced in April 2016 ahead of the referendum. The authors were among only a handful of prominent economists who publicly challenged the Treasury conclusion that a Brexit vote would produce 'an immediate and profound economic shock', while making the UK significantly poorer in the long run.[1]

The Treasury report was designed to produce a precise, headline-grabbing forecast that would generate a wave of anti-Brexit news coverage and which could then be cited repeatedly by the Prime Minister and Chancellor during the final weeks of the campaign. That is precisely what happened.

The central prediction of this 'authoritative study' was that every UK household would be £4,300 worse off because of Brexit. This was based on the economy growing by almost 30 per cent between 2017 and 2030 outside the EU, but by 6.2 percentage points less than if we stayed in. The Treasury's analysis, though, relied on a series of wholly unrealistic assumptions – such as the UK becoming far more protectionist outside the EU (the opposite will be the case) while failing to cut a trade deal with any non-EU nation (a view already exposed as unduly pessimistic).

The centrepiece of 'Project Fear', though, was the Treasury's 'immediate and profound economic shock' forecast. The UK economy would shrink by 1 per cent in the third quarter of 2016 alone, the Treasury said, in the aftermath of any

Brexit vote. That would be followed by a further 0.4 per cent contraction during the fourth quarter. In order to cope, the UK would then need 'an emergency budget', Chancellor George Osborne insisted, raising fears about spending cuts and punitive tax hikes.[2]

These lurid pre-referendum assertions – based on assumptions that were demonstrably false – went almost wholly unchallenged by the UK's economics profession. The outcome, as we pointed out in the Introduction, was precisely the opposite of what the Treasury had forecast.

The authors argued ahead of the referendum that the economy would grow in the immediate aftermath of any vote to leave the EU, helped by a weaker pound – which is what happened.[3] During the campaign, the authors also said that once the Article 50 talks started, the most likely profile of the economy during the two-year negotiations would be a 'Nike swoosh' – with near-term uncertainty impacting investment and confidence, ahead of a later recovery.[4] It is certainly the case that uncertainty linked to the Article 50 negotiation could drag on the economy in the short-term. At the time of writing, GDP growth has slowed during the first half of 2017 – although that may also be linked to the calling of an unexpected general election. As one projects ahead, and once the UK has actually left the EU, our economic prospects improve.

Rather than damaging our prosperity, we believe that Brexit will benefit Britain. We view leaving the EU not as a burden, but as an opportunity. Brexit allows the UK to make policy choices that precisely suit our economy – empowering our democracy too. To appreciate the potential of Brexit, we would put it alongside some of the other landmark years for the UK economy. When future historians look back, they will surely see Britain's decision to leave the EU as one of the most important events in our economic, political and social history. If we seize this opportunity, then 2016, when the referendum was held, or perhaps more likely 2019, when we are scheduled to leave, will join a short but important list of historic economic turning points.

Over the past couple of centuries, in our view four similar years stand out, each of which proved to be transformative for the UK economy – namely: 1846, 1931, 1945 and 1979. If we make Brexit a success, then 2019 could be added to that list.

It is hard to overstate the significance of the 1846 Repeal of Corn Laws. The UK's large landowners and the establishment were defeated by Conservative

Prime Minister Sir Robert Peel, Richard Cobden MP, the Anti-Corn Law League and a moral crusade to change the balance of economic power, away from the elite to the common people. By imposing restrictions and tariffs on imported grain, the mercantilist Corn Laws kept grain prices high, favouring domestic producers with consumers paying higher prices. The repeal – which saw food prices fall and poor workers benefit – signalled a new direction. We have a similar opportunity today, as the UK leaves the protectionist EU that favours lobbyists, big businesses and producers. The benefits to poorer households that stem from moving towards free and fair trade with the entire world harks back to 1846.[5]

Brexit also has shades of 1931 – another momentous year, when the UK left the gold standard. Freed from the constraints of that rigid currency and monetary system, the pound fell sharply and the economy thrived. While the 1930s were a difficult decade for the USA, the UK economy did relatively well and grew solidly. Determining one's own economic policy carries significant advantages. This is true now, as it was then.

We also have a chance to learn the lessons of 1945, another truly remarkable moment in our economic history – and not just because it marked the end of World War Two. The country was financially on its knees, but Labour Prime Minister Clement Attlee, having won a decisive election victory, enacted a transformational agenda, creating a modern welfare state. Sir William Beveridge's celebrated 1942 report identified the 'five giant evils to be overcome – disease, want, ignorance, squalor and idleness'. The response was the NHS, national insurance, free compulsory secondary schooling up until the age of fifteen, a mass home-building and slum clearance programme and initially low levels of unemployment'.

Then there is 1979, which turned out to be the start of the Thatcher revolution that transformed the supply side of the UK economy. Thatcher's policies created social divisions but delivered stronger growth.

While she won three elections, Margaret Thatcher was not always popular – and her name still evokes bitterness across some parts of the country. But it is hard to argue, in retrospect, that the UK of the late 1970s was a well-functioning economy. That is why the broad thrust of her policies is now widely seen as successful, positioning the UK for the subsequent changes in the global economic environment. It is important not to lose sight of the global context now.

The 2017 Conservative election manifesto identified the five challenges for the new government as, 'the need for a strong economy, Brexit and the changing world, enduring social divisions, an ageing society, fast-changing technology'. This is a reasonable frame of reference. There were also some positive aspects in the Labour manifesto, as we have discussed, not least the emphasis on public services and better infrastructure.

Chancellor Philip Hammond has said, since the referendum, that the British people did not vote to become poorer. Of course they didn't, and neither should they expect such an outcome. But voters did – and still do – expect their political leaders to demonstrate leadership, respect democracy, deliver on the referendum result and take advantage of the opportunities presented by being outside the insular, protectionist construct that is the EU. While the media focus is on the negotiations, it is vitally important to get the domestic policy agenda right too.

There may clearly be some near-term uncertainty, particularly given the hung parliament. But the further ahead one projects, the better the outlook under Brexit, and the more superior the performance of an outward-looking Britain becomes compared to remaining inside an unreformed EU.[6]

THE VISION THING

We believe that Brexit provides a unique opportunity to reinvigorate the British economy, boosting domestic demand and regional UK growth while repositioning us internationally. We can maintain a close relationship with the EU while also strengthening our commercial links with the rest of the world. The UK needs to get policy-making right at the local, regional and global level.

People tend to have strong, natural affinities with local organisations and individuals, such as a local MP or hospital. Local entities are often seen as people-friendly and reassuring. Such considerations go to the heart of a key issue reflected in the Brexit referendum – that family, work and place all matter. Place can often be overlooked. Time and again, a degree of bureaucratic control is imposed on people, reflecting the actions of remote structures with which few associate. The EU is a prime example. Place is often associated with a lack of social mobility, where success is measured in terms of how far one has managed to move from their childhood home. But is this rational, and does it reflect what the economy really needs?[7] While a degree of labour mobility is vital to make a market economy function, surely it would be better if good opportunities were also available locally. Would it not make more sense, economically and otherwise, if young qualified British people did not feel they had to move to London, or overseas, in order to be 'successful'?

In economic terms, it is necessary to create an enabling environment at the local level. Leaving the EU returns competencies to the UK in many areas, but at the same time there are other policy improvements we must make. The fact they have not been made should not be blamed on the UK membership of the EU. Managing non-EU immigration, for instance, could have been addressed without Brexit. Boosting our educational system and improving skills training, while making greater inroads into poverty, could all have happened while inside the EU.

Wage growth in the UK has been relatively subdued in recent years, and the broader picture is one of Britain as a low-wage, relatively low-investment and low-productivity economy. Apart from the lowest income decile, where there is progress, the next three lowest deciles achieve little in the way of social mobility, according to research by think tank Centre for Social Justice (CSJ).[8] This led the CSJ to identify five pathways that need to be addressed for those 'stuck' in such income deciles – family breakdown, educational failure, unemployment, addiction and serious personal debt – while proposing radical ways to confront these issues.

It may seem strange to be talking about a broken economic model given that the UK has, over recent years, shown relatively strong economic growth and high rates of employment. Unemployment is now at a forty-two year low. Britain also ranks favourably when it comes to technological change, placing third in the world according to a recent study on global innovation.[9] This highlights, if anything, that the picture is nuanced and mixed. One size does not fit all and policy must reflect this. London must be enabled to compete internationally – which includes, for instance, retaining the scope to attract skilled labour in a post-Brexit world.[10] There is a need, though, to boost other cities and regions. As such, fiscal devolution should now become a reality, as we discussed in Chapter 12, including greater control by regional authorities over local infrastructure spending. While linking local taxation to local spending, fiscal devolution should also encourage competition between regions, as different parts of the country strive to attract businesses and investment.

If we are to thrive after Brexit, UK policymakers must recognise that parts of the present economic system are broken and need to change. We should be rewarding the entire population, whether they voted Leave or Remain, by delivering a domestic economic policy that works. We referred to this in Chapter 8 as a rejection of hypernormalisation. At the same time, though, Britain must seize the opportunity of leaving the EU to reposition itself in a rapidly changing and fast-growing global economy.

To ensure a truly successful Brexit, our domestic policy agenda, EU relations and global interactions need to work in a mutually reinforcing manner. While there is currently a relentless focus on the EU exit negotiations, this is only one aspect of our future policy, albeit one that is important. But there are many other facets of our domestic and global policy-making that can also be advanced that don't depend upon our EU discussions. There are opportunities afforded to us by Brexit, regardless of how the 'divorce proceedings' work out.

Naturally, as we have said, there will be challenges. It is not easy to leave a complex commercial, legal and political construct after more than four decades. This process is made harder still in the wake of an unsettling election that produced a largely unexpected result, making the government more vulnerable to parliamentary ambush. Such complexity is manageable but, aside from handling detailed policy change and political conflict, this also requires articulating a clear and inspiring vision of how the UK economy and broader society can thrive outside the EU.

Ambition is needed, in terms of the kind of economy we want the UK to be. An upbeat assessment of post-Brexit Britain, combined with bold and constructive policies, will influence not only domestic thinking but also how international investors and the rest of the world view the UK. Our thought processes have been anchored in the EU for over forty years – an observation that applies particularly to the UK's political and media class. It will take time to change our collective view of ourselves, not least given inevitable near-term uncertainty.[11] We have lately seen, according to the Cambridge historian Robert Tombs, 'the revival of an old and familiar malady: declinism, a periodic fear that the nation has declined and is declining from some earlier time of strength, cohesion and success'. The reality is that 'Britain is a strong and wealthy nation', countered Tombs. 'Let's behave like one.' Such behaviour involves not only identifying our strengths and playing to them, but enabling the economy to innovate, adapt and succeed.

Humility is needed, too. This is vitally important for anyone intervening in an economy. While the market mechanism only operates well if there is proper regulation, and efforts are made to temper its worst excesses, we should be realistic in terms of what can be achieved over and above largely market-based outcomes. Intervention can work, but can also have unintended consequences. Micromanagement should be avoided. The default approach should be to trust market outcomes, while tempering any social fallout.

Economies are impacted by so many factors – local, national and global – that we cannot easily predict how interventionist policies will work out, even if previously successful. While the public sector has a vital role, we stress once again the core principle of creating an enabling environment that allows private enterprise to flourish. The simpler things are, the better the outcomes will be. When it comes to policy, less is often more – a principle that could hardly be more alien to Brussels.

While Brexit allows us to reclaim competencies in several areas, how much change do we need, alongside leaving the EU, to help the economy succeed? Change is necessary and inevitable – but not necessarily too much. For many of us, change is generally unwelcome. Too often it is forced upon us – by our employers, or politicians – frequently without consultation. Change can be disruptive and even frightening. And change that is imposed without permission and contrary to the general consensus tends eventually to unravel. That, after all, is the story of the incremental yet significant changes in the UK's relationship with the EU since joining the common market back in 1973.

IT'S THE INFRASTRUCTURE, STUPID

The UK needs to put investing, innovation and infrastructure at the centre of its economic thinking, as discussed in Chapter 8. The other 'I' is incentives. Regardless of politics, the factor most likely to make people act in a certain way is economic incentives.

Our DNA makes each of us unique, but it is our bodies and minds that make us function. Infrastructure sounds like a dry economic word but it is vital for the economy if it is to achieve its potential. Improving our infrastructure gets our economic body and mind in shape. No piece of infrastructure is insignificant – all of it is helping to drive the broader whole, in the same way as arteries pump oxygen-filled blood to our head, heart and hands. Moving on from Brexit, we need to place greater emphasis on the many different components of infrastructure: hard, soft and institutional.

Hard infrastructure refers to physical assets like roads, railways and bridges, as well as access to reliable and reasonably priced utilities such as cheap energy, housing and broadband. When it comes to hard infrastructure provision, the UK has fallen behind and needs to catch up, not only to drive growth but also to address the regional imbalances exposed so starkly during our Brexit referendum.

The government should take advantage of low long-term interest rates to raise funds for infrastructure projects that generate revenue streams and future growth, while also helping pension funds and asset managers to direct long-term institutional savings into such projects. We need new national airports beyond the south-east, new toll roads and enhanced rail links – with HS3 being prioritised so it can transform our northern cities into a second UK growth centre. We agreed with the call in the Labour Party manifesto for a £250 billion fund, built up over a decade, to invest in long-term infrastructure needs. In addition to government seed money, this should ideally be funded through long-term infrastructure bonds aimed at UK institutions who need to match long-term liabilities with investments generating a steady income stream.

Housing is an important part of this debate – and, in our view, should be the absolute focus of the government's domestic economic policy. People have been incentivised to own a house, as house prices are continuing to rise. This drives up prices further, which then diverts disproportionate shares of post-tax incomes into mortgage and rental payments, which impacts broader consumer demand. The resulting longer commutes, as people move out further so they can afford to buy, not only lowers productivity but also negatively impacts family life and happiness. Not only do more homes need to be built, for purchase and rental, as discussed in Chapter 11, but the taxation of housing needs to change – starting with a sharp reduction of stamp duty, to boost turnover in the secondary market for housing.

Soft infrastructure involves creating the right mix of education and skills so that the economy can succeed, with more people realising their potential, adding to the country's future economic success. This strengthens the case for a migration system more closely matching the UK's requirements for both skilled and unskilled labour. It bolsters the argument for better and more widespread training of UK-based workers. University attendance has risen sharply over recent years while, with some notable local exceptions, vocational courses and apprenticeships have been scaled back. Both trends should be reversed.

The election also raised questions regarding the funding of tertiary education. The current system – a graduate tax of sorts, charging students punitive rates of interest – is not the most efficient way to proceed. As we review university funding, all options should be considered, including certain institutions issuing bonds. We need to foster the UK's leading universities so they compete with their US counterparts and contribute to domestic commerce.

The government needs to incentivise – and, in some cases, fully fund – more students that follow much-needed vocational training. Such 'upskilling' is vital given the technological changes already under way, covering a vast array of areas, including artificial intelligence, robotics, green technology, stem-cell research and financial technology among others. These developments should make us positive about future growth prospects globally. The UK needs to ensure it is positioned to benefit, with our workforce suitably equipped, and it requires a re-gional policy that encourages clusters of activity, centred around existing innova-tion hotspots such as universities, helped by better transport links, infrastructure and increased research and development. The UK – and not just London – needs to be seen globally as a good place to conduct business 'in' and 'from'.

Too much of the recent commentary regarding technology is either utopian or dystopian, as Amy Studdart has written, framing such trends as powerful forces we cannot channel.[12] Studdart asks how we might create a framework that ensures change enhances democracy, open markets and the rule of law. One of the central tenets of successful start-ups in this new technological age, as she highlights, is 'the idea of human-centric design'. We need to reflect that in our approach to domestic economic policy-making post Brexit: a human-centric design with a regional focus, and training and upskilling at its heart.

The UK, like all major industrialised economies, faces major questions over the coming years regarding automation, the world of work, and the benefits and returns of skills as opposed to capital investment in robotics and machines. Work and wages are impacted by many factors: trade unions, globalisation and technology. The impact of each is changing in directions no one can predict.

How, for instance, are technological changes likely to affect employment patterns among the poorest in society – some of whom voted for Brexit, in the hope that their prospects, and those of their children, would improve? How do we avoid unskilled workers doing only the dirty, dangerous and demeaning jobs? As the nature of work changes, does the government need to start taking the idea of a state-issued minimum income seriously? While instinctively against such an intervention, with its potentially dulling impact on incentives, the pace of automation and technological change means both authors are prepared to keep an open mind.

Underpinning this is the need to uphold workers' rights. There is no doubt that some of those who backed Brexit saw it as an opportunity to have a bonfire of the regulations, establishing the UK as some kind of European Hong Kong. Others, in contrast, saw it as an opportunity to take a more mixed economy route, with more state control. Most, though, including the authors, view Brexit as a chance to pass our own laws and attempt to make improvements based on a revamped British model.

Whether in economic or foreign policy terms, the UK has often given the impression of managing decline, rather than having the confidence and drive that comes from seeing better days ahead. Leaving the EU, as we have argued, provides Britain with a unique, unparalleled opportunity to rebalance the domestic economy while repositioning ourselves globally. It is not just about leaving the EU, but also about the policies we adopt and the vision we paint for our economic and cultural future. Efforts to improve our soft infrastructure are most obviously about education and vocational training. But they also include the creation of a sense of national purpose that drives our post-Brexit economy forward.

Finally, there is our institutional infrastructure – which also needs to evolve and improve. There is too little focus on the need for our economic institutional infrastructure to change – in particular the Bank of England and HM Treasury. When it comes to macroeconomic policy-making, we seem to be very forgiving of institutions that have done little to improve the structure of the economy and have arguably caused much harm.

Both the Bank of England and the Treasury need far more knowledge of the global economy, in particular experience of the emerging countries that are already driving global growth. There is not enough serious insight in either institution into the workings of companies across a range of sectors. Both bodies, vital to our national well-being, also need to stand up authoritatively to often myopic politicians. During the EU referendum, neither institution showed much capacity for rational analysis or independent thought – and are subsequently, in the eyes of much of the population, diminished as a result. We feel that, in general, there has been a failure of macroeconomic management and long-term strategic economic thinking, both in the run-up to and since the 2008 global financial crisis.

The Bank of England exists to 'promote the good of the people of the UK by maintaining monetary and financial stability', according to its website. But how is it promoting 'the good of the people' and who ultimately benefits? What is the wider impact of monetary policy decisions on society; how do they affect the most disadvantaged? Has the maintenance of cheap credit allowed countless households to live beyond their means? Or has credit enhanced living standards beyond compressed wages and state welfare? Is it the Bank's fault that ever-rising house prices, reinforced by ultra-low interest rates, have seen even professional workers priced out of owning property in relatively cheap areas? Or have buoyant house prices in many regions sparked the construction of more affordable homes?

What should the Treasury do differently? Despite years of austerity, public spending does not appear to be under control. The UK has run a persistent budget deficit for almost two decades. Public spending continues to soar above the tax take – which, despite successive governments finding ever more ingenious ways of taxing individual households and firms, struggles to remain above 38–40 per cent of GDP for any sustained length of time.

There is a need to allow flexibility in fiscal policy, of course, and this would suggest avoiding arbitrary fiscal rules.[13] Yet we need more fiscal discipline. Over recent years various rules have been implemented, only to be reversed. All too often we have gone from feast to famine in public spending. Rather than the fiscal equivalent of a diet, what we really need is a change of fiscal lifestyle, to get our public finances permanently back into shape.

The real issue is that the UK needs to decide on the appropriate size of the state, with implications for tax policy and government spending. We favour a radical approach, bearing down on public spending, consistent with the tax take that the economy appears able to raise. Alternatively, if the country chooses that it wants government spending to be higher, then we need to be honest about the steps needed to make this happen. It is simply not acceptable to keep borrowing, foisting costs onto future generations.

Even at ultra-low interest rates, the government already spends a huge amount on debt interest – more than on public order and safety, equivalent to one third of the sum spent on the NHS, almost the same as spending on defence and schools.[14] While there is certainly a loud and vociferous political demand for higher government expenditure, and more borrowing to finance such current spending, there is probably a larger political market for maintaining some vestige of fiscal responsibility and reordering our spending priorities so as to avoid loading ever more debts onto our children and grandchildren.

It is also vital to retain the confidence of international financial markets, which keep market borrowing rates relatively low. Over the next couple of years, stronger growth in nominal GDP – economic growth plus inflation – if combined with continued low government borrowing rates, will allow the budget deficit to fall as a share of national income. However, this welcome cyclical improvement, were it to materialise, should not divert attention from the need to improve the longer-term public finances, particularly given an ageing population.

Two wrongs do not make a right. If spending and deficits are not brought under control in good times – the first wrong – that shouldn't mean active fiscal policies should not be used to help counter an economic downturn – the second wrong. There is a role for active fiscal policy but also an overwhelming need to improve fiscal balances, running annual surpluses to pay down national debts when times are good. Yet the UK has only twice run an annual budget surplus in the last forty years.

BRITAIN AND THE WORLD

The relatively buoyant post-referendum performance of the UK economy was largely predictable, resembling in many respects what happened after Black Wednesday in 1992 – when the pound was ejected from the ill-fated Exchange Rate Mechanism. What happened in June 2016, as in the early 1990s, was seen as disastrous by the policy-making establishment, but the resulting competitive boost from a weaker currency has served the UK economy well, allowing it to rebalance.

Admittedly inflation has recently risen. From June 2016 to February 2017, there was a general rise in global inflation, not helped by firmer oil prices. Since then, inflation in other major economies has eased, while UK price pressures have become more acute.[15] The Bank of England and the markets expect inflation to peak in the second half of 2017, before easing as domestic cost pressures remain subdued. This would see the current squeeze on real incomes – with inflation rising more than wages – reversed during 2018 as the Article 50 talks progress.

Although we are generally positive about Britain's economic prospects, the next few years could be difficult. The UK economy, after all, is at a late stage in the cycle, after seven successive years of expansion. Moreover, in the wake of the 2008 banking crisis, monetary policy has acted as a shock absorber across Western economies, with low rates and QE. Central banks including the Bank of England may follow the lead of the US Federal Reserve and start gradually raising interest rates. While global monetary policy tightening is necessary, it is unclear how the world's major economies and financial markets will respond to higher rates and a reversal of QE.

For the UK, the uncertainty associated with triggering Article 50 and the risk of another general election could well impact investment. Having said that, the scale of both domestic and inward investment since the EU referendum has been encouraging, not least from leading firms such as Google, Apple and Boeing. At the end of 2016, Google announced plans to double the size of its European headquarters in King's Cross, London.[16] This state-of-the-art centre, designed by Thomas Heatherwick, is expected to house around 2,500 employees, many of whom will be tech engineers.[17]

The future of international finance is becoming more interlinked with technology, and such inward investment is a positive endorsement of the UK's future prospects.[18] Moreover, foreign direct investment into the UK has soared since the referendum vote, as we discuss in our Conclusion. Many firms are looking through the near-term uncertainty and fulfilling previous commitments, or making fresh decisions to invest in the UK.

The UK should now be preparing, at a faster pace, for functions that will come back under our control from March 2019. We need everything from extra patrol boats to police our fishing waters to investment to enhance the customs clearance facilities at our ports. The autumn Budget of 2017 needs to be, more than anything, a 'preparing for Brexit' Budget – in stark contrast to that of March 2017, which barely mentioned that we were leaving the EU.

Too much of the referendum debate gave the wrong impression that, by leaving the EU, the UK would be retreating from the world. The very opposite is true. After Brexit, Britain has the ability to decide whether it wants to create a more business-friendly environment to succeed in the global economy, equipping our people with the skills to compete, while enabling domestic and foreign UK-based firms to succeed or instead adopt a different approach and practise protectionism.

In contrast to warnings of economic isolation, Brexit provides the UK with an opportunity to reaffirm its status as one of the world's most open and tolerant societies. Managed immigration will mean ministers and Parliament establish clear rules, while enshrining our long-standing commitment to take in genuine refugees and ensure the economy gets the supply of both skilled and unskilled labour that it needs.

There are also strong economic benefits of the UK regaining its historic role as an advocate of free trade. Gradually removing high EU tariffs on food and other consumer goods would benefit UK households and importers, boosting the economy – a point often overlooked. It should be stressed that tariff rates are falling around the world and non-tariff barriers – key for trade in services – are a major part of trade negotiations. Once outside the EU, the UK can look to negotiate away NTBs, working with other major service-sector exporters, helping us strike future FTAs.

There are respectable arguments in favour of not cutting tariffs entirely at the outset, as we discussed in Chapter 6. These include the economic dislocation to sectors currently behind the tariff wall – such as agriculture and some parts of manufacturing.[19] While we do not favour subsidising producers at the expense of consumers, we are conscious of the regional impact of exposing some domestic sectors to global competition. Tariffs should be reduced gradually but steadily, in our view, alongside possible temporary 'transition' payments within certain sectors.

Even with such transition measures, there is much scope after Brexit for the UK to return to the forefront of worldwide efforts to secure free trade among major economies. Keeping some tariffs, in fact, helps us to negotiate away trade barriers maintained by other countries, as we help to foster global free trade – a role impossible for the UK to play inside the protectionist EU.

A fully sovereign Britain, exploiting its links with Europe but not bound by them, while harnessing its influence across the rest of the world, will also be extremely well placed to help shape the direction of global governance. Far from being 'isolated', we will have greater influence over the global standards increasingly governing cross-border commerce. Much of the law impacting the single market – including on food standards, autos and climate change – is now made by global institutions and handed to the EU, which in turn transfers it to member states. It is vital that British politicians and officials are heard at the global level, rather than being limited by being forced to adopt EU-derived positions across a range of important issues.

The same is true in terms of debate on the environment – a key area for us all. Although there is no suggestion the UK will leave international agreements, we reiterate the importance of remaining a signatory to the Paris COP 21 agreement. The UK could also, after leaving the EU, implement its own emissions trading scheme (ETS), along with a UK-wide carbon tax.[20] With the European ETS falling under the ECJ, a UK-specific scheme could take on a leadership role to link with ETS initiatives elsewhere. It is certainly the case that the UK's desire to simplify its carbon pricing policy, with just one carbon price after 2021, might be easier to achieve outside the EU ETS.

The outlook for any economy depends upon the fundamentals, policy and confidence. Of all of these, confidence is the hardest to predict. The government has the Clean Brexit basics right in our view – leaving both the single market and the customs union. But we feel there is a long way to go in terms of convincing both domestic detractors and EU negotiation counterparts that suitable and sufficient preparations are being made to make operating outside these EU institutions a reality by March 2019. With more evidence of smart planning, together with a constructive, outward-looking message, we believe the government would succeed in generating more of a positive buzz around Brexit at home, while creating the sense of greater strength abroad. Both are vital if the UK is to succeed in these Article 50 negotiations, providing the best possible chance of thriving once we have left the EU.

CONCLUSION

CLEAN BREXIT

'Courage is resistance to fear, mastery of fear – not absence of fear.'
MARK TWAIN[1]

The UK has exercised its democratic right to leave the EU. Both authors publicly argued, ahead of the June 2016 referendum, for Brexit. We have outlined in this book why and how being outside the EU is to the UK's advantage, economically and otherwise. But we are leaving the EU, not Europe. Britain will benefit enormously from retaining close trading, diplomatic and other ties with the EU 27. If Brexit is carried out correctly, though, it can be a win-win for both the UK and EU.

While Brexit is a big opportunity for Britain, it is not by itself a guarantee of national success. We will benefit from being outside the EU, not least in democratic terms as national sovereignty is returned, but the extent of the economic advantages depends on what we do once we leave. Brexit certainly frees the UK from the constraints of the EU, empowering the country to become economically and strategically stronger. How we respond to this opportunity, in particular the economic policies we choose to implement, is among the most important questions Britain faces over the coming decade – yet has received very little attention.

CLEAN BREAK

Brexit only means Brexit if we are outside the two main legal constructs of the EU – the single market and the customs union. Within the single market, our laws stay under ECJ jurisdiction and Britain would have to continue making multi-billion-pound annual payments to Brussels while observing freedom of movement rules. This is not Brexit and much of the electorate would not accept it as such.

The benefits of single market membership are often exaggerated. Membership is by no means required in order to have access to the single market and to be able to trade successfully with the EU. The US conducts hundreds of billions of dollars of EU trade each year, from outside the single market and with no EU free trade agreement. China is the EU's second largest trading partner – again, from outside the single market.

The UK can keep trading successfully with the EU, paying an average tariff of between 2 per cent and 4 per cent until such time as we cut an FTA with the EU.[2] In many areas where tariffs apply they should be a manageable business cost, not a deterrent to trade, and would not apply on services. In some areas, though, like autos and agriculture, they would be higher – which is why the government is seeking sector-specific deals with the EU, and may provide tariff-related assistance to these sectors.

Even with no such overarching FTA with the EU, access to the single market is automatic, unless the EU decides to act in a completely irrational manner, breaking international trade rules – a strategy that would cost powerful EU exporters hundreds of billions of euros in lost revenues. This is unlikely, given the EU's large trade surplus in goods with Britain and the desire of influential businesses both in the UK and the EU 27 eventually to see zero-for-zero tariffs, once the politicians have stopped arguing.

Despite the UK urging the EU for many years to complete the single market, trade in services, in which Britain excels, is barely covered. That's one reason the UK already conducts the majority of its trade with counties outside the EU. We have a deficit on our diminishing trade within the single market and a surplus on our growing trade outside the single market. This suggests 'membership' is not nearly as vital as we are so often told.

Many large firms want the UK to stay in the single market, as they benefit from the status quo. The regulatory and compliance costs help keep smaller rivals in check and, for some, membership facilitates large-scale cross-border corporate tax avoidance. The single market also guarantees an unlimited supply of low-wage labour, subsidised by the state via tax credits, which suppresses domestic wages, especially for low-skilled jobs.

Being outside the EU's protectionist customs union also brings benefits, lowering consumer prices, while allowing us to cut trade deals with countries across the globe. Being a customs union member forces Britain to impose the common external tariff on non-EU imports – which raises prices for UK shoppers. Free of the customs union, food in the UK could be significantly cheaper.

While we could lose access to FTAs the EU has cut with other countries, such deals are not structured to help service-sector exporters like the UK, being driven largely by French and German interests. The EU has also failed to cut FTAs with the US, China, Brazil and the world's other largest economies – due to the complexity of negotiating as a bloc of twenty-eight, often with conflicting interests. The EU's recently announced trade deal with Japan, greeted with much fanfare in Brussels, is merely a provisional political agreement.

The world's fifth largest economy, the UK has a much better chance of securing trade deals with large economies negotiating alone – as Switzerland did with China, striking an FTA in 2013, after two years of talks. With the EU accounting for less than 20 per cent of the global economy, it makes sense to forge deeper trade links not just with the US, but also the fast-growing emerging markets that will increasingly dominate global commerce. This is much easier outside the EU's protectionist customs union.

This book has advocated Clean Brexit – leaving the single market and customs union without trying to negotiate a bespoke deal that would break the EU's fundamental rules. The chances of forcing the EU into a trade-off between single market membership and open borders are remote. That's because if the EU bends these central rules, considering the growing discontent over the Continent's lack of border controls, any flexibility shown towards the UK could well see EU electorates elsewhere demanding their own exit referendums. The European project could implode. As such, a Soft Brexit would become what we deem a Messy Brexit.

Consider, also, that a treaty-busting UK–EU deal would need to be ratified by twenty-seven EU Parliaments and a bunch of regional assemblies – and even then could be vetoed by an increasingly hostile European Parliament. That may be impossible before March 2019. An inevitably bitter negotiation over the EU's core principles would, at best, seriously harm UK–EU relations, undermining future cooperation on a range of issues. It could also spark a systemic EU-wide crisis, traumatising pan-European politics for a generation.

The chances of a stalemate, or any deal being blocked, are high. As the Article

50 period expires, the UK would face a cliff edge, amidst a frenzy of closed-door, last-minute bargaining. In the UK and across Europe, voters would despair at a Messy Brexit, characterised by chaos and cross-border finger-pointing and a woeful lack of planning. The related uncertainty would seriously damage business sentiment – and faith in our political classes.

Under a Clean Brexit, in contrast, it is clear from the outset that the UK will be outside the single market and customs union, allowing the relevant legislative and practical preparations to be made. The UK's negotiations with the EU, while they will still no doubt be complex and testing, avoid attempts to breach EU treaties. In the Prime Minister's Lancaster House speech of January 2017 and the UK's Article 50 letter two months later, a Clean Brexit was clearly at the centre of the government's thinking. This is the right approach.

The June 2017 election, however, and the resulting hung parliament and febrile Westminster atmosphere, has made the implementation of Brexit more complex. With the government vulnerable in both the Commons and the Lords, it is vital that ministers counter the scare stories being spread by those attempting to reverse the result of the June 2016 referendum.

It is by no means 'a disaster', for instance, to leave the EU with no agreement in place. Not agreeing an FTA within the Article 50 period is a perfectly acceptable outcome – and, in our view, could happen. That's why we recommend setting a 'no deal' deadline for the autumn of 2018, to force the initiative, after which the focus of attention would switch from trying to negotiate an FTA with the EU to all the other aspects of departure that must be agreed, not least the various protocols required to trade under WTO rules.

Unless 'no deal' is seen as a viable option, the UK's negotiating hand will be seriously undermined, so all the preparations must be made ahead of March 2019 for us to trade under WTO rules. Much of this work is happening, which gives us confidence in a successful outcome, whether it be an agreement on aviation and broadcasting with the EU, or mutual recognition agreements putting the frameworks in place for trade deals across the globe. WTO rules provide a good platform for the UK to strike a future FTA with the EU, once the Brexit process has passed.

Many of the alarmist stories about a Brexit cliff edge are resolved by the government's Repeal Bill, which is in its early Commons stages at the time of writing. All EU law is to be brought onto the UK statute book ahead of 'Brexit day' – but now under Westminster's control. The biggest cliff-edge danger, in fact, is that presented by any attempted Soft Brexit negotiation with the EU – or the second referendum being demanded by some in the Lords – given the extremely uncertain nature of the final outcome.

Rather than a cliff edge, it makes more sense to talk of a bridge from EU membership, back to full UK independence. Before anyone steps onto a bridge, they need to know its length and where it is taking them. There should, then, once we have agreed a deal with the EU, be a Temporary Transition Arrangement for Britain (T-Tab) to smooth the process of leaving. The deal must be time-limited, definitely not open-ended. Some firms have predicated their business models on the grounds of being in the EU, and sectors like autos, farming or the City that are closely intertwined with the EU will benefit from a transition period. T-Tab must not, though, become a stepping stone to re-enter the EU – which means negotiations over the precise legal structure used, and any involvement of the ECJ, are likely to be fraught.

The UK will, of course, continue to trade and collaborate with the EU extensively after Brexit. Political rhetoric suggesting that we are 'cutting ourselves off' or 'pulling up the drawbridge' is infantile and absurd. As well as ongoing cross-Channel commerce, Britain will contribute resources, political energy and support to a host of pan-European initiatives, from security and law enforcement to science and technology to educational and cultural exchange, as do many other non-EU countries. It cannot be said often enough that we are leaving the EU, not Europe.

BEYOND BREXIT

Brexit has the potential to deliver many benefits for the UK. Directly elected MPs will once again have the final say over Britain's laws, borders, taxes and trade negotiations. This is what the people voted for in the June 2016 EU referendum, and this is what the government and Parliament must deliver.

On the economic front, as we leave the EU, Britain needs to forge domestic policies based on strong growth, buoyant wages and high investment. The UK's industrial policy should, in general, be less about 'picking winners' than creating the enabling environment for business that we have outlined in the second half of this book. This means low and simple taxation, world-class transport and broadband connectivity, reasonably priced energy, a steady supply of both skilled and unskilled labour and maximum access to international export markets. There is a particular need to boost skills and training, linking the world of education with that of work, while providing the soft and hard infrastructure to create the best possible climate for innovation and investment.

There should be considerable emphasis on encouraging the UK's small and medium-sized enterprises – which account for over half of growth, two thirds of employment and often spark technological progress. We believe SMEs have been held back by the EU, with all UK firms having absorbed the cost and effort of complying with notoriously bureaucratic EU regulations even though less than 10 per cent of them export to the EU. Industries in fields from biotechnology to agribusiness, energy and fintech will now have the opportunity to innovate and expand in ways that were not previously possible.

Freed from EU state aid rules and regional 'structural fund' restrictions, there is huge potential for post-Brexit regional policy, boosting growth beyond London and the south-east. Closing the productivity gap between the capital and the rest of the nation requires more regional infrastructure spending. A well-targeted infrastructure programme could pay huge economic dividends, with the government utilising infrastructure bonds that channel institutional savings into revenue-generating projects, together with a National Transformation Fund seeded by central government.

Brexit should, meanwhile, spark additional devolution to Scotland and Wales, providing scope for more fiscal independence within the UK. We also believe that new post-Brexit farming and fishing policies will help spread wealth and enterprise more evenly across the country, as would the development of half a dozen or so UK 'free ports'.

Securing our future prosperity depends in large part on building a knowledge-based economy. That means putting the UK's universities at the heart of efforts to channel our huge intellectual property to commercial ends. One of Britain's greatest assets and sources of export revenue, our universities attract talent from around the world. This brings the UK huge advantages in terms of building worldwide connections – and it is vital students are removed from headline immigration numbers, allowing this sector to flourish commercially and culturally.

Our leading universities can play a catalytic role in generating not just areas of dynamism and enterprise across the UK's nations and regions, but in boosting British trade across the globe.

The UK's strong universities sector contrasts with a patchy system of vocational training. UK-based firms have underinvested in staff skills and training for many years, in part due to the EU's freedom of movement rules. Securing a high-wage, high-productivity economy means, above all, more investment in skills. It is vital that vocational training acquires a new enhanced status, not least at the heart of government – with its own Cabinet position.

Britain needs to provide more homes, freeing households from the enormous debt burdens that come from bloated house prices. The UK should build new homes on a large scale, taking immediate steps to double the rate of house-building to 300,000 new homes each year over the next decade, pressing the large developers to convert the huge backlog of planning permissions into marketable homes. A National Development Corporation should be used to convert state-owned land into marketable plots for builders, with local authorities channelling profits from 'planning gain' – the huge increase in land values once planning consent has been granted – into local infrastructure.

It is vital that, early on during the Article 50 period, preparations are made to return the UK to a system of managed immigration. This must provide the overseas labour and talent the economy needs, while restoring badly dented public confidence in UK border controls. Britain, should, of course, maintain its long-standing policy of providing a haven for genuine refugees – that is not in question. But just as creating an immigration system that is business-friendly and humane will reassure many who voted Remain, demonstrating that the UK government is now in charge, and immigration will be managed, will reassure many others who voted Leave.

It is also important to stress that Brexit must not mean an erosion of workers' rights and a regulatory race to the bottom. We do not believe it will. While favouring free markets more than some countries, the UK has also been a pioneer of much of the workers' rights legislation now taken for granted across the EU. Many existing UK-derived rules on pay and labour conditions are already more progressive than those elsewhere in the EU – such as our minimum wage and equal pay legislation. Workers' rights should be protected, and indeed with sovereignty returning to Westminster, Parliament will be beholden to the British people in ensuring that this is the case.

Uncertainty surrounding the UK's Article 50 negotiations could easily deter investment temporarily and, depending upon policy, impact economic confidence. That is one reason we have advocated a Clean Brexit that provides clarity on the outcome, allowing more time to prepare and adjust. It is vital that, ahead of March 2019, the UK makes practical preparations for technology upgrades at UK ports and border controls, to securing recognition agreements on matters ranging from aviation to broadcasting. The authors are well aware that, across Whitehall, such preparations are taking place. Amidst the vagaries of Westminster politics, they must continue. They also need to be funded, with the Treasury showing urgency in providing the resources in areas that are essential to Brexit's success.

The UK's economic prospects outside the EU are generally good, with Brexit taking place as the global economy appears finally to be recovering from the 2008 financial crisis. The negativity both before and since the referendum regarding the potential economic impact of Brexit has been alarmist and rather shocking. UK exports to the EU are around 12 per cent of GDP. As such, the fortunes of over 85 per cent of the British economy are not directly affected by the terms of its trade relationship with the EU. If the UK does not strike an FTA with the EU, British exports to the EU 27 would be subject to the EU's Common External Tariff – levied at an average rate of between 2 per cent and 4 per cent. If the value of UK exports sold in the EU then dropped to the entire extent of an implied 4 per cent price rise, this would amount to a fall of less than 0.5 per cent in our GDP. This is a worst-case scenario, of course, as UK exporters in practice would lower their margins to maintain sales, while seeking markets beyond the EU.

To promote the notion that UK GDP could be 10 per cent lower than it otherwise would be once we leave the EU – one of the Treasury's pre-referendum scenarios – was deeply irresponsible. The infamous forecast of 'an immediate and profound economic shock' following a vote to leave the EU has also been shown to be extremely wide of the mark. Since June 2016, the UK economy has held up well, growing by 2 per cent during the year as a whole. The Treasury forecasted that within a year of a vote to leave the EU, 500,000 jobs would be lost. Unemployment has actually fallen, from 4.9 per cent to 4.5 per cent – it lowest level since 1975, when we voted to stay in the EEC.

We do not deny that the UK faces big challenges – including the twin budget and current account deficits, high household indebtedness and the short-termism of UK firms. Low productivity and low wages are issues we could have done more to tackle prior to leaving the EU. But now that Brexit is happening, we must use the new regulatory and spending freedoms to our best advantage.

During the first half of 2017, real incomes have been squeezed as a result of higher inflation, caused in part by a fall in the pound since our EU referendum. Many factors, including globalisation and technology, are restraining wage growth, which is why we need such an intense focus on skills, training and other measures to raise UK productivity. A weaker pound was anyway long overdue, taking into account the UK's large current account deficit. Certainly, a more competitive exchange rate has helped exports, not least in the manufacturing sector. The CBI's quarterly industrial trends survey shows that in the three months to July 2017, manufacturers' production grew at its strongest pace since 1995.[3]

In contrast to firms fleeing the country after a Brexit vote, as many economists predicted, foreign direct investment into the UK has soared. According to the OECD, FDI rose from $33 billion in 2015 to no less than $254 billion in 2016, with more than 70 per cent of that total coming after the June vote.[4] While inward investment can change sharply from year to year, these are impressive figures by any standards, demonstrating confidence in the UK economy. The UK remains Europe's No. 1 destination for inward investment and that seems unlikely to change once we have left the EU, with the UK building on its reputation as a global hub.

As this book goes to press, there has been a flurry of positive economic developments. In late July, BMW announced it is to build the electric Mini in the UK – with Cowley seeing off fierce competition from factories in Germany and the Netherlands. The budget airline easyJet announced its largest ever intake of new cabin crew staff members, with half of these recruits to be based at Gatwick, suggesting that London will not be losing its hub status anytime soon. Following in the footsteps of Google a few months earlier, Amazon confirmed a huge investment in London, creating 450 hi-tech jobs. The company praised the UK for being a 'brilliant location for talent', as a result of our outstanding universities and strength in engineering, science and fashion.

Such investments, and there have been many since June 2016, are often 'despite Brexit', according to much of the mainstream press. It strikes the authors that, while leaving the EU will be complicated and cause uncertainty, the economics profession should accept that Brexit need not be the disaster that so many have predicted. Leaving the EU is no guarantee of economic success, as we have said. But it provides opportunities that can help secure success, as long as we make the right policy choices, both at home and abroad.

WITH EUROPE, *NOT* OF EUROPE

As the global centre of economic gravity shifts away from the West, and the world economy begins to recover, Brexit provides a one-off opportunity to reposition Britain in a fast-changing world. The UK has the ability to take a leadership role in many global organisations such as the WTO and NATO, working with like-minded countries to drive the global agenda.

It is no exaggeration that Britain can become the global champion of free trade. Unhindered by EU collective bargaining, the UK can reframe the global trade debate, tackling tariff barriers and opening up opportunities.[5] And Britain can work with the US, among others, to cut the non-tariff barriers that block trade in services. For too long, progress in world trade liberalisation has been stalled by the unwillingness of the EU and other Western nations to open their agricultural markets to global competition. The UK can break the logjam through a landmark 'agriculture for services' agreement – that would benefit UK consumers, while doing much to improve attitudes towards Western nations in some of the world's poorest countries.

Over the coming years, the UK needs to forge trade deals with the US, China, India, Australasia and a host of emerging economies, gaining market share in the nations that already account for the majority of global commerce. There are encouraging signs of progress. The ubiquity of English law and language, and our strong Commonwealth links, put the UK in a strong position to negotiate trade deals with the rest of the world. Such deals will help secure access to the fastest-growing markets on earth, the economic superpowers of tomorrow. None of this is possible under a 'jobs-first Soft Brexit'.

In general, we should be trading far more with Asia and Africa (the world's two most populous continents). The UK can encourage groups of Commonwealth nations to form plurilateral free trade groups – WTO rules allow and even encourage such multi-country arrangements. We should take advantage of the dominance of Chinese trade in the supply chain nexus, as the One Belt, One Road programme opens up. In many industries, regulatory standards are now set at the global level, superseding the EU – which, free of the complexity of negotiating as a bloc, should help Britain cut new trade deals.

Striking FTAs takes time. But that does not stop trade from growing. Trade happens when like-minded people based in different countries see an opportunity to do business. Most trade in the world happens outside formal FTAs, under WTO rules. Simply raising our sights from the EU, channelling our commercial and diplomatic attention in a way that reflects the emerging shape of global economy, rather than our four-decade institutional fixation on the EU, will generate more trade, even before formal FTAs are struck.

The UK is the EU's biggest military power, second largest economy, second largest financial contributor and one of its most effective policy advocates. We are not leaving because the UK is 'isolationist' or because British voters are 'stupid'. The public backed Leave because the EU has become rigid, protectionist and dogmatic on issues including business regulation and the UK's financial contribution, as well as border controls.

This book has compared the EU to the RMS *Titanic*. Like the ocean liner, some people feel we must remain in a big trade bloc like the EU. While not doomed like the *Titanic*, the EU needs to change course if it is to survive. Built on noble intentions, the bloc has become unaccountable, bloated and too susceptible to opaque corporate lobbying. We sincerely hope Brexit is a trigger for reforms that make the EU more flexible, outward-looking and democratic. That would be to the benefit of the UK, the EU and the rest of the world.

We remain deeply concerned, though, about the single currency. While the Eurozone is showing signs of cyclical recovery, the euro remains a fundamentally flawed structure. It is avoiding implosion only due to hundreds of billions of euros of central bank largesse and an assumption that, eventually, Germany will bail out those nations struggling to live with an exchange rate which, for them, is far too high.

'The crisis of European monetary union will drag on, and it cannot be resolved without confronting either the supranational ambitions of the EU or the democratic nature of sovereign national governments – one or other will have to give,' says Lord (Mervyn) King. 'The tragedy of monetary union in Europe is not that it might collapse but that, given the degree of political commitment among the leaders of Europe, it might continue, bringing economic stagnation to the largest currency bloc in the world.'[6]

The billionaire financier George Soros, speaking at one of the EC's flagship economic summits in June 2017, joined those calling for a less centralised, more flexible EU. 'The EU is now in an existential crisis … and if it carries on with business as usual, there is little hope for an improvement,' said Soros. 'Instead of a "multi-speed" Europe we should aim for a "multi-track" Europe that would allow member states a wider variety of choices.'[7]

It may be that Brexit, and the issues it brings to the fore – not just as part of the UK policy debate, but across the EU – eventually ushers in a looser, less remote and more dynamic EU. This seems unlikely, though, with the EU heading in the direction of increased centralisation and control. It may well be that the single currency remains in place until what is, in our view, its inevitable implosion. Such a verdict, once heretical, is increasingly becoming accepted by mainstream analysts – as we have discussed.

As such, the Eurozone will continue to generate north–south tensions. Member states like Italy and Greece, locked into an overvalued exchange rate, will remain scarred by stagnation and tragically high unemployment, while voters in Germany, the Netherlands and other wealthier parts of the Eurozone complain about bailouts. And across the EU, the migrant crisis will keep stoking east–west tensions, with voters everywhere alarmed at how freedom of movement has encouraged trans-Mediterranean human trafficking, while new EU member states become increasingly reluctant to accept their quotas of migrants and refugees.

It is astonishing that, when Italy hosted the annual G7 meeting in Sicily in May 2017, the migrant crisis was barely referenced and received only a token mention in the communiqué. It is this determination to ignore problems raised by an ongoing push for EU integration that has caused the rise of extremism across the EU.

Although Macron won the French presidency in 2017, the vote share of the

Front National was double that of the previous 2012 election. In the Netherlands, the far-right Party for Freedom came second in the 2017 Dutch general election, winning over 30 per cent more seats than in 2012. In Germany, the far-right Alternative für Deutschland Party, founded only in 2013, now has representatives in thirteen out of Germany's sixteen state Parliaments. While Angela Merkel should prevail in the election of September 2017, it is noteworthy that 45 per cent of Germans now say immigration is the most important issue facing their country, a larger percentage than in any other EU nation.[8]

In July 2017, the Italian anti-establishment Five Star Movement revived its calls for a referendum on euro membership.[9] Founded by comedian Beppe Grillo, this ultra-populist party is neck and neck in the polls with the ruling Partito Democratico, ahead of elections due in the spring of 2018. The debt Italy owes to the rest of Europe is so large – equivalent to 25 per cent of its GDP – that a default could shatter the Eurozone, which in turn would trigger the worst financial crisis since 2007.

We believe the UK's best interests are served outside the EU. This is not just because of the economic advantages and issues of sovereignty, but also because the EU, in our view, with an unworkable single currency at its heart, faces a serious systemic crisis. While the UK can continue to trade and cooperate with the EU across a range of headings, not least helping with the humanitarian relief effort in the Mediterranean, perhaps the best thing Britain can do for the rest of Europe is to demonstrate that it is possible to leave the EU and prosper.

Prime Minister Theresa May now needs to make the positive case for Brexit that she failed to make during the June 2017 election campaign. Many at Westminster want to ignore the EU referendum result and derail the government's plans. Much hinges on how public opinion develops during the Article 50 talks. That, in turn, depends on how the government conducts itself and the quality of the arguments it makes.

Leaving the EU is about passing our own laws, diverting Brussels-bound funds back to UK public services – including the NHS – and boosting trade with the fastest-growing parts of the world. The Prime Minister must state, repeatedly, that numerous major economies conduct EU trade happily without the onerous and costly conditions of single market membership – and the UK can do the same. She must highlight the fact that being outside the customs union brings benefits to UK consumers and businesses, that trading under WTO rules is perfectly normal and that it is totally acceptable to leave the EU with no FTA in place. This makes political sense, not only on the domestic front, but in terms of the UK's Article 50 talks. Senior politicians from all parties, in fact, should recognise the will of the people and admit that Soft Brexit is a cynical ruse, thus helping to ensure that Britain positions itself well for a future outside both the single market and the customs union.

Corporate interests determined to maintain the EU protections that benefit them will continue to resist Brexit. When protectionist barriers are removed, the losers are concentrated and vocal, while the beneficiaries – the general public – are silent and diffuse. The government needs to help industries adjust, while countering the inevitable scare stories. Ridiculous reports about the dangers of 'US chlorinated chicken' in July 2017, in the wake of overtures towards a UK–US free trade deal, will no doubt be revived in many forms.

Leaving the EU, while presenting short-term challenges, is a chance for the UK to modernise, upskill and recast its entire economy. Done properly, and used imaginatively, Brexit can generate a wave of prosperity that spreads beyond London and the south-east. The Prime Minister and her government, as we have stressed, need to lay out a positive vision of the UK outside the EU that demonstrates why we are leaving – and why Soft Brexit actually amounts to Messy Brexit, leaving both the UK and EU worse off.

Those trying to subvert Brexit, while extremely vocal and backed by considerable corporate money, are a small minority. They in no way 'respect the will of the people', as they constantly claim. A poll conducted in June 2017, after the general election, suggested that 70 per cent of the public feel that Brexit now needs to happen – as we highlighted in the Introduction. Reversing the vote not only risks serious public discontent, it would also genuinely alarm investors in the UK and beyond.

'We are with Europe, but not of it,' as Winston Churchill said of the UK in 1930. 'We are linked but not compromised. We are interested and associated but not absorbed.'[10] These words, cited at the start of this book, capture an important nuance in the UK's national identity. We joined the EEC in 1975 for economic, rather than political reasons. The truth is that the UK has always been an awkward partner of the EU.

Even the most ardent Remain campaigners don't share the vision of a federal Europe. Surveys suggest only a tiny percentage of UK voters believe in 'ever closer union' – just 6 per cent in December 2016.[11] Yet that is what has happened since 1975, and will continue to happen, given successive treaties and other centralising measures. When it comes to the EU, there is no status quo. This is a point the Remain side, including those still calling for a second referendum, have never managed to answer.

We have tried, throughout this book, to address the concerns of those who voted against the UK's departure from the EU. Our advocacy of a Clean Brexit is designed specifically to limit disruption and uncertainty, while fulfilling the public's stated desire to leave. Making a success of Brexit is about achieving a clean break, keeping UK–EU relations as steady as possible, while positioning Britain to succeed in a fast-changing global economy. This requires a credible, ambitious domestic economic policy agenda. It also means embracing the world, realising that globalisation is irreversible and that geographic proximity, while still significant, now means less than it ever has.

There is a need, then, for us to move on. We must be realistic about the near-term challenges of Brexit, but also optimistic about the longer-term opportunities. We believe our twenty-five negotiating principles and twenty-five economic recommendations provide a solid framework for future success. Brexit permits us to think boldly and radically. It calls for great leadership, both in government and business, but it also calls for national unity, or at least an end to this enduring sense of rancour. It is time to get beyond grief and resentment and to combine our energies in a common endeavour. Let's use this unfrozen moment to create a new era of national prosperity as a nation in Europe, but not the EU.

AFTERWORD

In June 2016, over 17 million people voted in a referendum for the UK to leave the EU – the biggest act of democracy in British history. In the general election a year later, more than 80 per cent of voters put their cross against parties campaigning on manifestos vowing to honour that referendum result and leave the EU. It is simply not true to say that the British government no longer has a mandate for Brexit.

The outcome of the June 2017 general election – and the resulting hung parliament – may have made the process of Brexit more politically complicated, but it does not change the principle. The British public, granted a referendum, declared that they wanted the UK Parliament to have the final say over their laws, taxes, borders and trade negotiations. It is vital to our democracy, and our country, that this now happens.

In this timely book that is full of insights, Liam Halligan and Gerard Lyons provide a powerful and compelling analysis of the UK's Article 50 negotiations and our economic prospects beyond. It is, as I would expect from these two writers, comprehensive and technically detailed, yet highly readable and politically astute.

This book focuses on the economic advantages of Brexit – laying out the benefits of 'access' to the single market without 'membership', while operating outside the EU's protectionist customs union. Halligan and Lyons also provide the negotiating principles – what they call 'Clean Brexit' – that give the UK the best chance of leaving the EU in a manner that minimises uncertainty for businesses and the public, while doing everything possible to maintain good relations with our European neighbours.

Some Members of Parliament are doggedly promoting so-called Soft Brexit as a reasonable compromise between Remain and Leave voters. Yet Soft Brexit amounts to staying in the EU in all but name. Continued membership of the single market means the UK's laws, money and borders remain under EU control. Customs union membership also requires the UK to keep collecting tariffs on imports from beyond the EU, money we then send to Brussels, while preventing us from securing trade deals elsewhere. This is not Brexit – and it is sophistry to claim otherwise.

'If the single market is so good for the UK,' write Halligan and Lyons, 'why do we trade less with the EU than with the rest of the world? Why is our EU trade shrinking as our non-EU trade expands? Why do we have a large deficit on our EU trade, but a sizeable surplus on our trade outside the EU?' Being in the customs union, meanwhile, does indeed result in UK consumers 'paying more, on a range of imports from outside the EU, to shield uncompetitive producers in other EU states from cheaper global prices', as the authors explain. It also forbids the UK from 'cutting trade deals with nations outside the EU – countries that account for four fifths of the global economy and are the world's fastest-growing markets'.

We have, amidst the political hurly-burly, lost sight of the fundamental economic reasons why we are leaving the EU. By providing such a clear explanation of the advantages, along with a thoughtful vision of how Britain can thrive as an independent nation beyond Brexit, this book provides an important public service.

'Too much of the referendum debate gave the wrong impression that, by leaving the EU, the UK would be retreating from the world. The very opposite is true,' write Halligan and Lyons. I agree and, as such, am delighted at the encouraging signs in recent months regarding the prospects for UK trade deals with the US, China and Australasia among others.

In this, the age of globalisation and rapid technological advance, it is an increasingly bureaucratic and inflexible EU that is insular and backward-looking. By allowing us to strike out and reclaim our status as one of the world's premier trading nations, Brexit provides a unique and exciting opportunity to build a more vibrant and prosperous UK.

Even more important than questions of economics, though, are questions of democracy and trust. Soft Brexit, backed by a host of commercial and institutional interests that benefit from the 'status quo' of EU membership, amounts to a cynical denial of the referendum result. Those promoting the notion of another referendum are also only doing so because they refuse to accept the outcome of the one we already had.

Just imagine if a second referendum 'on the deal' did loom over these Article 50 negotiations. The UK's bargaining position would be fatally undermined, as Halligan and Lyons make clear. 'The EU – keen to retain Britain's multi-billion-pound annual budget contribution, while discouraging other member states from leaving – would have every incentive to offer the UK the worst deal imaginable,' the authors explain. 'This would make it more likely, in turn, that the terms were rejected when the second referendum was held, with the UK then remaining in the EU – precisely the outcome that Brussels wants'.

Since the June 2016 referendum, many across our political and media classes have continued to fight the referendum campaign. The British public is wiser, with polls showing they want politicians to get on with it. Even after attempts by ultra-Remainers to spin the 2017 general election result as a vote against leaving Brexit, some 70 per cent of voters say the referendum result must be honoured.

Yet subtle and shameful schemes to subvert democracy are still being cooked up by opportunistic politicians and others intent on blocking Brexit. The parliamentary arithmetic means the government is susceptible to attacks from Remain supporters from all parties, not only in the Commons but also the Lords.

Much of this will take place in code, with talk of remaining in the single market or customs unions appearing to be a benign way of imprisoning us in the European Union. There are many 'experts' who disdain the electorate, resent their wisdom and loathe being overruled by those whom they hold in contempt. Yet the voters are clear-sighted and the constitutional stability provided by British democracy is considerable. The elite, the would-be oligarchs, cannot be allowed to prevail.

Fortunately, while the process may encounter squalls, Brexit will still happen, whatever the intelligentsia think. Having triggered Article 50, come March 2019, the UK will be legally outside the European Union. What is needed now is for supporters of democracy to come together, to make sure that there is no backsliding, no pretend Brexit and that the will of the people is fully respected.

To this end, Halligan and Lyons have made a significant contribution. By cutting through the political spin and focusing on the economic and diplomatic realities, they have produced a valuable guide to the why and how of leaving the

EU. A work that combines urgent polemic with considered research and scholarship, *Clean Brexit* deserves a wide readership among politicians, policy-makers and the broader public.

Jacob Rees-Mogg MP
Somerset, August 2017

NOTES

Preface

1   *Saturday Evening Post*, 15.02.30, 'The United States of Europe', republished in *The Collected Essays of Sir Winston Churchill, Volume II: Churchill and Politics*, (London: Library of Imperial History, 1976), pp. 176–86.

Introduction

1   HM Treasury, 'The Immediate Economic Impact of Leaving the EU', May 2016, CM 9292, p. 3. https://www.gov.uk/government/uploads/system/uploads/attachment_data/file/524967/hm_treasury_analysis_the_immediate_economic_impact_of_leaving_the_eu_web.pdf

2   *The Independent*, 21.06.16, 'Remain "80 per cent likely to win" EU vote, as Leave odds lengthen'. http://www.independent.co.uk/news/uk/politics/eu-referendum-latest-odds-80-per-cent-live-betfair-coral-bookies-remain-leave-brexit-winning-ahead-a7093296.html

3   Many Remain campaigners, not least David Cameron, repeatedly warned that voting for Brexit would be 'a leap in the dark'. Perhaps they were unaware of the honorable origins of the phrase. It entered common usage after being used by Conservative Prime Minister Edward Smith Stanley in support of the 1867 Reform Act, which extended voting rights beyond the landed gentry to include some of the urban working class. 'No doubt we are making a great experiment, taking a leap in the dark,' Stanley declared. 'But I have the greatest confidence in the sound sense of my fellow countrymen.' The cartoonist John Tenniel captured the phrase in a famous *Punch* illustration, cementing it into the political lexicon. The 1867 Reform Act, which consolidated Tory support at the expense of Gladstone's Liberals, is viewed cynically by some historians. Yet this 'leap in the dark' still represented a very significant extension of British democracy.

4   Reputable studies had anyway previously pointed to 'a sterling overvaluation in 2015 of about 5–15 per cent' – and that was before the pound climbed steeply ahead of the referendum, on the widespread assumption Remain would win. See International Monetary Fund, UK Country Report, No.16/58, February 2016, p. 10. https://www.imf.org/external/pubs/ft/scr/2016/cr1658.pdf – page=11

5   HM Treasury, 'The Immediate Economic Impact of Leaving the EU', May 2017, CM 9292, p. 3. https://www.gov.uk/government/uploads/system/uploads/attachment_data/file/524967/hm_treasury_analysis_the_immediate_economic_impact_of_leaving_the_eu_web.pdf

6   Economists generally define 'recession' as two consecutive quarters of negative GDP growth.

7   Between June 2016 and February 2017, CPI inflation rose from 1 per cent to 2.3 per cent in the US, from 0.3 per cent to 2.2 per cent in Germany, and from 0.1 per cent to 2 per cent in the Eurozone. Over this period, CPI inflation rose from 0.5 per cent to 2.3 per cent in the UK. Since then, UK inflation has risen to 2.7 per cent in April and 2.9 per cent in May before dipping again in June.

8   See CBI Press Team, 25.07.17, 'Manufacturers report strong output growth', http://www.cbi.org.uk/news/manufacturers-report-strong-output-growth/

9   Article 50 of the Lisbon Treaty gives any EU member the right to leave and outlines the procedure for doing so. Before the Treaty was signed in 2007, there was no legal way to leave. Article 50 gives the leaving country two years to negotiate an exit deal. Once in motion, it cannot be stopped or extended beyond two years, unless there is unanimous consent among EU member states.

10 The authors coined this phrase in mid-2016, in various speeches and newspaper articles. Some of the themes contained in this book were then developed in 'Clean Brexit', an essay published by the think tank Policy Exchange in January 2017. https://policyexchange.org.uk/wp-content/uploads/2017/01/Policy-Exchange-Clean-Brexit-16th-January-2017.pdf

11 The EU's 'four freedoms' are: freedom of movement of goods, people, services and capital across borders. These key principles lie at the heart of the EU and underpin the 'single market', originally known as the 'common market', and are enshrined in various EU treaties.

12 The figures quoted here are the authors' calculations using the interactive World Bank database. In 1973, the nominal GDP of the existing six member states (EU 6) was $958.8 billion (21.7 per cent of a world economy then worth $4,589.2 billion). When the UK joined, along with Denmark and the Republic of Ireland, the combined economy of the then nine EU members (EU 9) was $1,189.5 billion (25.9 per cent). By 2016, the GDP of the twenty-eight EU members was $16,100 billion and the world economy was $75,500 billion. Out of interest, in 2016, the GDP of the original EU 6 was $9,100 billion, or 12 per cent of the world economy, and the EU 9 was $12,300 billion, or 16.3 per cent. See http://data.worldbank.org/indicator/NY.GDP.MKTP.CD?locations=EU and http://data.worldbank.org/indicator/NY.GDP.MKTP.CD?end=2016&start=1973. The EU 28, as a group, would have been 34.1 per cent of the world economy in 1980 compared to just over 20 per cent now. See Full Fact, 13.02.17, 'The EU has shrunk as a percentage of the world economy'. https://fullfact.org/europe/eu-has-shrunk-percentage-world-economy/ and the IMF interactive database http://www.imf.org/external/datamapper/NGDPD@WEO/OEMDC/ADVEC/WEOWORLD/EU

13 See PwC, 'The Long View: How will the global economic order change by 2050?', February 2017. https://www.pwc.com/gx/en/world-2050/assets/pwc-world-in-2050-summary-report-feb-2017.pdf

14 Balance of Payments Stat Bulletin, 23.12.16, Tables B & C

15 Note that balance of payments figures can be subject to frequent revisions. The data we use is from the Office for National Statistics, *Statistical Bulletin*, 30.06.2017, 'Balance of Payments: Jan-Mar 2017'.

16 There are, in some areas, 'mutual recognition agreements' between countries. While not formal free trade agreements, they can sometimes be important in facilitating trade – as we highlight in Chapter 6. https://ec.europa.eu/growth/single-market/goods/international-aspects/mutual-recognition-agreements_en

17 This alarmist prediction was widely accepted by much of the economics profession, but was criticised by some independent thinkers – not least the authors. See Liam Halligan, *Daily Telegraph*, 23.04.16, 'A pro-EU "study" straight from the Ministry of Truth'. http://www.telegraph.co.uk/business/2016/04/23/a-pro-eu-study-straight-from-the-ministry-of-truth/ and Gerard Lyons, *The Sun*, 09.06.16, 'How George Osborne got Europe numbers so totally tangled'. https://www.thesun.co.uk/news/1252856/economist-rubbishes-chancellors-4300-brexit-claim-as-dodgy-division/

18 Polling data from January 2016 suggested the owners of small- and medium-sized enterprises (SMEs) were quite evenly split, with 42 per cent saying they would vote Leave in an EU referendum and 47 per cent backing Remain. The equivalent figures among CEOs at large businesses were 7 per cent and 93 per cent. See Stephan Shakespeare, YouGov, 25.01.16, 'Small business owners more Eurosceptic than big business'. https://yougov.co.uk/news/2016/01/25/eu-referendum-small-businesses-more-eurosceptic/

19 See Jonathan Hill, comments at Prosperity UK Conference, London, 25.04.17. See http://www.prosperity-uk.com/speeches-research/

20 The poll, conducted by YouGov, was based on a survey conducted between 12 and 13 June 2017, several days after the election. In it, just 21 per cent of respondents said they wanted Brexit to be reversed, with 9 per cent saying 'don't know'. It is interesting that this poll was highlighted by the influential political activist and writer Owen Jones, who campaigned extensively for Remain. 'As a Remainer who is a democrat,' said Jones, 'I accept and respect the referendum result, which is the view I've had ever since we lost.' See *Medium*, 23.07.17, 'Why I'm a Remainer who accepts the EU referendum result'. https://medium.com/@OwenJones84/why-im-a-remainer-who-accepts-the-eu-referendum-result-d198dbc99c2

Chapter 1: The European Union at sixty

1 From Jean Monnet, *Memoirs of Jean Monnet, The Architect and Master Builder of the European Economic Community* (London: Doubleday, 1978), p. 417.

2 The signatories were Christian Pineau on behalf of France, Paul-Henri Spaak from Belgium, Joseph Bech from Luxembourg, Joseph Luns from the Netherlands, Antonio Segni from Italy and Konrad Adenauer from the Federal Republic of Germany. The Treaty was ratified by National Parliaments over the following months and came into force on 01.01.58.

3 Stephen, George. *An Awkward Partner: Britain in the European Community* (Oxford: Oxford University Press, 1998), p. 5.

4 Politico, 17.06.10, 'De Gaulle's complicated legacy'. http://www.politico.eu/article/de-gaulles-complicated-legacy

5 This phrase was originally used by Tsar Nicolas I of Russia, while discussing the mid-nineteenth-century Ottoman Empire. See Harold Temperley, *England and the Near East* (London: Longmans, Greens & Co., 1936), p. 272. Since being applied to the UK in the 1970s, 'sick man of Europe' has been used to describe, *inter alia*, Germany after reunification and at various points France, Italy and Greece, as their economies have struggled to grow after adopting the single currency.

6 Benn's letter was reproduced in *The Spectator* on 18 January 1975. *The Spectator* was one of only two national publications calling for the UK to leave the EEC ahead of the 1975 referendum. The other was the far-left *Morning Star*.

7 The turnout was 64.62 per cent and the vote was 17,378,581 *v.* 8,470,073. Out of interest, the vote in favour of remaining in 1975 was less than the vote to leave in 2016 (17,410,742).

8 See footnote 12 in introduction.

9 Originally a stand-alone arrangement outside the auspices of the EU, the Schengen Convention was incorporated into EU law under the 1999 Treaty of Amsterdam. The UK is not part of the Schengen Convention. In a leaflet distributed to all UK households ahead of the June 2016 referendum, the then government said 'we control our own borders' within the EU. That is not strictly true. Being outside Schengen means EU nationals must show a passport as they enter the UK. But all EU nationals still have the right to live, work and claim benefits in Britain, as long as the UK remains in the EU. We will discuss this further in Chapter 14.

10 'Ah, but a man's reach should exceed his grasp' is a line from Robert Browning's poem 'Andrea del Sarto' ('The Faultless Painter'), published in his 1855 poetry collection, *Men and Women*.

11 European Commission, 25.03.07, 'Declaration on the occasion of the 50th Anniversary of the signature of the Treaties of Rome'. http://europa.eu/50/docs/berlin_declaration_en.pdf

12 Giscard d'Estaing's first recorded public admittance that the Treaty of Lisbon was indeed a reworked version of the rejected European Constitution was in July 2007, five months before the Treaty was signed. It came in response to a question posed by one of the authors at a conference in London. See Liam Halligan, *Daily Telegraph*, 01.07.07, 'New treaty is just "constitution in disguise"'. http://www.telegraph.co.uk/news/world-news/1556175/New-treaty-is-just-constitution-in-disguise.html

13 In 2007, Prime Minister David Cameron had given a 'cast-iron guarantee' that a UK referendum would be held on the Lisbon Treaty, which also created the post of EU President and reversed more than fifty previously negotiated British vetoes over various aspects of EU policy. Cameron repeated his pledge in 2009, before U-turning once other EU nations had ratified the Treaty.

14 European Commission, 25.03.17, 'The Rome Declaration of the leaders of twenty-seven member states and of the European Council, the European Parliament and the European Commission'. http://www.consilium.europa.eu/press-releases-pdf/2017/3/47244656633_en.pdf

15 'Address of his holiness Pope Francis to the Heads of State and government of the European Union in Italy for the celebration of the 60th Anniversary of the Treaty of Rome', 24.03.17. http://w2.vatican.va/content/francesco/en/speeches/2017/march/documents/papa-francesco_20170324_capi-unione-europea.html

16 House of Commons Library, Briefing Paper Number 5871, 12.07.17, 'Youth Unemployment Statistics'. Youth unemployment rates in Q4, 2016. The EU 28 average was 18.1 per cent.

17 *After Brexit: The battle for Europe*, BBC4 television documentary, 14.02.17. At the time of writing, this documentary has unfortunately been removed from BBC iPlayer.

18 *Financial Times*, 22.02.17, 'Brussels warns Italy to cut public debt by April'. https://www.ft.com/content/adc3ab4c-f905-11e6-9516-2d969e0d3b65

19 In the 'big bang' enlargement of 2004, the Czech Republic, Estonia, Hungary, Latvia, Lithuania, Poland, Slovakia and Slovenia became EU members, along with Cyprus and Malta. They were joined by Bulgaria and Romania in 2007 and Croatia in 2013.

20 Ruben, Atoyan et al, 'Emigration and its Economic Impact on Eastern Europe', IMF Staff Discussion Note, SDN/16/07, July 2016. https://www.imf.org/external/pubs/ft/sdn/2016/sdn1607.pdf

21 Dmiter, Toshkov et al, 'The "Old" and the "New" Europeans: Analyses of Public Opinion on EU Enlargement in Review', *MAXCAP Working Paper Series*, No. 2, April 2014. 'Maximizing the integration capacity of the European Union: Lessons of and prospects for enlargement and beyond' (MAXCAP event).

22 Eurostat, 16.03.17, 'Asylum in EU member states', News Release 46/20. http://ec.europa.eu/eurostat/documents/2995521/7921609/3-16032017-BP-EN.pdf/e5fa98bb-5d9d-4297-9168-d07c67d1c9e1

23 European Commission, 'Public Opinion in the European Union – Standard Eurobarometer 86', December 2016, p. 15, Exhibit QA9.

24 Greek voters rejected a bailout package in July 2015. The Danish electorate refused to accept a dilution of a previously negotiated opt-out relating to justice and home affairs in December 2015. In April 2016, a Dutch referendum rejected an EU–Ukraine Association Agreement – a development widely interpreted as a more general anti-EU protest. In October 2016, Hungary held a referendum on whether the country should accept its EU quota of 1,300 asylum-seekers without approval from the country's National Assembly. The proposal was rejected by a reported 98 per cent of those who voted. But the 44 per cent turnout was too low for the poll to be recognised as internationally valid.

25 Reuters, 18.07.17, 'Leading light of Italy's 5-Star revives euro referendum pledge'. http://www.reuters.com/article/us-italy-5star-euro-referendum-idUSKBN1A30TI. Italy's constitution bans referendums on matters

governed by international treaties. So any vote on euro membership would be 'advisory'. A vote to leave the single currency, though, would put huge pressure on political leaders. It would also spark extreme volatility on financial markets, since Italy leaving the euro and reintroducing a devalued lira would amount to an effective default on all euro-denominated debt.

26 Reuters, 08.05.17, 'Many French voters yet to be convinced by Macron'. http://www.reuters.com/article/us-france-election-morning-reactions-idUSKBN1841GD

27 Thomas Hocks, 'Germany's Elections Won't Be a Populist Takeover', Harvard Kennedy School blog, March 2017. https://harvardkennedyschoolreview.com/germanys-elections-wont-be-a-populist-takeover/

28 European Commission, 'Public Opinion in the European Union – Standard Eurobarometer 86', December 2016, p. 11, Exhibit QA3.

29 Reuters, 07.01.17, 'Germany's Gabriel says EU break-up no longer unthinkable'. http://www.reuters.com/article/us-germany-europe-idUSKBN14R0G8

Chapter 2: How the world has changed

1 *The Guardian*, 26.11.15, 'People think I live in a cave all year and come out in December, shouting It's Chriiisstmaaasss!' https://www.theguardian.com/music/2015/nov/26/noddy-holder-people-think-i-live-in-a-cave-all-year-and-come-out-in-december-shouting-its-chriiisstmaaasss

2 In 2017, UK government debt is just under 90 per cent of GDP – a peacetime high.

3 In July 1957, at a speech in Bedford, Conservative Prime Minister Harold Macmillan gave a very upbeat assessment of the UK's economic prospects. 'Indeed let us be frank about it – most of our people have never had it so good.' The phrase came to define an era, contrasting with the austerity of the immediate post-war years.

4 'Stagflation', a portmanteau of 'stagnation' and 'inflation', describes a situation where inflation is high, growth is low and unemployment remains high. It presents policymakers with tough choices, because actions designed to lower inflation may make unemployment worse. The term is often attributed to Conservative MP Iain Macleod, who used it in a parliamentary debate on 17 November 1965, after which it became widely used among politicians, journalists and economists. 'We now have the worst of both worlds – not just inflation on the one side or stagnation on the other, but both of them together,' said Macleod. 'We have a sort of "stagflation" situation – and history, in modern terms, is indeed being made.' Stagflation, not limited to the UK, was prevalent among half a dozen major economies during the decade from 1973. See John Helliwell, 'Comparative Macroeconomics of Stagflation,' *Journal of Economic Literature*, 26 (1) March 1988: 1–28.

5 International Monetary Fund, 'Annual Report 1973', Washington, DC, 1973.

6 Standard Chartered Bank, Global Research Team, 'The Super-Cycle Report', 2010. https://www.sc.com/id/_documents/press-releases/en/The Super-cycle Report-12112010-final.pdf

7 As the website of the European Commission Director-General for Trade states: 'Over the next 10 to 15 years, 90 per cent of world demand will be generated outside Europe'. See 'Trade, Growth and Jobs: European Commission contribution to the European Council', February 2013. http://trade.ec.europa.eu/doclib/docs/2013/april/tradoc_151052.pdf

8 McKinsey Global Institute, 'Rome Redux: New Priorities for the European Union at 60', Discussion Paper, March 2017, p. 20.

9 China's 'Belt Road' initiative was unveiled by President Xi at the end of 2013. Sometimes referred to as 'One Belt, One Road', it is an adventurous plan to recreate China's ties with a host of countries across the globe, overland (via the 'Silk Road Economic Belt') and via sea (via the 'Maritime Silk Road'). There are multiple routes and initiatives, with cities already identified along both the 'Belt' and the 'Road'. The Maritime Silk Road runs from the Chinese coast and ports such as Fuzhou, Guangzhou and Haikou, through Southeast Asia to Kuala Lumpur and Jakarta, south Asia to Colombo, through east Africa to Mombasa, the Mediterranean to Athens and Venice. In May 2017, President Xi hosted a Belt Road Summit in Beijing, attended by around thirty world leaders. While the summit was boycotted by many Western countries, worried about China's growing influence, UK Chancellor Philip Hammond did attend.

10 See United Nations Department of Economic and Social Affairs, Population Division, via the website https://esa.un.org/unpd/wpp/DataQuery/ (Choose Total Population then Europe then select years). These historic and projected population figures for 'Europe' include the USSR then Russia. The same numbers excluding USSR/Russia are 473 million (1957), 543 million (1975), 594 million (2015) and 578 million (2050).

11 African Development Bank, African Economic Outlook, 2014, p. 41.

12 The 'internet of things' (IoT) refers to the connection of devices to the internet other than typically internet-enabled devices such as computers and smartphones. Through IoT, cars, kitchen appliances and even heart monitors can all be connected to the internet. For a discussion of the impact, see, 'Industrial Internet of Things: Unleashing the Potential of Connected Products and Services' from The World Economic Forum in association with Accenture. http://reports.weforum.org/industrial-internet-of-things/

13 The 'green economy' refers to the low-carbon technologies that can help reduce climate change and in the process provide a boost to economies across the globe – not just in terms of the environmental impact of the technologies themselves, but the related growth in investment and employment. The number of jobs in the global renewable energy industry, for instance, including solar, wind, hydro and other 'clean energy' sectors, grew to 8.1 million in 2015, up from 7.7 million the year before. The International Renewable Energy Agency. forecasts that number will increase to 24 million by 2030, assuming the share of renewables in the global energy mix doubles. See *Financial Times*, 25.05.16, 'Green jobs grow as oil employment falls'. https://www.ft.com/content/7da1638a-2293-11e6-aa98-db1e01fabc0c

14 3D printing is also known as additive manufacturing, and refers to a process whereby a computer creates a three–dimensional object from a digital model. During the print–process the printer starts at the bottom and builds the object layer by layer.

15 'Big data' relates to the automated collection and organisation of huge data sets that, when analysed, can help provide policy solutions and commercial gains. The uses of big data extend beyond retail and marketing to manufacturing, construction, education, public administration and finance. By 2015, the 'big data' economy in the US was worth €115.5 billion, directly employing 11.6 million people, with its EU equivalent valued at €54.4 billion, generating 6 million jobs. A recent European Parliament Research Service Briefing forecast that big data practices could add 1.9 per cent to EU GDP between 2014 and 2020. See Eulalia Claros and Ron Davies, 'Economic impact of Big Data', European Parliamentary Research Service Briefing, PE 589.801, September 2016.

16 See Paul Ormerod and Bridget Rosewell, 'Europe Report: A Win-Win Situation', Report for the Mayor of London, Greater London Authority, 2014.

17 See the Centre for Social Justice, '48:52 Healing a Divided Britain', October 2016.

18 See 'UKTI Inward Investment Report 2014 to 2015', 17.06.15. https://www.gov.uk/government/publications/ukti-inward-investment-report-2014-to-2015/ukti-inward-investment-report-2014-to-2015-online-viewing

19 See Katie Simmons and Bruce Stokes, 'Populism and Global Engagement: Europe, North America and Emerging Economies', Pew Research Institute, 15.12.16. http://www.pewglobal.org/2016/12/15/populism-and-global-engagement-europe-north-america-and-emerging-economies/ Slide 17.

Chapter 3: What kind of Brexit?

1 Michel Barnier, former French Foreign Minister and European Commission Chief Brexit Negotiator, 06.12.16.

2 The single market is designed to guarantee the free movement of goods, capital, services and people (the 'four freedoms') within the EU – although, in practice, trade in services remains significantly restricted. Originally referred to as the 'common market', then the 'internal market', the name has changed as its scope has been extended.

3 The UK voted in 1975 to remain a member of the common market. It is axiomatic that ongoing membership of the single market – an arrangement that, due to successive treaties over the last four decades, now constitutes a far greater pooling of sovereignty than the common market – would, after the June 2016 referendum, be an affront to democracy.

4 Balance of Payments Stat Bulletin, 23.12.16, Tables B & C.

5 ONS suggests the Rotterdam Effect could account for 'around 4 percentage points' of the UK's goods exports to the EU. See UK Balance of Payments, The Pink Book 2016, Background Notes, p. 27.

6 ONS, 25.05.16, UK Perspectives 2016: Trade with the EU and beyond. http://visual.ons.gov.uk/uk-perspectives-2016-trade-with-the-eu-and-beyond/

7 ONS Balance of Payments Stat Bulletin, 23.12.16, Tables B & C.

8 Anna Soubry, a Conservative minister who vigorously backed Remain, said on *Question Time* ahead of the vote that, outside the single market, UK exports to the EU would 'fall to almost absolutely zero'. Quoted in Iain Dale, 'Why Ken Clarke's memoirs aren't worth what Macmillan will pay for them', *Conservative Home*, 18.03.16. http://www.conservativehome.com/thecolumnists/2016/03/iain-dale-why-ken-clarkes-memoirs-arent-worth-what-macmillan-will-pay-for-them.html

9 European Commission, 'Top Trading Partners', 2016, Directorate General for Trade, G-2, 15/02/17 http://trade.ec.europa.eu/doclib/docs/2006/september/tradoc_122530.02.2017.pdf

10 'The EU in the world – International Trade', Eurostat. http://ec.europa.eu/eurostat/statistics-explained/index.php/The_EU_in_the_world_-_international_trade

11 Dominic Webb and Lorna Booth, 'Brexit: Trade Aspects', Briefing Paper 7694, House of Commons Library, 21.03.17, p. 14.

12 Article 8 of the Treaty of Lisbon requires the EU to seek out cooperation with countries on its borders. 'The Union shall develop a special relationship with neighbouring countries,' the Treaty states, 'aiming to establish an area of prosperity and good neighbourliness founded on the values of the Union and characterised by close and peaceful relations based on cooperation'.

13 The gross UK contribution to the EEC/EU from 1973 to 2014 was £484 billion in constant June 2014 prices. The net contribution, taking account of payments back to the UK as part of various EU-administered schemes, was £157 billion. These figures were calculated by Vote Leave – using a standard methodology and the official government GDP deflator. https://d3n8a8pro7vhmx.cloudfront.net/voteleave/pages/214/attachments/original/1451513263/VLBudgetNote.pdf?1451513263

14 See Professor Stephen Bush, 'Britain's Referendum Decision and its Effects', Technomica, 2016.

15 Fabienne Ilzkovitz et al., 'A contribution to the Single Market Review', European Commission Directorate-General for Economic and Financial Affairs, Economic Paper No. 271, EC Brussels, January 2007.

16 See Michael Burrage, 'Myth and Paradox of the Single Market', Civitas, London, January 2016. http://www.civitas.org.uk/content/files/mythandparadox.pdf

17 See Open Europe, http://openeurope.org.uk/intelligence/economic-policy-and-trade/single-market-in-services/

18 European Court of Auditors, 'Has the Commission ensured effective implementation of the Services Directive?' Special report No. 5/2016, March 2016. http://www.eca.europa.eu/Lists/ECADocuments/SR16_05/SR_SERVICES_EN.pdf

19 In a letter written to the *Telegraph* in February 2012, the governments of twelve EU member states, led by then UK Prime Minister David Cameron, committed themselves to 'open up the services markets' across the EU. 'Services now account for almost four-fifths of our economy and yet there is much that needs to be done to open up services markets on the scale that is needed,' the letter stated. 'We must act with urgency, nationally and at the European level, to remove the restrictions that hinder access and competition and to raise standards of implementation and enforcement to achieve mutual recognition across the single market.' See *Telegraph*, 20.02.12, 'David Cameron and EU leaders call for growth plan in Europe'. http://www.telegraph.co.uk/finance/financialcrisis/9093478/David-Cameron-and-EU-leaders-callfor-growth-plan-in-Europe-full-letter.html. This letter is cited in Stephen Booth, Christopher Howarth and Mats Persson, 'Kick-starting growth: How to reignite the EU's single market in services and boost growth by €300bn', Open Europe, May 2013. http://openeurope.org.uk/intelligence/economic-policy-and-trade/single-market-in-services/ The report also says: 'There are currently around 800 regulated professions across the EU, 25 per cent of which are regulated in only one member state, which creates barriers to professionals seeking to provide services outside their own country.'

20 See, for instance, Chuka Umunna, *Prospect*, 27.06.17, 'Chuka Umunna: MPs of all parties must stand up for our Single Market membership'. https://www.prospectmagazine.co.uk/politics/single-market-membership-is-a-win-win-for-britain

21 Michael Burrage, 'It's Quite OK to Walk Away', Civitas, London, April 2017, p. 21.

22 Patrick Minford and Edgar Miller, 'What shall we do if the EU will not play ball?', Economists for Free Trade, March 2017.

23 The share of UK companies exporting to the EU is often stated as 8 per cent, but estimates based on HMRC data at https://fullfact.org/europe/how-many-businesses-export-eu/ suggest the figure is closer to 5 per cent.

24 Dominic Webb and Lorna Booth, 21.03.17, 'Brexit: Trade Aspects', Briefing Paper 7694, House of Commons Library, p. 8.

25 World Trade Organization, WTO Tariff Profiles 2016, p. 81. Trade-weighted average.

26 The problems encountered by the EU in finalising the recent Canada–EU Trade Agreement (CETA) – not least bloody-minded last-ditch opposition by farmers in Wallonia – reminds us of the difficulties the EU has in securing trade deals. The terms of CETA were agreed in August 2014 but, at the time of writing, the agreement is yet to be ratified by all twenty-eight EU member states and Parliaments. While popular among most Canadians, CETA has prompted protests in various EU countries, particularly over food standards and perceived environmental dangers.

27 *Financial Times*, 05.07.17, 'EU strikes trade deal with Japan'. https://www.ft.com/content/20248b48-6193-11e7-91a7-502f7ee26895.

28 No dispute resolution mechanism has been agreed between the EU and Japan and the two sides have barely begun to discuss highly sensitive issues such as protection for Japanese pork and dairy producers and safeguards for EU carmakers. Talks on these issues are not scheduled to finish until 2019, after which the deal will need to be approved by all EU member states (and various regional assemblies). Even at this very early stage, the EU–Japan political agreement on trade indicates that tariffs will remain in place for another seven years.

29 These four economies with EU FTAs that rank in the world's top-twenty economies are, as of 2017, South Korea (twelfth), Turkey (sixteenth), Mexico (seventeenth) and Switzerland (twentieth). See 'World Economic Outlook Database', International Monetary Fund, 19.04.17. The other nations where the EU has a trade agreement in force are: Akrotiri & Dhekelia, Albania, Algeria, Andorra, Bosnia & Herzegovina, Chile, Egypt, Faroe Islands, Georgia, Bailiwick of Guernsey, Iceland, Isle of Man, Israel, Bailiwick of Jersey, Jordan, Kosovo, Lebanon, Liechtenstein, Macedonia, Moldova, Monaco, Montenegro, Morocco, Norway, Palestinian Authority, San Marino, Serbia, South Africa and Tunisia.

30 Member states pass tariffs collected to the EU but keep 20 per cent to cover the cost of collection. See 'A guide to the EU budget' by Matthew Keep, 30.01.17, House of Commons Library, Briefing Paper No. 06455. http://researchbriefings.files.parliament.uk/documents/SN06455/SN06455.pdf. Customs duties accounted for 13.6 per cent of the EU revenues of €137.3 billion in 2015. See https://ec.europa.eu/taxation_customs/facts-figures/customs-duties-mean-revenue_en

31 See http://www.economistsforbrexit.co.uk. Overpriced food within the EU should be no surprise. The July 1971 White Paper on the UK's entry to the European Economic Community states that 'membership will affect food prices gradually over a period of about 6 years, with an increase of about 2.5 per cent each year in retail prices', p. 23. The EU's Common Agricultural Policy will be explored in more detail in Chapter 8.

32 For the EU's most recent tariff schedule, see http://stat.wto.org/TariffProfiles/E28_e.htm

33 This point has been made forcefully by Francis Hoar of Field Court Chambers, Gray's Inn, a member of http://www.laywersforbritain.org.

34 At present, goods entering the UK from outside the EU require an import declaration. Usually this is done via the logistics providers carrying the goods as agents. Once we leave the customs union, UK–EU trade will be subject to such requirements, with costs varying from a few pounds to '£25 plus for declaring a sea container'. Then there is the cost of physical inspections, from between £52 to £1,540 per consignment. See Professor Andrew Grainger, 'The Unforeseen Cost of Brexit – Customs', *The Conversation*, 22.07.16.

35 The North American Free Trade Agreement, signed by Canada, Mexico and the United States, creates a trilateral trade bloc in North America. It came into force in January 1994.

36 Strictly speaking, all members of the EU are also members of the EEA. But Norway, Liechtenstein and Iceland are not in the EU, so identify as EEA members.

37 Norway's EU payments, 04.08.16, Full Fact. https://fullfact.org/europe/norway-eu-payments/

38 In principle, EEA members are subject to judgments by the court of the European Free Trade Association (EFTA), based in Luxembourg. In practice, this court largely accepts and adopts legal precedents based on EU policy and law not just relating to the 'four freedoms' of goods, persons, services and capital, but transport, competition, social policy, the environment and state aid to companies. In other words, despite Brexit, broad aspects of the UK's domestic law and policy-making would remain bound by supranational court judgments.

39 See Shanker Singham, 'Cost of EEA Membership for UK', Legatum Institute Special Trade Commission Briefing, November 2016.

40 Peter Lilley, *Conservative Home*, 19.09.16, 'Brexit should be swift. Here's how to do it'. http://www.conservativehome.com/platform/2016/09/peter-lilley-brexit-should-be-swift-heres-how-to-do-it.html

41 While Switzerland considered joining the EEA in 1992 along with Norway, Iceland and Liechtenstein, the Swiss public rejected the proposition in a referendum.

42 In the aftermath of the UK's Brexit vote, some called for Britain and Switzerland to work together. After all, in the words of one former Swiss ambassador to London, Switzerland is trying to achieve 'exactly the same trade-off as the UK'. Since mid-2016, Brussels has toughened its stance towards Switzerland, as any Swiss success in securing a better trade-off between trade access and border controls could act as a precedent for the UK. *Financial Times*, 18.09.16, 'Switzerland: An immigration model for Brexit or a cautionary tale?'. https://www.ft.com/content/4c8efca6-7b28-11e6-b837-eb4b4333ee43

43 See Table 9.1 of the annual 'UK Balance of Payments Report: The Pink Book 2016', released 29.07.16. The figures quoted here are annual data for 2015.

44 'The government's negotiating objectives for exiting the EU,' Prime Minister's Speech, Lancaster House, 17.01.17 https://www.gov.uk/government/speeches/the-governments-negotiating-objectives-for-exiting-the-eu-pm-speech

Chapter 4: What kind of European Union?

1 *The Scotsman*, 19.05.10, 'Euro on the brink with whole continent "in jeopardy"'. http://news.scotsman.com/world/Euro-on-the-brink-with.6306724.jp

2 *New York Times*, 25.03.17, 'EU leaders sign Rome Declaration and proclaim a "Common Future" (minus Britain)'. https://www.nytimes.com/2017/03/25/world/europe/rome-declaration-european-union.html

3 *Globe & Mail*, 25.03.17, 'Protests, marches as anxious EU marks anniversary'. http://www.theglobeandmail.com/news/world/pro-and-anti-demonstration-as-eu-marks-anniversary/article34428358/

4 http://www.consilium.europa.eu/press-releases-pdf/2017/3/47244656633_en.pdf

5 Reuters, 25.03.17, 'EU leaders renew fraying Union's vows on sixtieth anniversary'. http://www.reuters.com/article/us-eu-summit-idUSKBN16W01Y

6 *The Times*, 02.04.17, 'In 30 years this will look like any old blip'. http://www.thetimes.co.uk/article/in-30-years-this-will-look-like-any-old-blip-xlmf09mcz

7 Quarter-on-quarter data. Eurostat Press Release, 29.04.16, 'GDP up by 0.6% in the euro area and by 0.5% in

the EU28'. http://ec.europa.eu/eurostat/documents/2995521/7244000/2-29042016-CP-EN.pdf/a6c3bcf4-f79b-4137-a279-ec11e15f9930

8   *New York Times*, 29.04.16, 'Europe's Economy, After 8-Year Detour, Is Fitfully Back on Track'. https://www.nytimes.com/2016/04/30/business/international/eurozone-economy-q1

9   Joseph Stiglitz, *The Euro*, (London: Allen Lane, 2016).

10 *Financial Times*, 22.02.17 'Brussels warns Italy to cut public debt by April' https://www.ft.com/content/adc3ab4c-f905-11e6-9516-2d969e0d3b65

11 In January 2017, Peter Navarro, President Trump's top trade adviser, accused Germany of gaining an unfair trade advantage from euro membership. Germany 'continues to exploit other countries in the EU as well as the US with an "implicit Deutsche Mark" that is grossly undervalued,' he said. See *The Guardian*, 31.01.17, 'Trump's trade adviser says Germany uses euro to "exploit" US and EU'. https://www.theguardian.com/business/2017/jan/31/trump-trade-adviser-germany-euro-us-eu-peter-navarro

12 The European Council is charged with defining the EU's overall political direction and priorities. The quotation is from 'The Presidency Conclusions, European Council meeting in Laeken', 15.12.01. DOC/01/18 http://europa.eu/rapid/press-release_DOC-01-18_en.htm

13 Kenneth Clarke MP, *The Times*, 15.05.02.

14 The Stability and Growth Pact, enacted in 1997, was created to establish rules designed to ensure that all countries within monetary union help maintain the value of the euro by enforcing fiscal responsibility – with annual budget deficits at 3 per cent of GDP or less, and national debts limited to 60 per cent of GDP. By 2003, both Germany and France were consistently breaking the rules, uniting to make sure that neither faced sanctions for doing so.

15 'Even at the outset of this global financial crisis during the first half of 2008, interest rate spreads between government bonds in France, Spain, Germany and Italy have been considerable. In other words, the markets feel that, despite endless political statements about "solidarity", "political will" and "ever closer union", it is by no means impossible that the Eurozone could break up.' See Liam Halligan, *Daily Telegraph*, 08.06.08, 'After ten years the euro is facing up to its first serious test'. http://www.telegraph.co.uk/finance/comment/liamhalligan/2791249/After-ten-years-the-euro-is-facing-up-to-its-first-serious-test.html

16 José Manuel Barroso, European Commission President, 5.02.10. Cited by Derk Jan Eppink MEP, European Parliament, 13.03.12. http://www.europarl.europa.eu/sides/getDoc.do?pubRef=-//EP//TEXT+CRE+20120313+ITEM-006+DOC+XML+V0//EN

17 'The Community shall not be liable for or assume the commitments of central governments, regional, local or other public authorities, other bodies governed by public law, or public undertakings of any Member State.' Article 104b, Maastricht Treaty, 1992.

18 *Il Sore 24 Ore*, 06.01.10, 'La Bce: tassi fermi e nessun aiuto ai conti della Grecia'. http://www.ilsole24ore.com/art/SoleOnLine4/Finanza e Mercati/2010/01/bce-tassi-fermi-nessun-aiuto-grecia.shtml

19 Reuters, 29.01.10, 'Greece: EU says no bailout'. http://uk.reuters.com/article/idUKTRE60R3BX20100129

20 *Deutsche Welle*, 01.03.10 'Angela Merkel rules out German bailout for Greece'. http://www.dw-world.de/dw/article/0,,5299788,00.html

21 Bloomberg, 24.03.10, 'EU economy chief concerned over Eurozone stability'.

22 'Greece represents just 2 per cent of the Eurozone's overall economy. A bath plug, though, accounts for around 2 per cent of the internal surface area of a bath. If Greece leaves, and the country's debts are redenominated in deeply devalued drachma, creditors of all "peripheral" Eurozone nations, having been pretty skittish for several years and more recently becoming frazzled, could end up enduring collective nervous breakdown. In that event, the single currency would simply drain away'. See Liam Halligan, *Daily Telegraph*, 19.05.12, 'We could all be losers in this Greek poker game'. http://www.telegraph.co.uk/finance/comment/9277190/We-could-all-be-losers-in-this-Greek-poker-game.html

23 A particular bone of contention among German voters is that Greece 'cheated' in order to enter the Eurozone. 'Supposedly, we have no money for tax cuts, no money for school upgrades, no money to maintain parks, no money to fix our streets … but suddenly our politicians have billions of euros for the Greeks who have deceived Europe,' declared the German tabloid *Bild* on 28.04.10. Greece joined the euro in 2001 on the basis of figures showing a budget deficit below 3 per cent of GDP, as required under the Maastricht Treaty. The Greek government later admitted these numbers were false. 'The Commission has been provided with incorrect figures for six years,' said Greek Prime Minister George Papandreou in an interview just a week after the Greek bailout had been agreed. 'Part of the responsibility was on Greece, but the Eurozone also lacked the tools to notice that.' *El Pais*, 23.05.10, 'Que nos den tiempo para realizar los cambios que tenemos que hacer'. http://elpais.com/diario/2010/05/23/internacional/1274565601_850215.html See also BBC News, 15.11.14, 'Greece admits fudging euro entry'. http://news.bbc.co.uk/1/hi/business/4012869.stm The investment bank Goldman Sachs has been accused of arranging a highly profitable secret £2.8 billion off-the-books 'cross-currency

swap' designed to flatter Greek accounts around the time of euro entry. See Robert Reich in *The Nation*, 16.07.15, 'How Goldman Sachs Profited From the Greek Debt Crisis'. https://www.thenation.com/article/goldmans-greek-gambit/ Goldman Sachs denies any wrongdoing.

24 *Daily Telegraph*, 05.05.10, 'Euro tumbles, stock falls as European debt fears grip investors'. http://www.telegraph.co.uk/finance/financetopics/financialcrisis/7682396/Greece-debt-contagion-fears- batter-euro.html

25 *Der Spiegel*, 19.04.10, 'We cannot allow Greece to turn into a second Lehman Brothers'. http://www.spiegel.de/international/europe/0,1518,689766,00.html

26 *The Scotsman*, 19.05.10, 'Euro on the brink with whole continent "in jeopardy"'. http://news.scotsman.com/world/Euro-on-the-brink-with.6306724.jp

27 *Der Spiegel*, 18.05.10, 'Bailout plan is all about rescuing banks and rich Greeks'. http://www.spiegel.de/international/germany/0,1518,695245,00.html

28 When government debt is above 100 per cent of GDP and the interest rate on that debt exceeds the rate of economic growth, then an economy is said to be in a 'debt trap'. This is akin to an individual over-spending on a credit card, then not being able to afford the monthly interest bill. A country in this situation can try running a budget surplus by suppressing spending, as has been imposed on Greece. But the result will inevitably be weak growth, compounding the debt burden.

29 *The Times*, 06.05.17, 'May needs more time for Brexit says Varoufakis'. https://www.thetimes.co.uk/edition/news/may-needs-more-time-for-brexit-says-varoufakis-qgszc5p0w

30 For a discussion about the dangers of QE, including testimony from leading investors, economists and policy makers, see Liam Halligan, BBC Radio 4 *Analysis*, 27.10.13, 'Quantitative Easing: Miracle Cure or Dangerous Addiction?' http://www.bbc.co.uk/programmes/b03dfpjt

31 Edward Yardeni and Mali Quintana, 24.05.17, 'Global economic briefing: central bank balance sheets', Yardeni Research Inc. (See Fig. 8 and Fig. 10). http://www.yardeni.com/pub/peacockfedecbassets.pdf

32 *Daily Telegraph*, 16.11.11, 'Barack Obama "deeply concerned" about euro crisis'. http://www.telegraph.co.uk/finance/financialcrisis/8893313/Barack-Obama-deeply-concerned-about-euro-crisis.html The US President wasn't alone. 'Until European countries build firewalls for their financial system, we'll continue to see market volatility,' said Canadian Finance Minister Jim Flaherty during the same month. 'Some of us are frustrated by the failure of clear and decisive action in Europe.' Reuters, 16.11.11, 'Flaherty: Bond volatility to continue without firewalls'. http://ca.reuters.com/article/businessNews/idCATRE7AF0BZ20111116

33 Mario Draghi, 26.07.12, 'Remarks at Global Investment Conference in London'. https://www.ecb.europa.eu/press/key/date/2012/html/sp120726.en.html

34 *Financial Times*, 22.01.16, 'European Central Bank unleashes quantitative easing'. https://www.ft.com/content/aedf6a66-a231-11e4-bbb8-00144feab7de

35 TARGET2 is the name given to the Trans-European Automated Real-time Gross Settlement System. It is designed to adjust accounts automatically between the branches of the ECB's family of central banks during the regular course of trade and investment across the Eurozone. In reality, the balances have been gradually chalked up as IOUs and equivalent debts to such an extent that TARGET2 has become a mechanism to facilitate semi-permanent transfers from wealthy to poorer Eurozone countries on an enormous scale. As of April 2017, Germany's Bundesbank is owed €843 billion by the ECB's TARGET2 mechanism – a figure approaching 30 per cent of annual German GDP. The Banca d'Italia, on the other hand, owes €364 billion – equivalent to over 20 per cent of Italian GDP. Spain's TARGET2 liabilities to the ECB are €328 billion, almost 30 per cent of Spanish GDP, while those of Greece are €72 billion, almost 40 per cent of Greek GDP. To some extent, these imbalances reflect capital flight from poor to rich Eurozone nations, but their ongoing non-settlement means they also amount to huge yet undeclared intra-Eurozone subsidies. If any country were to leave the Eurozone and default on these TARGET2 balances, other Eurozone countries would, in theory, be liable to plug the default gap according to their percentage weight in the Eurozone economy. At the time of writing, TARGET2 imbalances are up at levels last seen in 2012, when Greece was on the verge of being forced out of the Eurozone.

36 At the end of April 2017, the ECB's balance sheet was $4,440 billion, while that of the Fed was $4,430 billion. See Yardeni and Quintana (op. cit.), Figure 10. Both were outstripped by the Bank of Japan, which in the same month registered a $4,520 balance sheet. http://www.yardeni.com/pub/peacockfedecbassets.pdf

37 In November 2016, the Bundesbank warned that persistently low interest rates were encouraging the build-up of risks that posed a 'threat' to German financial stability, while also undermining the profitability of German banks. The German central bank further highlighted the 'duration' risks of funded pension providers forced by low rates to 'increasingly diversify their assets by region and sector' given their much longer-term obligations to policyholders. See 'Deutsche Bundesbank Financial Stability Review' 2016, pp. 49 & 56. https://www.bundesbank.de/Redaktion/EN/Downloads/Publications/Financial_Stability_Review/2016_financial_stability_review.html Also Bloomberg, 16.11.16, 'Bundesbank Says Low Interest Rates Encouraging Risk Build-Up'. https://www.bloomberg.com/news/articles/2016-11-16/bundesbank-says-low-interest-rates-encouraging-build-up-of-risk

38　See *Der Spiegel*, 08.04.16, 'Germany Takes Aim at the European Central Bank'. http://www.spiegel.de/international/europe/conflict-grows-between-germany-and-the-ecb-a-1086245.html and *Financial Times*, 10.04.16, 'Germany blames Mario Draghi for rise of rightwing AfD Party'. https://www.ft.com/content/bc0175c4-ff2b-11e5-9cc4-27926f2b110c

39　The ECB has designed its Outright Monetary Transactions programme so national central banks are responsible for any losses incurred on their own government's bonds – to address German concerns. The original plaintiffs then complained the inclusion of purchases of corporate debt discriminates against smaller businesses, which generally don't issue bonds. *Financial Times*, 16.05.16, 'European Central Bank faces renewed pressure in Germany'. https://www.ft.com/content/5683ba6e-1b5e-11e6-b286-cddde55ca122

40　Deutsche Bundesbank, 30.04.17, TARGET2 Balance. https://www.bundesbank.de/Redaktion/EN/Standardartikel/Tasks/Payment_systems/target2_balance.html

41　European Central Bank, *Financial Stability Review*, May 2017. The document refers to 'abrupt' 're-pricings' and 'adjustments' no fewer than fifteen times. https://www.ecb.europa.eu/pub/pdf/other/ecb.financialstabilityreview201705.en.pdf?60c526239a8ecb2b6a81cfedd898ccod

42　International Monetary Fund, April 2017. Transcript of the Press Conference on the Release of April 2017 Global Financial Stability Report. https://www.imf.org/en/News/Articles/2017/04/20/tr041817-transcript-on-the-release-of-Spring-2017-Global-Financial-Stability-Report

43　European Central Bank, Financial Stability Review, May 2017, p. 158. https://www.ecb.europa.eu/pub/pdf/other/ecb.financialstabilityreview201705.en.pdf?60c526239a8ecb2b6a81cfedd898ccod

44　Vítor Constâncio, 03.02.17, 'Resolving Europe's NPL Burden: Challenges and Benefits', speech by ECB vice-president.

45　See McKinsey Global Institute, 'Rome Redux: New Priorities for the European Union at 60', Discussion Paper, March 2017, p. 8.

46　Mesnard et al, European Parliament Briefing, PE 574.400, 'Non-Performing Loans in the Banking Union: stocktaking and challenges'. http://www.europarl.europa.eu/RegData/etudes/BRIE/2016/574400/IPOL_BRI(2016)574400_EN.pdf

47　The Italian government, in consultation with the ECB, is considering rescue plans for Monte dei Paschi di Siena, Italy's oldest bank, as well as Banca Popolare di Vicenza and Veneto Banca, two smaller regional lenders that have struggled to raise commercial finance. Reuters, 27.03.17, 'ECB's Nouy sees Monte Paschi rescue soon, working on more'. http://uk.reuters.com/article/uk-monte-dei-paschi-ecb-bailout-idUKKBN16Y1S9

48　In a recent article for the *Official Monetary and Financial Institutions Forum*, a highly respected independent think tank on central banks, Professor Frank Westermann of Osnabrück University highlights changes in the euro area's international investment position compared to non-euro countries. He demonstrates that offshore financial centres have become the largest net asset holders in the ECB's statistics, with a current balance of over €500 billion, compared to almost nothing before the 2008 crisis. Westermann suggest this pattern reflects financial markets 'taking advantage of QE' to sell their euro-denominated bonds to the ECB, then buying 'European real estate and equities', doing this to 'hedge their risks against a partial or complete euro break-up'. The result, says Westermann, is that 'if the euro should break up, they are well positioned to protect their wealth, while the Bundesbank will need to explain to German taxpayers why it viewed more than €700 billion worth of TARGET2 claims as a safe investment'. See Frank Westermann, 'ECB TARGET2 balances keep rising', *OMFIF*, 29.11.16. https://www.omfif.org/analysis/commentary/2016/november/ecb-target-2-balances-keep-rising/

49　L. Giordano et al., 'The determinants of government yield spreads in the euro area', Commissione Nazionale per le Società e la Borsa (CONSOB), Working Paper 71, October 2012. http://www.consob.it/documenti/quaderni/qdf71en.pdf

50　Dmiter Toshkov et al., 'The "Old" and the "New" Europeans: Analyses of Public Opinion on EU Enlargement in Review', MAXCAP Working Paper Series, No. 2, April 2014, 'Maximizing the integration capacity of the European Union: Lessons of and prospects for enlargement and beyond' (MAXCAP).

51　EuroStat, 16.03.17, 'Asylum in EU member states', News Release 46/201. http://ec.europa.eu/eurostat/documents/2995521/7921609/3-16032017-BP-EN.pdf/e5fa98bb-5d9d-4297-9168-d07c67d1c9e1

52　Under the terms of the EU's Dublin Convention, established in 1990, the responsible member state for any asylum seeker is usually the state through which the individual first entered the EU.

53　Migrants and asylum seekers cost Germany's federal government €21.7 billion in 2016, according to a Finance Ministry report, not including additional provision of public services in future years. This includes €9.3 billion to help states and municipalities cope with funding living costs, €1.4 billion on reception and registration and €2.1 billion on integration services. In addition to federal expenditure, local governments estimate spending an additional €21 billion a year, rising to €30 billion by 2020. The tabloid *Bild* has reported that Germany's internal security budget is also set to climb by a third in 2017, from €6.1 billion to €8.3 billion, due to the influx of more than 1 million asylum seekers into Germany since 2015. Ferdinand Fichtner, a department head at the Institute for Economic Research (DIW Berlin), argues the sharp rise in immigration could ultimately benefit the German economy, describing the federal and municipal outlays as a 'huge stimulus package'. See *Frankfurter Allgemeine Zeitung*, 27.01.17, 'Flüchtlingskrise kostet mehr als 20 Milliarden Euro im Jahr'. http://m.faz.net/aktuell/wirtschaft/wirtschaftspolitik/bundesfinanzministerium-fluechtlingskrise-kostet-mehr-als-20-milliarden-euro-im-jahr-14766733.html

54 Aleks Szczerbiak and Paul Taggart, 18.05.17, 'How has Brexit, and other EU crises, affected party Euroscepticism across Europe?', London School of Economics European Institute. http://blogs.lse.ac.uk/europpblog/2017/05/18/how-has-brexit-affected-euroscepticism-across-europe/ See also Mark Galeotti in bne Intelli News.

55 Reuters, 18.05.17, 'Poland defies EU over taking in asylum-seekers'. http://www.reuters.com/article/us-europe-migrants-eu-poland-idUSKCN18E2JN?il=0. Within the EU, the Visegrád countries have, in response to the migrant crisis, negotiated as a bloc. While resisting EU quotas on registering asylum seekers, they have meanwhile paid lip service to the importance of the Schengen Agreement, given the large numbers of their nationals who migrate, temporarily or permanently, to wealthier EU nations in search of highly paid work. See bne IntelliNews, 02.03.17, 'Visegrád Four reiterate call for EU reform'. http://www.intellinews.com/visegrad-four-reiterate-call-for-eu-reform-116873/

56 Reuters, 27.04.17, 'French would-be president Macron says would seek Poland sanctions'. http://uk.reuters.com/article/uk-france-election-poland-idUKKBN17T362 Macron made this call during his presidential campaign, following a political row over a French tumble dryer factory that was being closed, with production moving to Poland.

57 Katie Simmons and Bruce Stokes, 15.12.16, 'Populism and Global Engagement: Europe, North America and Emerging Economies', Pew Research Institute. http://www.pewglobal.org/2016/12/15/populism-and-global-engagement-europe-north-america-and-emerging-economies/

58 Eurobarometer is a series of public opinion surveys, regularly conducted on behalf of the European Commission across EU member states since 1973. Addressing a wide variety of topical issues, the Eurobarometer results are published by the European Commission's Directorate-General (Communication).

59 IMF World Economic Outlook, July 2017. http://www.imf.org/en/Publications/WEO/Issues/2017/07/07/world-economic-outlook-update-july-2017

60 *New York Times*, 29.04.16, 'Europe's Economy, After 8-Year Detour, Is Fitfully Back on Track'. https://www.nytimes.com/2016/04/30/business/international/eurozone-economy-q1

61 Reuters, 18.04.16, 'Next ECB president must be German, Merkel's Bavarian allies say'. http://www.reuters.com/article/us-germany-ecb-idUSKCN0XF0IX

62 *After Brexit: The Battle for Europe*, BBC 4 television documentary, 14.02.17.

63 Guy Verhofstadt, *Europe's Last Chance: Why the European States Must Form a More Perfect Union* (London: Basic Books, 2016).

64 European Commission, *Public Opinion in the European Union – Standard Eurobarometer 86*, December 2016, p. 15, Exhibit QA9.

65 See Simmons and Stokes, op. cit., Slide 17

66 Ibid.

67 European Union, 1975, Report by Mr Leo Tindemans to the European Council, *Bulletin of the European Communities*, Supplement 1/76. http://aei.pitt.edu/942/1/political_tindemans_report.pdf

68 *Le Figaro*, 30.08.94, 'The Three Concentric Circles: Interview with former French Prime Minister, Edouard Balladur', quoted in Jean-Claude Piris, *The Future of Europe: Towards a Two-Speed EU?* (Cambridge: Cambridge University Press, 2012), p. 68.

69 Reuters, 03.02.17, 'EU founders speak of possible "multispeed" future after Brexit'. http://www.reuters.com/article/us-eu-future-idUSKBN15I2WX

70 European Commission, March 2017, 'White Paper on the future of Europe: Reflections and Scenarios for the EU 27 by 2025'. https://ec.europa.eu/commission/sites/beta-political/files/white_paper_on_the_future_of_europe_en.pdf In July 2015, the so-called Five President's Report had emphasised a far more federalist European model. Presented by European Commission President Jean-Claude Juncker, President of the Euro Summit Donald Tusk, President of the Eurogroup Jeroen Dijsselbloem, ECB President Mario Draghi and the President of the European Parliament Martin Schulz, it outlined plans on how to 'deepen' and 'complete' monetary union. These included the introduction of a 'European deposit insurance scheme' and the creation of 'a future euro area treasury'. Set alongside this ambitious July 2015 document, Juncker's March 2017 White Paper appeared to amount to a significant retreat in his push for EU federalism. European Commission, 'The Five Presidents' Report: Completing Europe's Economic and Monetary Union', June 2015. https://ec.europa.eu/commission/publications/five-presidents-report-completing-europes-economic-and-monetary-union_en

71 Tigran Poghosyan et al., 'The Role of Fiscal Transfers in Smoothing Regional Shocks: Evidence from Existing

Federations, European Stability Mechanism', Working Paper Series 18, 2016, pp. 29–31. https://www.esm.
europa.eu/sites/default/files/wp18final.pdf

72 The Global Competitiveness Report, 2016–2017 World Economic Forum, Geneva, 2016. http://www3.wefo-
rum.org/docs/GCR2016-2017/05FullReport/TheGlobalCompetitivenessReport2016-2017_FINAL.pdf

73 Donald MacDougall et al., 'Report of the study group on the role of Public Finance in European Integration', EEC, Brussels, April 1977, pp. 13–14. http://ec.europa.eu/archives/emu_history/documentation/chap-
ter8/19770401en73macdougallrepvol1.pdf

74 In 2000, in an interview with one of the authors, MacDougall stated: 'I do hope I'm wrong, but I suspect
monetary union under the present circumstances runs the risk of setting back, rather than promoting closer
European integration.' See Liam Halligan, *Sunday Business*, 22.10.00, 'Voice from past warns on future' and
also *Daily Telegraph*, 01.05.10, 'Chronicle of a disaster foretold plays out on the streets of Athens'. http://
www.telegraph.co.uk/finance/comment/7664328/Chronicle-of-a-disaster-foretold-plays-out-on-the-streets-of-
Athens.html

75 Reuters, 11.01.17, 'Euro will fail in 10 years without reform, Emmanuel Macron says'. https://www.theguardian.
com/world/2017/jan/11/euro-will-fail-in-10-years-without-reform-emmanuel-macron

76 *Der Spiegel*, 15.05.17, 'Frenemy in the Making? Merkel Views Macron with Skepticism and Hope'. http://
www.spiegel.de/international/europe/frenemy-in-the-making-merkel-views-macron-with-skepticism-and-
hope-a-1147822.html

77 Jacques Rueff, 'L'Europe se fera par la monnaie ou ne se fera pas', *Revue Synthèses*, No. 45, 1950. Emmanuel-
Mourlon-Druol 'The Euro Crisis: A Historical Perspective', LSE Strategic Update, June 2011. http://eprints.lse.
ac.uk/43647/1/The Euro Crisis A Historical Perspective.pdf

Chapter 5: Early UK–EU skirmishes

1 *Wall Street Journal*, 09.05.11, 'Luxembourg Lies on Secret Meeting'. https://blogs.wsj.com/brussels/2011/05/09/
luxembourg-lies-on-secret-meeting/

2 *Frankfurter Allgemeine Zeitung*, 01.05.17, 'EU-Kommission befürchtet Scheitern der Verhandlungen'. http://
www.faz.net/aktuell/brexit/eu-kommission-skeptisch-vor-brexit-verhandlungen-14993673.html

3 Reuters, 03.05.17, 'PM May says EU seeking to affect result of British election'. http://www.reuters.com/
article/britain-election-brexit-may-idUSL8N1I55WX

4 Cited in *Der Spiegel*, 09.05.11, 'The Only Real Option Left for Greece Is Debt Restructuring'. http://www.
spiegel.de/international/europe/the-world-from-berlin-the-only-real-option-left-for-greece-is-debt-restructur-
ing-a-761475.html

5 *Wall Street Journal*, 09.05.11, 'Luxembourg Lies on Secret Meeting'. https://blogs.wsj.com/brussels/2011/05/09/
luxembourg-lies-on-secret-meeting/

6 Euractiv, 10.01.14, 'Why Merkel doesn't support Juncker for Commission president'. https://www.euractiv.
com/section/future-eu/news/why-merkel-doesn-t-support-juncker-for-commission-president/

7 *Der Spiegel*, 06.05.17, 'Merkel verärgert über Juncker nach Brexit-Dinner'. http://www.spiegel.de/politik/aus-
land/angela-merkel-veraergert-ueber-jean-claude-juncker-nach-brexit-dinner-a-1146299.html

8 BBC News, 26.06.17, 'Brexit: Merkel says "no need to be nasty" in leaving talks'. http://www.bbc.co.uk/news/
world-europe-36630326

9 *Financial Times*, 22.06.16, 'EU "foolish" to erect trade barriers against Britain'. A few days before the UK's
EU referendum, Markus Kerber, managing director of the BDI employers' group, attempted to cut through
combative political rhetoric, putting forward a more commercially oriented point of view: 'Imposing trade
barriers, imposing protectionist measures between our two countries – or between the two political centres,
the EU on the one hand and the UK on the other – would be a very, very foolish thing in the twenty-first
century,' said Kerber. 'I would not want Great Britain to stop producing the Mini – why would I?' he said. 'The
Mini is manufactured in the UK by the German motor group BMW.' The BDI – *Bundesverband der Deutschen
Industrie* – represents thirty-seven sector associations and 100,000 companies, employing around 8 million
people in Germany – approximately one fifth of the workforce.

10 *Washington Post*, 19.06.17, 'Merkel seeks "good agreement" with UK on Brexit'. https://www.washingtonpost.
com/world/europe/boris-johnson-looks-for-happy-brexit-resolution/2017/06/19/156756c2-54c3-11e7-840b-
512026319da7_story.html?utm_term=.b66d7a627cad. The VDMA – *Verband Deutscher Maschinen und Anla-
genbau* – represents 3,200 businesses with 1 million employees in Germany, making industrial machinery.

11 Office for National Statistics, Statistical Bulletin, 07.07.17, 'UK Trade: May'. The 2016 data for goods is cited
here. Note that the latest annual data for goods and services is 2015, contained in 'UK Balance of Payments:
The Pink Book 2016', released 29.07.16. This shows, in Table 9, that the total trade in goods and services in
2015 between the UK and EU was £357 billion in goods and £157 billion in services. The UK ran a trade deficit
of £90 billion and a surplus in services of £21 billion, for a total deficit in goods and services of £69 billion.

12　These German figures and the bilateral country data is from ONS, Statistic Bulletin, 10.03.17, 'UK Trade: Jan'.

13　*Daily Telegraph*, 06.07.17, 'Macron the Menace: Why the new French president is Britain's Brexit nemesis'. http://www.telegraph.co.uk/news/2017/07/06/macron-menace-new-french-president-britains-brexit-nemesis/

14　See World Bank Migration and Remittances database, 2016. http://www.worldbank.org/en/topic/migrationremittancesdiasporaissues/brief/migration-remittances-data

15　Reuters, 10.03.17, 'Carmakers eye more UK suppliers to handle hard Brexit'. http://uk.reuters.com/article/us-autoshow-geneva-britain-eu-idUKKBN16H0LF

16　*The Guardian*, 25.07.17, 'BMW pledges to build new e-Mini at UK car plant'. https://www.theguardian.com/business/2017/jul/25/bmw-pledges-build-new-e-mini-uk-car-plant-cowley

17　Annual Business and Finance Outlook, May 2017, OECD: Paris. http://www.oecd-ilibrary.org/finance-and-investment/oecd-business-and-finance-outlook-2017_9789264274891-en

18　The next highest ranking EU financial centre is Luxembourg in the eighteenth spot. Frankfurt, often cited as a rival to London, ranks twenty-third in the world. These rankings are discussed in more detail in Chapter 9. See Global Financial Centres Index, Long Finance, March 2017. http://www.longfinance.net/images/gfci/gfci_21.pdf

19　Reuters, 04.02.17, 'Germany's Schäuble wants "reasonable" Brexit deal for London'. http://uk.reuters.com/article/uk-britain-eu-germany-idUKKBN15J0GL

20　*Financial Times*, 26.01.17, 'Spain backs early trade talks in Brexit negotiations'. https://www.ft.com/content/40075c22-e314-11e6-9645-c9357a75844a

21　*Financial Times*, 03.05.17, 'Brussels hoists gross Brexit "bill" to €100bn'. https://www.ft.com/content/cc7eed42-2f49-11e7-9555-23ef563ecf9a

22　*The Sun*, 18.05.17, 'Chief EU negotiator Michel Barnier rejects claims Britain will be slapped with a €100bn Brexit bill'. https://www.thesun.co.uk/news/3589517/chief-eu-negotiator-michel-barnier-rejects-claims-britain-will-be-slapped-with-a-e100bn-brexit-bill/ See also *Daily Telegraph*, 07.05.17, '€100bn Brexit bill is "legally impossible" to enforce, European Commission's own lawyers admit'. http://www.telegraph.co.uk/news/2017/05/06/100bn-brexit-bill-legally-impossible-enforce-european-commissions/

23　'Divorce settlement or leaving the club? A breakdown of the Brexit bill', Bruegel Working Paper Issue 3, 2017. http://bruegel.org/wp-content/uploads/2017/03/WP_2017_03-.pdf

24　'Analysing the EU Exit Charge: An ICAEW Brief', May 2017. http://www.icaew.com/technical/economy/brexit/analysing-the-eu-exit-charge

25　02.03.17, 'Brexit and the EU budget', House of Lords European Union Committee, 15th Report of Session 2016-17. https://publications.parliament.uk/pa/ld201617/ldselect/ldeucom/125/12502.htm Professor Iain Begg of the LSE stated that 'the overall subscribed capital of the EIB is €232 billion ... of which 16.1 per cent is British'. The EIB in its Financial Report 2015 lists overall subscribed capital of €243.3 billion, of which €21.7 billion was called up as of December 2015. On that basis, the UK's contribution to the called up capital is 16.1 per cent of €21.7 billion, which is €3.5 billion. 'A more useful measure of the EIB's assets may be the listing of own funds (its equity), which includes reserves, and profits for the financial year,' says the Lords report. 'This amounted to €63.3 billion in 2015. A 16.1 per cent stake of this sum, were it to be put into play, amounts to €10.1 billion.'

26　*The Guardian*, 04.03.17, 'Brexit: UK could quit EU without paying a penny, say Lords'. https://www.theguardian.com/politics/2017/mar/04/uk-could-quit-eu-without-paying-a-penny-say-lords

27　'Reflection paper on the future of EU finances', European Commission, June 2017. https://ec.europa.eu/commission/sites/beta-political/files/reflection-paper-eu-finances_en.pdf

28　*The Independent*, 21.03.17, 'Brexit: EU will take UK to International Court if it refuses to pay £50bn divorce bill, "leaked document" says'. http://www.independent.co.uk/news/uk/politics/brexit-latest-divorce-bill-eu-take-uk-court-leaked-strategy-documents-a7641406.html

29　*Daily Telegraph*, 06.08.17, 'UK ready to pay €40bn Brexit bill, but only if EU talks trade'. http://www.telegraph.co.uk/news/2017/08/05/uk-ready-pay-40bn-brexit-bill-eu-talks-trade/?WT.mc_id=tmgliveapp_iosshare_ApPQnmboJ6lw

30　See Hansard Online, House of Commons, 'Next Steps in Leaving the European Union', 10.10.2016, Vol. 615. https://hansard.parliament.uk/Commons/2016-10-10/debates/6CE5F6BB-3AA4-4332-BF7A577DB35BDB77/NextStepsInLeavingTheEuropeanUnion

31　Terry McGuinness, 11.07.17, 'Brexit: what impact on those currently exercising free movement rights?', House of Commons Library, Briefing Paper No. 787.

32　See Liam Halligan and Gerard Lyons, 'Clean Brexit', Policy Exchange, January 2017. https://policyexchange.org.uk/wp-content/uploads/2017/01/Policy-Exchange-Clean-Brexit-16th-January-2017.pdf

33　The Vienna Convention on the Law of Treaties 1969 – sometimes known as 'the Treaty on Treaties' – contains articles that are based on 'acquired rights', which individuals build up over time and hold despite any changes in future treaties enacted by their nation. Moreover, 'acquired rights' were acknowledged in Greenland's withdrawal from the European Economic Community (EEC) in 1985. Under the term 'vested rights', the European

Commission said that Greenland should retain the 'substance' of free movement rights for workers from the EEC at the time of withdrawal.

34 See HM Government, 'The United Kingdom's Exit from the European Union: Safeguarding the Position of EU Citizens Living in the UK and UK Nationals Living in the EU', June 2017, Cm 9464. https://www.gov.uk/government/uploads/system/uploads/attachment_data/file/621848/60093_Cm9464_NSS_SDR_Web.pdf

35 The EU has also rejected the UK's offer of continued participation in the European Health Insurance Card scheme – a reciprocal agreement that means foreign hospitals accept treatment costs will be paid by the NHS, and vice versa. *Daily Telegraph*, 20.07.17, 'Britons face losing healthcare in Europe as EU toughens Brexit stance'. http://www.telegraph.co.uk/news/2017/07/20/britons-face-losing-healthcare-europe-eu-toughens-brexit-stance/ The EHIC scheme already works overwhelmingly in the EU's favour, with the UK paying more than £670 million to EU countries for the healthcare of UK citizens abroad, while claiming back less than £50 million from EU nations, even though there are significantly more EU citizens in the UK than UK citizens in the EU. The government has indicated it will anyway pay for the healthcare of UK citizens living in the EU unilaterally. See Sky News, 02.03.16, 'NHS "Scandal" as UK Pays Millions to EU'. http://news.sky.com/story/nhs-scandal-as-uk-pays-millions-to-eu-10189381

36 There was disagreement on fourteen and 'amber' – or partial agreement – on eight. See 19.07.17, 'Comparison of EU/UK positions on citizens' rights'. https://www.gov.uk/government/uploads/system/uploads/attachment_data/file/631038/Joint_technical_note_on_the_comparison_of_EU-UK_positions_on_citizens__rights.pdf

37 Politico, 20.07.17. http://www.politico.eu/article/michel-barnier-fundamental-divergence-with-uk-over-post-brexit-rights-of-citizens/

38 *The Independent*, 02.10.16, 'Theresa May – her full Brexit speech to Conservative conference'. http://www.independent.co.uk/news/uk/politics/theresa-may-conference-speech-article-50-brexit-eu-a7341926.html While a detailed examination of the history and powers of the ECJ is beyond the scope of this book, it should be noted that since the 2009 implementation of the Charter of Fundamental Rights, which seeks to standardise individual rights across the EU, there has been a fierce debate about where the power of the ECJ ends. The Luxembourg-based court has displayed a widely recognised tendency to expand its jurisdiction – so-called competence creep. Previous British and Polish claims to opt-outs preventing the extension of EU law into national courts, meanwhile, have both been overturned. As such, the Prime Minister's words of October 2016 signalled an end to British efforts to restrict ECJ jurisdiction, in favour of ending that jurisdiction altogether.

39 Franklin Dehousse, 29.05.17, 'The European Union is exaggerating in its demands for Brexit, especially about the ECJ's future role', Egmont Royal Institute for International Relations. http://www.egmontinstitute.be/eu-exaggerating-in-its-demands-for-brexit/

40 *The Guardian*, 9.07.17, Guy Verhofstadt, 'Improve the Brexit offer to EU citizens, or we'll veto the deal'. https://www.theguardian.com/commentisfree/2017/jul/09/brexit-offer-eu-citzens-veto-british-porposal-european-parliament

41 *The Independent*, 25.06.17, 'UK willing to do deal on European Court of Justice's influence after Brexit, says David Davis'. http://www.independent.co.uk/news/uk/politics/david-davis-brexit-european-court-of-justice-influence-a7807076.html

42 See 31.07.17, 'the3million and British in Europe issue joint response to EU and UK offers on citizens'. https://www.the3million.org.uk and https://docs.wixstatic.com/ugd/0d3854_c43534aebbb14aafac038e9e7dc60ba2.pdf

43 For a list of agencies see 'The Tangled Web: Dealing with EU Agencies after Brexit', Report from The Private Study Group, May 2017. www.theredcell.co.uk

44 House of Commons Library, 11.07.17, Briefing Paper No. CBP 8036, 'Euratom'. http://researchbriefings.files.parliament.uk/documents/CBP-8036/CBP-8036.pdf

45 See 'United Kingdom's exit from and new partnership with the European Union – White Paper', Cm 9417, February 2017 (and updates). This White Paper says the European Union (Amendment) Act 2008 'makes clear' that, in UK law, references to the EU include Euratom. So the Euratom Treaty 'imports Article 50 into its provisions'. https://www.gov.uk/government/publications/the-united-kingdoms-exit-from-and-new-partnership-with-the-european-union-white-paper

46 'Leaving the EU: negotiation priorities for energy and climate change policy', House of Commons Business, Energy and Industrial Strategy Committee, Hc909, May 2017. https://publications.parliament.uk/pa/cm201617/cmselect/cmbeis/909/909.pdf

47 See 'Small Modular Reactors – once in a lifetime opportunity for the UK,' Rolls-Royce plc, May 2016. https://www.rolls-royce.com/~/media/Files/R/Rolls-Royce/documents/customers/nuclear/smr-booklet-28-sep.pdf

48 'Leaving the EU, the Euratom Treaty Part 2: A Framework for the Future', Institute for Mechanical Engineering, May 2017. https://www.imeche.org/policy-and-press/reports/detail/leaving-the-eu-the-euratom-treaty-part-2-a-framework-for-the-future

49 JET is run by the European Consortium for the Development of Fusion Energy, which gets about half of its

funding from the EU's Euratom Horizon 2020 programme. A magnetic-confinement plasma-physics experiment, JET is studying how nuclei can be made to fuse together to unleash large amounts of clean energy. The EU currently funds 88 per cent of the costs of JET, which is contracted to 2018. 'JET is a prized facility at the centre of the UK's global leadership in nuclear fusion research,' said Industry Secretary Greg Clark, confirming in June 2017 that the UK will pay towards the funding of JET until 2020, beyond the contracted period. JET is the precursor to the ITER fusion-energy demonstrator, currently being built in France, and supports 1,300 UK jobs. See PhysicsWorld.com, 28.06.17, 'UK will fund Joint European Torus beyond Brexit'. http://physicsworld.com/cws/article/news/2017/jun/28/uk-will-fund-joint-european-torus-beyond-brexit

50 'It is actually necessary to leave Euratom when you leave the EU for the pragmatic legal reason that the institutions are inseparable from the European Commission, the Council and the European Court of Justice,' said Brexit Minister Steve Baker in July 2017, at the height of the row. Baker was speaking on the BBC Radio 4 *Today Programme* on 13.07.17.

51 *Daily Telegraph*, 13.07.17, 'Flights to Europe could be suspended in a post-Brexit legal vacuum, airports warn'. http://www.telegraph.co.uk/travel/news/british-airports-warn-flights-to-europe-will-be-grounded-aviation/

52 'UK aviation industry – Socio-economic report', Sustainable Aviation, 2016. http://www.sustainableaviation.co.uk/wp-content/uploads/2016/01/SA-Socio-Economic-Report.pdf

53 The ten busiest airports in Europe are Heathrow (75,676,223 passengers in 2016), Paris Charles de Gaulle (65,933,145), Amsterdam Schiphol (63,625,664), Frankfurt (60,792,308), Istanbul Ataturk (60,119,215), Madrid Barajas (50,420,583), Barcelona (44,154,693), Gatwick (43,136,800), Munich (42,277,692) and Rome (40,463,208). Manchester ranks twentieth (25,600,000) and Stansted is twenty-second (24,3000,000). See http://www.airliners.net/forum/viewtopic.php?t=1352841

54 EU agreements currently govern UK airline access to seventeen non-EU countries – including Canada and Israel, as well as the US.

55 BBC2, *Newsnight*, 01.08.17.

56 See Andrew Lilico, *Daily Telegraph*, 27.02.17, 'Of course we will stay in some EU agencies after Brexit – that's common sense, not weakness'. http://www.telegraph.co.uk/news/2017/03/27/course-will-stay-eu-bodies-brexit-common-sense-not-weakness/

57 Such provision is outlined in Article VII of the regulations that set up Horizon 2020. See Scientists for Britain, http://www.scientistsforbritain.uk, including work by Dr Lee Upcraft and Dr Chris Lee.

58 'In the early 1990s, Britain was recognised as one of the best places in the world to test new drugs on patients – decisions were quick and bureaucratic obstacles were few,' writes Bell. 'The introduction of the European Clinical Trials Directive in 2004 ended all this … Britain is more inclined towards a relatively liberal risk-based regulatory environment that allows fields to move quickly – to reflect on ethical issues but not to over-regulate. The EU, by contrast, has a record of deep regulatory conservatism, attempting to legislate and control many aspects of science that are not deemed here in the UK to present a significant danger.' See John Bell, *Financial Times*, 25.08.16, 'Brexit offers opportunities for UK scientists'. https://www.ft.com/content/5db36726-5740-11e6-9f70-badea1b336d4?mhq5j=e4

59 Field Fisher, 09.03.17, 'The UK staking its claim in the future of space – Brexit and beyond'. http://www.fieldfisher.com/publications/2017/03/satellite-finance-february-2017-the-uk-staking-its-claim-in-the-future-of-space-brexit-and-beyond – sthash.ODII6kSC.dpbs

60 Bloomberg, 28.06.17, 'EU Willing to Soften Brexit Position Over Court's Role, Officials Say'. https://www.bloomberg.com/news/articles/2017-06-28/eu-said-willing-to-soften-brexit-position-over-court-s-role Germany's Foreign Minister, Sigmar Gabriel, has raised the prospect of 'a joint court that is staffed by Europeans and Britons' which in principle follows the ECJ's rulings. See *The Independent*, 19.06.17, 'Europe may offer "soft Brexit" and let UK stay in Single Market, hints German Foreign Minister'. http://www.independent.co.uk/news/uk/politics/brexit-uk-may-secure-soft-eu-withdrawl-european-single-market-theresa-may-david-davis-german-foreign-a7796721.html

61 *The Independent*, 25.06.17, 'UK willing to do deal on European Court of Justice's influence after Brexit, says David Davis'. http://www.independent.co.uk/news/uk/politics/david-davis-brexit-european-court-of-justice-influence-a7807076.html

Chapter 6: WTO rules and transition

1 *Thoughts and Details on Scarcity*, 1795.

2 @daviddavismp, 26.05.17. https://twitter.com/daviddavismp/status/735770073822961664

3 More than 50,000 pieces of EU legislation have been passed since 1990. As such, transferring European legislation into UK law is the most efficient way to ensure continuity. Some of these laws will need redrafting – as they assume the UK is an EU member or refer to EU institutions the UK is leaving. Given the time needed to do this, the Repeal Bill contains provisions – known as 'Henry VIII clauses' in parliamentary slang – that

allow ministers to pass statutory instruments to amend or remove both primary and secondary legislation. Under Section 7 of the bill, ministers can correct 'deficiencies' such as legislation referring to the UK as an EU member or to EU agencies the UK will have left. These proposed powers – which cannot be used to change taxation, create a criminal offence, alter human rights legislation or change the 1998 Northern Ireland Act which implemented the Good Friday Agreement – expire two years after the UK leaves the EU. Section 9 of the Repeal Bill gives ministers substantially broader powers to 'make any provision that could be made by an Act of Parliament (including modifying this Act)' so long as 'the Minister considers such provision should be in force on or before exit day'. These powers are subject to restrictions similar to those under Section 7 but expire on the day the UK leaves the EU.

4   The European Union's draft negotiation principles:
   •   The EU wishes to have the United Kingdom as a close partner in the future
   •   Preserving the integrity of the Single Market means that the UK will not be able to participate on a sector-by-sector basis
   •   The EU 'four freedoms' are indivisible and there can be no cherry-picking
   •   A non-member of the Union cannot have the same rights and benefits as a member
   •   The EU will negotiate as a bloc, rather than 27 individual countries, so as not to undercut the position of the Union
   •   Brexit negotiations will take place as a single package. They will only be considered settled when all individual items are agreed
   •   The UK and EU must agree on their future relationship, but these discussions can only take place when there is sufficient clarity on the process of the UK's withdrawal from the Union
   •   The EU is open to a transitional membership agreement, but this must be very clearly defined, time-limited and dependent on the UK maintaining EU membership obligations
   •   Negotiations must be completed by 29 March 2019
   •   No part of these negotiations can affect Gibraltar without an agreement between the UK and Spain

5   Andrew Tyrie, 'Giving Meaning to Brexit', Open Europe, September 2016. http://openeurope.org.uk/intelligence/britain-and-the-eu/giving-brexit-meaning/

6   Jean Pisani-Ferry et al., 'Europe after Brexit: A proposal for a continental partnership, Bruegel'. File://localhost/August 2016 http/::bruegel.org:wp-content:uploads:2016:08:EU-UK-20160829-final-1.pdf

7   *The Economist*, 25.03.17, 'The future of the European Union'. https://www.economist.com/news/special-report/21719188-it-marks-its-60th-birthday-european-union-poor-shape-it-needs-more

8   Fabian Zuleeg is chief executive of the European Policy Centre – a think tank with very close links to the EC and across the major EU governments on mainland Europe. In late July 2017, Zuleeg wrote a coruscating attack on the notion of Soft Brexit – which was immediately retweeted by Sabine Weyand, the EU's Deputy Chief Negotiator. Referring to voices 'outside government demanding that the UK reconsider its position', Zuleeg described as 'misguided' any notion the EU 27 would accept a Soft Brexit deal. 'What is missing in these discussions is a real appreciation of the view from the other side of the channel,' said Zuleeg. 'Allowing cherry-picking of benefits would act as a signal to others inside the EU that a Europe à la carte is obtainable, opening the Pandora's box of disintegration.' Fabian Zuleeg, 24.07.17, 'Reality bites: the Brexit negotiations seen from the other side of the Channel', European Policy Centre. http://www.epc.eu/pub_details.php?cat_id=4&pub_id=7865&year=2017

9   'The government's negotiating objectives for exiting the EU', Prime Minister's speech, Lancaster House, 17.01.17. https://www.gov.uk/government/speeches/the-governments-negotiating-objectives-for-exiting-the-eu-pm-speech

10   Julian Braithwaite, 23.01.17, 'Ensuring a smooth transition in the WTO as we leave the EU', FCO Blog. https://blogs.fco.gov.uk/julianbraithwaite/2017/01/23/ensuring-a-smooth-transition-in-the-wto-as-we-leave-the-eu/

11   *Financial Times*, 25.05.16, 'WTO warns on tortuous Brexit trade talks'. https://www.ft.com/content/745d0ea2-222d-11e6-9d4d-c11776a5124d

12   Sky News, 26.10.16, 'Brexit will not cause UK trade "disruption" – WTO boss'. http://news.sky.com/story/brexit-will-not-cause-uk-trade-disruption-wto-boss-10632803

13   In establishing our schedules, the UK needs 'equivalence of concessions', which means UK tariffs are 'not less favourable' to other WTO members than those currently adopted by the EU. Thus, the tariffs we impose on others would be equivalent to, or less than, those we have now. The choice is ours. The key point is that it should not be a problem as long as the UK does not want to become more protectionist than the EU currently is, and there is no reason to think we would, or should. One reason we are likely to simply adopt the EU's tariffs at the outset is to ease this transition.

14   If the UK's proposed schedules hit objections after Brexit – with another country opposing them for commercial or political reasons – mediation talks and hearings begin, which can take years to resolve. In the meantime, the UK trades on the basis of its proposed schedules. The EU itself has had ninety-seven cases as a complainant

at the WTO, against a total of seventeen countries. Of these, thirty-three were against the US, ten with India and eight with both China and Brazil. For WTO dispute cases involving the EU see https://www.wto.org/english/thewto_e/countries_e/european_communities_e.htm – members_may04

15 *The Guardian*, 20.02.17, 'Post-Brexit customs gridlock could choke UK trade, experts warn'. https://www.theguardian.com/uk-news/2017/feb/20/post-brexit-customs-gridlock-could-choke-uk-trade-experts-warn

16 Food and non-alcoholic drink imports from the EU to the UK totaled £24.6 billion in 2015. HMRC data cited in 'Food and Drink Federation – UK–EU Food and Drink Statistics 2015'. https://www.fdf.org.uk/eu-referendum-food-drink-statistics.aspx

17 Agreed at the WTO Ministerial Conference in Bali, the Agreement on Trade Facilitation is a much-delayed technical agreement on customs harmonisation. Commenting on the implementation in February 2017, the European Commission said: 'This agreement aims to simplify and clarify international import and export procedures, customs formalities and transit requirements … It will make trade-related administration easier and less costly, thus helping to provide an important and much needed boost to global economic growth … EU customs authorities will play a leading role in the implementation of this agreement, acting both as an example to follow and as an engine for further progress in trade facilitation within the EU and at international level … The agreement will also help improve transparency, increase possibilities for small and medium-sized companies to participate in global value chains.' https://ec.europa.eu/taxation_customs/general-information-customs/trade-facilitation_en

18 Bernard Jenkin MP, 09.12.16, 'Free and Fair Trade: A Simple, Clear, Effective Guide to Leaving the EU', Politeia Blog. http://www.bernardjenkin.com/latest-news/202-free-and-fair-trade-a-simple--clear--effective-plan-to-leave-the-eu

19 See Eurostat Statistics Explained, 24.07.17, 'Intra-EU trade in goods – recent trends'. http://ec.europa.eu/eurostat/statistics-explained/index.php/Intra-EU_trade_in_goods_-_recent_trends

20 *The Guardian*, 30.03.17, 'David Davis says Article 50 letter was not a threat to EU on security'. https://www.thegua,rdian.com/politics/2017/mar/30/david-davis-says-article-50-letter-was-no-threat-to-eu-on-security

21 See Nigel Lawson, Introduction to Liam Halligan and Gerard Lyons, 'Clean Brexit', Policy Exchange, January 2017. https://policyexchange.org.uk/wp-content/uploads/2017/01/Policy-Exchange-Clean-Brexit-16th-January-2017.pdf

22 See Patrick Minford and Edgar Miller, 'What shall we do if the EU will not play ball?', Economists for Free Trade, March 2017. 'The prize from the UK adopting global free trade today (UFT) is an additional long-term GDP gain of 4 per cent and a fall of 8 per cent in consumer prices, compared to remaining in the Single Market. These gains are achieved even if other countries do not reduce their tariffs against the UK. This does not include additional benefits gained from decreased regulation, eliminating annual EU budget contributions … If no FTA is agreed with the EU and the EU raises import tariffs against the UK, the UK should not reciprocate, as this will lose half the gain from achieving global free trade, will disrupt manufacturing supply chains, and is likely to harden the EU's resolve not to climb down over the long term.'

23 Roger Bootle, *Daily Telegraph*, 19.02.17, 'Why Britain should consider Unilateral Free Trade'. http://www.telegraph.co.uk/business/2017/02/19/britain-should-consider-unilateral-free-trade/

24 See Gerard Lyons, *The Guardian*, 14.06.16, 'Brexit would help UK manufacturing survive in a global market'. http://www.theguardian.com/business/economics-blog/2016/jun/14/brexit-uk-manufacturing-global-market-eu-referendum?client=safari

25 Data taken from United States Census Bureau, 04.08.17, 'Exhibit 20 – US Trade in Goods and Services by Selected Countries and Areas – BOP Basis', p. 26, and European Commission Trade Statistics, converted with average annual exchange rates. http://ec.europa.eu/trade/policy/eu-position-in-world-trade/statistics/

26 Liam Halligan and Gerard Lyons, 'Clean Brexit', Policy Exchange, January 2017. https://policyexchange.org.uk/wp-content/uploads/2017/01/Policy-Exchange-Clean-Brexit-16th January-2017.pdf

27 'The government's negotiating objectives for exiting the EU', speech by Prime Minister Theresa May, Lancaster House, 17.01.17. https://www.gov.uk/government/speeches the-governments-negotiating-objectives-for-exiting-the-eu-pm-speech

28 In late July 2017, International Trade Secretary Liam Fox – among the most long-standing Brexit advocates – signalled his support for a transition, as long as it expired ahead of a general election scheduled for 2022. 'Having waited for over forty years to leave the EU, twenty-four months would be a rounding error,' he said. 'It's not a huge deal and neither is it an ideological one … I think we would want to get it out of the way before the election.' *The Sun*, 23.07.17, 'Liam Fox signals Brexit transitional deal could last to 2022'. https://www.thesun.co.uk/news/4079471/liam-fox-signals-brexit-transitional-deal-could-last-to-2022-keeping-britain-under-eu-rules-for-extra-3-years/

29 With £32 billion turnover in 2016, £28 billion of exports and 120,000 direct employees, the UK's aerospace industry is the largest in Europe and second largest in the world. Britain's space sector has a turnover of £14 billion, while delivering £5 billion of exports and employing 40,000 staff. The UK's lead in space data led

the European Space Agency to establish the European Centre for Space Application and Telecommunications at Harwell, south Oxfordshire. The UK has agreed to keep contributing to ESA at least until 2020, as mentioned in Chapter 5. For data and information on the UK's aerospace, defence, security and space industries, see ADS Group, '2017 Industry Facts & Figures: A Guide to the UK's Aerospace, Defence, Security & Space Sectors'. https://www.adsgroup.org.uk/wp-content/uploads/sites/21/2017/06/ADS-Annual-Facts-2017.pdf

30 On 07.07.17, for instance, Brexit Secretary David Davis hosted senior business leaders at Chevening, the seventeenth-century grace-and-favour house used by certain Cabinet ministers, to discuss and listen to their views on Brexit.

31 See, for instance, Politico, 06.07.17, 'Big business spies its chance to alter the course of Brexit'. https://www.google.co.uk/amp/www.politico.eu/article/big-business-brexit-chevening-reception-david-davis/amp/

32 Private correspondence with authors, July 2017.

33 Private correspondence with Lord Owen. As a EU member, the UK is already a member of the EEA. Owen warns, though, that if the Article 50 negotiations 'get rough', the EU could 'irrationally refuse continuing EEA membership for the UK after leaving the EU in March 2019'. Were that to happen, Owen suggests Britain should take the issue to international law dispute resolution procedures under the Vienna Convention, during which 'it is very likely that a reasonable interpretation of the EEAA would allow the UK to remain' within EEA during a transition period. 'The European Commission's view that leaving the EU automatically means leaving the EEA is likely to be judged as far too absolute,' argues Owen. 'It is wholly within the spirit of the EEAA for the UK to continue tariff-free trade with the EU, along with the advanced set of measures for customs and trade facilitation which minimises impediments to the movement of goods,' he says. If the UK is successful at the Vienna Court, Owen argues that it would then be necessary to put time-limited EEAA membership into the overall Article 50 agreement. As such, the EU 27 and the European Parliament, having voted on that agreement, would be bound into accepting a fixed UK transition period – although it would also be subject to acceptance by EEA members not in the EU, such as Norway. 'This procedure would close down any possible later House of Commons amendment to prolong EAA membership, whether for a year or more or indefinitely,' says Owen. 'This is because any House of Commons vote on an Article 50 agreement is a vote on an international treaty – which can only be a simple "yes" or "no" and is not amendable.'

34 There is an ongoing lack of clarity over whether the UK stays in or leaves the EEA as it leaves the EU. The confusion arises because although Britain has signed up to the EEA as a member state of the EU, it also signed up to the EEA as an individual state as a legal requirement.

35 Institute of Directors, 'Bridging the Brexit Gap – Options for Transition', IoD Policy Paper, August 2017. https://www.iod.com/Portals/0/PDFs/Campaigns and Reports/Europe and trade/Bridging-the-Brexit-Gap.pdf?ver=2017-08-03-101139-523

36 *The Guardian*, 30.03.17, 'David Davis says Article 50 letter was not a threat to EU on security'. https://www.theguardian.com/politics/2017/mar/30/david-davis-says-article-50-letter-was-no-threat-to-eu-on-security

37 The UK–France Defence Co-operation Treaty was signed in November 2010. 'This co-operation is intended to improve collective defence capability through UK and French forces working more closely together,' said the UK government, 'contributing to more capable and effective forces, and ultimately improving the collective capability of NATO and European defence'. The Treaty was signed at Lancaster House.

38 *The Guardian*, 15.12.16, 'Brexit in a single shot'. https://www.facebook.com/theguardian/posts/10154847126496323

Chapter 7: Global negotiations

1 *Saturday Evening Post*, 26.10.29, 'What Life Means to Einstein: An Interview by George Sylvester Viereck'.

2 Danny Quah, 'The Global Economy's Shifting Centre of Gravity', Global Policy, Vol. 2, Issue 1, January 2011.

3 Authors' calculation based on latest UN population data on India and on the average age of the Indian population.

4 Speech by UK Secretary of State for International Trade, to UK–India Joint Economic and Trade Committee, 7.11.2016. https://www.ukibc.com/uk-secretary-state-international-trade-speech-jetco/

5 John Ross, 'Why the Belt & Road Region will be the main locomotive of the world economy', Feedblitz, Key Trends in Globalisation, May 2017. In his study, Ross uses the IMF's data and current growth forecasts for 2016–21.

6 For a useful overview of emerging middle-class trends across the emerging markets, see Homi Kharas, *Pew Trusts Magazine*, 05.07.16, 'How a Growing Global Middle Class Could Save the World's Economy'. http://magazine.pewtrusts.org/en/archive/trend-summer-2016/how-a-growing-global-middle-class-could-save-the-worlds-economy

7 The figures for UK FDI are $49 billion during the first three months of 2016, followed by $20 billion, $36 billion and $147 billion in the subsequent three quarters. See 'Foreign Direct Investment Statistics: Data, Analysis and Forecasts', April 2017, OECD, Paris. http://www.oecd.org/corporate/mne/statistics.htm.

8 In July 2017, the Department for International Trade reported that during the year following the referendum, the number of foreign direct investment projects into the UK rose 2 per cent to 2,265. Admittedly the number of jobs created was down slightly by 7 per cent on the previous year, but it was still an impressive performance, with 107,898 posts created. See Department for International Trade, 'Inward Investment Results 2016–17', July 2017. There were 2,265 FDI projects, of which 1,237 were new investments (up 9 per cent on the previous year), 782 were expansions (down 5 per cent) and 246 were mergers and acquisitions (down 6 per cent).

9 *Daily Telegraph*, 26.05.17, Ryan Bourne, 'Brexit doom mongers are looking ahead, but they may be wrong again'.

10 See Graham Gudgin, Ken Coutts and Neil Gibson, 'The Macroeconomic Impact of Brexit', Centre for Business Research, University of Cambridge, Working Paper No. 483, January 2017, pp. 20–21.

11 Henry Newman, Stephen Booth, Aarti Shankar, Alex Greer & Vincenzo Scarpetta, 'Global Britain: Priorities for trade beyond the European Union', Open Europe, April 2017.

12 See Office for National Statistics, Statistical Bulletin, 30.06.17, 'Balance of Payments: Jan–Mar 2017'.

13 See 24.07.17, 'Liam Fox champions global free trade'. https://www.gov.uk/government/speeches/liam-fox-champions-global-free-trade and 20.07.17, 'Beyond Brexit: Britain and the global economy'. https://www.gov.uk/government/speeches/beyond-brexit-britain-and-the-global-economy

14 For a useful overview, see Klaus Schwab, 14.01.16, 'The Fourth Industrial Revolution: what it means, how to respond', World Economic Forum. https://www.weforum.org/agenda/2016/01/the-fourth-industrial-revolution-what-it-means-and-how-to-respond/

15 Hansard, House of Commons, 'Fourth Industrial Revolution', 08.09.16, Vol. 614. http://www.parliament.uk

16 Anthony Hilton, *Evening Standard*, 18.05.17, 'Which party is even remotely ready for the tech revolution?'

17 Alan Mak MP, 'Masters of the Revolution: Why the Fourth Industrial Revolution should be at the heart of Britain's new Industrial Strategy', Free Enterprise Group, November 2016.

18 Authors' calculation based on published data. Elsewhere in the book we have made reference to the increase in the working age population in Africa, citing the 'African Economic Outlook', 2015 and 2016. On p. xii of the 2015 edition, we read: 'The workforce is expected to increase by 910 million people between 2010 and 2050, of which 830 million in sub-Saharan Africa and 80 million in north Africa. Creating more productive jobs, a major stake in Africa's structural transformation, becomes even more pressing. The estimated numbers of youth joining labour markets in 2015 are about 19 million in sub-Saharan Africa and 4 million in north Africa. Over the next fifteen years, the figures will be 370 million and 65 million respectively, or a yearly average of 24.6 million and 4.3 million new entrants. The upcoming growth in Africa's workforce represents two thirds of the growth in the workforce worldwide.' Meanwhile there are various references to India and China on World Bank (data.worldbank.org) and UN sites. According to p. 23 of Standard Chartered's 'Super-cycle report', India's working age population increases by 118 million in 2010–20 and by 95 million in 2020–30, while China's contracts, by 4 million and 51 million respectively, over those time periods.

19 Even allowing for the fact that the EU itself is a large single market, so does not need a trade deal with itself, the scale of the FTAs it has signed – accounting for economies with a combined GDP of $7,700 billion, compared to global GDP approaching $78,000 billion – is disappointing. The EU 27 market for the UK is $13,800 billion.

20 The China–Switzerland trade deal, signed in May 2013, came into force in July 2014. The agreement removes bilateral tariffs and trade barriers on goods and services and provides intellectual property protection. It also includes investment promotion, technical cooperation and environmental protection, along with a platform for future bilateral economic cooperation, notably in banking. Bern and Beijing signed, in addition, a three-year currency swap agreement, allowing the Swiss central bank to purchase up to US$2.4 billion of Chinese bonds. Zürich was later designated as a trading hub for the Chinese yuan, a status already granted to London.

21 See Michael Burrage, 'Myth and Paradox of the Single Market', Civitas, London, January 2016, p. 43, Fig. 1. http://www.civitas.org.uk/content/files/mythandparadox.pdf.

22 'It would be logical to expect [that a UK–US trade deal] might be high on the Commerce Department's list of priorities' – aide to Wilbur Ross, incoming US Trade Secretary, 17.12.16 . '[The UK] will take a front seat and I think it will be our priority to make sure we deal with them on a trade agreement initially but in all respects in a way that demonstrates the long-term friendship we've had for so long' – Bob Corker, Chairman, US Senate Foreign Relations Committee, 09.01.17. Paul Ryan, the Speaker of the US House of Representatives, went further, saying on a visit to London in April 2017 that 'the US stands ready to forge a new trade agreement with Great Britain as soon as possible, so that we may further tap into the great potential between our people.' See *Daily Telegraph*, 19.04.17, 'Paul Ryan announces US is ready to forge a new bilateral trade deal with UK "as soon as possible".' http://www.telegraph.co.uk/news/2017/04/19/paul-ryan-announces-us-ready-forge-new-bilateral-trade-deal/ These statements contrast with the view of Barack Obama, who said the opposite when he was President. *The Guardian*, 22.04.16, 'Obama: Brexit would put UK "back of the queue" for trade talks'. https://www.theguardian.com/politics/2016/apr/22/barack-obama-brexit-uk-back-of-queue-for-trade-talks And in late

July 2017, President Trump tweeted: 'Working on major Trade Deal with the UK. Could be very big & exciting. JOBS!'

23 These quotes were contained in a presentation by the Royal Commonwealth Society, delivered by Tim Hewish to the GTMC annual conference in Monaco on 5.06.17.

24 These figures came from the same presentation in Monaco on 05.06.17.

25 Cited in James Cleverly MP and Tim Hewish, Free Enterprise Group, 'Reconnecting with the Commonwealth: the UK's free trade opportunities', 10.01.17, p. 24. https://www.freeenterprise.org.uk/reconnecting-with-the-commonwealth-the-uks-free-trade-opportunities/

26 On 23.06.17 in London, DealGlobe and the Hurun Report released the '2017 Special Report on China Cross-Border M&A'. This report highlighted the favourable view taken towards post-Brexit Britain by Chinese entrepreneurs – a message emphasised at the report launch by Rupert Hoogewerf, chairman of the Hurun Report. In terms of Chinese outbound M&A, the top destinations in the world are the US, Hong Kong, Germany and then the UK.

27 The Free Enterprise Group comprises several dozen Conservatives MPs, convened by James Cleverly MP. Founded in 2010 by the Rt Hon. Elizabeth Truss MP, now Chief Secretary to the Treasury, FEG had close links to the Treasury and then Chancellor George Osborne during the 2010–15 parliament.

28 Foreword to the earlier cited Free Enterprise Group report.

29 Department for Business, Innovation and Skills, 'Trade and Investment for Growth', February 2011. https://www.gov.uk/government/uploads/system/uploads/attachment_data/file/228941/8015.pdf

30 See 'Keep Trade Easy – what small firms want from Brexit', Federation of Small Businesses, March 2017. http://www.fsb.org.uk/docs/default-source/fsb-org-uk/keep-trade-easy_-what-small-firms-want-from-brexit-21-march-2017.pdf?sfvrsn=0

31 See http://smeforgrowth.co.uk/index.php/category/confederation-of-british-industry/

32 See, for instance, 'Brexit means success: Evaluating the impact on the economy of the West Midlands Combined Authority and Wider Economy', West Midlands Economic Forum, January 2017.

33 See Rishi Sunak, 'The Free Ports Opportunity: How Brexit could boost trade, manufacturing and the North', Centre for Policy Studies, November 2016.

34 The Times, Gerard Lyons, 06.05.16, 'We don't need trade deals to boom after Brexit'

35 Shanker Singham, 'A Blueprint for UK Trade Policy', Legatum Institute Special Trade Commission Briefing, April 2017.

36 Daily Telegraph, 25.12.09, 'The Queen's Christmas Message'. http://www.telegraph.co.uk/news/newsvideo/royalfamilyvideo/6880071/The-Queens-Christmas-message-2009-in-full.html

37 David Howell, Old Links & New Ties: Power and Persuasion in an Age of Networks (London: I. B. Tauris, 2014).

38 In the Queen's Speech of June 2017, it was noted that the UK government 'will host the Commonwealth Summit in April 2018 to cement its relevance to this, and future generations'.

39 McKinsey Global Institute, March 2016, 'Digital Globalization: The New Era of Global Flows', McKinsey & Company.

40 The June 2017 Queen's Speech stated that the UK 'will seek to maintain a deep and special relationship with European allies and forge new trading relationships across the globe'. The speech further flagged up 'new bills on trade and customs that will help to implement an independent trade policy, and support to help British businesses export to markets around the world'.

41 In his Geneva speech on 20.07.17 cited earlier, International Trade Secretary Liam Fox noted that 'research by the OECD shows that protectionist instincts have grown since the financial crisis of 2008. By 2010, G7 and G20 countries were estimated to be operating some 300 non-tariff barriers to trade – by 2015 this had mushroomed to over 1,200'. https://www.gov.uk/government/speeches/beyond-brexit-britain-and-the-global-economy

42 While it is hard to quantify protectionism, Global Trade Alert collates input from different organisations to provide analysis on protectionist trends across the world. See globaltradealtert.org.

43 World Bank, 'Global Economic Prospects – a Fragile Recovery', June 2017. https://openknowledge.worldbank.org/bitstream/handle/10986/26800/9781464810244.pdf?sequence=13&isAllowed=y Also, in their July 2017 update to their world economic outlook, the IMF forecast the volume of global trade in goods and services rising from 2.6 per cent in 2015 and 2.3 per cent in 2016 to 4 per cent in 2017 and 3.9 per cent in 2018.

44 Only about a dozen countries across the world are not in the WTO. See http://www.wto.org

45 Liam Halligan, Daily Telegraph, 03.12.06, 'The process of economic de-colonisation is not yet complete', interview with Pascal Lamy. http://www.telegraph.co.uk/finance/migrationtemp/2951735/The-process-of-economic-de-colonisation-is-not-yet-complete.html

46 Professor Tim Congdon, Speech to Bruges Group, September 2016

47 Statement by President Clinton, Geneva WTO ministerial conference, 1998. https://www.wto.org/english/thewto_e/minist_e/min98_e/anniv_e/clinton_e.htm

48 Luis de la Calle, comments at Prosperity UK conference, London, April 2017.

49 Crawford Falconer, comments at Prosperity UK conference, London, April 2017. During the summer of 2017, Falconer joined the Department for International Trade as Chief Trade Negotiation Adviser, helping the UK government to strike trade deals with non-EU nations.

50 The Asian Infrastructure Investment Bank (AIIB) is a Beijing-based, China-led development bank. When the UK government announced Britain was to be a founder member of the AIIB, which could one day rival the World Bank, a White House official accused London of 'constantly accommodating' China. The US said Western countries 'could help shape the standards and rules' these institutions will adopt 'by staying on the outside'. The UK was defiant, though. 'Forging links between the UK and Asian economies to give our companies the best opportunity to work and invest in the world's fastest-growing markets is a key part of our long-term economic plan,' declared then Chancellor George Osborne. 'Joining the AIIB at the founding stage will create an unrivalled opportunity for the UK and Asia to invest and grow together.' Once the UK had announced it would be a founder member, Germany, France and other large Western economies followed suit. See Liam Halligan, 20.03.15, 'US glowers as allies hop aboard China's AIIB', Invisible Hand column, *bne-InteiliNews*. http://www.intellinews.com/invisible-hand-us-glowers-as-allies-hop-aboard-china-s-aiib-500445377/?archive=bne

51 This point was well made in Roland Smith, 'The Liberal Case For Leave', Adam Smith Institute blog. 30.03.16. https://www.adamsmith.org/the-liberal-case-for-leave/

52 Even though the US announced its withdrawal from the Paris Agreement in early June 2017, the other signatories intend to proceed with implementation.

Chapter 8: Economic and industrial landscape

1 'The economy, stupid' is a phrase coined by James Carville, a strategist who worked on Bill Clinton's successful 1992 presidential campaign. In the wake of a US recession, Clinton's focus on the economy helped him to beat George H. W. Bush in the race for the White House. Although the phrase was meant for an internal audience of campaign workers, it quickly became Clinton's most important mass audience slogan. Since then, slightly rephrased as 'It's the economy, stupid', Carville's words have been used by politicians the world over to emphasise the importance of living standards in any electoral contest.

2 See Bank of England home page and link to Inflation Report Press Conference, 03.08.2017. http://www.bankofengland.co.uk/publications/Pages/inflationreport/2017/aug.aspx

3 Economic Bulletin May 2016, European Central Bank. See p. 83, chart 7.

4 According to the Office for National Statistics, GVA measuring the economy's breakdown is: low-to-medium technology manufacturing 5.6 per cent; medium-to-high technology manufacturing 5.1 per cent; knowledge-intensive services account 29.5 per cent, with financial services alone being 9.4 per cent; other services 46.7 per cent and, within this, health and social care is the largest at 7.8 per cent; and finally, other areas are 13 per cent, of which construction is 6.7 per cent.

5 This is a controversial and complex subject largely beyond the scope of this book. Yet fiscal and demographic pressures put welfare at the heart of any serious discussion of long-term UK economic policy – and, indeed, one of the main economic suggestions of *Clean Brexit* is a Royal Commission to examine a more contributory Bismarckian welfare system. William Beveridge was the social reformer who designed the NHS in the early 1940s and the Bismarck model is named after Prussian Otto von Bismarck, who invented the more contributory German welfare state in the mid-nineteenth century. Strictly speaking, the NHS and the UK's broader system of public services already contains elements of both. So discussions are a matter of degree.

6 The EU's competences are set out and conferred upon in successive EU treaties. Over time, the number of competencies transferred has been considerable. In some areas, such as a common approach to the environment and an emissions trading scheme, this has worked, but in others it has not. See 'Final reports in review of EU Balance of Competencies published', 18.12.14. https://www.gov.uk/government/news/final-reports-in-review-of-eu-balance-of-competences-published

7 'There are different types of competence: exclusive, shared and supporting,' according to the Foreign Office. 'Only the EU can act in areas where it has exclusive competence, such as the customs union and common commercial policy. In areas of shared competence, such as the single market, environment and energy, either the EU or the member states may act, but the member states may be prevented from acting once the EU has done so. In areas of supporting competence, such as education, culture and tourism, both the EU and member states may act, but action by the EU does not prevent the member states from taking action of their own.' See 'Review of the Balance of Competencies between the United Kingdom and the European Union', presented to Parliament by the Secretary of State for Foreign and Commonwealth Affairs, July 2012, p. 13. https://www.gov.uk/government/uploads/system/uploads/attachment_data/file/35458/eu-balance-of-competences-review.pdf

8 That treaty's competencies included, of course, a customs union; the free movement of goods; a common commercial policy; free movement of persons, services and capital; a common agricultural policy; a common

transport policy; a competition policy; the coordination of economic policies; a common market; the European Social Fund; and the European Investment Bank.

9 The Single European Act of 1986 related to the single market and the environment. The 1992 Maastricht Treaty involved common foreign and security policy, justice and home affairs, economic and monetary union, education and culture. The 1997 Amsterdam Treaty then dealt with employment, social policy and discrimination, while the 2007 Lisbon Treaty covered energy, civil protection, data protection and even sport and space.

10 The UK has negotiated some opt-outs from the Schengen Agreement, the Charter of Fundamental Rights of the EU, the area of freedom, security and justice and, of course, from economic and monetary union. While outside the single currency, though, the UK contributed to two euro bailouts: €3 billion to Ireland in November 2010 and €3.5 billion to Portugal in May 2011. The UK was also liable for some of the bailout to Greece, as this was funded via the EU budget, but it was agreed non-euro countries would be covered for any loss via the ECB. The UK has, in addition, contributed via the IMF, while making a bilateral loan to Ireland in 2010, largely to minimise contagion to UK banks.

11 'Labour's Plan for Science', 1.10.63, reprint of speech by Harold Wilson MP, leader of the Labour Party, at the annual party conference in Scarborough. http://nottspolitics.org/wp-content/uploads/2013/06/Labours-Plan-for-science.pdf. For insightful contemporary commentary on Wilson's speech, see Theo Blackwell, '"White heat" 50 years on', *Progress*, 01.10.13. http://www.progressonline.org.uk/2013/10/01/white-heat-50-years-on/

12 See Robert Wade, LSE, 10.05.17, 'Picking winners'. http://www.lse.ac.uk/News/Research-Highlights/Economy/Picking-winners

13 See Prime Minister Theresa May's letter to Donald Tusk triggering Article 50, 29.03.17, p. 5. https://www.gov.uk/government/uploads/system/uploads/attachment_data/file/604079/Prime_Ministers_letter_to_European_Council_President_Donald_Tusk.pdf

14 See Exiting the European Union Committee, Written evidence submitted by the 'Society of Motor Manufacturers and Traders (OBJ0098)' to the Select Committee on Exiting the EU, December 2016. http://data.parliament.uk/writtenevidence/committeeevidence.svc/evidencedocument/exiting-the-european-union-committee/the-uks-negotiating-objectives-for-its-withdrawal-from-the-eu/written/44283.html

15 UK Pink Book, 2016, Table 2.1. Based on 77.3 per cent of exports going to the EU, this would be £19.8 billion, implying a £1.9 billion tariff. Another lower estimate based on exports of £15.6 billion comes from 'Brexit: the automotive industry reacts', 24.06.16, by Richard Aucock on http://www.motoringresearch.com. With a tariff of 9.6 per cent, this is £1.6 billion.

16 While 56 per cent of UK car exports got to the EU, 12 per cent of EU (minus the UK) car exports go to the UK. At Standard International Trade Classification (SITC) two-digit level, EU exports to the UK are still larger than UK exports to the EU, according to research cited by the Trade Observatory Centre at Sussex University in 'A Special Deal for the Car Industry: How Would It Work?', 16.11.16. https://blogs.sussex.ac.uk/uktpo/2016/11/16/a-special-deal-for-the-car-industry-how-could-it-work/

17 See a discussion of this Deloitte report on openeurope.org.uk. In the year of withdrawal, German car exports would fall by 255,000 units, down a massive 32 per cent, putting approximately 18,000 jobs in Germany at direct risk.

18 The allocation of CAP funding per capita over the 2014–20 period are: England €330; Scotland €855; Wales €841; Northern Ireland €1,372. Source: Department for the Environment, Food and Rural Affairs, 'UK CAP allocations announced', 08.11.13. http://www.gov.uk/government/news/uk-cap-allocations-announced

19 *The Independent*, 30.06.17, 'EU farming subsidies: One in five biggest recipients are billionaires and millionaires on UK rich list'. https://inews.co.uk/essentials/news/environment/britains-wealthiest-people-raking-in-millions-in-farm-subsidies/

20 The CAP is a cornerstone of the EU, costing nearly 40 per cent of its budget, or €58 billion a year. Set up in 1957 to sustain the EU's food supplies by boosting agricultural productivity, the CAP provides financial support to some 12 million farmers across Europe

21 See Institute for Government (instituteforgovernment.org.uk) section on common agricultural policy.

22 In a survey of UK farmers ahead of the EU referendum, *Farmers' Weekly*, 29.04.16, 'Survey reveals 58 per cent of farmers back EU exit'. http://www.fwi.co.uk/news/exclusive-survey-reveals-farmers-back-eu-exit.htm

23 'The government will … match the current level of agricultural funding until 2020, providing certainty to our agricultural community, which plays a vital role in our country.' Chancellor Philip Hammond, 13.08.16. https://www.gov.uk/government/news/chancellor-philip-hammond-guarantees-eu-funding-beyond-date-uk-leaves-the-eu

24 'We will continue to commit the same cash total in funds for farm support until the end of the Parliament', Conservative Party manifesto, 'Forward Together: Our Plan for a Stronger Britain and a Prosperous Future', p. 26.

25 'Recommendations for Post-Brexit Agricultural Policy', Landworkers' Alliance, June 2017. https://drive.google.com/file/d/0B6eRd6MaabyucmdySjBLaTRScjQ/view

26 The watershed year for New Zealand agricultural reform was 1984, the country's experience showing that withdrawing subsidies requires strong political support but can have a dramatic and positive impact. See Ralph Lattimore, 'Paper prepared for the North American Agrifood Market Integration Consortium Meetings', Calgary, Canada, May 2006. 'Twenty years on, the results of the farm subsidy reforms are clear. Sufficient time has passed for technological improvements to be generated and adopted ... It is now possible to confirm that there is a dividend payable from subsidy reform ...The rate of total factor productivity growth more than doubled from 0.7 per cent over the high sub sidy period, 1972–84, to 1.9 per cent thereafter. Real farm incomes have now recovered and in some cases are significantly higher than they were during the period of high subsidies. Likewise, real farmland prices are higher than they were under high subsidies.'

27 See http://www.economistsforbrexit.co.uk. Overpriced food within the EU should be no surprise. The July 1971 White Paper on the UK's entry to the European Economic Community states that 'membership will affect food prices gradually over a period of about 6 years, with an increase of about 2.5 per cent each year in retail prices', p. 23. Within the EU, huge additional expense is loaded on to consumers who might wish to buy products from outside the bloc: on dairy products tariffs are 54 per cent, on sugar 31 per cent and on cereals 22 per cent.

28 See HM Government, 'Review of the Balance of Competencies between the United Kingdom and the European Union: Agriculture', summer 2014, p. 35.

29 This figure is for 2015. It is cited in 'Brexit, Agriculture and Agricultural Policy', Centre for Policy Studies, January 2017. This paper was written by Sir Richard Packer, former Permanent Secretary, Department of Agriculture.

30 Warwick Lightfoot, Policy Exchange, 01.08.17, 'Farming Tomorrow'. The report also points to that while the highest-income households spend 7.5 per cent of total expenditure on food and non-alcoholic drinks, the figure for the bottom decline is 17.3 per cent.

31 When striking any trade deals involving agriculture, the UK must take account of so-called tariff rate quotas (TRQs). These are the agreed amounts of certain products that can be imported without incurring tariffs, according to WTO rules. A significant amount of New Zealand lamb, for instance, can be imported free of tariffs because it falls under a TRQ. This complication needs to be acknowledged, and is a factor in our new WTO schedules, but it should not deter us from a radical new approach to agriculture. Again, these issues are readily identifiable and should be seen as transition costs or opportunities to rethink the way we support farming, with money perhaps shifting away from larger to smaller landowners. See 'The Implications of Brexit for UK Agriculture', a report for the Yorkshire Agricultural Society, 2016. http://yas.co.uk/uploads/files/YAS_FSN_Brexit_-_Full_Report.pdf

32 John Ashworth,'The Betrayal of Britain's Fishing', 2016, Campaign for an Independent Britain.

33 Norway voted against joining the EU in both 1972 and 1994. These outcomes were heavily influenced by concerns that the CPF would negatively impact the country's fishing industry. Concerns about fishing quotas also caused Iceland to abandon its EU accession talks in 2013–14.

34 In 2002, when Minister of State for Europe Peter Hain proposed in secret that the sovereignty of Gibraltar be split between Spain and the UK, 24.01.12. http://www.dailymail.co.uk/news/article-2090845/Tony-Blair-signed-secret-deal-Gibraltar-Spain.html?google_editors_picks=true

35 Ashworth, op. cit., p. 17.

36 John Ashworth, 'Seizing the moment: The opportunities for fisheries after Brexit', 2017, Campaign for an Independent Britain.

37 The London Fisheries Convention was signed in 1964, and grants reciprocal fishing rights with France, Belgium, Germany, Ireland and the Netherlands in an area 6–12 nautical miles from each countries' respective coastline. The EU's Common Fisheries Policy, in contrast, allows vessels from all EU nations to fish beyond the twelve-mile limit, subject to quotas.

38 See Open Europe, 16.03.15, 'Top 100 EU rules cost Britain £33.3bn'. http://openeurope.org.uk/intelligence/britain-and-the-eu/top-100-eu-rules-cost-britain-33-3bn/

39 For more details see Douglas McWilliams, The Flat White Economy, (London: Gerald Duckworth, 2015). The book details the emergence of east London as a leading centre of tech-related commerce, becoming a prototype for digital cities around the world.

40 EU rules stipulate the minimum rate of value-added tax for goods sold within the EU must be 5 per cent. The UK has some zero-rated products – such as most food and childrens' clothes – but only on goods where zero-rating predated our EEC membership or as a result of specific derogations negotiated with Brussels.

41 See Bob Lyddon, 'The UK's Lost GDP and Tax Revenues', Global Britain, 2016. http://globalbritain.co.uk/wp-content/uploads/2016/12/The-Brexit-Papers-4-Lost-GDP-Tax-revenues.pdf

42 The term 'hypernormalisation' is taken from Alexei Yurchak's 2006 book Everything was Forever, Until it was

No More: The Last Soviet Generation, about life in the USSR during the 1970s and 1980s. Yurchak argued that everyone knew the system was failing, but because no one could imagine any alternative to the status quo, politicians and citizens maintained the pretence that society was functioning properly. Over time, this delusion became self-fulfilling and was accepted as real – a form of behaviour that Yurchak termed 'hypernormalisation'.

43 Over this period, spending in public order and safety (including the police force) fell from £35 billion to ·£34 billion, spending on personal social services was flat in nominal terms, rising from £31 billion to £32 billion, and while transport spending rose from £24 billion to £37 billion, the figure is probably still too low.

44 See William White, 'Ultra-Easy Money: Digging the Hole Deeper?', Adam Smith Lecture delivered at the Annual Meeting of the National Association for Business Economics, 11.11.16. http://williamwhite.ca/sites/default/files/11369_2016_12_OnlinePDF.pdf

45 Bank for International Settlements, 87th Annual Report, Basel, June 2017, p. 68. https://www.bis.org/publ/arpdf/ar2017e.pdf

46 Quoted in Liam Halligan, *Daily Telegraph*, 14.03.09, 'Leaving it to the experts who don't know what they're doing'. http://www.telegraph.co.uk/finance/comment/liamhalligan/4991881/Leaving-it-to-the-experts-who-dont-know-what-theyre-doing.html

Chapter 9: Why the City will thrive

1 *New Statesman and Nation*, 10 July 1937.

2 The data on this page can be found in *TheCityUK*, 01.11.16, 'Key Facts about the UK as an international financial centre'. https://www.thecityuk.com/research/key-facts-about-the-uk-as-an-international-financial-centre-2016/

3 Gerard Lyons spoke on the importance of closing the Macmillan Gap when he delivered 'The Peston Lecture' in 2014 at Queen Mary College, University of London, in honour of the leading UK economist and former government advisor Professor Lord Maurice Peston (1931–2016).

4 This is an issue we address in other chapters, in the context of the need for a more balanced UK economy. In terms of the City, the focus has been on a host of areas, such as strengthening its resilience to shocks and improving its governance.

5 London tops the rankings of international financial centres. The next highest ranked in Europe is Zurich at eleventh with Geneva at twentieth – but neither of these Swiss cities is in the EU. While there is much financial expertise elsewhere in the EU, the cities that hope to grab business from London are low down the global list – Luxembourg is eighteenth, Frankfurt twenty-third, Paris twenty-ninth, Dublin thirty-first and Amsterdam fortieth. See 'The Global Financial Centres Index 21', March 2017, Finanical Centres Forum and zyen.com

6 Moody's, 19.09.16, 'Banks – Europe: Impact on Financial Institutions' "Passports" following the UK's exit from the EU' is available on www.moodys.com. See also *Daily Telegraph*, 19.09.16, 'Banks can cope with loss of EU passports after Brexit, says Moody's'.

7 There has been much evidence that the City has performed well since mid-2016, despite Brexit-related uncertainty – and that far fewer financial institutions are set to leave the City than previously feared. See *Bloomberg*, 01.03.17, 'The Brexit bank exodus could be more like a trickle'. https://www.bloomberg.com/news/articles/2017-03-01/brexit-exodus-starts-with-a-trickle-as-some-say-banks-bluffing?cmpid=BBBXT0301317

8 See testimony of Lord Turnbull, ex-Head of the Civil Service and formerly non-executive director at Prudential, to Treasury Select Committee in late June 2016. See *Daily Telegraph*, 28.06.16. http://www.telegraph.co.uk/business/2016/06/28/brexit-will-allow-insurers-to-escape-absolutely-dreadful-eu-regu/

9 'Insurance bosses tell MPs stronger after Brexit'. http://www.telegraph.co.uk/business/2017/01/25/british-insurers-will-competitive-brexit

10 Dark trading refers to transactions taking place within 'dark pools', named as such because they are not open and transparent, but private exchanges for trading securities not accessible by the investing public.

11 See HM Government, 'Competences between the United Kingdom and the European Union – The Single Market: Financial Services and the Free Movement of Capital', summer 2014, p. 58. 'There were concerns from a broad range of stakeholders that the UK has a disproportionately low level of influence considering the national importance of the UK's financial sector in terms of its size and contribution to the economy compared to other Member States.' The UK accounts for 36 per cent of the EU's financial wholesale market and 61 per cent of the EU's net exports in financial services, yet it has far less formal influence in EU institutions – accounting for 9.5 per cent of seats in the European Parliament and just over 8 per cent of votes in the European Council. https://www.gov.uk/government/uploads/system/uploads/attachment_data/file/332874/2902400_BoC_FreedomOfCapital_acc.pdf

12 Ibid, p. 74

13 One of the authors – Gerard Lyons – was on the Advisory Board of the Open Europe think tank that fully supported the then PM in his case to push for EU-wide reform. See Open Europe's EU Reform Index, constructed in

2015, which highlighted thirty areas the UK might seek to reform. Open Europe, 'EU Reform Index: Evaluating 30 potential proposals for EU renegotiation', May 2015.

14 'Total taxpayer support for UK banks peaked at £1.2 trillion between 2007 and 2010'. See Alex Brazier, Executive Director, in a Foreword in Bank of England, Financial Stability Paper No. 42, July 2017, 'Simulating stress across the financial system: the resilience of corporate bond markets and the role of investment funds'.

15 Sam Woods letter, 07.04 2017. http://www.bankofengland.co.uk/pra/Documents/about/letter070417.pdf

16 See letter 13.01.2017 from Andrew Bailey, CEO of Financial Conduct Authority, to Andrew Tyrie MP, Chairman of Treasury Select Committee. http://www.parliament.uk/documents/commons-committees/treasury/Correspondence/13-01-17-Andrew-Bailey-to-Chair-re-UK%27s-future-economic-relationship-with-the-EU.pdf

17 The EEA includes EU countries and also Iceland, Liechtenstein and Norway. It allows them to be part of the EU's single market, as explained in Chapter 3.

18 See letter 17.08.16 from Andrew Bailey, CEO of Financial Conduct Authority, to Andrew Tyrie MP, Chairman of Treasury Select Committee. Passporting rights for some financial service companies, mainly in the retail sector, enables them to sell their financial services/products either directly within other EU member states or via a branch regulated by the UK regulator. Without passports, companies must operate through a local subsidiary authorised and regulated by the national regulator. https://www.parliament.uk/documents/commons-committees/treasury/Correspondence/AJB-to-Andrew-Tyrie-Passporting.PDF

19 See European Commission, 24.03.2017, report from the Commission to the Council and the European Parliament – 'Accelerating the capital markets union: addressing national barriers to capital flows'. https://ec.europa.eu/info/sites/info/files/170227-report-capital-barriers_en.pdf

20 See Barnabas Reynolds, 2016, 'A Blueprint for Brexit: The Future of Global Financial Services and Markets in the UK', *Politeia*. http://www.politeia.co.uk/wp-content/Politeia%20Documents/2016/Nov%20-%20A%20Blueprint%20for%20Brexit/%27A%20Blueprint%20for%20Brexit%27%20Nov%202017.pdf

21 For more detailed information of 'equivalence', see International Regulatory Strategy Group, 'The EU's third country regimes and alternatives to passporting', Hogan Lovells, January 2017. http://www.hoganlovellsbrexit.com/_uploads/downloads/TheEUsThirdCountryRegimesandAlternativestoPassporting.pdf

22 Prosperity UK conference, County Hall, London, 26.04.17.

23 *Daily Telegraph*, 20.05.17, http://www.telegraph.co.uk/business/2017/05/20/eu-threat-move-euro-clearing-away-london-tool-whip-britain/

24 *Daily Telegraph*, 30.05.17, 'Deal or no deal, there's "ample room" for the EU to trade freely with the City of London after Brexit, says OECD'. http://www.telegraph.co.uk/business/2017/05/30/deal-no-deal-ample-room-eu-trade-freely-city-london-brexit-says/

25 Prosperity UK conference, County Hall, London, 26.04.17.

26 *Evening Standard*, 23.06.17, 'ECB ratchets up battle to seize London's euro clearing industry'. https://uk.news.yahoo.com/ecb-ratchets-battle-seize-london-102700272.html

27 *The Guardian*, 23.06.17, 'London could lose out as ECB seeks control of euro clearing after Brexit'. https://www.theguardian.com/business/2017/jun/23/london-ecb-euro-clearing-brexit-european-central-bank

28 See a report to the President from Treasury Secretary Steven Mnuchin and Counsellor to the Secretary Craig Phillips, 'A Financial System that creates economic opportunities: Banks and Credit Unions', June 2017. The report provides further evidence of the proactive way the US intends to use the financial sector to drive growth. This is good for the US economy, and one should expect further measures to help bolster Wall Street too. But a more aggressive stance towards the promotion of New York could pose challenges to the City of London – challenges it may well be better placed to address from outside the EU.

Chapter 10: Immigration

1 Stephen Kinnock, *The Guardian*, 19.09.16, 'My cure for a divided Britain? A programme of managed immigration'. https://www.theguardian.com/commentisfree/2016/sep/19/cure-divided-britain-managed-immigration-work-permits.

2 Britain will be a more 'insular and inward-looking country' if it votes to leave the EU, said Prime Minister David Cameron during the last twenty-four hours of the June 2016 referendum campaign. See *Daily Mail*, 21.06.17, 'Cameron: UK "would be more insular and inward-looking post-Brexit".' A few days earlier, Tony Blair and two former Deputy Prime Ministers, Nick Clegg and Lord Heseltine, had urged voters to reject 'division, isolationism and blame' by choosing to stay in the EU. *The Guardian*, 18.06.17, 'Senior politicians back EU membership: "We must reject division and isolation."' https://www.theguardian.com/politics/2016/jun/18/politicians-eu-membership-blair-clegg-brexit-referendum

3 According to the IMF, using market exchange rates, the size of the world economy at the end of 2016 was $75,278 billion, of which the EU was $16,408 billion and the UK was $2,629 billion. Thus, the EU 27 would

have been $13,779 billion or 18.3 per cent of the global economy. So the rest of the world, excluding the EU 27 was 81.7 per cent and excluding the EU 27 and UK was 78.2 per cent.

4 The EU has, since 1971, operated a Generalised Scheme of Preferences aimed at assisting developing countries – these GSPs have been reformed in recent years. See European Commission, 28.01.16, 'Report on the Generalised Scheme of Preferences covering the period 2014–15'. http://trade.ec.europa.eu/doclib/docs/2016/january/tradoc_154180.pdf. Despite this, there is much evidence to suggest damage is caused to poorer countries by EU trade polices. See, for instance, 'How the EU Starves Africa' by Brian Denny, Trade Unionists Against the EU (http://www.tuaeu.co.uk/how-the-eu-starves-africa/) or *The Guardian*, 16.01.15, 'EU trade agreements threaten to crush Kenya's blooming flower trade'. https://www.google.co.uk/amp/s/amp.theguardian.com/sustainable-business/2015/jan/16/kenya-flower-trade-eu-pressure

5 For more details see 'Long Term International Net Migration' tables. https://www.ons.gov.uk/employmentandlabourmarket/peopleinwork/employmentandemployeetypes/bulletins/uklabourmarket/dec2016

6 See David Metcalfe, 'MAC report: Immigration and the Labour Market', August 2016. https://www.gov.uk/government/uploads/system/uploads/attachment_data/file/547697/MAC-_report_immigration_and_the_labour_market.pdf%5D

7 For a useful discussion of immigration see Cambridge University's Professor Robert Rowthorn, 'The Costs and Benefits of Large-scale Immigration', *Civitas*, December 2015. Rowthorn notes that 'unskilled workers have suffered some reduction in their wages due to competition from immigrants' and also highlights the pressure placed on public services.

8 A report from the government's Migration Advisory Committee (MAC) concluded that immigration has put 'extra pressure on housing, education, health and transport services'. See Metcalfe, op. cit. https://www.gov.uk/government/uploads/system/uploads/attachment_data/file/547697/MAC-_report_immigration_and_the_labour_market.pdf%5D

9 'Migration Statistics', House of Commons Library, Briefing Paper No. SN06077, June 2017. file://localhost/Users/user/Downloads/SN06077 (1).pdf

10 Christian Dustmann et al., 'The impact of EU enlargement on migration flows', Home Office Online Report 25/03, 2003. p. 58. http://www.ucl.ac.uk/~uctpb21/reports/HomeOffice25_03.pdf

11 Select Committee on Economic Affairs, First Report, Appendix 9: 'Measuring And Predicting Immigration From Eastern Europe', 2008. https://publications.parliament.uk/pa/ld200708/ldselect/ldeconaf/82/8220.htm

12 Invitation to join the government of Britain, Conservative Party manifesto, March 2010, p. 21. https://www.conservatives.com/~/media/Files/Manifesto2010

13 UKIP won just one Westminster seat in 2015, despite winning 13 per cent of the popular vote. The SNP took fifty-six seats on 5 per cent of votes cast, while the Lib Dems took eight seats on 8 per cent. Perhaps the most striking aspect of UKIP's 2015 performance was that the party came second in no less than 120 seats – almost twice the number of runner-up slots achieved by the Lib Dems, and two thirds that of the Conservatives. In 2010, UKIP had not come second in a single constituency. It is almost certain that, had Cameron not called an EU referendum, which he did soon after the 2015 general election, UKIP support would have risen further in a subsequent general election.

14 'Long Term International Net Migration' tables. https://www.ons.gov.uk/employmentandlabourmarket/peopleinwork/employmentandemployeetypes/bulletins/uklabourmarket/dec2016

15 The UK's PBS of immigration, applying to non-EU immigrants only, categorises immigrants into one of four tiers depending on their ability to contribute to the economy. Tier 1 immigrants are either exceptionally talented or wealthy – including entrepreneurs, noted artists and high-net-worth individuals. Tier 2 are skilled workers who can fill jobs that are not adequately filled by the host population – as well as including intra-company transfers. Tier 3 used to include unskilled workers but was scrapped in 2010. Tier 4 are students and Tier 5 are temporary migrants. The surest way to score enough points to qualify is to have a professional qualification on the 'shortage occupation list' – which includes doctors, nurses, IT specialists and engineers.

16 *Daily Telegraph*, 24.08.16, 'Low skilled migrants would have to apply for work permits under plans being considered by ministers'. http://www.telegraph.co.uk/news/2016/08/24/low-skilled-migrants-will-have-to-apply-for-work-permits-under-p/ Since 2017, Sir David Metcalf has been the first Director of Labour Market Enforcement – or 'labour market tsar' – appointed by the government to oversee a crackdown on rogue employers. As well as being the former Chair of MAC, he is also a founding member of the Low Pay Commission. In his new role, Sir David sets priorities for Britain's three main labour market enforcement agencies, the Gangmasters and Labour Abuse Authority, Employment Agency Standards Inspectorate and HMRC's National Minimum Wage enforcement team.

17 The MAC report cited earlier – Metcalf, op. cit. – concluded that an influx of low-skilled workers has had

'possible implications for cohesion and integration' because of 'rapidly changing populations' in some parts of the country.

18   See, for instance, an interview given by Labour deputy leader Tom Watson in February 2017. 'I think you can actually say London requires more liberal immigration policies but there are other parts of the country where immigration may be putting pressure on public services like schools and hospitals – that's why I think when we come out of the EU we can have an immigration policy that maybe addresses both those issues,' said Watson. 'These are nascent ideas, we're not ready to make them robust in a manifesto yet but they're certainly the debate that is going on in the Labour Party right now and in wider circles.' See *The Independent*, 12.02.17, 'Labour plans regional immigration system to tighten controls outside London'. http://www.independent.co.uk/news/uk/politics/labour-immigration-controls-regional-london-brexit-a7575826.html

19   In May 2017, six new 'metro mayors' were elected to lead combined authorities in England. Combined authorities are groups of local councils that have come together to take on powers devolved from central government relating to issues such as transport, housing, planning, skills and economic development. The areas which elected metro mayors were: Cambridgeshire and Peterborough (James Palmer, Conservative); Greater Manchester (Andy Burnham, Labour); Liverpool City Region (Steve Rotherham, Labour); Tees Valley (Ben Houchen, Conservative); West of England (Tim Bowles, Conservative) and West Midlands (Andy Street, Conservative).

20   'Regional visas – a unique immigration solution?', City of London Corporation and PwC, October 2016. https://www.cityoflondon.gov.uk/business/economic-research-and-information/research-publications/Documents/Research 2016/regional-visas.pdf

21   See NatCen Social Research, 21.11.16. http://www.natcen.ac.uk/news-media/press-releases/2016/november/voters-want-uk-to-stay-in-the-eu-single-market-but-be-able-to-control-immigration/

22   Stephen Kinnock, *The Guardian*, 19.09.16, 'My cure for a divided Britain? A programme of managed immigration'. https://www.theguardian.com/commentisfree/2016/sep/19/cure-divided-britain-managed-immigration-work-permits

23   Vince Cable, *New Statesman*, 04.01.17, 'Why it's time to end EU free movement'. http://www.newstatesman.com/politics/uk/2017/01/why-its-time-end-eu-free-movement

24   From 'The Europe Report', Mayor of London.

25   Of all NHS staff, 87.7 per cent (960,847) are British, 5.5 per cent are from the EU and 6.7 per cent from the rest of the world. Of doctors, 9.8 per cent are from the EU and 7.4 per cent of nurses. See Carl Baker, 10.04.17, House of Commons Library, Briefing Paper No. 7783, 'NHS staff from overseas: statistics'. http://researchbriefings.files.parliament.uk/documents/CBP-7783/CBP-7783.pdf. For a discussion on some of these issues see MigrationWatchUK, 'Public Services and Infrastructure | Key Topics'. https://www.migrationwatchuk.org/key-topics/public-services-infrastructure

26   'The Economic Impact of International Students', research by Oxford Economics for Universities UK, March 2017. http://www.universitiesuk.ac.uk/policy-and-analysis/reports/Documents/2017/briefing-economic-impact-international-students.pdf

27   Labour MP Frank Field – who co-chairs a parliamentary group on migration with Conservative MP Nicholas Soames – has promoted this idea. 'Of course we want vice-chancellors to earn their salaries by expanding their universities,' says Field. 'But they also need to be given the duty of making sure their overseas students return home – and if vice-chancellors fail to fulfil their duties on overseas students, their quota should be brought down and part of their salary docked.' See *The Sun*, 01.05.17, 'University chiefs must foot the bill if foreign students stay in UK, says Commons migration committee chief'. https://www.thesun.co.uk/news/3456918/university-chiefs-must-foot-the-bill-if-foreign-students-stay-in-uk-says-commons-migration-committee-chief/

28   The UK is the world's fifth most popular migrant destination, with 8,540,000 foreign-born residents, amounting to 13.2 per cent of the population. This figure was 3.2 per cent in 1960, 6.0 per cent in 1980 and 8.0 per cent in 2000. The US is the world's most popular migrant destination, with 46,627,000 foreign-born residents (14.5 per cent), followed by Germany with 12,006,000 (14.9 per cent), Russia with 11,643,000 (8.1 per cent) and Saudi Arabia with 10,186,000 (32 per cent). See United Nations, Department of Economic and Social Affairs, 2015, 'Trends in International Migrant Stock: Migrants by Destination and Origin' (United Nations database, POP/DB/MIG/Stock/Rev.2015). http://www.un.org/en/development/desa/population/migration/data/estimates2/estimates15.shtml

29   Politico, 04.07.17, 'For Europe and migrants, it looks like 2015 all over again'. http://www.politico.eu/article/for-europe-and-migrants-it-looks-like-2015-all-over-again/

30   Eurostat, Median incomes, 2016. http://ec.europa.eu/eurostat/web/gdp-and-beyond/quality-of-life/median-incom

Chapter 11: Housing and young people

1 Sajid Javid MP, Communities Secretary, speech to Conservative Party conference, 03.10.16. http://press.conservatives.com/post/151284016515/javid-speech-to-conservative-party-conference

2 See Liam Halligan, *The Spectator*, 05.11.16, 'Home to Roost'. https://www.spectator.co.uk/2016/11/britains-lack-of-house-building-has-come-home-to-roost/

3 See Kate Barker, review of 'House Supply – Delivering Stability: Securing our Future Housing Needs' HM Treasury, 2004. http://webarchive.nationalarchives.gov.uk/20120704150618/http://www.hm-treasury.gov.uk/d/barker_review_execsum_91.pdf

4 See 'Laying the Foundations: A Housing Strategy for England', HM Government, 2011. https://www.gov.uk/government/uploads/system/uploads/attachment_data/file/7532/2033676.pdf

5 Sajid Javid MP, Communities Secretary, speech to Conservative Party conference, 03.10.16. http://press.conservatives.com/post/151284016515/javid-speech-to-conservative-party-conference

6 'Building More Homes', House of Lords Economic Affairs Select Committee, HL Paper 20.07.16, p. 24. https://publications.parliament.uk/pa/ld201617/ldselect/ldeconaf/20/20.pdf

7 Marcus McPhillips, 'Phantom Homes – Planning Permissions, Completions and Profits', Shelter Research Briefing, July 2017. https://england.shelter.org.uk/__data/assets/pdf_file/0005/1396778/2017_07_07_Phantom_Homes_-_Profits,_Planning_Permissions_and_Completions.pdf

8 About 3.7 million workers in Britain endured a daily commute of two hours or more in 2015, according to the Trades Union Congress – an increase of 900,000 since 2010. London had the highest concentration of long-commuters – 930,000. A commute of four hours a day could add up to more than 5.5 weeks a year if you discount five weeks' holiday.

9 See https://www.gov.uk/government/speeches/queens-speech-2017. Also 'Fixing our Broken Housing Market', Department of Communities and Local Government, Cm 9352, February 2017. https://www.gov.uk/government/uploads/system/uploads/attachment_data/file/590464/Fixing_our_broken_housing_market_-_print_ready_version.pdf

10 Under existing 'New Towns' legislation, national government can set up HDCs – which, crucially, can buy land at 'existing use' value. Arable land, for instance, is purchased as arable land, bringing a healthy upside once residential planning is granted – guaranteeing ring-fenced cash for extra local infrastructure. Under current 'Section 106' negotiations, powerful house-builders hold most of the cards and often spend less on local amenities than councils expect.

11 See 'London: The Global Powerhouse', Mayor of London, February 2016, pp. 61–7. https://www.london.gov.uk/sites/default/files/gla_the_london_economy_report_full_low_res.pdf. As the Mirrlees Review on tax system reform said: 'The taxation of housing is a mess. Council tax is still based on 1991 valuations and is unnecessarily regressive. Stamp duty is among the most inefficient and damaging of all taxes. And renting is needlessly penalised by the tax system. Stamp duty should be abolished and council tax reformed so that payments are based on up to date valuations.' IFS Mirrlees Review: 'Reforming the Tax System for the 21st Century', 2011. http://www.ifs.org.uk/publications/mirrleesreview/

12 See, for instance, *The Guardian*, 26.06.17, 'Nostalgic elderly Brexiters have stolen my future' (https://www.theguardian.com/commentisfree/2016/jun/26/education-erasmus-brexit-referendum) and *Daily Telegraph*, 24.06.16, 'Millennials' "fury" over baby boomers' vote for Brexit'. http://www.telegraph.co.uk/news/2016/06/24/millenials-fury-over-baby-boomers-vote-for-brexit/

13 In the 2015 general election, David Cameron's Conservatives gained 36 per cent of votes among 30–39-year-olds, compared to 34 per cent for Ed Miliband's Labour Party. In 2017, the position was transformed, with Jeremy Corbyn's Labour Party taking 55 per cent of the votes within the same age range, while Theresa May's Conservatives won just 29 per cent.

Chapter 12: Nations and regions

1 BBC, EU referendum: Results in maps and charts, 24.06.16. http://www.bbc.co.uk/news/uk-politics-36616028. See also *Financial Times* http://ig.ft.com/sites/elections/2016/uk/eu-referendum/index.html and *Daily Telegraph* http://www.telegraph.co.uk/news/0/leave-or-remain-eu-referendum-results-and-live-maps/

2 The five London boroughs with a Leave majority were Barking and Dagenham, Bexley, Havering, Hillingdon and Sutton.

3 Open Europe, 'Off Target: The case for bringing regional policy back home', January 2012. The European Commission's own QUEST model shows that the effectiveness of EU structural and regional funds on GDP was negative in no fewer than eight countries, the UK being one of them. This analysis was from 2000–2006, but reinforces the conclusion reached by Open Europe. (See Column 1 of Table 3 – QUEST Cumulative SCF (Structural and Cohesion Funds), 'Review of the Balance of Competencies between the UK and the EU: Cohesion Policy', summer 2014, p. 47.

4   HM Government, 'Review of the Balance of Competences between the United Kingdom and the European Union: Cohesion Policy', Summer 2014

5   See European Commission, 'The EU Regional Competitiveness Index 2016', Working Papers WP 02/2017, plus scorecards available via http://ec.europa.eu/regional_policy/en/information/maps/regional_competitiveness/ This is the only measure to provide a European perspective on competitiveness of all so-called Nomenclature of Units for Territorial Statistics (NUTS-2) regions in the EU, although in this case NUTS in the same functional urban area are combined. NUTS are levels of local administration, and NUTS-2 refers to large counties or combined smaller counties.

6   William Hague, *Daily Telegraph*, 22.12.15, 'Why I will be voting to stay in Europe'. http://www.telegraph.co.uk/news/newstopics/eureferendum/12064244/Why-I-will-be-voting-to-stay-in-Europe.html

7   Constitutional Reform Group, 13.07.16, 'Act of Union Bill', Explanatory Notes and 48-page bill. The group, convened by former Conservative Cabinet minister Lord Salisbury, includes the former Liberal Democrat leader Sir Menzies Campbell, the former Labour Northern Ireland and Wales Secretary Peter Hain, the former House of Commons clerk Lord Lisvane and the former Ulster Unionist politician David Burnside. The group believes that, in the aftermath of the Brexit vote, the governance of England, Scotland, Wales and Northern Ireland should be reinvented within a new voluntary union, devolving power to each constituent part of the UK in order to save the Union.

8   Mark Carney, 'The economics of currency unions', speech in Edinburgh, 29.01.14. http://www.bankofengland.co.uk/publications/Documents/speeches/2014/speech706.pdf. *Daily Express*, 09.09.14, 'Independent Scotland Won't be able to keep the pound, warns Bank of England', https://www.express.co.uk/news/politics/508800/Bank-of-England-Yes-Campaign-Pound-Coin-EU-Scottish-Independence

9   See Gerard Lyons, *Financial Times*, 23.03.98, 'History shows EMU's success depend on political union', reprinted in https://www.sc.com/privatebank/_pdf/en/Global Focus May Final.pdf

10 Since 1978, the 'Barnett Formula' has been used to distribute UK wealth across Northern Ireland, Scotland, England and Wales. Devised by Joel Barnett, Chief Secretary to the Treasury under Jim Callaghan's Labour government, the formula stipulates how much of any broad government spending increase is sent to the four parts of the UK. Introduced as a temporary measure, the formula was adopted by subsequent governments amid fears that withdrawing it could severely damage the Union. Estimates of government spending per person have consistently shown the highest levels in Northern Ireland, followed by Scotland, then Wales and finally England. Many English MPs have called for reform of the Barnett Formula and, in 2014, Barnett himself referred to it as 'a terrible mistake' and 'a national embarrassment'. See *Daily Telegraph*, 16.09.14, 'My funding formula for Scotland is a "terrible mistake", Lord Barnett admits'. http://www.telegraph.co.uk/news/uknews/scottish-independence/11100400/My-funding-formula-for-Scotland-is-a-terrible-mistake-Lord-Barnett-admits.html

11 Bill Jamieson, *The Scotsman*, 24.08.16, 'Scotland's problems are bigger than Brexit'. https://www.google.co.uk/amp/www.scotsman.com/news/opinion/bill-jamieson-scotland-s-problems-are-bigger-than-brexit-1-4211925/amp

12 Speech by Economy Secretary Keith Brown to SNP Spring Conference, 18.03.2017. He also noted the life sciences sector grew 29 per cent from 2010 to £4.2 billion and is expected to almost double by 2025. https://www.snp.org/speech_by_economy_secretary_keith_brown_to_the_2017_snp_spring_conference

13 On 21.07.17, Environment Secretary Michael Gove said, 'We now have an historic opportunity to review our policies on agriculture, land use, biodiversity, woodlands, marine conservation, fisheries, pesticide licensing, chemical regulation, animal welfare, habitat management, waste, water purity, air quality and so much more.' His words were welcomed by various Scottish farming and fisheries bodies and, cautiously, by various environmental groups.

14 See *Daily Telegraph*, 29.06.16, 'Gordon Brown tells Scots: UK's single market worth more than EU's'. http://www.telegraph.co.uk/news/2016/06/29/gordon-brown-tells-scots-uks-single-market-worth-far-more-than-e/

15 The UK's two remaining Trafalgar-class submarines, HM Submarines *Talent* and *Triumph*, currently based in Plymouth, are due to move to the Clyde in 2019 and 2020 respectively. The last four Astute-class submarines, which will eventually replace the Trafalgar class, are due to be commissioned into the Royal Navy between 2018 and 2024. The Ministry of Defence has pumped £1.3 billion into consolidating the UK's submarine infrastructure, making the Clyde, in the words of Defence Secretary Michael Fallon, 'Britain's submarine hub'. In February 2017, the government announced that a £4 million submarine school will be built at the base, providing academic and technical training for all Royal Naval personnel entering the submarine service from 2022. See *Plymouth Herald*, 03.02.17, 'Plymouth submarines to move to Scotland by 2020'.

16 'MOD seals the deal on nine new Maritime Patrol Aircraft to keep UK safe', MOD Press Release, 11.07.16. https://www.gov.uk/government/news/mod-seals-the-deal-on-nine-new-maritime-patrol-aircraft-to-keep-uk-safe http://www.plymouthherald.co.uk/8203-plymouth-submarines-to-move-to-scotland-by-2020/story-30110141-detail/story.html

17 Janes, 04.10.16, 'Lossiemouth to host sixth RAF Typhoon squadron'. http://www.janes.com/article/64329/lossiemouth-to-host-sixth-raf-typhoon-squadron

18 See Kenny Richmond and Jonathan Slow, 'Self-employment in Scotland: trends and its implications for productivity', Fraser of Allander Institute, University of Strathclyde, Glasgow, Economic Commentary, June 2017. https://www.strath.ac.uk/media/1newwebsite/departmentsubject/strathclydebusinessschool/fraserofallander/Self-employment_in_Scotland,_trends_and_implications_for_productivity.pdf

19 Quote from Andy Willox, BBC News, 05.07.17, 'Scottish economy rebounds in first quarter of 2017'. http://www.bbc.co.uk/news/uk-scotland-40498752

20 FDI Intelligence, 21.07.16, 'A post-Brexit future for Welsh FDI'. http://www.fdiintelligence.com/News/A-post-Brexit-future-for-Welsh-FDI

21 Office of the Secretary of State for Wales, 06.07.17, 'Foreign investors see opportunities in Wales'. https://www.gov.uk/government/news/foreign-investors-see-opportunities-in-wales

22 A detailed analysis of the Wales–EU relationship can be found at 'Securing Wales' Future: Transition from the European Union to a new relationship with Europe', Welsh government, 2017. https://beta.gov.wales/sites/default/files/2017-01/30683 Securing Wales¹ Future_ENGLISH_WEB.pdf

23 See HM Government, 'Review of the Balance of Competencies between the United Kingdom and the European Union: Cohesion Policy', summer 2014.

24 See David Williamson, Wales Online, 12.07.2017, 'Everything you need to know about the public sector pay freeze in Wales – and what it really meant for workers'. http://www.walesonline.co.uk/news/politics/everything-you-need-know-public-13276653

25 See Wales Online, 06.12.2016, 'Full Pisa results 2016 show Wales' schools are still adrift of the rest of the UK'. http://www.walesonline.co.uk/news/education/full-pisa-results-2016-show-12278551. The previous Pisa 2013 results were also poor. http://www.bbc.co.uk/news/uk-wales-25196974

26 See http://www.eib.org

27 See p. 22 of 'Securing Wales' Future: Transition from the European Union to a new relationship with Europe', 2017, a White Paper developed jointly by the Welsh Government and Plaid Cymru.

28 South Wales Metro is a new transport system for the 'Cardiff Capital Region'. See the Welsh Government, http://gov.wales/topics/transport/public/metro/?lang=en

29 See pp. 11–12, 'For the Many Not The Few', Labour Party manifesto 2017.

30 *Daily Mail*, 13.07.17, 'Spanish train maker CAF to open new £30m factory in South Wales creating 300 jobs'. http://www.thisismoney.co.uk/money/news/article-4694098/Spanish-train-maker-CAF-open-factory-South-Wales.html#ixzz4naRqPIDN

31 See Office for National Statistics, 23.05.17, 'Country and regional public sector finances: Financial year ending March 2016'. https://www.ons.gov.uk/economy/governmentpublicsectorandtaxes/publicsectorfinance/articles/countryandregionalpublicsectorfinances/2015to2016

32 See 'London: the Global Powerhouse', Report by the Mayor of London, Greater London Authority, February 2016, p. 22. 'London accounts for one quarter of the UK economy, and its ratio has been growing in recent years. It is not uncommon for a capital city to dominate its economy. Lisbon is one third of Portugal's economy, Stockholm is around 30 per cent of Sweden's economy, and Vienna – often ranked as one of the most desirable cities in which to live – is about 27 per cent of Austria's economy. These are a bigger proportion of their economy than London is of the UK. But when it comes to large countries it is less common for the capital city to dominate in the way London does. The other exceptions might be Madrid, which is about 18 per cent of Spain, and Seoul, a mega city of over 10 million people which is about 20 per cent of South Korea's economy. In terms of major Western European economies, Paris is just under a tenth of France's economy, while Berlin is about a twentieth of Germany's. In the US, Washington is a small part of the economy, hence London is compared to New York.'

33 Chancellor Philip Hammond, speech to Conservative Party conference. http://www.ibtimes.co.uk/read-chancellor-philip-hammonds-full-speech-conservative-conference-1584555

34 See McKinsey & Company, 'Urban World: Mapping the economic power of cities', March 2011 (http://www.mckinsey.com/global-themes/urbanization/urban-world-mapping-the-economic-power-of-cities) and United Nations, 'World Urbanization Prospects', 2014 Revision (https://esa.un.org/unpd/wup/publications/files/wup2014-highlights.Pdf), and World Economic Forum, 'The Competitiveness of Cities', August 2014. http://www3.weforum.org/docs/GAC/2014/WEF_GAC_CompetitivenessOfCities_Report_2014.pdf

35 Rolls-Royce is sometimes cited as an example of how government intervention can succeed. It was forced into receivership in February 1971, without receiving any government help, as Prime Minister Edward Heath's stated view was that 'industry must stand on its own two feet'. The government then nationalised Rolls-Royce and it continued as a newly formed company Rolls-Royce Ltd (1971) and was later privatised.

36 See Mayor of London, London Finance Commission report, 'Devolution: a capital idea', January 2017, chaired

by Professor Tony Travers. This report set out the benefits of fiscal devolution. Gerard Lyons testified and gave evidence to the Commission. This report builds on a previous report by a previous London Finance Commission, 'Raising the capital', May 2013.

37 See John Plender, *Financial Times*, 25.04.17, 'UK public finance: councils build a credit bubble'. https://www. ft.com/content/84892c56-1a17-11e7-bcac-6d03d067f81f

Chapter 13: Ireland

1 Ray Bassett was Ireland's ambassador to Canada from 2010 until 2016. He was part of the Irish government talks team during the Belfast (Good Friday) Agreement negotiations and, throughout his career, held diplomatic posts in Belfast, London, Canberra and Copenhagen as well as Ottawa. See Ray Bassett, 'After Brexit, Will Ireland be Next to Exit?', Policy Exchange, June 2017. https://policyexchange.org.uk/publication/after-brexit-will-ireland-be-next-to-exit/

2 European Commission Press Release, 11.05.17, 'Speech by Michel Barnier at the Joint Houses of the Oireachtas (Houses of Parliament of Ireland), Dublin'. http://europa.eu/rapid/press-release_SPEECH-17-1276_en.htm. See also Lisa O'Carroll, *The Guardian*, 11.05.17, 'Brexit will not jeopardise peace in Ireland, EU's chief negotiator says'. https://www.theguardian.com/world/2017/may/11/michel-barnier-brexit-will-not-jeopardise-peace-in-ireland-eu-chief-negotiator-says

3 *Belfast Telegraph*, 25.05.17, 'No new customs points planned for Irish border after Brexit, says Revenue chief'. http://www.belfasttelegraph.co.uk/news/northern-ireland/no-new-customs-points-planned-for-irish-border-after-brexit-says-revenue-chief-35754851.html

4 *Irish Independent*, 22.07.17, 'Nigel Farage accuses EU of "stoking Irish nationalism to make Brexit difficult"'. http://www.independent.ie/business/brexit/nigel-farage-accuses-eu-of-stoking-irish-nationalism-to-make-brexit-difficult-35675658.html?utm_content=buffer9aa1c&utm_medium=social&utm_source=twitter. com&utm_campaign=buffer

5 Bertie Ahern, BBC Radio 4, *Today Programme*, 10.05.17.

6 RTE television documentary, *Brexit, Trump and Us*, 22.05.17. https://www.youtube.com/watch?v=a_FMuC2HXLc

7 Under the terms of such an agreement, a minority party pledges to vote with the government on budget legislation and any no confidence vote. From 1977 to 1979, Jim Callaghan's Labour Party retained power thanks to a confidence and supply deal with the Liberal Party, known as the Lib–Lab Pact.

8 In 2013, Finance Minister Michael Noonan acknowledged that Ireland had 'taken one for the team'. Regarding the 2010 bailout, which left the Irish state deeply indebted, Noonan said 'while some of it was our own fault, a lot of the action was taken at the direction of the European Central Bank to prevent contagion spreading to the European banking system'. See TheJournal.ie, 21.02.13, 'Noonan: Europe now owes Ireland after "taking one for the team"'. http://www.thejournal.ie/noonan-bloomberg-team-803873-Feb2013/ This was, to a large degree, a statement of the obvious. As one of the authors wrote at the time of the bailout: 'Ireland is now being forced to borrow money from the European Financial Stability Facility (EFSF), the multi-billion euro war chest set up after May's Greek crisis to deal with future euro emergencies. Why? One reason is that the eurocrats are engaged in a misguided attempt to calm down the markets in the hope that yields stay relatively low for Spain and Portugal, countries whose financing needs are far greater and more immediate ... For this Irish bailout is about a lot more than Ireland. It's about the bullheaded determination of other European governments, including the UK, to keep avoiding the harsh truths that the Irish, having made their fair share of mistakes in recent years, have now begun to face. This bailout is mostly about the euro elite's dogged refusal to acknowledge the structural flaws at the heart of the entire single currency project.' See Liam Halligan, *Daily Telegraph*, 20.11.10, 'Plucky Irish felled by the twisted, self-serving logic of the eurozone'. http://www. telegraph.co.uk/finance/comment/liamhalligan/8148757/Plucky-Irish-felled-by-the-twisted-self-serving-logic-of-the-eurozone.html

9 Ray Bassett, 'After Brexit, Will Ireland be Next to Exit?', Policy Exchange, June 2017. https://policyexchange. org.uk/publication/after-brexit-will-ireland-be-next-to-exit/

10 *Irish Times*, 08.04.17, 'German bosses say Brexit may have silver lining for Ireland'. http://www.irishtimes.com/business/economy/german-bosses-say-brexit-may-have-silver-lining-for-ireland-1.3041045

11 BBC News, 21.07.17, 'Bank of America picks Dublin for EU hub'. http://www.bbc.co.uk/news/business-40680013

12 Ireland: Trade Statistics, Global Edge https://globaledge.msu.edu/countries/ireland/tradestats

13 *Irish Independent*, 05.04.17, 'Brexit is too important to be left to Bureaucrats'. http://www.davidmcwilliams. ie/2017/04/05/brexit-is-too-important-to-be-left-to-bureaucrats

14 GDP per head in the Republic of Ireland was equivalent to $62,562 in 2016, according to the International Monetary Fund, placing the Republic fourth in the world. The UK was nineteenth with $40,092. See World Economic Outlook Database, April 2017, accessed on 18 April 2017.

Chapter 14: Respecting the referendum

1   *Good Morning Britain*, 27.03.17. See *Daily Telegraph*, 27.03.17, 'Alastair Campbell: Believe me, Brexit can be stopped' http://www.telegraph.co.uk/news/2017/03/27/believe-brexit-can-stopped-watch-nigel-farage-alistair-campbell/

2   'Why the government believes voting to remain in the EU is the best decision for the UK'. https://www.gov.uk/government/uploads/system/uploads/attachment_data/file/515068/why-the-government-believes-that-voting-to-remain-in-the-european-union-is-the-best-decision-for-the-uk.pdf

3   The leaflet stated, for instance, that 'the UK is not part of the EU's border-free zone'. EU membership was presented as essential to 'controlling immigration', keeping Britain safe from terrorists and 'securing our borders'. This is, at best, disingenuous. Britain is not part of the Schengen Agreement, so EU nationals do indeed have to show a passport on entering the UK, unlike when they move, for instance, between Portugal and Spain. But EU nationals still have the right to live and work in Britain under the EU's freedom of movement rules, despite the leaflet claiming the UK has 'special status in the EU' allowing us to 'keep control of our borders'. The leaflet goes on to warn voters that leaving the EU would jeopardise access to cheap flights and healthcare while on holiday in the EU, leading also to higher mobile phone roaming charges. More than 3 million jobs could be threatened because they are linked to EU exports, the leaflet suggested, with Brexit causing '10 years of uncertainty' and 'an economic shock'.

4   Only one in five British voters think the UK should stay in the EU on its current terms of membership, or with greater powers handed over to Brussels. And just 2 per cent believe the UK should unite with the rest of the EU to form a single government, pursuing 'ever closer union'. See British Social Attitudes survey by NatCen, 28.06.17.

5   This was the EU (Notification of Withdrawal) Bill, with the vote taking place on 08.02.17.

6   Technically, the amendment said that the UK should not leave the EU unless it secures departure terms which 'deliver the exact same benefits the UK has as a member of the single market and customs union' – a requirement that is highly subjective even on the moment of departure, let alone in the future. The amendment was tabled by Labour MP Chuka Umunna. Some forty-nine of his parliamentary colleagues defied their party whip to vote with him.

7   The degree of parliamentary scrutiny of Brexit is further guaranteed by the fact that, following the June 2017 election and a vote among MPs, some nineteen out of twenty-four of the key House of Commons Select Committees – almost four out of five – are chaired by an MP who voted to stay in the EU. These include the highly influential Brexit Committee (chaired by former Labour shadow Foreign Secretary Hilary Benn) and the Treasury Select Committee (chaired by former Conservative Education Secretary Nicky Morgan). Made up of cross-party groups of MPs, Commons committees have powers to call ministers to give evidence, launch investigations and produce reports that shape the political debate.

8   'Change Britain's Future', Liberal Democrat election manifesto, May 2017. https://www.libdems.org.uk/manifesto.

9   Prof. John Curtice, 13.07.17, 'Has the election seen a change in attitudes towards Brexit?', The UK in a Changing Europe blog, ESRC and King's College, London. http://ukandeu.ac.uk/has-the-election-seen-a-change-in-attitudes-towards-brexit/

10 'For the Many, not the Few', Labour manifesto, May 2017. http://www.labour.org.uk/page/-/Images/manifesto-2017/Labour Manifesto 2017.pdf

11 *Daily Mirror*, 23.07.17, 'Jeremy Corbyn grilled over Brexit as he insists Britain has to quit the EU single market'. http://changebritain.us15.list-manage2.com/track/click?u=19200c5d3464a1dffcoc5c9db&id=f824f71173&ce=053718ica4

12 *The Guardian*, 24.07.17, 'Brexit means leaving the single market and the customs union. Here's why'. https://www.theguardian.com/commentisfree/2017/jul/24/leaving-eu-single-market-customs-union-brexit-britain-europe

13 *Daily Telegraph*, 27.07.17, 'Labour Brexit split widens as Sir Keir Starmer says we must not "sweep options off the table"'. http://www.telegraph.co.uk/news/2017/07/27/labour-brexit-split-widens-sir-keir-starmer-says-must-not-sweep/

14 BBC News, 26.07.17, 'John McDonnell not ruling out single market membership'. http://www.bbc.co.uk/news/uk-politics-40726213

15 Balance of Payments Stat Bulletin, 23.12.16, Tables B & C.

16 The EU's 'four freedoms' are: freedom of movement of goods, people, services and capital across borders. These key principles lie at the heart of the EU and underpin the single market, originally known as the Common Market, and are enshrined in various EU treaties.

17 Fabian Zuleeg, 24.07.17, 'Reality bites: the Brexit negotiations seen from the other side of the Channel', European Policy Centre. http://www.epc.eu/pub_details.php?cat_id=4&pub_id=7865&year=2017

18 *Bristol Post*, 18.04.17, 'Brenda from Bristol's furious reaction to the general election'. http://www.bristolpost.co.uk/news/bristol-news/watch-brendas-furious-reaction-general-27526

19 *The Sun*, 19.09.17, 'Vince Cable slaps down Lib Dem leader Tim Farron's plans for second EU referendum'.

https://www.thesun.co.uk/news/1813743/vince-cable-slaps-down-lib-dem-leader-tim-farrons-plans-for-second-eu-referendum/

20 Vince Cable, *The Sun*, 19.07.17, 'Vince Cable ditches opposition to second EU referendum as he takes over as leader of the Liberal Democrats'. https://www.thesun.co.uk/news/politics/4055996/vince-cable-liberal-democrats-leader-referendum/

21 BBC News, 09.07.17, 'Brexit may never happen – Sir Vince Cable'. http://www.bbc.co.uk/news/uk-politics-40547733

22 Vince Cable, *New Statesman*, 04.01.17, 'Why it's time to end EU free movement'. http://www.newstatesman.com/politics/uk/2017/01/why-its-time-end-eu-free-movement

23 See Gideon Rachman, *Financial Times*, 17.07.17, 'The campaign to stop Brexit is gathering pace. The most obvious sign is the increasing chatter about a second referendum. At the moment it is still mainly former politicians, such as Tony Blair and Nick Clegg, who are explicit about their desire to prevent the UK leaving the EU. Active politicians tend to talk about a "soft Brexit". For some, this is simply a convenient code, or a staging post, for their real goal – stopping Brexit altogether.' https://www.ft.com/content/b3630088-6ac6-11e7-b9c7-15af748b60d0

24 'The government's negotiating objectives for exiting the EU', speech by Prime Minister Theresa May, Lancaster House, 17.01.17. https://www.gov.uk/government/speeches/the-governments-negotiating-objectives-for-exiting-the-eu-pm-speech

25 Forsyth later said: 'Be aware that what is going on here is the House of Lords, stuffed full of people who've had jobs in Europe and are committed to Europe … is trying to frustrate the will of the elected House of Commons.' BBC Radio 4, *Any Questions*, 11.03.17. http://www.bbc.co.uk/programmes/b08h0g4w

26 After Labour's landslide general election victory in 1945, there were only sixteen Labour peers in the Lords, led by Lord Addison. Because the Labour government had a clear electoral mandate to follow contentious measures such as nationalisation and the introduction of the welfare state, it was decided the House of Lords, with its then large in-built Conservative majority, should not oppose such legislation at second reading. This arrangement is sometimes called the Salisbury-Addison convention.

27 'As we leave the European Union, we will no longer be members of the single market or customs union but we will seek a deep and special partnership including a comprehensive free trade and customs agreement.' See 'Forward, Together', Conservative election manifesto, May 2017, p. 36. https://s3.eu-west-2.amazonaws.com/manifesto2017/Manifesto2017.pdf

28 See Liam Halligan, *Daily Telegraph*, 07.05.17, 'Negotiation over dinner leaves a bad taste' (http://www.telegraph.co.uk/business/2017/05/06/negotiation-dinner-leaves-bad-taste/) and James Forsyth, *The Spectator*, 08.07.17, 'Why hasn't the Remain dog barked in this election?'. https://www.spectator.co.uk/2017/06/why-hasnt-the-remain-dog-barked-in-this-election/

29 The DUP manifesto published just before the June 2017 election supports a 'comprehensive free trade and customs agreement with the EU' and 'progress on new free trade deals with the rest of the world'. While these two statements clearly imply being outside the single market and the customs union, they do not refer to these institutions by name. This may be a procedural loophole the government's enemies attempt to exploit, with opposition parties in the Lords arguing that the Salisbury Convention does not hold on a combined majority, given that one of the relevant manifestos was not explicit.

30 Hansard, House of Lords, 21.06.17, Vol. 783, Col. 16. https://hansard.parliament.uk/Lords/2017-06-21/debates/4F52BED7-7AA0-49A9-BAFC-2985A01349DB/Queen'SSpeech – contribution-E73D28EB-F79B-4823-9BC9-4BE7BE5160E7

31 Politics Home, 23.02.17, 'Lord Newby: Article 50 bill is "not the end, it's just the beginning"'. https://www.politicshome.com/news/europe/eu-policy-agenda/brexit/house/house-magazine/83596/lord-newby-article-50-bill-not-end

32 'I do not believe that a convention drawn up sixty years ago on relations between a wholly hereditary Conservative-dominated House and a Labour government who had 48 per cent of the vote should apply in the same way to the position in which we find ourselves today,' said Lord McNally, then Liberal Democrat leader in the Lords. See House of Lords, Deb 17.05.05, cc. 20–21.

33 See 'Lessons from the process of Government formation after the 2010 General Election', House of Commons Political and Constitutional Reform Committee – Vol. 1, January 2011. Evidence submitted by the Hansard Society, Ev. 62, Para. 7. https://publications.parliament.uk/pa/cm201011/cmselect/cmpolcon/528/528.pdf

34 Paul Marshall, *Financial Times*, 29.03.17, 'At last we can embrace the business of building up prosperity'. https://www.ft.com/content/c35124e8-13e6-11e7-b0c1-37e417ee6c76

35 *Good Morning Britain*, 27.03.17. See *Daily Telegraph*, 27.03.17, 'Alastair Campbell: Believe me, Brexit can be stopped'. http://www.telegraph.co.uk/news/2017/03/27/believe-brexit-can-stopped-watch-nigel-farage-alistair-campbell/

Chapter 15: Remaking global Britain

1   For comments on the Treasury's underlying assumptions, made just after the report was published, see Liam Halligan, *Daily Telegraph*, 23.04.16, 'A pro-EU "study" straight from the Ministry of Truth'. http://www.telegraph.co.uk/business/2016/04/23/a-pro-eu-study-straight-from-the-ministry-of-truth. See also Gerard Lyons, *The Sun*, 09.06.16 'How George Osborne got Europe Numbers So Totally Tangled'. https://www.thesun.co.uk/news/1252856/economist-rubbishes-chancellors-4300-brexit-claim-as-dodgy-division/

2   *The Guardian*, 15.06.16, 'George Osborne: vote for Brexit and face £30 billion of taxes and spending cuts'. https://www.theguardian.com/politics/2016/jun/14/osborne-predicts-30bn-hole-in-public-finance-if-uk-votes-to-leave-eu

3   'Economists for Brexit' was one of very few groups accurately to predict the UK's economic performance in the aftermath of the Leave vote, using the 'Liverpool model' of two of its members – Professors Patrick Minford and Kent Matthews. This group has now been reformed as 'Economists for Free Trade'. https://www.economistsforfreetrade.com/. Gerard Lyons was co-founder with Patrick Minford of Economists for Brexit.

4   In his report for the Mayor of London, cited earlier, 'London the Global Powerhouse', Lyons referred to leaving the EU as 'an economic shock' and used the 'tick' or 'Nike swoosh' analogy to describe the trajectory of growth during the Article 50 negotiation, with a temporary slowdown then turning into recovery. He was positive about the post-referendum outlook, and expected the economy to perform well – following a path similar to that after 'Black Wednesday' in 1992, when the pound left the EU's Exchange Rate Mechanism.

5   See 'Free Trade and other Fundamental doctrines of the Manchester School', edited by Francis W. Hirst (Harper & Brothers, 1903) for a good description of the issues. The scale and the length of the battle to repeal the Corn Laws were considerable. Ebenezer Elliott authored popular 'Corn Law Rhymes', Joseph Hume gave a well-received speech in Wolverhampton in May 1933, a full thirteen years before success was achieved. While, on 28 September 1843, the Anti-Corn Law League held its first monthly meeting in Covent Garden. 'The vast space was crowded in every corner' as a report was read detailing the operations of the League. 'Subscriptions exceeded £50,000. Over nine million tracts and stamped publications had been distributed during the year, and 651 lectures delivered under the auspices of the league.'

6   A 2014 report for the Mayor of London, 'The Europe Report: A Win-Win Situation', contained the results of a detailed econometric forecasting exercise by economists Professor Paul Ormerod and Bridget Rosewell. The report showed that, over a twenty-year period, taking in two business cycles, the two best scenarios for the UK were to leave the EU and adopt a global approach (this was referred to as 'Brave new world') or to remain in a truly reformed EU ('One regime, two systems'). These scenarios were both far better than remaining in an unreformed EU ('Business as usual'), or leaving but then adopting an insular, protectionist stance ('Inward-looking').

7   This point has been made in *The Road to Somewhere* by David Goodhart (London: C. Hurst & Co., 2017). It was amplified by the Labour peer Professor Lord Maurice Glasman at a discussion group organised by Global Britain and the Commission for National Renewal in June 2017.

8   Centre for Social Justice, 'The five pathways to poverty: tackling the root causes and breaking the cycle of poverty', 2007. http://www.centreforsocialjustice.org.uk/policy/breakthrough-britain

9   See Cornell University, 'Global Innovation Index 2016'. The top six nations for innovation were Switzerland, then Sweden, UK, USA, Finland and Singapore.

10 It is not uncommon for capital cities to dominate their economy, but less so among bigger countries. London accounts for one quarter of UK GDP. London's productivity outperforms the UK by 72 per cent; it is not uncommon to see this picture in other countries too, given the tendency for capitals to attract clusters of high value-added roles. Paris outperforms France by 67 per cent; New York, while not the political capital of the US, outperforms the broader nation by 36 per cent.

11 Professor Robert Tombs, *The Spectator*, 08.07.17, 'Down with Declinism'.

12 Amy Studdart, 20.03.17, 'How Technology is Unraveling the Global Order'. https://medium.com/out-of-order/why-technology-is-unravelling-the-global-order-9a7463db62bb

13 There are numerous data sources and analyses of government spending and revenue. In this context, see Helen Miller and Barra Roantree, IFS Briefing Note No. 198, 01.05.17, 'Tax revenues: where does the money come from and what the next government's challenges?', or Tom Clark and Andrew Dilnot, IFS, 2002, 'Long-term Trends in British Taxation and Spending'.

14 See HM Treasury spring Budget, 2017. https://www.gov.uk/government/publications/spring-budget-2017-documents/spring-budget-2017. Total managed expenditure in 2017/18 was expected to be around £802 billion. Debt interest was £46 billion, spending on defence was £48 billion, public order and safety was £34 billion, health £149 billion. Also data on spending can be found here: https://tradingeconomics.com/united-kingdom/government-spending-to-gdp

15 Between June 2016 and February 2017, inflation rose from 0.3 per cent to 2.2 per cent in Germany and from

0.1 per cent to 2.0 per cent across the broader Eurozone. Since then, inflation has eased to 1.6 per cent and 1.3 per cent respectively. In the UK, inflation rose from 0.5 per cent to 2.3 per cent between June 2016 and February 2017 and has since increased to 2.9 per cent. A larger rise in inflation occurred when sterling fell after the 2007/08 financial crisis, but that was not sustained.

16 See BBC Report by Kamal Ahmed, 15.11.2016. http://www.bbc.co.uk/news/business-37988095

17 See *The Independent*, 06.07.17, 'Foreign investment to UK creates fewer jobs as Brexit looms'. Despite the headline of this piece, it reports data from the Department for International Trade that, 'The UK attracted over 2,200 new inward investment projects in 2016–17, a record rate.' The headline was based on 'jobs created in 2015/16 [by inward investment] were 82,650, falling to 75,226 in 2016/17' with the number of firms expanding their UK investment down from 821 to 782. http://www.independent.co.uk/news/uk/politics/brexit-foreign-investment-effect-fdi-uk-liam-fox-tim-farron-department-international-trade-eu-us-a7826601.html

18 See Gerard Lyons, *The Sun*, 02.08.2017, 'Why London's Brexit-proof'.

19 Gerard Lyons, *The Guardian*, 14.06.16, 'Brexit would help UK manufacturing survive in a global market'. http://www.theguardian.com/business/economics-blog/2016/jun/14/brexit-uk-manufacturing-global-market-eu-referendum?client=safari

20 For a good summary, see the Grantham Institute, Imperial College London, 'Carbon pricing in the UK post-Brexit: tax or trade? – A discussion paper', April 2017.

Conclusion: Clean Brexit

1 From *Pudd'nhead Wilson* by Mark Twain.

2 See IndexMundi's summary of tariffs using World Bank data. http://www.indexmundi.com/facts/european-union/tariff-rate. For instance in 2014 the EU's 'tariff rate, most favoured nation, simple mean, manufactured product' was 4.05 per cent while its 'tariff rate, most favored nation, weighted mean, all products' was 2.41 per cent.

3 See CBI Press Team, 25.07.17, 'Manufacturers report strong output growth'. http://www.cbi.org.uk/news/manufacturers-report-strong-output-growth/

4 The figures for UK FDI are $49 billion during the first three months of 2016, followed by $20 billion, $36 billion and $147 billion in the subsequent three quarters. See 'Foreign Direct Investment Statistics: Data, Analysis and Forecasts', April 2017, OECD, Paris. http://www.oecd.org/corporate/mne/statistics.htm

5 Liam Fox, Secretary of State for International Trade, has been making this case. See Reuters, 20.07.17, 'Britain's Fox to call for new WTO trade round'. http://www.reuters.com/article/us-britain-eu-trade-wto-idUSKBN1A50W3?il=0

6 Mervyn King, *New York Review of Books*, 18.08.16, 'Which Europe Now?'

7 Brussels Economic Forum Keynote Speech, 01.06.17, given at the flagship annual economic event of the European Commission. http://ec.europa.eu/economy_finance/bef2017/media/speech/2-soros-bef_en.pdf

8 European Commission, 'Public Opinion in the European Union – Standard Eurobarometer 86', December 2016, p. 11, Exhibit QA3.

9 Reuters, 18.07.17, 'Leading light of Italy's 5-Star revives euro referendum pledge', http://www.reuters.com/article/us-italy-5star-euro-referendum-idUSKBN1A30TI

10 *Saturday Evening Post*, 15.02.30, 'The United States of Europe'. Republished in *The Collected Essays of Sir Winston Churchill, Vol. II: Churchill and Politics* (London: Library of Imperial History, 1976), pp. 176–86.

11 Six per cent of respondents wanted 'more powers to be transferred to the EU'. See Katie Simmons and Bruce Stokes, 'Populism and Global Engagement: Europe, North America and Emerging Economies', *Pew Research Institute*, 15.12.16. http://www.pewglobal.org/2016/12/15/populism-and-global-engagement-europe-north-america-and-emerging-economies/

SELECT BIBLIOGRAPHY

ADS Group, '2017 Industry Facts & Figures: A Guide to the UK's Aerospace, Defence, Security & Space Sectors', Farnborough, UK

African Development Bank, 'African Economic Outlook 2014'

Ashworth, John, 'Seizing the moment: The opportunities for UK fisheries after Brexit', Campaign for an Independent Britain, 2017

Ashworth, John, 'The Betrayal of Britain's Fishing', Campaign for an Independent Britain, 2016

Atoyan, Ruben, et al., 'Emigration and its Economic Impact on Eastern Europe', IMF Staff Discussion Note, SDN/16/07, July 2016

Baker, Carl, 'NHS staff from overseas: statistics', House of Commons Library, Briefing Paper No. 7783, April 2017

Bank for International Settlements, '87th Annual Report', Basel, June 2017

Barker, Kate, Review of 'House Supply – Delivering Stability: Securing our Future Housing Needs', HM Treasury, 2004

Bassett, Ray, 'After Brexit, Will Ireland be Next to Exit?', Policy Exchange, June 2017

Booth, Stephen; Howarth, Christopher and Persson, Mats, 'Kick-starting growth: How to reignite the EU's single market in services and boost growth by €300bn', Open Europe, May 2013

Bruegel, 'Divorce settlement or leaving the club? A breakdown of the Brexit bill', Working Paper, Issue 3, 2017

Burrage, Michael, 'It's Quite OK to Walk Away', Civitas, London, April 2017

Burrage, Michael, 'Myth and Paradox of the Single Market', Civitas, London, January 2016

Bush, Stephen, 'Britain's Referendum Decision and its Effects', Technomica, 2016

Centre for Social Justice, 'The five pathways to poverty: tackling the root causes and breaking the cycle of poverty', 2007

Centre for Social Justice, '48:52 Healing a Divided Britain', October 2016

Churchill, Winston, *The Collected Essays of Sir Winston Churchill: Vol. II: Churchill and Politics*, Library of Imperial History, London, 1976

City of London Corporation, 'Regional visas – a unique immigration solution?', Report written in conjunction with PwC, October 2016

Claros, Eulalia and Davies, Ron, 'Economic impact of Big Data', European Parliamentary Research Service Briefing PE 589.801, September 2016

Cleverly, James and Hewish, Tim, 'Reconnecting with the Commonwealth: the UK's free trade opportunities', Free Enterprise Group, January 2017

Constitutional Reform Group, 'Act of Union Bill', 13 July 2016

Department for Business, Innovation and Skills, 'Trade and Investment for Growth', February 2011

Department for Communities and Local Government, 'Fixing our Broken Housing Market', Cm 9352, February 2017

Dustmann, Christian, et al., 'The impact of EU enlargement on migration flows', Home Office Online Report 25/03, 2003

European Central Bank, *Financial Stability Review*, May 2017

European Commission, 'Public Opinion in the European Union – Standard Eurobarometer 86', December 2016

European Commission, 'The EU Regional Competitiveness Index 2016', Working Papers WP 02/2017, February 2017

European Commission, 'The Five Presidents' Report: Completing Europe's Economic and Monetary Union', June 2015

European Commission, 'Trade, Growth and Jobs: European Commission contribution to the European Council', February 2013

European Commission, 'Reflection paper on the future of EU finances', June 2017

European Commission, 'White Paper on the future of Europe: Reflections and Scenarios for the EU 27 by 2025', March 2017

European Court of Auditors, 'Has the Commission ensured effective implementation of the Services Directive?', Special report No. 5/2016, March 2016

European Union, Report by Mr. Leo Tindemans, to the European Council, *Bulletin of the European Communities*, Supplement 1/76, 1975

Federation of Small Businesses, 'Keep Trade Easy – What small firms want from Brexit', March 2017

George, Stephen, *An Awkward Partner: Britain in the European Community*, Oxford University Press, 1998

Giordano, L. et al., 'The determinants of government yield spreads in the euro area', Commissione Nazionale per le Società e la Borsa (CONSOB), Working Paper 71, October 2012

Goodhart, David, *The Road to Somewhere: The Populist Revolt and the Future of Politics*, Hurst & Co., London 2017

Grantham Institute, 'Carbon pricing in the UK post-Brexit: tax or trade? – A discussion paper', Imperial College London, April 2017

Gudgin, Graham et al., 'The Macroeconomic Impact of Brexit', Centre for Business Research, University of Cambridge, Working Paper No. 483, January 2017

Halligan, Liam and Lyons, Gerard, 'Clean Brexit', Policy Exchange, January 2017

Hawkins, Oliver, 'Migration Statistics', House of Commons Library, Briefing Paper SN06077, June 2017

Helliwell, John, 'Comparative Macroeconomics of Stagflation', *Journal of Economic Literature*, 26 (1) March 1988: 1–28

HM Government, 'Competences between the United Kingdom and the European Union – The Single Market', July 2013

HM Government, 'Competences between the United Kingdom and the European Union – The Single Market, Financial Services and the Free Movement of Capital', summer 2014

HM Government, 'Laying the Foundations: A Housing Strategy for England', UK government Cabinet Office, 2011

HM Government, 'Review of the Balance of Competences between the United Kingdom and the European Union: Agriculture', summer 2014

HM Government, 'Review of the Balance of Competences between the United Kingdom and the European Union: Cohesion Policy', Foreign Office, Cm 8415, July 2014

HM Government, 'The United Kingdom's Exit from the European Union: Safeguarding the Position of EU Citizens Living in the UK and UK Nationals Living in the EU', Cm 9464, June 2017

HM Treasury, 'The Immediate Economic Impact of Leaving the EU', Cm 9292, May 2017

Hocks, Thomas, 'Germany's Elections Won't Be a Populist Takeover', Harvard Kennedy School blog, March 2017

McGuinness, Terry and Oliver Hawkins, 'Brexit: what impact on those currently exercising free movement rights?', House of Commons Library, Briefing Paper CBP-7871, July 2017

House of Commons, Official Report, 'Parliamentary Debates (Hansard)', Vol. 614, No. 34, September 2016

House of Commons Political and Constitutional Reform Committee, 'Lessons from the process of Government formation after the 2010 General Election', Vol. 1, January 2011

House of Lords Economic Affairs Select Committee, 'Building More Homes', 1st Report of Session 2016–17, HL Paper 20, July 2016

House of Lords European Union Committee, 'Brexit and the EU budget', 15th Report of Session 2016–17, March 2017

Howell, David, *Old Links and New Ties: Power and Persuasion in an Age of Networks*, I. B. Tauris, London, 2014

ICAEW, 'Analysing the EU exit charge', ICAEW Brief, May 2017

Ilzkovitz, Fabienne et al., 'A contribution to the Single Market Review', European Commission Directorate-General for Economic and Financial Affairs, Economic Paper No. 271, EC Brussels, January 2007

Institute for Fiscal Studies, 'Reforming the Tax System for the 21st Century: The Mirrlees Review', 2011

Institute of Directors, 'Bridging the Brexit Gap – Options for Transition', Policy Paper, August 2017

International Monetary Fund, 'Annual Report 1973', Washington, DC, 1973

International Monetary Fund, 'UK Country Report, IMF Country Report No. 16/58', February 2016

International Monetary Fund, 'World Economic Outlook Database', Washington, DC, April 2017

International Regulatory Strategy Group, 'The EU's third country regimes and Alternatives to Passporting', Hogan Lovells, January 2017

King, Mervyn, *The End of Alchemy: Money, Banking, and the Future of the Global Economy*, Little, Brown, London, 2016

Landworkers' Alliance, 'Recommendations for Post-Brexit Agricultural Policy', June 2017

Lattimore, Ralph, 'Paper prepared for the North American Agrifood Market Integration Consortium Meetings', Calgary, May 2006

Lightfoot, Warwick, 'Farming Tomorrow: British agriculture after Brexit', Policy Exchange, August 2017

Lyddon, Bob, 'The UK's Lost GDP and Tax Revenues', Global Britain, 2016

Mak, Alan, 'Masters of the Revolution: Why the Fourth Industrial Revolution should be at the heart of Britain's new Industrial Strategy', Free Enterprise Group, November 2016

Mayor of London, 'The Europe Report: A Win-Win Situation', Greater London Authority, August 2014

Mayor of London, 'London: The Global Powerhouse', Greater London Authority, February 2016

Mayor of London, London Finance Commission, 'Devolution: a Capital Idea', Greater London Authority, January 2017

MacDougall, Donald et al., 'Report of the study group on the role of Public Finance in European Integration', EEC, Brussels, April 1977

McKinsey & Company, 'Urban World: Mapping the economic power of cities', March 2011

McKinsey Global Institute, 'Rome Redux: New Priorities for the European Union at 60', March 2017

McPhillips, Marcus, '"Phantom Homes" – Planning Permissions, Completions and Profits', Shelter Research Briefing, July 2017

McWilliams, Douglas, *The Flat White Economy: How the Digital Economy is Transforming London and Other Cities of the Future*, Duckworth Overlook, London, 2015

Mesnard, B., et al., 'Non-Performing Loans in the Banking Union: Stocktaking and Challenges', European Parliament Briefing PE 574.400, March 2016

Metcalf, David, 'Migration Advisory Committee (MAC) report: Immigration and the Labour Market', August 2016

Mills, John, 'Britain's Achilles Heel: Our Uncompetitive Pound', Civitas, 2017

Minford, Patrick and Miller, Edgar, 'What shall we do if the EU will not play ball?', Economists for Free Trade, March 2017

Monnet, Jean, *Memoirs: The Architect and Master Builder of the European Economic Community*, translated by Richard Mayne, Doubleday Books, London, 1978

Mourlon-Druol, Emmanuel, 'The Euro Crisis: A Historical Perspective', London School of Economics Strategic Update, June 2011

Newman, Henry; Booth, Stephen; Shankar, Aarti; Greer, Alex; and Scarpetta, Vincenzo, 'Global Britain: Priorities for trade beyond the European Union', Open Europe, April 2017

Open Europe, 'Off Target: The case for bringing regional policy back home', January 2012

Open Europe, 'Kick-starting growth: how to reignite the EU's single market in services', May 2013

Ormerod, Professor Paul and Rosewell, Bridget, 'A Report Commissioned by the GLA from Volterra Economic Consultancy', pp. 67–110 of the Appendices to the Europe Report, Mayor of London, Greater London Authority, 2014

Packer, Richard, 'Brexit, Agriculture and Agricultural Policy', Centre for Policy Studies, January 2017

Piris, Jean-Claude, *The Future of Europe: Towards a Two-Speed EU?*, Cambridge University Press, Cambridge, 2012

Pisani-Ferry, Jean et al., 'Europe after Brexit: A proposal for a continental partnership', Bruegel, August 2016

Poghosyan, Tigran et al., 'The Role of Fiscal Transfers in Smoothing Regional Shocks: Evidence from Existing Federations, European Stability Mechanism', Working Paper Series 18, 2016

PwC, 'The Long View: How will the global economic order change by 2050?', February 2017

Quah, Danny, 'The Global Economy's Shifting Centre of Gravity', Global Policy, Vol. 2, Issue 1, January 2011

Reynolds, Barnabas, 'A Blueprint for Brexit: The Future of Global Financial Services and Markets in the UK', Politeia, 2016

Richmond, Kenny and Slow, Jonathan, 'Self-employment in Scotland: trends and its implications for productivity', Fraser of Allander Institute Economic Commentary, University of Strathclyde, Glasgow, June 2017

Rowthorn, Robert, 'The Costs and Benefits of Large-scale Immigration', Civitas, December 2015

Schwab, Klaus, 'The Fourth Industrial Revolution: what it means, how to respond', World Economic Forum, Geneva, January 2016

Select Committee on Economic Affairs, First Report, 'Measuring and Predicting Immigration Flows from Eastern Europe', 2008

Simmons, Katie and Stokes, Bruce, 'Populism and Global Engagement: Europe, North America and Emerging Economies', Pew Research Institute, December 2016

Singham, Shanker A., 'Cost of EEA Membership for UK', Legatum Institute Special Trade Commission Briefing, November 2016

Singham, Shanker A., 'A Blueprint for UK Trade Policy', Legatum Institute Special Trade Commission Briefing, April 2017

Stephen, George, *An Awkward Partner: Britain in the European Community*, Oxford University Press, 1998

Stiglitz, Joseph, *The Euro: And its Threat to the Future of Europe*, Allen Lane, London, 2016

Standard Chartered Bank, 'The Super-Cycle Report', 2010

Temperley, Harold, *England and the Near East*, Longmans, Greens and Company, New York, 1936

Toshkov, Dimiter et al., 'The "Old" and the "New" Europeans: Analyses of Public Opinion on EU Enlargement in Review', *MAXCAP Working Paper Series*, No. 02, April 2014

Tyrie, Andrew, 'Giving Meaning to Brexit', Open Europe, September 2016

United Nations, 'Trends in International Migrant Stock: Migrants by Destination and Origin', UN Department of Economic and Social Affairs, 2015

United Nations, 'World Urbanization Prospects', 2014 Revision

Verhofstadt, Guy, *Europe's Last Chance: Why the European States Must Form a More Perfect Union*, Basic Books, New York. 2016

Webb, Dominic and Booth, Lorna, 'Brexit: Trade Aspects', Briefing Paper 7694, House of Commons Library, March 2017

Welsh Government, 'Securing Wales' Future', 2017

World Bank Group, 'Global Economic Prospect: A Fragile Recovery', June 2017

World Economic Forum, 'The Global Competitiveness Report, 2016–2017', Geneva, 2016

World Economic Forum, 'The Competitiveness of Cities', August 2014

Yorkshire Agricultural Society, 'The Implications of Brexit for UK Agriculture', January 2016

Yurchak, Alexei, *Everything was Forever, Until it was No More: The Last Soviet Generation*, Princeton University Press, New Jersey, 2005

ACKNOWLEDGEMENTS

Clean Brexit has been written quickly and covers contemporary, fast-moving and in many cases rather complex ideas and events. Our family and friends have heard us both say over the summer of 2017 that writing these chapters, and keeping up with the latest developments, has been 'like painting an express train on roller skates'.

While some of the commentary and analysis in this book will inevitably be 'overtaken by events', we hope the information and predictions in *Clean Brexit*, and the policy recommendations and analytical framework we have provided, will prove useful during the Article 50 negotiations and beyond.

The authors would like to thank, above all, Iain Dale – Managing Director of Biteback Publishing – who has been unwavering in his support of *Clean Brexit*. This book, during its gestation, has been impacted by numerous unforeseen events – not least a 'snap' general election campaign. Iain has remained encouraging throughout, seeing value in an up-to-the-minute account of Britain's departure from the EU, written by two economists who are broadly positive about the UK's prospects. We owe a great deal to the superb team at Biteback for pulling out the stops to publish *Clean Brexit* as quickly as possible. Olivia Beattie and Bernadette Marron have been model professionals – cool and calm, yet full of kindness and good advice. We are most grateful to them.

The authors coined the phrase 'Clean Brexit' during the autumn of 2016 – as we felt the distinction between 'Hard Brexit' and 'Soft Brexit' was inaccurate and deliberately misleading. We are grateful to the think tank Policy Exchange – which published our joint pamphlet, 'Clean Brexit', in early January 2017, ahead of the Prime Minister's Lancaster House speech later that month.

We would like to thank the countless ministers, shadow ministers, MPs, civil servants, academics, journalists, investors and policy advisors with whom we have discussed Brexit – and its implications for the UK, Europe and the wider world – both before and since the June 2016 referendum. They are too numerous to name and many would not want to be named anyway.

We are, though, most grateful to the Rt Hon. Gisela Stuart and Jacob Rees-Mogg MP for taking the time to write the Foreword and Afterword to *Clean Brexit*. And also to Gerard Benedict Lyons, Nicholas Garrott and other anonymous readers who have commented on draft chapters.

The authors have, since the referendum was called and held, given numerous presentations and taken part in many public debates on the subject of Brexit. Venues have included the National Institute of Economic and Social Research, the CFA Institute, the Official Monetary Financial Institutions Forum, Open Europe, Policy Exchange, Poiteia, the Centre for European Reform, the British Chambers of Commerce, Bloomberg, Thomson Reuters, as well as numerous universities and financial and legal firms across the City, Europe and the wider world. Brexit is an emotive subject and some have taken issue with our analysis. But we are grateful to the audiences at each of these events for their (mostly!) constructive and informative feedback.

Writing a book is a big distraction – and we are grateful to professional colleagues who have shown encouragement and forbearance. Liam would to thank, in particular, James Quinn, Ben Marlow and Allister Heath at the *Telegraph* and Jerome Booth of New Sparta Asset Management – as well as Ilias Melas. Gerard is grateful to Charlotte Ransom and Tom Salter at Netwealth Investments and also to fellow economists who formed 'Economists for Brexit'.

We would also like to thank our literary agents – respectively, Toby Mundy of TMA and Charlie Campbell of Kingsford Campbell.

The people who suffer, though, are those whom we love the most. The authors cannot thank enough our respective families – Lucy, Ailis, Maeve and Ned and Annette, Elf, Lulu and Gerard Jnr – who have shown great patience and understanding, while putting up with much obsessive conversation, as we have worked to complete this book over the summer holidays. It should go without saying, but we will say it anyway – we dedicate our efforts to them.

Liam Halligan and Gerard Lyons
August 2017

AUTHOR BIOGRAPHIES

LIAM HALLIGAN – @LIAMHALLIGAN

Liam Halligan has written his weekly Economic Agenda column in the *Sunday Telegraph* since 2003 – which enjoys a wide international following and has been recognised with a British Press Award. A senior columnist at UnHerd.com and resident panelist on CNN Talk, he also has extensive business experience in both the media and asset management. Halligan took degrees in economics from the University of Warwick and St Antony's College, Oxford and has held economic research posts at the International Monetary Fund, the Social Market Foundation and the London School of Economics. He has reported from Moscow for *The Economist*, been political correspondent for the *Financial Times* and for eight years was economics correspondent at *Channel 4 News* – where he won the Wincott Business Broadcasting Award an unprecedented four times. Raised in Kingsbury, he lives in Saffron Walden with Lucy and their three children.

GERARD LYONS – @DRGERARDLYONS

Dr Gerard Lyons is one of the UK's leading economists and has regularly topped polls of City forecasters. He is a regular commentator on television, radio and in the press. Lyons has testified to committees of the US Senate and Congress, in both Houses of the UK Parliament and given economic presentations in the Great Hall of the People, Beijing, at Davos and across the globe. Lyons spent twenty-seven years in senior roles in the City at Chase, Swiss Bank, DKB International and Standard Chartered Bank. He was chief economic advisor to Boris Johnson in his second term as Mayor of London. Lyons now has a portfolio of roles in finance, universities and economics, including chief economic strategist at Netwealth Investments and independent non-executive director of Bank of China (UK). Originally from Kilburn, he is married to Annette, has three children and lives in Kent.

INDEX